Atlantic Canada Bed & Breakfasts

Third Edition

1997-98

Formac Publishing Company Limited
Halifax, Nova Scotia

Formac Publishing acknowledges the support of the Nova Scotia Department of Education and Culture in the development of writing and publishing in Canada.

COVER: Detail from a painting by Joy Laking, Bass River, Nova Scotia

Canadian Cataloguing in Publication Data

Atlantic Canada bed & breakfasts.
    3rd. ed.
    ISBN 0-88780-402-0

1. Bed and breakfast accommodations — Atlantic Provinces — Guidebooks. 2. Atlantic Provinces — Guidebooks. I. Title: Atlantic Canada bed and breakfasts.

TX907.5.C22A85 1997   647.94715'03   C97-950009-5

Formac Publishing Company Ltd., Publishers
5502 Atlantic Street
Halifax, Nova Scotia
B3H 1G4

Printed and bound in Canada.

Distributed in the United States by:
Seven Hills Book Distributors
49 Central Avenue, Cincinnati, Ohio 45202

Distributed in the United Kingdom by:
World Leisure Marketing
9 Downing Road
West Meadows Industrial Estate
Derby DE21 6HA England

Contents

Introduction

Welcome to the first-ever complete guide to bed and breakfasts and small country inns in Atlantic Canada!

You'll be surprised by the friendly and hospitable attitude toward visitors you'll encounter everywhere in the four Atlantic provinces. In this part of the world, people take time to enjoy life and to get to know travellers and people 'from away'.

And one of the great appeals of bed and breakfast accommodation is that you meet and become acquainted with Maritimers and Newfoundlanders in their own homes. There's no better way to learn about the unique and diverse approaches to life you'll find in the communities of this region.

This guide has been compiled to give you a complete list of every bed and breakfast and small inn facility in Atlantic Canada. To prepare it, we obtained lists of all licensed accommodation from each of the four provinces. We then compiled detailed information on all of these properties, and put it together in this one handy book. The result is a unique resource for travellers — one single source, listing every B&B we could find in the region.

What is a B&B?

Of course B&Bs are only one of the many different kinds of accommodation you can choose. To compile the listings for this book we referred to the criteria used by the four provincial governments in preparing their tourist information material, and to other publications on B&Bs. For this guide, a B&B is:

- Accommodation in a home which guests share with their host
- With one or more guest bedrooms
- With a common living room for guests to use
- Where guests are offered breakfast

Often inns fit the above description of a B&B, but they have licensed dining rooms where dinner and often lunch is served, as well as breakfast. This year, we've expanded our range of listings to include small country inns which meet the other B&B criteria, and have identified them as such.

Tourist or guest homes are also similar to B&Bs, and although they don't always offer breakfast, they fall into the same category as B&Bs in provincial government material, so these accommodations have also been included in our listings.

Locations

While many B&Bs are located in the villages, towns and cities of the region, others are in smaller centres or in rural areas. As you'll see, for each listing we've provided the full address and often included directions about how to find the house. When an accommodation is not located in one of the larger communitites in the region, it is listed under the name of the nearest town or village. We've used the same method as is used in the provincial travel guides to decide locations for spots in rural areas or smaller centres.

Help us keep this guide up to date

As you'll see, we've tried to provide a complete description of each B&B and small inn — what it offers, and what features are available in the surrounding area to guests. There is also information about prices and terms. The information was compiled in March-April 1997.

Of course things are always changing. You should always reconfirm items that are important to you when you are booking your accommodation. On occasion you may find that some of the information in this guide may be out of date; please let us know. We'll be updating all our listings each time we go back to press, so that this volume is kept as up-to-date and as current as possible.

What the stars mean

For each property, we've provided information on their current rating according to the Canada Selection Accommodation Rating Program. Here's what the stars mean:

★	Basic, clean, comfortable
★★	Basic, clean, comfortable with some amenities
★★★	Better quality, more amenities and services
★★★★	High quality, extended facilities, amenities and services

More information

This guide is one of a growing series of guidebooks to the Atlantic Canada region which we have published. Our guides are independent — they're compiled by authors and editors based on their judgment about what visitors should know about and see. We don't seek or accept fees or anything else in exchange for listings or mentions in our books. That way, you can rely on our books as a source of trustworthy information.

On the back cover, you'll see several of the guides you can select for information on the unique heritage, culture, peoples and places of Atlantic Canada. They're available through bookstores everywhere.

Another great source of basic information on the four Atlantic provinces are the provincial departments of tourism. If you call their toll-free (in North America) phone numbers, you can obtain comprehensive basic information on tourist facilities in all provinces. Provincial literature is available free.

The numbers are:

New Brunswick	1-800-561-0123
Newfoundland	1-800-563-6353
Nova Scotia	1-800-565-0000
PEI	1-800-463-4734

We hope that you'll find this book helpful as you travel the Atlantic provinces!

The publishers

Chapter 1

New Brunswick

Alma
Captain's Inn ★★★
John & Elsie O'Regan, Main Street,
Alma, E0A 1B0
(506) 887-2017
Fax (506) 887-2074
Rte. 114, Exit 430 • Waterfront
property overlooking Bay of Fundy
• Ten o/n units, private B&S • Cable
TV and telephone in rooms and liv-
ing room • Non-smoking only
FEATURES: Air-conditioning •
Housekeeping unit available • Walk
to beach • Off-street parking •
Vacation packages
*RATES: $46-$50 (1), $55-$68 (2),
$7-$10 add'l person • Full breakfast
• Open year-round • MC, Visa
accepted • TIANB Member*

Alma
Cleveland Place ★★★
Patricia West, North Main Street,
Alma, E0A 1B0
(506) 887-2213

 Rte. 114 •
Historic village
home on water-
front property •
Three o/n units,
one shared B&S • Cable TV in liv-
ing room • Telephone in rooms •
Non-smoking only
FEATURES: Laundry facilities •
Walk to beach • Off-street parking •
Book shop and artisans barn
*RATES: $50-$60 (1), $60-$75 (2) •
Discount for 2-night stay • Full
breakfast • Open year-round • MC,
Visa accepted •*

Alma
Florentine Manor ★★★ ½
Mary Tingley, RR 2, Albert,
E0A 1A0
Tel & Fax (506) 882-2271
Toll free 1-800-665-2271
Rte. 915 • Heritage property near
Mary's Point Bird Sanctuary • Nine
o/n units, private B&S • Cable TV
in living room • Non-smoking only
FEATURES: Meals on request •
Drive to beach • Off-street parking
*RATES: $50-$60(1), • $65-$95 (2),
$10 add'l person • Full breakfast •
Open year-round • MC, Visa
accepted • NBBBA; NBHIA; TIANB
Member*

Alma
Parkland Village Inn ★★ ½
Allan & Donna Pittman, Alma,
E0A 1B0
(506) 887-2313
Rte. 114, Exit 430 • Waterfront
property • Five o/n units, private
B&S • Cable TV and telephone in
rooms and sitting room • Non-
smoking rooms available
FEATURES: Walk to beach •
Laundry facilities • Off-street parking • Licensed restaurant and lounge
*RATES: $45 (1), $55-$65 (2), $5
add'l person • Weekly and off-season rates • Open April-Nov. • Off-
season by reservation • MC, Visa
accepted • TIANB member*

Alma
School's Out
Bed & Breakfast ★★
Ethel Duffy, Albert, RR 2,
Albert County, E0A 1A0
(506) 882-2630
Rte. 915 • Three o/n units, one
shared B&S • Cable TV in sitting
room • Non-smoking only
FEATURES: Drive to beach • Off-
street parking
*RATES: $30 (1), $40-$45 (2) • Full
breakfast • Open May-Oct. •
NBBBA Member*

Alma
Sandpiper
Bed & Breakfast ★ ½
Stephen & Patrica Marshall, RR 2,
Albert, E0A 1A0
(506) 882-2744
Rte. 915, exit at Mary's Point Rd. •
135-year-old home close to Mary's
Point • Two o/n units, one shared
B&S • Cable TV in sitting room •
Pets permitted, ususally on leash •
Non-smoking only
FEATURES: Drive to beach •
Meals on request • Off-street parking
*RATES: $40 (1), $45 (2) • Full
breakfast • Open May-Oct. • Off-
season by reservation • Visa accepted*

Apohaqui
Apohaqui Inn ★★★
Louise Cosman, Foster Street,
Apohaqui, E0G 1A0
(506) 433-4149
Off Rte. 1 • Seven o/n units, private
B&S • Cable TV in living room •
Non-smoking only
FEATURES: Laundry facilities •
Meals on request • Air-conditioning
• Off-street parking
*RATES: $35 (1), $45-$60 (2), $8
add'l person • Full breakfast • Open
year-round • MC, Visa accepted •
NBBBA; TIANB Member*

Back Bay
The Beach House ★★ ½
Peggy Matheson, Back Bay,
E0G 1B0
(506) 755-2675/0732
Fax (506) 755-6688
Rte. 772S • Waterfront property •
Four o/n units, shared B&S • Cable
TV in sitting room • Non-smoking
only
FEATURES: Off-street parking •
Walk to beach
*RATES: $40 (1-2), $10 add'l per-
son • Full breakfast • Open May-
Sept. • Visa accepted • NBBBA
Member*

Bathurst
Auberge Les Amis
De La Nature ★★★ ½
Jocelyn Desgagné, 2183 Lincour
Road, Robertville, E0B 2K0
Tel & Fax (506) 783-4797
Toll free 1-800-327-9999
Rte. 11, Exit 318 • Five o/n units,
private B&S • Cable TV in lounge •
Non-smoking only
FEATURES: Laundry facilities •
Licensed dining room • Hot tub •
Drive to beach • Off-street parking
*RATES: $55-$65 (1-2) •
Continental or full breakfast • Open
year-round • MC, Visa accepted •
TIANB Member*

Bathurst
The Harbour Inn
Bed & Breakfast ★★ ½
Barbara Richard, 262 Main Street,
Bathurst, E2A 2A8
(506) 546-4757
Rte. 134 • Waterfront property •
Three o/n units, one shared B&S •

TV in lounge
FEATURES: Drive 20 minutes to beach • Off-street parking
RATES: $35 (1), $40-$45 (2), $9 add'l person • Full breakfast • Open year-round

Bathurst
Les Peupliers/ The Poplars ★★
Marianne Schwartz, Kent Lodge Road, Beresford, E0B 1H0
(506) 546-5271
E-mail mariane@nbnet.nb.ca
Rte. 1 • Waterfront property • Two o/n units, private and shared B&S • Cable TV and telephone in rooms • Pets welcome • Non-smoking only
FEATURES: Golf • Walk to beach • Off-street parking
RATES: $45 (2), $60 (family) • Open June-Sept. • DC, DIS, ER, MC, Visa accepted • NBBBA Member

Bertrand
Chez Claude et Pauline ★★ ½
784, boulevarde des Acadiens, Bertrand, E0B 1J0
(506) 727-2368
Fax (506) 727-6815
Rte. 11 • One two-bedroom o/n unit, private B&S • TV in room • Telephone in room
FEATURES: Laundry facilities • Housekeeping facilities • Drive to beach • Off-street parking • 3 km to Acadian Historical Village
RATES: $80 (2), $10 add'l person •Full breakfast • Open May-Sept. • Off-season by reservation • Visa accepted

Bertrand
Hébergement Clément ★★ ½
856, boulevarde des Acadiens, Bertrand, E0B 1J0
(506) 727-2322
Rte. 11 • Three o/n units, one shared B&S • TV in living room • Non-smoking rooms available
FEATURES: Drive to beach • Off-street parking • Cycling and walking trail
RATES: $44 (2), $10 add'l person • Full breakfast • Open June-Sept. • Off-season by reservation

Blackville
Dungarven Manor Bed & Breakfast ★★ ½
Darlene Underhill, 45 Alcorn Drive, Blackville, E0C 1C0
(506) 843-6312
Rte. 8 • Unique home in heart of salmon country • Four o/n units, one shared B&S • Cable TV/VCR in sitting room
FEATURES: Off-street parking • Waterslide on site
RATES: $35 (1), $45-$55 (2), $5 add'l person • Open May-Oct. • NBBBA Member

Blackville
Oak Hill Bed & Breakfast ★★ ½
Joan Coughlan, RR 1, Upper Blackville, E0C 2C0
(506) 843-2805
Rte. 8 • Three o/n units, one shared B&S • Non-smoking rooms available
RATES: $35 (1), $40-$45 (2) • Full breakfast • Open year-round

Bouctouche
Au Bord de la Mer
Bed & Breakfast ★★
Rita Caissie, RR 1, Sainte-Anne-de-Kent, E0A 2V0
(506) 743-5329
Off Rte. 11, on Rte. 505; on Rte. 475, Exit 42 • Two o/n units, private and shared B&S • Cable TV in rooms
FEATURES: Air-conditioning • Housekeeping facilities and kitchen available • Drive to beach • Off-street parking
RATES: $45 (1), $55 (2) • *Open June-Sept.*

Bouctouche
Aux Pétits Oiseaux ★★ ½
Guylaine Castonguay & Maurice Cullen, 124, chemin du Couvent, Bouctouche, E0A 1G0
(506) 743-8196
Off Rte. 11 on 475, Exit 32 • Two o/n units, one shared B&S • Cable TV in sitting room • Children under 6 yrs free • Non-smoking only
FEATURES: Drive to beach, golf course and Le Pays de la Sagouine • Halfway between Parlee Beach and Kouchibouguac National Park • Off-street parking
RATES: $40-$45 (1-2), $10 add'l person • *Full breakfast* • *Open year-round*

Bouctouche
Domaine-sur-Mer ★ ½
Eveline Haché, RR 3, Bouctouche, E0A 1G0
(506) 743-6582
Rte. 535 • Two o/n units, one shared B&S • Cable TV in sitting room • Telephone in rooms • Non-smoking only
FEATURES: Walk to beach • Off-street parking

RATES: Rates not available • *Continental breakfast* • *Open year-round* • *NBBBA Member*

Bouctouche
J and J
Bed & Breakfast ★★
Jackie Dominique, RR 3, Bouctouche, E0A 1G0
(506) 743-9012
Rte. 134 • Two o/n units, one shared B&S • Cable TV in rooms and lounge • Non-smoking rooms available
FEATURES: Laundry facilities • Drive to beach • Off-street parking
RATES: $45 (2), $10 add'l person • *Full breakfast* • *Open May-Oct.*

Cambridge-Narrows
Cambridge-Narrows
Bed & Breakfast ★★ ½
Susan Steeves, Washademoak Lake, Cambridge-Narrows, E0E 1E0
Tel & Fax (506) 488-2000
Off Rte. 715, Exit 343 • 120-year-old farmhouse overlooking Washademoak Lake • Three o/n units, private B&S • Cable TV • No alcohol • Non-smoking only
FEATURES: Laundry facilities • Swimming pool • Housekeeping facilities • Walk to beach • Boating, windsurfing and waterskiing • Off-street parking
RATES: $25 (1), $35-40 (2), $5 add'l person • *Full breakfast* • *Open year-round* • *Pantel; NBBBA Member*

Campbellton
Aylesford Inn
Bed & Breakfast ★★ ½
Jacques Tou Louse, 8 McMillan Avenue, Campbellton, E3N 1E9
(506) 759-7672

Off Rte. 11, Exit 134 • Six o/n units, private and shared B&S • Cable TV and telephone in rooms
FEATURES: Drive to beach • Off-street parking
RATES: $50 (1), $56-$60 (2), $8 add'l person • Continental or full breakfast • Open year-round • DIS, MC, Visa accepted • NBHIA; TIANB Member

Campobello Island
Owen House ★★★
Welshpool, Campobello Island, E0G 3H0
(506) 752-2977
Waterfront property • Nine o/n units, private and shared B&S • Cable TV in living room • Non-smoking only
FEATURES: Walk or drive to beach • Off-street parking
RATES: $60-$70 (1), $70-$98 (2), $15 add'l person • Open May-Oct. • Visa accepted

Cape Tormentine
Briggs Homestead ★★★ ½
Eric & Debbie Sloan, RR 1, Bayfield, E0A 1E0
(506) 538-2313
Rte. 955, Exit 15 or 16 • Restored fifth-generation family farmhouse on waterfront property • Four o/n units, private B&S • Cable TV in sitting room • Children under 12 yrs free • Non-smoking only
FEATURES: Laundry facilities • Air-conditioning • 8 km to Murray Beach • Off-street parking
RATES: $60 (1), $69.50 (2), $10 add'l person • Full breakfast • Open year-round • Visa accepted • NBBBA Member

Cape Tormentine
Hilltop Bed & Breakfast ★★ ½
Garth & Joan Trenholm, Main Street, Cape Tormentine, E0A 1H0
(506) 538-7747
Off Rte. 955 and Rte. 16, Exit 550 • Beautiful new home overlooking water • Three o/n units, one shared B&S • Cable TV in sitting room • Non-smoking only
FEATURES: Hot tub • Laundry facilities • Walk or drive to beach • Off-street parking • Classy Glass Tours available
RATES: $30 (1), $40-$50 (2), $10 add'l person • Full breakfast • Open year-round • NBBBA Member

Caraquet
Auberge Le Goéland (Seagull) ★★
44, boulevarde St. Pierre est, Caraquet, E1W 1B6
(506) 727-2919
Rte. 145 • Near the "Carrefour de la mer" and Caraquet Wharf • Four o/n units, shared B&S • Cable TV in common room • Non-smoking rooms available
FEATURES: Walk or drive to beach • Laundry facilities • Off-street parking
RATES: $35 (1), $35-$40 (2) • Full breakfast • Open May-Sept.

Caraquet
Chez Rhéa
Bed & Breakfast ★★
236, boulevarde St. Pierre ouest,
Caraquet, E1W 1A4
(506) 727-4275
Rte. 11 • Two o/n units, one shared
B&S • Cable TV in common room •
Non-smoking only
FEATURES: Walk or drive to
beach • Off-street parking
*RATES: $34 (1), $44-$48 (2), $8
add'l person • Open year-round*

Caraquet
Hotel Paulin ★★★
Gerard R. Paulin, 143, boulevarde
St. Pierre ouest, Caraquet, E1W 1B6
(506) 727-9981/3165
Rte. 11 • Waterfront property • Ten
o/n units, private and shared B&S •
Cable TV in sitting room
FEATURES: Licensed dining room
• Walk to beach • Off-street parking
*RATES: $40-$60 (1), $45-$85 (2) •
Open May-Oct. • MC, Visa accepted*

Caraquet
La Maison Touristique
Dugas ★★ ½
683 boulevarde St. Pierre ouest,
Caraquet, E1W 1A1
(506) 727-3195
Fax (506) 727-3193
Rte. 11 • Eighteen o/n units, shared
B&S • Cable TV in common room •
Non-smoking rooms available
FEATURES: Housekeeping units
available • Drive to beach • Off-
street parking • Vacation packages
*RATES: $25-$45 (1), $34-$55 (2),
$5 add'l person • Full breakfast •
Open year-round • MC, Visa
accepted*

Caraquet
Le Pignon Rouge ★★ ½
Raymond & Thérèse Albert,
338, boulevarde St. Pierre est,
Caraquet, E1W 1B4
(506) 727-5983
Rte. 145 • Waterfront property •
Three o/n units, shared B&S • Cable
TV in living room • Non-smoking
only
FEATURES: Walk or drive to
beach • Off-street parking •
Vacation packages
*RATES: $40-45 (1), $50-$55 (2),
$10 add'l person • Continental
breakfast • Open June-Sept. • Visa
accepted • Off-season by reserva-
tion*

Chance Harbour
Mariner's Inn ★★★ ½
Susan Postma, Mawhinney Cove
Road, RR 2, Chance Harbour,
Lepreau, E0G 2H0
(506) 659-2619
Fax (506) 659-1890
Toll free 1-888-783-2455
Off Rte. 1, Rte. 790, Exit 85 •
Waterfront property with elevated
ocean view and uninhabited forested
shoreline • Nine o/n units, private
B&S • Cable TV in common room •
Non-smoking only
FEATURES: Licensed dining room
• Walk or drive to beach • Off-street
parking • Vacation packages
*RATES: $65-$85 (1), $75-$95 (2),
$10 add'l person • Continental
breakfast • Open year-round • MC,
Visa accepted • TIANB Member*

Charlo
Aunt Maud's Place ★★★
Anne Coughlan, 996 Chaleur Street,
Charlo, E0B 1M0
(506) 684-2483
Rte. 134, Exit 375 • Older farm-

house (c. 1910) on twenty acres • Three o/n units, shared B&S • Cable TV in common room • Non-smoking only
FEATURES: Laundry facilities • Drive to beach • Nature trails • Bird-watching • Cycling • Off-street parking
RATES: $45 (1), $50-$60 (2), $10 add'l person • Full breakfast • Open May-Oct. • Off-season by reservation • Visa accepted • AAWBO; NBBBA; TIANB Member

Chipman
Speakman's
Bed & Breakfast ★★ ½
Sylvia Speakman, 162 Bridge Street, Chipman, E0E 1C0
(506) 339-6387
Rte. 10 • Three o/n units, one shared B&S • Cable TV in sitting room • Non-smoking rooms available
FEATURES: Laundry facilities • Meals on request • Outdoor swimming pool • Air-conditioning • Drive to beach • Off-street parking
RATES: $50 (2) • Full breakfast • Open year-round

Deer Island
Clam Cove Farm
Bed & Breakfast ★★★ ½
Marie Dolan, Fairhaven, Deer Island, E0G 1R0
(506) 747-2025
Rte. 772, Exit 40 or 43 • Waterfront property • Two o/n units, private B&S • TV and telephone in rooms • No alcohol • Non-smoking only
FEATURES: Outdoor swimming pool • Air-conditioning • Off-street parking • Close to beach
RATES: $60 (2), $5 add'l person • Full breakfast • Open year-round • Visa accepted • NBBBA Member

Deer Island
West Isles World
Bed & Breakfast ★★ ½
Audrey J. Cline, Lambert's Cove, Deer Island, E0G 2E0
(506) 747-2946
Rte. 772, Exit 43 or 40 • Waterfront property • Two o/n units, private B&S • Cable TV in rooms and sitting room • Non-smoking only
FEATURES: Meals on request • Walk or drive to beach • Off-street parking • Clothes dryer available • Vacation packages
RATES: $40 (1), $50 (2), $7 add'l person • Continental or full breakfast • Open May-Oct. • Reservations required • 3-day minimum stay

Dorchester
Rocklyn Inn
Bed & Breakfast ★★ ½
Mrs. Sylvia Yeoman, Dorchester, E0A 1M0
(506) 379-2205
Toll free 1-800-822-6633
Rte. 106, Exit 522 or 541 • National Historic Site (c. 1831); home of E.B. Chandler, a Father of Confederation • Four o/n units, private and shared B&S • Cable TV and telephone in rooms and lounge • Pets welcome • Non-smoking rooms available
FEATURES: Meals on request • Library of books and records • Piano • Heritage garden on five-acre property • Large summer house
RATES: $35 (1), $45 (2), $10 add'l person • Full breakfast • Open year-round • NBBBA Member

Edmundston
Beaulieu
Tourist Home ★★
Patsy-Ann Lynch, 255, rue de
Pouvoir, Edmundston, E3V 2Y6
(506) 735-5781
Off Rte. 2, Exit 18 • Five o/n units,
shared B&S; one housekeeping
suite • Cable TV in common room
FEATURES: Laundry facilities •
Off-street parking
*RATES: $20-30 (1), $22-$32 (2),
$3-$5 add'l person • Open in season*

Edmundston
Ginik's
Bed & Breakfast ★★ ½
Ginette Bossé, 241, rue Principale,
Saint-Jacques, E0L 1K0
(506) 739-6008
Rte. 2, Exit 8, 15 • Waterfront home
• Four o/n units, private & shared B;
two suites • Cable TV in rooms and
sitting room • Pets welcome • Non-
smoking only
FEATURES: Laundry facilities •
Hot tub • Air-conditioning •
Botanical garden • Cycling • Golf
course and aquatic park nearby •
Off-street parking
*RATES: $50 (1), $60-$75 (2), $10
add'l person • Full breakfast • Open
year-round • Off-season by
reservation • MC, Visa accepted •
NBBBA Member*

Edmundston
Le Fief ★★★
Sharon or Phil Bélanger, 87 Church
Street, Edmundston, E3V 1J6
(506) 735-0400
Rte. 2, Exit 18 • Six o/n units,
private & shared B&S • Cable TV
and telephone in rooms and sitting
room • Non-smoking only
FEATURES: Licensed dining room

• Air-conditioning • Kitchenette
available • Off-street parking •
Vacation packages
*RATES: $44.95-$54.95 (1),
$54.95-$74.95 (2), $10 add'l person
• Full breakfast • Open year-round •
Off-season by reservation • MC,
Visa accepted*

Florenceville
Wicklow House
Bed & Breakfast ★★★
Floyd & Irene Ritchie, RR 2,
Wicklow, E0J 1K0
(506) 278-3047
Rte. 2 • Three o/n units, private &
shared B&S • Cable TV and tele-
phone in rooms and sitting room •
Non-smoking only
FEATURES: Laundry facilities •
Air-conditioning • Off-street
parking
*RATES: $50-60 (2)• Full breakfast
• Open year-round • NBBBA
Member*

Fredericton Area
Appelot
Bed & Breakfast ★★★
Elsie Myshrall, RR 4, Hwy 105,
#1272, Fredericton, E3B 4X5
(506) 444-8083
Rte. 105 • Waterfront property •
Three o/n units, private and shared
B&S • Cable TV in living room •
Telephone in rooms • No alcohol •
Non-smoking only
FEATURES: Laundry facilities •
Drive to beach • Off-street parking
*RATES: $45 (1), $55-$60 (2), $15
add'l person • Full breakfast •
Open in season • Off-season by
reservation • NBBBA Member*

Fredericton Area
Carriage House Inn ★★★
Joan & Nathan Gorham, 230
University Avenue, Fredericton,
E3B 4H7
(506) 452-9924
Fax (506) 458-0799
Toll free 1-800-267-6068
Off Rte. 2 and 102, Exit 295 • Ten
o/n units, private and shared B&S •
Cable TV and telephone in rooms
and common room • Non-smoking
only
FEATURES: Laundry facilities •
Meals on request • Air-conditioning
• Drive to beach • Off-street parking
*RATES: $55-$70 (1), $60-$75 (2),
$12 add'l person • Full breakfast •
Open year-round • AE, DC, ER,
MC, Visa accepted • NBHIA;
TIANB Member*

Fredericton Area
Chickadee Lodge Bed & Breakfast ★★★
Vaughn & Bunny Schriver, Prince
William, E0H 1S0
(506) 363-2759
Off-season (506) 363-2288

Rte. 2, 5 km
from Kings
Landing •
Waterfront
property •
Five o/n units,
shared B&S • Cable TV in living
room • Non-smoking rooms
available
FEATURES: Laundry facilities •
Air-conditioning • Rowboats and
canoes available • Off-street parking
*RATES: $40-$45 (1), $50-$55 (2),
$10 add'l person • Full breakfast •
Open May-Nov. • MC, Visa accept-
ed • NBBBA Member*

Fredericton Area
Cornish Corner Inn ★★ ½
Sheelah Wagener, Main Street,
Stanley, E0H 1T0
(506) 367-2239
Off Rte. 8 • Seven o/n units, private
and shared B&S • Cable TV in sit-
ting room • Pets welcome • Non-
smoking rooms available
FEATURES: Laundry facilities •
Licensed dining room• Kitchenette
available • Off-street parking •
Vacation packages
*RATES: $30-$35 (1), $35-$45 (2),
$5 add'l person • Full breakfast •
Open year-round • AE, MC, Visa
accepted • NBHIA Member*

Fredericton Area
Country Lane ★★★
James & Sheila MacIsaac, Lakeville
Corner, RR 1, Ripples, E0E 1N0
(506) 385-2398
Fax (506) 385-1999
Rte. 690, Exit 325 • Waterfront
property • Two o/n units, one shared
B&S • Cable TV in sitting room •
Non-smoking only
FEATURES: Drive to beach • Off-
street parking • Barbecue • Pedal
boat and canoe available
*RATES: $42 (1), $52 (2), $15 add'l
person • Full breakfast • Open year-
round • MC, Visa accepted •
NBBBA Member*

Fredericton Area
Fowler House ★★★★
Rita Fowler, 2785 Woodstock Road,
Fredericton, E3C 1R1
(506) 459-7766
2 km from Fredericton, welcome
sign on Riverside • 1820s farmhouse with twenty-two acres of gardens on Saint John River • Two o/n
units, private and shared B&S •
Cable TV in sitting room
FEATURES: Laundry facilities •
Outdoor swimming pool • Off-street
parking • Near downtown, golf
course and Kings Landing
*RATES: $62 (1), $65 (2), $15 add'l
person • Full breakfast • Open May-
Nov. • Visa accepted • NBBBA
Member*

Fredericton Area
The Hawks Nest ★★★
Lorne & Kathleen Hawkins,
150 Rocky Road, Keswick Ridge,
E0H 1N0
(506) 363-3645
Off Rte. 2 and 105, Exit 274 • Three
o/n units, shared B&S • Cable TV in
common room • Non-smoking only
FEATURES: Laundry facilities •
Drive to beach • Off-street parking
*RATES: $40 (1), $55 (2) • Full
breakfast • Open year-round*

Gagetown
Broadview
Bed & Breakfast ★★ ¹/₂
Mildred Eveleigh, Queenstown,
Gagetown, E0G 1V0
(506) 488-2266&S
Rte. 102 • Three o/n units, shared
B&S • Cable TV in sitting room
FEATURES: Laundry facilities •
Restaurant • Off-street parking
*RATES: $35 (1), $45-$55 (2), $10
add'l person • Full breakfast •*

*Open in season • MC, Visa accepted
• NBBBA Member*

Gagetown
Doctor's Hill
Bed & Breakfast
and Crafts ★★ ¹/₂
16 Doctor's Hill Road, Gagetown,
E0G 1V0
(506) 488-8989
Rte. 102 • Three o/n units, private
and shared B&S • TV in sitting room
• No alcohol • Non-smoking only
FEATURES: Laundry facilities •
Craft shop on site • Homemade
jams and jellies • Coffee and sweet
on arrival • Air-conditioning • Drive
to beach • Off-street parking •
Meals on request • Vacation packages
*RATES: $40 (1), $55 (2), $10 add'l
person • Open Feb.-Dec. • Visa
accepted • NBBBA Member*

Gagetown
Hector House
Nanne Fawcett, 1 Hector Road,
Gagetown, E0G 1V0
(506) 488-2673
Rte. 102 • Historic house, secluded
yet close to amenities, on two acres
of waterfront property, overlooking
wildlife sanctuary • Three o/n units,
one shared B&S • Telephone in
rooms • Non-smoking only
FEATURES: On and off-street
parking • Laundry facilities • Walk
to beach
*RATES: $40 (1), $55 (2) • Open
year-round • MC, Visa accepted •
NBBBA: TIANB Member*

Gagetown
Hewlett House
~1785 ~ ★★★
Anne Fawcett, 4683 Queenstown, Gagetown, E0G 1V0
(506) 488-2673
Fax (506) 488-1011
Rte. 102 • Waterfront property • Three o/n units, one shared B, one private 1/2 B • Cable TV in living room • Telephone in rooms • Non-smoking only
FEATURES: Laundry facilities • Informal garden • Dock • Canoeing, sailing, swimming, cross-country skiing and snowshoeing • Walk to beach • Off-street parking • Vacation packages
RATES: $45-$52 (1), $60-$67 (2) • Full breakfast • Open year-round • MC, Visa accepted • TIANB Member

Gagetown
Steamers Stop Inn ★★★
Vic & Pat Stewart, Box 155, Front Street, Gagetown, E0G 1V0
(506) 488-2903
Fax (506) 488-1116
Off Rte. 102 • Waterfront property on Saint John River • Six o/n units, private B&S • Cable TV in sitting room • Non-smoking rooms available
FEATURES: Licensed dining room • Art gallery • On- and off-street parking
RATES: $65 (2), $15 add'l person • Continental breakfast • Open year-round • MC, Visa accepted • ACHI; NBHIA; TIANB Member

Grand Falls/Grand-Sault
Auberge Heritage
Tourist Home ★★ ¹/₂
Roger & Ginette Desmeules, Grand Falls, E3Z 1E6

(506) 473-4806
Rte. 2 • Three o/n units, shared B&S • Cable TV in common room • Pets welcome • Non-smoking rooms available
FEATURES: Laundry facilities • Air-conditioning • Golf course nearby • Drive to beach • Off-street parking
RATES: $40-$50 (1-2), $10 add'l person • Continental breakfast • Open May-Sept. • Visa accepted • NBBBA Member

Grand Falls/Grand-Sault
Coté
Bed & Breakfast ★★★
Norma Coté, 575 Broadway Street, Grand Falls, E3Z 1E6
(506) 473-1415
Fax (506) 473-1952
Rte. 2, Exits 75, 76 or 81 • Five o/n units, two private B&S, one shared B • Cable TV and telephone in rooms and sitting room • Non-smoking only
FEATURES: Air-conditioning • Drive to beach • Walk to gorge • Off-street parking
RATES: $40-$45 (1), $45-$65 (2), $10 add'l person • Full breakfast • Open year-round • MC, Visa accepted • NBBBA Member

Grand Falls/Grand-Sault
Maple Tourist Home
Bed & Breakfast ★★★ ½
Jim & Rachel Crawford, 142 Main
Street, Grand Falls, E3Z 1E1
(506) 473-1763
Off Rte. 2, Exit 76 or 81 • Built in
1934 • Three o/n units, one private
B, one shared B&S • Cable TV and
telephone in rooms and sitting room
• No alcohol • Non-smoking only
FEATURES: Laundry facilities •
Air-conditioning • Walk to beach •
Off-street parking
*RATES: $50-$55 (2), $10 add'l
person • Full breakfast •
Open year-round • MC, Visa
accepted • NBBBA Member*

Grand Falls/Grand-Sault
Mont Assomption
Bed & Breakfast ★★ ½
Mariette Gagnon & Vincent Ouellet,
Route 2, Grand Falls, E0J 1M0
(506) 473-3562
Toll free 1-800-509-7223
Rte. 2 • Twelve o/n units, private
and shared B&S • Cable TV in
living room • Non-smoking only
FEATURES: Laundry facilities •
Drive to beach
*RATES: $40 (1), $48 (2), $8 add'l
person • Continental breakfast •
Open year-round • MC, Visa
accepted • NBBBA; TIANB Member*

Grand Manan Island
Aristotle's Lantern ★★ ½
Helen Charters, North Head,
Grand Manan Island, E0G 2M0
(506) 662-3788
Rte. 776 • Waterfront property •
Three o/n units, shared B&S •
Cable TV in sitting room •
Non-smoking only
FEATURES: Afternoon tea room

and art gallery • Walk or drive
to beach • Whale-watching •
Off-street parking
*RATES: $50-$60 (2), $5 add'l
person • Full breakfast • Open
June-Sept. • Visa accepted*

Grand Manan Island
Baldwin's
Bed & Breakfast ★★★
Donald & Maureen Baldwin,
Seal Cove, Grand Manan Island,
E0G 3B0
(506) 662-8801
Rte. 776 • Waterfront property •
Two o/n units, one shared B&S •
Cable TV in living room •
Telephone in rooms • Non-smoking
rooms available
FEATURES: Laundry facilities •
Walk to beach • Bird-watching •
Hiking trails • Off-street parking
*RATES: $37 (1), $59 (2), $11 add'l
person • Full breakfast •
Open May-Oct. • GMTA Member*

Grand Manan Island
The Compass Rose ★★ ½
Nora & Ed Parker, North Head,
Grand Manan Island, E0G 2M0
(506) 662-8570
Off-season (514) 458-2607
Rte. 776 • Charming inn with
superlative view of Bay of Fundy •
Eight o/n units, shared B&S •
Non-smoking only
FEATURES: Laundry facilities •
Licensed dining room • Off-street
parking
*RATES: $49 (1), $59-$85 (2), $10
add'l person • Full breakfast •
Open May-Oct. • MC, Visa accepted
• HIAC; NBHIA; TIANB*

Grand Manan Island
The Fount Inn
Bed & Breakfast ★★ ½
Frances Bainbridge, Seal Cove,
Grand Manan Island, E0G 3B0
(506) 662-3725
Three o/n units, shared B&S •
Cable TV in rooms • No alcohol •
Non-smoking only
FEATURES: Laundry facilities •
Walk or drive to beach • Off-street
parking • Vacation packages
*RATES: $49(1), $59-$85 (2), $10
add'l person • Open year-round*

Grand Manan Island
The Inn At Whale Cove
Cottages ★★ ½
Laura Buckley, North Head,
Grand Manan Island, E0G 2M0
(506) 662-3181
Rte. 776, exit at Whistle Rd. •
Waterfront property • Three o/n
units, private B&S; one housekeep-
ing suite • Pets welcome
FEATURES: Licensed dining
room, recommended by *Where to
Eat in Canada* • Historic gourmet
food shop and take-out • Walk or
drive to beach • Off-street parking
*RATES: $65 (1), $75 (2) •
Continental or full breakfast • Open
May-Oct. • MC, Visa accepted •
GMTA; TIANB Member*

Grand Manan Island
Marathon Inn ★★ ½
Elizabeth Crompton, North Head,
Grand Manan Island, E0G 2M0
(506) 662-8144
Rte. 776 • In operation since 1871 •
Fifteen o/n units, private B&S •
Cable TV in rooms and lounge •
Non-smoking rooms available
FEATURES: Laundry facilities •
Licensed dining room and lounge

bar • Outdoor swimming pool •
Tennis court • Walk to beach • Off-
street parking
*RATES: $64-89 (1-2), $6 add'l per-
son • Open May-Oct. • Off-season
by reservation • MC, Visa accepted
• TIANB Member*

Grand Manan Island
McLaughlin's Wharf
Inn ★★ ½
Mrs. Brenda McLaughlin,
Seal Cove, Grand Manan Island,
E0G 3B0
(506) 662-8760
Rte. 776 • Waterfront property • Six
o/n units, shared B&S • Cable TV in
lounge • Non-smoking only
FEATURES: Licensed dining room
• Walk to beach • Off-street parking
*RATES: $59 (1), $69 (2), $10 add'l
person • Continental breakfast •
Open June-Sept. • Off-season by
reservation • AE, MC, Visa accepted*

Grand Manan Island
Rosalie's Guest
Home ★★
Rosalie Harvey, Seal Cove, Grand
Manan Island, E0G 3B0
(506) 662-3344
Rte. 776 • Three o/n units, shared
B&S • Cable TV in lounge
FEATURES: Drive to beach • Off-
street parking
*RATES: $35 (1), $45 (2) • Open
May-Oct.*

Grand Manan Island
Shorecrest Lodge Country Inn ★★ ½
Dennis & Robin Sesplankis, North Head, Grand Manan Island, E0G 2M0
(506) 662-3216
Off-season (410) 247-8310
Rte. 776 • Waterfront property • Ten o/n units, private B&S • Cable TV in lounge • Non-smoking only
FEATURES: Licensed dining room • Walk or drive to beach • Off-street parking
RATES: $55-$68 (1), $65-$79 (2), $8 add'l person • Continental breakfast • Open May-Oct. • Off-season by reservation • MC, Visa accepted

Grand Manan Island
Swallowtail Inn & Gifts ★★ ½
Catherine Neves, Sherman Ross & Crystal Cook, Swallowtail Road, North Head, Grand Manan Island, E0G 2M0
(506) 662-1900
Rte. 776 • Former residence of lighthouse keepers • Completely restored, with beautiful ocean views from all rooms • Six o/n units, shared B&S • Cable TV in sitting room • Non-smoking rooms available
FEATURES: Laundry facilities • Drive to beach • Off-street parking • Licensed dining room
RATES: $65 (1), $85 (2), $11 add'l person • Open May-Oct. • MC, Visa accepted

Grande-Anse
Auberge de L Anse ★★
Aurore Blanchard, 317, rue Acadie, Grande-Anse, E0B 1R0
(506) 732-5204/546-5667
Rte. 11 • Ten o/n units, private and shared B&S • Cable TV in rooms and lounge • Pets welcome
FEATURES: Walk or drive to beach • Off-street parking
RATES: $35 (1) $40-$45 (2), $5 add'l person • Full breakfast • Open June-Aug.

Grande-Anse
L'Auberge aux Portes de l'Acadie ★★★
Michelle Cormier, 108, rue Acadie, Grande-Anse, E0B 1R0
Tel/Fax (506) 732-5229
Rte. 11 • Two o/n units, private B&S • Cable TV in rooms • Non-smoking rooms available
FEATURES: Drive to beach • Off-street parking
RATES: $45 (1), $45-$49 (2), $9 add'l person • Continental breakfast • Open May-Oct. • Off-season by reservation • Visa accepted

Grande-Digue
Le Sous-Bois ★★ ½
Roger Tremblay, RR 1, Grande-Digue, E0A 1S0
(506) 576-1183
Route 530, Cap de Cocagne, Exit 37 • Two o/n units, private and shared B&S • Cable TV in common room • Telephone in rooms • Pets welcome • Non-smoking only
FEATURES: Laundry facilities • Walk or drive to beach • Swimming and board-sailing • Off-street parking
RATES: $40 (1), $50 (2) • Continental breakfast • Open year-round • AE, MC, Visa accepted

Hampton
Bamara Inn ★★ ½
Barbara McNamara, 316 Main
Street, Hampton, E0G 1Z0
(506) 832-9099
Off Rte. 1, on Rte. 121, Exit 143 or
145 • Historic sea captain's house •
Three o/n units, private B&S • TV
in rooms • Non-smoking rooms
available
FEATURES: Laundry facilities •
Licensed dining room • Walk to
beach • Off-street parking •
Vacation packages
*RATES: $50 (1), $75 (2), $15 add'l
person • Full breakfast • Open year-
round • DC, ER, MC, Visa accepted
• AAWBO; TIANB Member*

Hampton
Evelyn's
Bed & Breakfast ★★★
David & Evelyn Cassidy, Ox-Bow
Farm, Highway 121, RR 1, Kings
County, Bloomsfield, E0G1J0
(506) 832-4450
Rte. 121, Exit 1 • Working farm on
waterfront property • Four o/n units,
shared B&S • Cable TV and tele-
phone in rooms and sitting room •
Families welcome • Non-smoking
rooms available
FEATURES: Laundry facilities •
Meals on request • Outdoor swim-
ming pool • Hot tub • Walk or drive
to beach • Off-street parking
*RATES: $45 (1), $55-$65 (2), $10
add'l person • Full breakfast • Open
April-Oct. • Off-season by reservation • Visa accepted • NBBBA
Member*

Hampton
Island Haven ★★★
Cindy Arsenault, 252 Meadow
Drive, Darlings Island, E0G 1Z0
(506) 832-1987
E-mail islhaven@nbnet.nb.ca
Off Rte. 1, Exit 131 or 145 •
Waterfront property on picturesque
island retreat • One o/n unit, private
B&S • TV in sitting room • Families
welcome • Non-smoking only
FEATURES: French spoken • Off-
street parking • Laundry facilities •
Meals on request
*RATES: $45 (1), $55 (2), $10 add'l
person • Full breakfast • Open Jan.
-Nov. • Visa accepted • NBBBA
Member*

Hartland
Campbell's
Bed & Breakfast ★★★
Howard & Rosemary Campbell,
Hartland, E0J 1N0
(506) 375-4775/4014
Off Rte. 2, Exit 170 • Waterfront
property • Three o/n units,
private and shared B&S • Cable TV
in common room • Telephone in
rooms • Non-smoking only
FEATURES: Meals on request •
Air-conditioning • Kitchenette
available
*RATES: $30-$45 (1), $35-$45 (2),
$5-$10 add'l person • Full breakfast
• Open year-round • NBBBA;
TIANB Member*

Harvey Station
Myrna's Manor ★★ ½
Myrna Dery, RR 4, Harvey
Station, E0H 1H0
(506) 366-3127
Rte. 3, Exit 263 • Three o/n
units, private and shared B&S
• Cable TV in rooms and sit-
ting room • Pets welcome •
Non-smoking rooms available
FEATURES: Laundry facili-
ties • Restaurant • Drive to
beach • Off-street parking
*RATES: $35 (1), $45 (2), $8
add'l person • Full breakfast •
Open year-round*

Hillsborough
Lakewood Estate
Bed & Breakfast ★★★
Lynne Liptay, 100 Golf Club
Road, Hillsborough, E0A 1X0
(506) 734-3108
Rte. 114, exit at Lake Road •
Beautiful setting near golf
course • Two o/n units, private
B&S • Cable TV and tele-
phone in rooms and sitting
room • Non-smoking only
FEATURES: Laundry facilities • Elegant dining room •
Off-street parking • Walk to
beach
*RATES: $40-$50 (1), $50-$60
(2) • Full breakfast • Open
year-round •NBBBA Member*

Hillsborough
Rose Arbor
Bed & Breakfast ★★ ½
Glendine & Herman White,
244 Main Street, Hillsborough,
E0A 1X0
(506) 734-2644
Victorian home in town centre
• Four o/n units, shared B&S •
Cable TV in living room • No
alcohol • Pets permitted, usually on leash • Non-smoking
rooms available
FEATURES: Walk to local
attractions and services • Off-
street parking
*RATES: $45 (1), $65 (2), $10
add'l person • Open year-
round • Visa accepted •
NBBBA Member*

Hopewell Cape
Aiko's Villa
Bed & Breakfast ★★★
Aiko M. Hawkes,
Hopewell Cape, E0A 1Y0
(506) 734-3160
Off Rte. 114 at Museum • Two
o/n units, one private B&S,
one shared B • Cable TV in
sitting room • Telephone in
rooms • Non-smoking only
FEATURES: Laundry facilities • Drive to beach • Close
to Hopewell Cape Rocks
Provincial Park and Fundy
National Park • Off-street
parking • Vacation packages
*RATES: $35 (1), $40-$45 (2),
$10 add'l person • Full break-
fast • Open in season • Off-
season by reservation only •
NBBBA Member*

Hopewell Cape
Broadleaf Too
Bed & Breakfast ★★ ½
Vernon & Joyce Hudson,
Hopewell Hill, E0A 1Z0
(506) 882-2803/2349
Fax (502) 882-2075
Rte. 114, Exit 430, 488A or
540 • Three o/n units, shared
B&S • Cable TV in sitting
room
FEATURES: Laundry facili-

ties • Meals on request • Kitchenette available • Drive to beach • Off-street parking
RATES: $40 (1), $45-$50 (2), $10 add'l person • Full breakfast • Open year-round • NBBBA; NBFVA Member

Hopewell Cape
Dutch Treat Farm ★★★
Glenn and Pat Treat, RR 1, Hopewell Cape, E0A 1Y0
(506) 882-2569
Rte. 114, Exit 430, 540 or 488A • 140-year-old farmhouse on waterfront property with view of Grindstone Island • Three o/n units, one shared B&S • Cable TV in sitting room • Pets welcome • Non-smoking rooms available
FEATURES: Drive to beach • Off-street parking
RATES: $35 (1), $40-$50 (2), $10 add'l person • Full breakfast • Open June-Sept. • NBBBA Member

Hopewell Cape
Peck Colonial House Bed & Breakfast & Tea Room ★★ ¹/₂
Elaine Holmstrom, Hopewell Hill, E0A 1Z0
(506) 882-2114

Rte. 114, Exit 430, 540 or 488A • Three o/n units, one shared B&S • Cable TV in living room • Non-smoking only
FEATURES: Meals on request • Drive to beach • Off-street parking
RATES: $40 (1), $45-$50 (2), $10 add'l person • Full breakfast • Open year-round • Visa accepted • NBBBA; TIANB Member

Losier Settlement
Chez Prime Bed & Breakfast ★★
Jocelyne Losier, 8796 Rte. 11, Losier Settlement, E1X 3B9
(506) 395-6884
Rte. 11 and 160 • Four o/n units, shared B
FEATURES: Drive to beach • Off-street parking
RATES: $30 (1), $40-$45 (2), $7 add'l person • Full breakfast • Open in season • ATPA Member

Lower Jemseg
Post Road Bed & Breakfast ★★ ¹/₂
Jennie Carton, Young's Cove Road, RR 1, Lower Jemseg, E0E 1S0
(506) 488-2187
Exit 11 or 160 • Waterfront property • Three o/n units, shared B&S • Cable TV in sitting room
FEATURES: Laundry facilities • Off-street parking
RATES: $45-$50 (1), $55-$60 (2), $5 add'l person • Open Feb.-Nov. • MC, Visa accepted

Millville
Larsen Log Lodge
Bed & Breakfast ★★★★
Marianne Larsen, 658 Hawkins
Corner, RR 1, Millville, E0H 1M0
(506) 463-2731
Rte. 585, exit at Jct. 104 or 585 •
Rural retreat • Two o/n units, private B&S • TV and telephone in
rooms • Non-smoking only
FEATURES: Laundry facilities •
Meals on request • Hot tub • Drive
to beach • Off-street parking •
Vacation package
*RATES: $75-$90 (2), $7.50 add'l
person • Full breakfast • Open year-round • MC, Visa accepted •
NBBBA Member*

Minto
Bailey's Guest
Home & Motel ★ ½
Kevin Bailey, 2 Bridge Street,
Minto, E0E 1K0
(506) 327-4256
Off Rte. 10 • Eight o/n units, private
B&S • Cable TV in rooms
FEATURES: Housekeeping suites
and kitchenettes available • Off-street parking
*RATES: $35-$45(1), $40-$60 (2),
$10 add'l person • Open year-round
• Visa accepted*

Miramichi
Betts Homestead ★★★
Annie Betts, RR 1, 5069
Route 108, Millerton, E0C 1R0
(506) 622-2511
Fax (506) 622-5157
Rte. 108 at Millerton • Overlooks
river • Six o/n units, shared B&S •
Cable TV in living room
FEATURES: Laundry facilities •
Meals on request • Lawn games •
Canoe available • Off-street parking

*RATES: $40-$60 (1), $55-$65 (2),
$10 add'l person • Full breakfast •
Open year-round • Visa accepted •
MRTA Member*

Miramichi
Fourth Generation
Bed & Breakfast ★★ ½
John McLean & Marcel Quirion,
RR 1, Strathadam, Miramichi,
E1V 3M3
(506) 622-3221
Toll free 1-888-244-4411
Rte. 425, Exit 8 • Waterfront property • Three o/n units, one private
B&S, one shared B&S • Cable TV
and telephone in rooms and lounge •
Non-smoking only
FEATURES: Laundry facilities •
Drive to beach • Meals on request •
Bird-watching • Off-street parking
*RATES: $40-$50 (1), $45-$65 (2),
$10 add'l person • Full breakfast •
Open year-round • Visa accepted*

Miramichi
Sunny Side Inn ★★ ½
Troy Donahue & Carla Crawford,
65 Henderson Street, Miramichi,
E1N 2R4
(506) 773-4232
Toll free 1-800-852-7711
Rte. 11, Exit 119 or 120 • Restored
Gothic-style home (c. 1870) offers
unique accommodations and meeting facilities for up to 40 people •
Five o/n units, private and shared
B&S • Pets permitted, usually on
leash • Cable TV in living room •
Non-smoking only
FEATURES: Laundry facilities •
Drive to beach • Off-street parking •
Meals on request
*RATES: $40-$50 (1), $45-$60 (2) •
Continental or full breakfast • Open
June-Sept. • MC, Visa accepted •
NBBBA Member*

Moncton
Auberge Wild Rose Inn ★★★★ ½
Dianne Logan, 17 Baseline Road, Moncton, E1H 1N5
Tel & Fax (506) 383-9751
Rte. 134, Exit 502 or 504 • Colonial-style country inn overlooking lakeside golf course • Four o/n units, private B&S • Cable TV and telephone in rooms and sitting room • Non-smoking only
FEATURES: Evening refreshments • Drive to beach • Off-street parking • Laundry facilities • Air-conditioning • Meals on request
RATES: $65-$75 (2), $10 add'l person • Full breakfast • Open year-round • MC, Visa accepted

Moncton Area
Au Mille Fleurs ★★★
Celyne & Richard LaFleur, 30 Courteney, Moncton, E1C 9L2
(506) 853-7263
One o/n unit, private B&S • Cable TV and telephone in room • Pets welcome • Non-smoking only
FEATURES: Meals on request • Outdoor swimming pool • Drive to beach • Off-street parking
RATES: $50 (1), $55 (2), $10 add'l person • Open year-round • NBBBA Member

Moncton Area
Bonaccord House Bed & Breakfast ★★★ ½
250 Bonaccord Street, Moncton, E1C 5M6
(506) 388-1535
Fax (506) 853-7191
Five o/n units, private and shared B&S • Cable TV in living room • Telephone in rooms • Non-smoking only
FEATURES: Air-conditioning • Drive to beach • On- and off-street parking
RATES: $40-$45 (1), $50-$58 (2), $10 add'l person • Full breakfast • Open year-round • Visa accepted • TIANB; NBBBA; AAWBO Member

Moncton Area
Canadiana Inn ★★★
46 Archibald Street, Moncton, E1C 5H9
(506) 382-1054
Rte. 15, Exit 8 • Beautiful historic inn located in Moncton's tourist district • Seventeen o/n units, private B&S • Cable TV in rooms • Non-smoking rooms available
FEATURES: Laundry facilities • Meals on request • Drive to beach • Off-street parking
RATES: $60-$75 (1), $65-$110 (2), $10 add'l person • Full breakfast • Open March-Nov. • MC, Visa accepted • TIANB Member

Moncton Area
Downtown Bed & Breakfast ★★★
Alice Boudreau, 101 Alma Street, Moncton, E1C 4Y5
(506) 855-7108
Four o/n units, shared B&S • Cable TV in sitting room • Non-smoking rooms available
FEATURES: Laundry facilities • Drive to beach • On-street parking
RATES: $39-$45 (1), $49-$55 (2) • Full breakfast • Open year-round • NBBBA Member

Moncton Area
Le Petunia ★★ ½
Thérèse Leger, 53 Hillside Drive, Moncton, E1A 3S2
(506) 853-9367
Three o/n units, shared B&S • Cable TV in living room • Non-smoking only
FEATURES: Drive to beach • Close to university • Off-street parking
RATES: $35 (1), $40-$50 (2), $10 add'l person • Full breakfast • Open year-round • NBBBA Member

Moncton Area
McCarthy Bed & Breakfast ★★★
Gerry McCarthy, 82 Peter Street, Moncton, E1A 3W5
(506) 383-9152
Rte. 2, Exit 496A • Three o/n units, private and shared B&S • Cable TV and telephone in rooms and sitting room • Non-smoking only
FEATURES: Laundry facilities • Guest fridge • Drive to beach • Off-street parking
RATES: $28 (1), $38-$50 (2), $8 add'l person • Open May-Aug. • Off-season by reservation • AAA; CAA; NBBBA; TIANB Member

Moncton Area
Park View Bed & Breakfast ★★★ ½
Carson & Gladys Langille, 254 Cameron Street, Moncton, E1C 5Z3
(506) 382-4504
Three o/n units, shared B&S • Cable TV and telephone in rooms and living room • Non-smoking only
FEATURES: Laundry facilities • Air-conditioning • Drive to beach • On and off-street parking
RATES: $40 (1), $50 (2), $10 add'l person • Full breakfast • Open year-round • NBBBA Member

Moncton Area
Victoria Bed & Breakfast ★★★★★
Sharon LeBlanc, 71 Park Street, Moncton, E1C 2B2
Tel & Fax (506) 389-8296
Elegant heritage home (c. 1910) featuring gift shop with antiques • Three o/n units, private B&S • TV and telephone in rooms • Non-smoking only
FEATURES: Laundry facilities • Air-conditioning • Drive to beach • On- and off-street parking • Romance packages
RATES: $69-$75 (1), $79-$85 (2), $10 add'l person • Full breakfast • Open year-round • MC, Visa accepted • TIANB; NBBBA Member

Nash Creek
Hayes House Bed & Breakfast ★★ ½
Nash Creek, E0B 1Z0
(506) 237-5228/2252
Rte. 134, Exit 357 • Spacious 1910s home offers elegant comfort and scenic views of Bay of Chaleur • Five o/n units, private and shared B&S • Cable TV in sitting room • Non-smoking only
FEATURES: Walk to beach • Off-street parking
RATES: $50-$60 (2) • Breakfast • Open May-Oct. • Visa accepted

New Denmark
Nyborg's Bed & Breakfast ★★
Boyd & Joan Nyborg, Foley Brook Road, New Denmark, E0J 1T0
(506) 553-6490
Rte. 108 • Three o/n units, one shared B&S • Cable TV in living

room • Pets welcome • No alcohol • Non-smoking rooms available
FEATURES: Partial wheelchair accessibility • Off-street parking
RATES: *$35 (1), $45-$50 (2), $10 add'l person • Full breakfast • Open year-round • MC, Visa accepted • NBBBA Member*

New Mills
Auberge Blue Heron
Bed & Breakfast ★★ ½
James Hayes & Lynn Ranger, New Mills, E0B 1M0
(506) 237-5560
Fax (506) 237-5564
Rte. 134, Exit 375 or 357 • Stately manse (c. 1913) on waterfront property with wonderful views • Eight o/n units, private and shared B&S • Cable TV in sitting room • Non-smoking only
FEATURES: Furnished with antiques • Laundry facilities • Off-street parking • Meals on request • Vacation packages
RATES: *Rates not available • Open May-Oct. • Off-season by reservation • Full breakfast • MC, Visa accepted*

Nigadoo
La Fine Grobe Sur-Mer
(By The Sea) ★★
Georges Frachon, Nigadoo, E0B 2A0
(506) 783-3138/4071
Off Rte. 11 or 134, Exit 321 • Waterfront property • Two o/n units, private B&S • Cable TV in rooms
FEATURES: Licensed dining room • Air-conditioning • Off-street parking
RATES: *$39-$80 (2)• Open May-Dec. • AE, CB, DIS, DC, MC, Visa accepted • AAA; CAA; TIANB Member*

Perth-Andover
Baird House
Bed & Breakfast ★ ½
RR 4, Braidsville, Perth-Andover, E0J 1V0
(506) 272-2643
TransCanada Hwy • Three o/n units, shared B&S • Cable TV in sitting room • Non-smoking rooms available
FEATURES: Drive to beach • Off-street parking
RATES: *Rates not available • Open year-round*

Petitcodiac
3 J's
Bed & Breakfast ★★ ½
Edith Corey, RR 2, Petitcodiac, E0A 2H0
(506) 756-2958
Rte. 2 • Three o/n units, one shared B&S • Cable TV in lounge • Telephone in rooms • Pets welcome • Non-smoking only
FEATURES: Laundry facilities • Doll museum and historic cemetery on site • Off-street parking
RATES: *$25 (1), $40 (2), $8 add'l person • Full breakfast • Open year-round • NBBBA Member*

Petit-Rocher
Auberge d Anjou ★★★
Lione Landry, 587, rue Principale,
Petit-Rocher, E0B 2E0
(506) 783-0587
Fax (506) 783-5587
Rte. 134, Exit 326 • Seventeen o/n
units, private and shared B&S •
Cable TV and telephone in rooms
and sitting room • Non-smoking
rooms available
FEATURES: Laundry facilities •
Licensed dining room • Kitchenette
available • Walk to beach • Off-
street parking
*RATES: $40-$80 (1), $45-$85 (2),
$7 add'l person • Full breakfast •
Open year-round • AE, MC, Visa
accepted • AAPA; NBBBA Member*

Pocologan
By The Sea Bed & Breakfast ★★★
Carol Moore, Pocologan, E0G 2S0
(506) 755-2498
Rte. 1 • Three o/n units, one shared
B&S • Cable TV in living room •
Pets welcome • Non-smoking only
FEATURES: Laundry facilities •
Walk to beach • Off-street parking
*RATES: $25-$35 (1), $30-$40 (2),
$10 add'l person • Open in season*

Pocologan
Pocologan House Bed & Breakfast ★★
Bonny Girouard, General Delivery,
Pocologan, E0G 2S0
(506) 755-3055
Rte. 1 • Oceanfront property • Three
o/n units, shared B&S • Cable TV in
living room • No alcohol • Non-
smoking rooms available
FEATURES: Walk or drive to
beach • Seal-watching • Close to
U.S. border and Fundy Trail • Off-
street parking
*RATES: $40 (1), $45-$50 (2), $10
add'l person • Continental or full-
breakfast • Open year-round • Visa
accepted • NBBBA Member*

Pokemouche
Blanchard Chambre Pour Touriste ★★ ¹/₂
Marie May Blanchard, 12048 Route
11, Village Blanchard, E0B 2J0
(506) 727-2630
Rte. 11 • Two o/n units, shared
B&S • No alcohol • Non-smoking
only
FEATURES: Canoe and pedal boat
• Horseback riding • Cycling path •
Golf course • Airplane tours available • Drive to beach • Off-street
parking
*RATES: $43-$45 (2) • Continental
breakfast • Open June-Sept. • Visa
accepted*

Port Elgin
A & A Jacobs Bed & Breakfast ★★
Upper Cape Road, RR 2, Port Elgin,
E0A 2K0
(506) 538-9980
Off Hwy 16 • Two o/n units, one
shared B&S • Cable TV in living
room • Telephone in rooms • Non-
smoking only
FEATURES: Drive to beach • Off-
street parking • Vacation packages
*RATES: $35 (1), $45 (2), $10 add'l
person, $5 add'l child • Full break-
fast • Open April-Oct.*

Port Elgin
Indian Point Bed & Breakfast ★★
Albert & Anne Flad, Fort Road,
Port Elgin, E0A 2K0
(506) 538-7586

Rte. 15 or 16 • Waterfront property • Five o/n units, private B&S; one housekeeping suite • Cable TV in rooms • Non-smoking rooms available
FEATURES: Off-street parking • Laundry facilities • Walk to beach
RATES: $45 (1), $50-$55 (2), $8 add'l person • Full breakfast • Open year-round

Port Elgin
Little Shemogue Country Inn ★★★★
Klaus & Petra Sudbrack, RR 1, Port Elgin, E0A 2K0
(506) 538-2320
Fax (506) 538-7494
E-mail inn@nbnet.nb.ca
Hwy 15, Rte. 955 • Secluded retreat on oceanfront • Five o/n units, private B&S • Cable TV and telephone in rooms • Non-smoking only
FEATURES: Licensed dining room • Laundry facilities • Walk to private beach • Canoeing, swimming, biking and bird-watching • Sauna • Off-street parking • Vacation packages
RATES: $79-$98 (1-2), $20 add'l person • Full breakfast • Open year-round • MC, Visa accepted • ACHIAC; NBHIA Member

Port Elgin
Roga Farm Bed & Breakfast #1 ★★ ½
Adriana W. Rommens, Port Elgin, E0A 2K0
(506) 538-7763
TransCanada Hwy, Rte. 16 • Two o/n units, one private B&S, one shared B • Cable TV in rooms and lounge • Non-smoking only
FEATURES: Drive to beach • Off-street parking
RATES: $35 (1), $40-$45 (2), $10 add'l person • Full breakfast • Open year-round*

Renous
The Schofield Place ★★ ½
Dan & Kathy Richard, 14 Schofield Street, Renous, E0C 1X0
(506) 627-0807
Jct. 8 and 108 • Renovated century-old Miramichi homestead • Three o/n units, one shared B&S • Cable TV in sitting room • No alcohol • Non-smoking only
FEATURES: Country walks • Fishing • Off-street parking
RATES: $45 (2), $5 add'l person • Continental breakfast • Open year-round • MC, Visa accepted

Richibucto
L'Auberge O'Leary Inn ★★ ½
101, rue Main, Richibucto, E0A 2M0
(506) 523-7515
Rte. 134, Exit 57 • Waterfront property • Seven o/n units, private and shared B&S • Cable TV in lounge • Non-smoking only
FEATURES: Drive to beach • Off-street parking
RATES: $45 (1), $40-$50 (2), $10 add'l person • Continental breakfast • Open May-Sept.

Riverside-Albert
Cailswick Babbling Brook Bed & Breakfast ★★★
Eunice Cail, Riverside-Albert, E0A 2R0
(506) 882-2079

 Rte. 114 • Elegant Victorian home • Three

o/n units, one shared B&S • Cable TV in living room • Non-smoking only
FEATURES: Laundry facilities • Drive to beach • Close to Fundy National Park, Hopewell Cape Rocks, Bird Sanctuary and Cape Enrage Lighthouse • Families welcome • Off-street parking
RATES: *$35 (1), $45-$50 (2), $10 add'l person • Open year-round • NBBBA Member*

Sackville
The Different Drummer ★★★
Richard Hanrahan, Main Street, Sackville, E0A 3C0
(506) 536-1291
Fax (516) 536-8116
Rte. 2, Exit 541 • Turn-of-the-century home • Eight o/n units, private B&S • Cable TV in rooms and lounge • Non-smoking only
FEATURES: Off-street parking
RATES: *$47 (1), $55-$60 (2), $10 add'l person • Full breakfast • Open year-round • MC, Visa accepted • TIANB; TTA Member*

Sackville
The Harbourmaster's House ★★ ½
Sandra Cant, 30 Squire Street, Sackville, E0A 3C0
(506) 536-0452
Rte. 106 • Three o/n units, one shared B&S • Pets welcome • Non-smoking only
FEATURES: Laundry facilities • Drive to beach • Walk to town, university or waterfowl park • Off-street parking
RATES: *$35 (1), $45 (2) • Continental breakfast • Open May-Sept. • NBBBA Member*

Sackville
Marshlands Inn ★★★
R. Peter Weedon, 59 Bridge Street, Box 1440, Sackville, E0A 3C0
(506) 536-0170
Fax (506) 536-0721
Rte. 106, Exit 541 • Pre-Confederation home operating as an inn for over 60 years • Eighteen o/n units, private and shared B&S • Cable TV in rooms and parlour • Telephone in rooms • Non-smoking rooms available
FEATURES: Licensed dining room, recommended in *Where to Eat in Canada* for 25 consecutive years • Drive to beach • Off-street parking • Vacation packages
RATES: *$50-$69 (1), $55-$95 (2), $15 add'l person • Open year-round • DC, AE, ER, MC, VISA accepted • HIAAC; NBHIA; TIANB; TIANS Member*

Sackville
Savoy Arms Bed & Breakfast ★★★ ½
Bill & Jean Young, 55 Bridge Street, Sackville, E0A 3C0
Tel & Fax (506) 536-0790
Rte. 106, Exit 541 • Nineteenth-century home • Three o/n units, private B&S • Cable TV/VCR in lounge • Non-smoking only
FEATURES: Hot and cold drinks • Three sitting rooms with fireplaces • Deck • Drive to beach • Laundry facilities • Off-street parking
RATES: *$49.50 (1), $55 (2) • Full breakfast • Open year-round • NBBBA; TTA Member*

Sainte-Anne-de-Kent
Les Pins Maritimes ★★
Jeanne Brideau, Côte St. Anne,
Sainte-Anne-de-Kent, E0A 2V0
(506) 743-8450
Rte. 11, Exit 42 • Enchanting setting
near wharf on waterfront property •
Two o/n units, one shared B&S •
Non-smoking only
FEATURES: Walk to beach • Off-
street parking
*RATES: $50-$60 (1-2) • Open
July-Sept.*

Saint John Area
The Blossoms
Bed & Breakfast ★★★ ½
Bert & Berna Critchlow, RR 1,
Westfield, E0G 3J0
(506) 757-2962
Off Hwy 7, Exit 80 to Rte. 102 •
Waterfront property • Three o/n
units, private B&S • Cable TV and
telephone in rooms • Non-smoking
only
FEATURES: Meals on request •
Craft and gift store • Herbal gardens
and workshop • Walk to beach •
Off-street parking
*RATES: $45-$50 (1), $55-$65 (2),
$15 add'l person • Full breakfast •
Open June-Sept. • Visa accepted •
NBBBA Member*

Saint John Area
Earle of Leinster
"Inn Style"
Bed & Breakfast ★★★ ½
Lauree & Stephen Savoie, 96
Leinster Street, Saint John, E2L 1J3
(506) 652-3275
Off Rte. 1 or 100, Exit 111 or 113 •
Uptown, refurbished Victorian
manor (c. 1877) • Seven o/n units,
private B&S • Cable TV and telephone in rooms • Pets welcome •

Non-smoking rooms available
FEATURES: Laundry facilities •
Drive to beach • On-street parking
*RATES: $39.14-$59.13 (1), $43.48-
$67.83 (2), $8.70 add'l person •
Full breakfast • Open year-round •
MC, Visa accepted • NBBBA
Member*

Saint John Area
Five Chimneys
Bed & Breakfast ★★★ ½
Linda Gates, 238 Charlotte Street
West, Saint John, E2M 1Y3
(506) 635-1888
Fax (506) 635-8402
E-mail ajdg@nbnet.nb.ca
Off Rte. 1, Exit 109 • 1850s home
with 1990s comfort • Two o/n units,
private and shared B&S • Cable TV
and telephone in rooms and lounge •
Non-smoking only
FEATURES: Laundry facilities •
Meals on request • Walk to beach •
On- and off-street parking
*RATES: $50-$60 (1), $50-$65 (2),
$10 add'l person • Full breakfast •
Open year-round • MC, Visa
accepted • NBBBA Member*

Saint John Area
Garden House
Bed & Breakfast ★★★ ½
Diane Marks, 28 Garden Street,
Saint John, E2L 3K3
(506) 646-9093
Rte. 1, Exit 112 • Three o/n units,
private and shared B&S • Cable TV
in rooms and sitting room
FEATURES: Laundry facilities •
Meals on request • Drive to beach •
Off-street parking
*RATES: $38-$45 (1), $55-$70 (2),
$10 add'l person • Full breakfast •
Open year-round • Visa accepted •
NBBBA Member*

Saint John Area
Inn on the Cove ★★★ ½
Willa & Ross Mavis, 1371 Sand
Cove Road, PO Box 3113 Station
B, Saint John,
E2M 4X7
(506) 672-7799
Fax (506) 635-5455
E-mail inncove@nbnet.nb.ca
Hwy 1, Exit 107A • Waterfront
property on Bay of Fundy • Five o/n
units, private B&S • Cable TV in
lounge • Non-smoking only
FEATURES: Meals on request •
Home of *Tide's Table* TV cooking
program • Close to Irving Nature
Park • Off-street parking • Vacation
packages
*RATES: $65-$125 (2) • Full break-
fast • Open year-round • MC, Visa
accepted • ACIA; HIONB;
OAOANB; SJBOYT; TIANB
Member*

Saint John
Linden Manor ★★★ ½
Linda Molloy, 267 Charlotte Street
West, Saint John, E2M 1Y2
(506) 674-2754
Rte. 1, Exit 111 or 112 • Three o/n
units, private B&S • Cable TV in
sitting room • Telephone in rooms •
Non-smoking only
FEATURES: Off-street parking •
Laundry facilities • Drive to beach
*RATES: $55-$65 (2) • Full break-
fast • Open year-round • MC, Visa
accepted • NBBBA Member*

Saint John Area
Mahogany Manor ★★★
Wayne Harrison & Ross Leavitt,
220 Germain Street, Saint John,
E2L 2G4
(506) 636-8000
Rte. 1, Exit 111 or 112 • Three o/n
units, private B&S • Cable TV in

living room • Telephone in rooms •
Non-smoking only
FEATURES: Laundry facilities •
Drive to beach • Off-street parking
*RATES: $55-$65 (2) • Full break-
fast • Open year-round • MC, Visa
accepted • MRC Member*

Saint John Area
Manawagonish
Bed & Breakfast ★★ ½
Jean & Shelly Poirier, 941
Manawagonish Road, Saint John,
E2M 3X2
(506) 672-5843
Off Rte. 1 or Rte. 100, Exit 107B
North • Two o/n units, private and
shared B&S • Cable TV and tele-
phones in rooms and living room •
No alcohol • Non-smoking only
FEATURES: Air-conditioning •
Drive to beach • Off-street parking
*RATES: $35-$40 (1), $40-$55 (2),
$10 add'l person • Full breakfast •
Open year-round • Visa accepted*

Saint John Area
Mount Hope
Bed & Breakfast ★★ ½
690 Nerepis Road, RR 2, Westfield,
E0G 3J0
Tel & Fax (506) 757-8608
Rte. 177 • Historic homestead built
in 1786 by Col. Henry Nase •
Seventh-generation family home •
Two o/n units, private B&S • Cable
TV in rooms • Non-smoking only
FEATURES: Meals on request •
Walk or drive to beach • Off-street
parking
*RATES: $50 (2) • Full breakfast •
Open year-round • Visa accepted*

Saint John Area
O'Neill's
Bed & Breakfast ★★ ½
Mrs. Fay O'Neill, 982
Manawagonish Road, Saint John,
E2M 3X1
(506) 672-011
Rte. 1, Exit 107B • Three o/n units,
shared B&S • Cable TV in lounge •
Non-smoking only
FEATURES: Laundry facilities •
Off-street parking
*RATES: $45 (1), $49 (2) • Full or
Continental breakfast • Open year-
round • MC accepted*

Saint John
Parkerhouse
Inn & Restaurant ★★★★
Kathy & Gary Golding, 71 Sydney
Street, Saint John, E2L 1L5
(506) 652-5054
Fax (506) 636-8076
Rte. 1 or 100, Exit 117 • Historic
Victorian mansion in the heart of
uptown Saint John • Nine o/n units,
private B&S • Cable TV and tele-
phone in rooms • Non-smoking only
FEATURES: Furnished with
antiques • Original stained-glass
conservatory • Air-conditioning •
Drive to beach • Off-street parking •
Licensed dining room and lounge •
Meals on request
*RATES: $59-$99 (1-2), $10 add'l
person • Open year-round • AE,
MC, Visa accepted*

Saint John Area
Phyl's Beverly Hills
Bed & Breakfast ★★★ ½
Phyllis Finkle, 8 Beverly Hills
Drive, Grand Bay, E0G 1W0
(506) 738-2337
Rte. 7, Exit 80 or 90 • View of
water • Four o/n units, private B&S

• Cable TV and telephone in rooms
and sitting room • Non-smoking only
FEATURES: Laundry facilities •
Hot tub • Drive to beach • Solarium
overlooking Saint John River • Off-
street parking
*RATES: $50 (1), $65-$85 (2), $15
add'l person • Open year-round •
Visa accepted • NBBBA Member*

Saint John Area
Riverside
Bed & Breakfast ★★★
Thomas & Connie Greene, 272
Beulah Road, Saint John, E0G 1K0
(506) 468-2820
Rte. 102, Exit 80 • Waterfront prop-
erty • Two o/n units, private B&S •
Cable TV and telephone in rooms •
No alcohol • Non-smoking only
FEATURES: Laundry facilities •
Deck • Drive to beach • Off-street
parking
*RATES: $39 (1), $49 (2), $10 add'l
person • Continental or full break-
fast • Open June-Oct.*

Saint John Area
Shadow Lawn Country Inn ★★★★
3180 Rothesay Road, Rothesay, E2E 5A3
(506) 847-7539
Fax (506) 849-9238
Toll free 1-800-561-4166
Rte. 100, Exit 125B or 121 to 100E • Nine o/n units, private B&S • Cable TV and telephone in rooms • Non-smoking rooms available
FEATURES: Licensed dining room and lounge bar • Hot tub • Air conditioning • Kitchenette available • Walk or drive to beach • Off-street parking
RATES: $79-$125 (2), $15 add'l person • Continental or full breakfast • Open year-round • AE, CB, DC, ER, MC, Visa accepted • AAA; ACHI; CAA; HINB Member

Saint John Area
Travis House Bed & Breakfast ★★★ ½
Peter & Teresa Godin, 280 Douglas Avenue, Saint John, E2K 1E7
(506) 693-0475
Rte. 1, Exit 107 • Charming 1904 home set in beautiful grounds with water garden • Three o/n units, shared B&S • Cable TV in living room • Telephone in rooms • Non-smoking only
FEATURES: Laundry facilities • Next to Reversing Falls • Meals on request • Air-conditioning • Drive to beach • Off-street parking
RATES: $36.51-$45.21 (1), $45.21-$53.91 (2), $8.70 add'l person • Full breakfast • Open year-round

Saint John
The Westerly Winds Bed & Breakfast ★★ ½
888 Manawagonish Road, Saint John, E2M 3X2
(506) 652-8575
Rte. 1, Exit 107 • Two o/n units, shared B&S • Cable TV in sitting room • No alcohol • Non-smoking only
FEATURES: Laundry facilities • Off-street parking • Drive to beach
RATES: $45 (1-2) • Continental breakfast • Open year-round

Saint-Louis-de-Kent
Le Gîte de l'Oasis Acadienne Bed & Breakfast ★★
Victor Savoie & Nicole Daigle, 169 Saint-Louis Street, Saint-Louis-de-Kent, E0A 2Z0
(506) 876-1199
Fax (506) 876-1918
Rte. 134, Exit 69 • Waterfront property • Three o/n units, shared B&S • Cable TV in living room • Children under 3 yrs free • Non-smoking only
FEATURES: Laundry facilities • Drive to beach • Sea-kayak adventures arranged • Seal- and bird-watching • Off-street parking
RATES: $34 (1), $40 (2), $6 add'l person • Full breakfast • Open May-Oct. • Off-season by reservation • ATRK; NBBBA Member

Saint-Louis-de-Kent
Le Gîte des Vautour Bed & Breakfast ★★ ½
46, rue Lajeunesse, Saint-Louis-de-Kent, E0A 2Z0
(506) 876-4546
Three o/n units, one shared B&S • Cable TV in common room
FEATURES: Drive to beach •

Laundry facilities • Off-street parking
RATES: Rates not available • Open June-Sept.

Salisbury
Salisbury Bed & Breakfast ★★
Dorothy Archibald, Salisbury,
E0A 3E0
(506) 372-9754
Cellular (506) 863-4586
Rte. 112 • Three o/n units, one shared B&S • Cable TV in lounge • Telephone in rooms
FEATURES: Air-conditioning • Off-street parking
RATES: $30 (1), $40 (2) • Full breakfast • Open year-round • NBBBA Member

Shannon
McCrea's Farm Vacation ★★ ½
Jim & Anna McCrea, RR 2, Hatfield Point, Shannon, E0G 2A0
(506) 425-2753
Rte. 705 • Quiet, relaxing vacation home in the country • One o/n unit, private B&S • Telephone in room • Cable TV in sitting room • Pets permitted, usually on leash
FEATURES: Swimming, boating, fishing, hiking, hunting, skiing, sliding and many other outdoor activities • Walk or drive to beach • Laundry facilities • Off-street parking • Kitchenette available • Meals on request
RATES: $40 (1), $45 (2) • Full breakfast • Open year-round

Shediac
Auberge Belcourt Inn ★★★ ½
Alcide & Thérèse Arsenault, 112 Main Street, Shediac, E0A 3G0
(506) 532-6098
Rte. 133 • Elegant Victorian home • Seven o/n units, private and shared B&S • Cable TV in lounge
FEATURES: Drive to beach • Off-street parking
RATES: $79-$99 (2) • Full breakfast • Open April-Dec. • Off-season by reservation • AE, DC, ER, MC, Visa accepted • HIAC; NBHIA; TIANB Member

Shediac
Auberge Seaside Haven Inn ★★★
75 Calder Street, Shediac, E0A 3G0
(506) 532-9025
Rte. 133, Exit 2A, 31B or 37 • Rambling Victorian manor, furnished with antiques • Seven o/n units, private B&S • Cable TV in rooms • Non-smoking rooms available
FEATURES: Kitchenette available • Walk or drive to beach • On- or off-street parking
RATES: $50-$70(1), $50-$85 (2) • Continental breakfast • Open in season • Off-season by reservation • MC, Visa accepted

Shediac
The Bear's Den ★★ ½
Jack & Jeri Lynn, Cannon Croft Road, Shediac, E0A 3G0
(506) 532-8000
Rte. 15 or 133, Exit 31B or 1 • Waterfront property • Three o/n units, private and shared B&S • Cable TV in living room • Non-smoking only
FEATURES: Tennis, volleyball, horseshoes and croquet • Walk to private beach • Air-conditioning • Laundry facilities • Off-street parking • Hot tub
RATES: $65-$80 (1-2), $10 add'l person • Full breakfast • Open year-round

Shediac
Chez Françoise ★★ ½
Hélène Johanny, 93 Main Street, CP 715, Shediac, E0A 3G0
(506) 532-4233
Rte. 133 • Fifteen o/n units, private and shared B&S • Cable TV in lounge
FEATURES: Licensed dining room • Drive to beach • Off-street parking
RATES: $55-$80 (1-2), $10 add'l person • Breakfast • Open April-Dec. • Off-season by reservation • AE, DC, ER, MC, Visa accepted

Shediac
Le Gourmand Country Inn ★★ ½
634 Main Street, Shediac, E0A 3G0
(506) 532-4351
Fax (506) 532-1025
Rte. 133, Exit 37 • Located in the Parlee Beach area • Six o/n units, private B&S • Cable TV and telephone in rooms • Non-smoking only
FEATURES: Table d'hôte available in licensed dining room •

Laundry facilities • Drive to beach • Vacation packages
RATES: $75 (1-2) • Open year-round • AE, DC, ER, MC, Visa accepted • APEX; CRFA; TIANB Member

Shediac
Maison du Touriste Do, Ré, Mi (Tourist Home) ★★ ½
Rachel Poirier, 263 Main Street, Shediac, E0A 3G0
(506) 532-1132
Exit 2A, 31B or 37 • Historic senator's house in town centre • Five o/n units, shared B&S • Cable TV in rooms • Non-smoking only
FEATURES: Veranda • Fireplace and piano in living room • Minutes to Parlee Beach • Air-conditioning • Off-street parking
RATES: $59-$74 (1-2), $10 add'l person • Full breakfast • Open year-round • Off-season by reservation • MC, Visa accepted

Shediac
Morgan's Place/ Place Morgan ★★ ½
Monty V. & Georgette M. Morgan, 668 East Main Street, Shediac, E0A 3G0
(506) 532-8570
Rte. 133, Exit 31B, 37 or 2A • Three o/n units, shared B&S • Cable TV in rooms and living room • Non-smoking rooms available
FEATURES: Laundry facilities • Drive to beach • Off-street parking
RATES: $45-$50 (1), $50-$60 (2), $5-$10 add'l person • Continental or full breakfast • Open in season • TIANB Member

Shippagan
Chez Jeannine du Havre Shippagan ★★ ½
Jeannine Larocque, Shippagan at Ile Lameque, E0B 2P0
(506) 336-8884
Fax (506) 336-8822
Rte. 13 • Waterfront property on the harbour, offering a variety of water- or land-based activities • Five o/n units, shared B&S; one housekeeping suite • Non-smoking rooms available
FEATURES: Canoes, pedal boats, surfing and bicycling • Smelt fishing shacks • Kitchenette available • Laundry facilities • Off-street parking
RATES: $38 (1), $45 (2), $10 add'l person • Breakfast • Open year-round • DC, MC, Visa accepted

Shippagan
Hébergement Dugay ★★ ½
160 rue des Saules, Shippagan, E0B 2P0
(506) 336-9135
Two o/n units, one shared B&S • Cable TV and telephone in rooms • No alcohol • Pets welcome • Non-smoking rooms available
FEATURES: Laundry facilities • Near wharf, marina, marine centre and university • Housekeeping unit available • Drive to beach • Off-street parking • Vacation packages
RATES: $40 (2) • Breakfast extra

Shippagan
Maison Touristique Mallet ★★ ½
Alice Mallet, RR 2, CP 4, Site 20, Haut Shippagan, E0B 2P0
(506) 336-4167
Rte. 113 • Waterfront property • Eight o/n units, private and shared B&S • Cable TV in rooms and common room • Non-smoking only
FEATURES: Walk or drive to beach • Off-street parking
RATES: $30-$40 (2), $10 add'l person • Open year-round • MC, Visa accepted • TIANB Member

Shippagan
O Meunier Tudor ★★
Jeanne-Mance Noel, 279, boulevarde J. D. Gauthier, Shippagan, E0B 2P0
(506) 336-9490
Fax (506) 344-0363
Rte. 113, Exit 310 • Three o/n units, shared B&S • Cable TV in living room • Non-smoking only
FEATURES: Housekeeping unit available • Drive to restaurants, beach, aquarium and Miscou Island • Off-street parking
RATES: $45 (2) • Continental breakfast • Open April-Sept • Off-season by reservation

St. Andrews
A. Hiram Walker Estate Heritage Inn ★★★★★
Elizabeth Cooney, 109 Reed Avenue, St. Andrews, E0G 2X0
(506) 529-4210
Fax (506) 529-4311
Toll free 1-800-470-4088
Rte. 127, Exit 14 or 29 • Five o/n units, private B&S • Cable TV and telephone in rooms • Non-smoking only
FEATURES: Laundry facilities • Outdoor swimming pool • Close to golf course • Meals on request • Walk to beach • Off-street parking
RATES: $115-$265 (2) • Full breakfast • Open year-round • MC, Visa accepted • ACHIA; NBHIA; TIANB Member

St. Andrews
Along the Shore Bed & Breakfast ★★★

Linda Thompson, RR 1, Bayside, St. Andrews, E0G 2X0
(506) 529-4323
Rte. 127, Exit 14 • Waterfront property • Two o/n units, private B&S • Cable TV in living room • Telephone in rooms • Non-smoking only
FEATURES: Hiking trails • Walk to beach • Off-street parking • Vacation packages
RATES: $50-$65 (2), $10 add'l person • Full breakfast • Open May-Nov. • Off-season by reservation • MC, Visa accepted

St. Andrews
Chamcook Forest Lodge Bed & Breakfast ★★★

Don & Jenny Menton, RR 2, St. Andrews, E0G 2X0
(506) 529-4778
Rte 127, Exit 14 or 29 • Victorian farmhouse (c.1884) on Chamcook Mountain, overlooking Passamaquoddy Bay • Three o/n units, shared B&S • Cable TV in sitting room • Non-smoking only
FEATURES: Spanish and Portuguese spoken • Laundry facilities • Petting zoo • Drive to beach • Off-street parking • Vacation packages
RATES: $40-$50 (1), $50-$65 (2), $5-$10 add'l person • Continental or full breakfast • Open year-round • MC, Visa accepted • NBBBA; TIANB Member

St. Andrews
Garden Gate Bed & Breakfast ★★★ ½

Constance Saunders, 364 Montague Street, St. Andrews, E0G 2X0
(506) 529-4453
Rte. 127, Exit 14 or 29 • Four o/n units, private B&S • Cable TV and telephone in rooms • Non-smoking rooms available
FEATURES: Drive to beach • Off-street parking • Laundry facilities
RATES: $75 (2), $10 add'l person • Full breakfast • Open in season • Visa accepted

St. Andrews
Hanson House ★★ ½

Ann McIntosh, 62 Edward Street, St. Andrews, E0G 2X0
(506) 529-4947
Rte. 127, Exit 14 or 29 • Gracious 1840s Georgian-style home on quiet street • Four o/n units, shared B&S • Cable TV in living room • Pets welcome • Non-smoking only
FEATURES: Drive to beach • Off-street parking
RATES: $45-$55 (1), $60-$70 (2), $8 add'l person • Full breakfast • Open May-Oct. • Off-season by reservation • MC accepted • QRTA Member

St. Andrews
Harris Hatch Inn ★★★★

Robert Estes & Jura Everett, 142 Queen Street, St. Andrews, E0G 2X0
(506) 529-4713
Off Rte. 127 or 1, Exit 14 or 29 • Two o/n units, private B&S • Cable TV in rooms and sitting room • Non-smoking only
FEATURES: Laundry facilities • Off-street parking • Walk to beach •

Air-conditioning • Meals on request
RATES: $85-$95 (2) • Full breakfast • Open May-Oct. • Off-season
by reservation • AE, DC, MC, Visa
accepted • NBBBA; TIANB Member

St. Andrews
Heritage Guest House ★★ ½
Erma Trudeau, 100 Queen Street,
PO Box 476, St. Andrews, E0G
2X0
(506) 529-3875
Rte. 127, Exit 14 or 29 • Three o/n
units, private B&S • Cable TV in
rooms
FEATURES: Laundry facilities •
Kitchenette available • Walk or
drive to beach • Off-street parking
RATES: $45-$50 (1), $50-$60 (2),
$5 add'l person • Continental
breakfast • Open in season • Off-
season by reservation • NBBBA
Member

St. Andrews
It's the Cat's Meow
★★★ ½
Bonnie Nelson, 62 Water Street, St.
Andrews, E0G 2X0
(506) 529-4717
Rte. 127 • Colonial-style home with
harbour view and secluded gardens
on waterfront property • Two o/n
units, private B&S • Cable TV and
telephone in rooms • Non-smoking
only
FEATURES: Laundry facilities •
Drive to beach • Rug-hooking
instruction • Off-street parking
RATES: $75-$85 (2), add'l person
$15 • Continental or full breakfast •
Open May-Oct. • Off-season by
reservation • MC, Visa accepted •
NBBBA; TIANB Member

St. Andrews
Kingsbrae Arms ★★★★★
219 King Street, St. Andrews,
E0G 2X0
(506) 529-1897/1187
Fax (506) 529-1197
E-mail kingbrae@nbnet.nb.ca
Rte. 127 • Old-world service in his-
toric waterfront mansion (c. 1897)
next to Kingsbrae Gardens • Nine
o/n units, private B&S (whirlpools)
• Cable TV and telephone in rooms
and sitting rooms • Non-smoking
only
FEATURES: Meals on request •
Air-conditioning • Drive to beach •
Kitchenette available • Laundry
facilities • Off-street parking •
Outdoor swimming pool
RATES: $150-$400 (2) • Full
breakfast • Open year-round • MC,
Visa accepted

St. Andrews
Pansy Patch B&B ★★★★
59 Carleton Street, St. Andrews,
E0G 2X0
(506) 529-3834
Fax (506) 529-9042
Toll free 1-888-PANSY PATCH
(726-7972)

Rte. 1, Exit 14 or 29 to Rte. 127, adjacent to Algonquin Resort • Most photographed home in New Brunswick • Canadian heritage property with seaside vista • Nine o/n units, private B&S • Cable TV/VCR in living room • Telephone in rooms • Non-smoking only
FEATURES: Laundry facilities • Licensed dining room • Tennis and racquetball courts • Bike rentals • Outdoor swimming pool, hot tub and sauna • Walk to beach • Off-street parking • Vacation packages
RATES: $105-$140 (1), $115-$180 (2), $15 add'l person • Full breakfast • Open year-round • MC, Visa accepted • AAA; CAA; NBBBA; TIANB Member

St. Andrews
Rossmount Inn ★★★
Webber Burns, RR 2, St. Andrews, E0G 2X0
(506) 529-3351
Fax (506) 529-1920
Rte. 127, Exit 14 or 29 • Eighteen o/n units, private B&S • Cable TV in living room • Non-smoking rooms available
FEATURES: Licensed dining room and lounge bar • Outdoor swimming pool • Drive to beach • Off-street parking

RATES: $65-$85 (1), $75-$95 (2), $10 add'l person • Full breakfast • Open year-round • MC, Visa accepted • AAA; CAA; TIANB; UCT Member

St. Andrews
Seascape Bed & Breakfast ★★ ½
Chris Ross, 190 Parr Street, St. Andrews, E0G 2X0
(506) 529-3872
Cape-style home (c. 1860) decorated with art and antiques • Three blocks from city centre and beaches • Two o/n units
RATES: Rates not available • Open year-round

St. Andrews
Treadwell Inn ★★★
129 Water Street, St. Andrews, E0G 2X0
(506) 529-1011
Fax (506) 529-4826
Rte. 127, Exit 14 or 29 • Waterfront property; home built in 1880 • Six o/n units, private B&S • Cable TV in rooms and lounge • Non-smoking only
FEATURES: Partial wheelchair accessibility • Laundry facilities • Kitchenette available • Walk or drive to beach • On- and off-street parking
RATES: $75-$95 (1), $85-$145 (2) $10 add'l person • Full breakfast • Open June-Sept. • MC, Visa accepted • AAA; CAA; NBBBA Member

St. George
Bonny River House Bed & Breakfast ★★★ ½
Eleanor Dougherty, RR 3, Bonny River, St. George, E0G 2Y0
(506) 755-2248

Rte. 770, Exit 40 or 43 • Waterfront property • Three o/n units, private B&S • Cable TV in lounge • Non-smoking only
FEATURES: Drive to beach • Off-street parking
RATES: $45-$55 (2), $10 add'l person • Full breakfast • Open May-Oct. • Off-season by reservation • Visa accepted • NBBBA; TIANB Member

St. Martins
Bayview
Bed & Breakfast ★★
Main Street, St. Martins, E0G 2Z0
(506) 833-4723
Rte. 111, Exit 125 • Three o/n units, one shared B&S • Cable TV in lounge • Non-smoking rooms available
FEATURES: Laundry facilities • Meals on request • Kitchenette available • Walk to beach • Off-street parking
RATES: $48-$50 (2), $8 add'l person • Open April-Oct.• AE, MC, Visa accepted

St. Martins
Fundy Breeze
Lodge ★★★
Main Street, St. Martins, E0G 2Z0
(506) 833-4723
Off Rte. 111 • Waterfront property • Three o/n units, one shared B&S • Cable TV in lounge • Non-smoking rooms available
FEATURES: Laundry facilities • Restaurant • Walk to beach • Off-street parking
RATES: $48-$50 (2), $8 add'l person • Open April-Nov.• AE, MC, Visa accepted

St. Martins
The Quaco Inn ★★★★ ½
Betty Ann & Bill Murray, Beach Street, Box 15, St. Martins, E0G 2Z0
(506) 833-4772
Off Rte. 111 • Restored Victorian heritage inn on Bay of Fundy • Waterfront property • Seven o/n units, private B&S • Cable TV in living room • Telephone in rooms • Non-smoking only
FEATURES: Laundry facilities • Licensed dining room • Hot tub • Air-conditioning • Walk to beach, harbour and nature trails • Off-street parking • Vacation packages
RATES: $65-$85 (1-2), $10 add'l person • Continental or full breakfast • Open year-round • MC, Visa accepted • CRFA; HIAC; NBHIA Member

St. Martins
St. Martins
Country Inn ★★★★ ½
Myrna & Al LeClair, St. Martins, E0G 2Z0
(506) 833-4534
Toll free 1-800-565-5257
Rte. 111, Exit 125 • Waterfront property • Sixteen o/n units, private B&S • Cable TV in lounge • Telephone in rooms • Non-smoking rooms available
FEATURES: Partial wheelchair accessibility • Laundry facilities • Licensed dining room and lounge bar • Air-conditioning • Off-street parking • Vacation packages
RATES: $70 (1), $95-$125 (2), $10 add'l person • Full breakfast • Open Jan.-June • MC, Visa accepted • CIA; CAA; NBHIA Member

St. Martins
Weslan Inn ★★★★
45 Main Street, St. Martins,
E0G 2Z0
Tel & Fax (506) 833-2531
Rte. 111, Exit 1 or 125 • Historic
sea captain's home overlooking Bay
of Fundy • Three o/n units, private
B&S; one housekeeping suite •
Cable TV and telephone in rooms •
Non-smoking only
FEATURES: Laundry facilities •
Drive to beach • Off-street parking •
Hot tub
RATES: *$80-$90 (1), $90-$100 (2),
$10 add'l person • Open year-round
• MC, Visa accepted*

St. Stephen
Bay's Edge
Bed & Breakfast ★★★
Duncan & Florence McGeachy,
RR 3, St. Stephen, E3L 2Y1
(506) 466-5401
Off Rte. 1 on Ledge Road •
Waterfront property • Two o/n units,
private B&S • Cable TV in sitting
room • Non-smoking only
FEATURES: Outdoor swimming
pool • Walk to beach • Laundry
facilities • Off-street parking
RATES: *$50-$55 (1), $57-$58 (2),
$8 add'l person • Full breakfast •
Open May-Oct.• Off-season by
reservation • MC, Visa accepted •
IODE; KIWANIS; NBBBA Member*

St. Stephen
Blair House
Bed & Breakfast ★★★
Betty Whittingham, 38 Prince
William Street, St. Stephen,
E3L 2W5
Tel & Fax (506) 466-2233
Off Rte. 1, 3rd house past the church
on left • Three o/n units, private

B&S • Cable
TV in sitting
room •
Telephone in
rooms • Non-
smoking only
FEATURES: Laundry facilities •
Drive to beach • Off-street parking
• Evening refreshments
RATES: *$40-$46 (1), $48-$56 (2),
$10 add'l person • Full breakfast •
Open year-round • MC, Visa
accepted • IODE; NBBBA; TIANB
Member*

St. Stephen
Elim Lodge
Bed & Breakfast ★★★
Doran & Anne Hooper, 477
Milltown Boulevard, St. Stephen,
E3L 1K2
(506) 466-3521
Cellular (506) 466-8971
Off Rte. 1 • 1850s riverside home •
Three o/n units, private B&S •
Clock radio in rooms • Cable TV in
living room • No alcohol • Non-
smoking only
FEATURES: French spoken •
Laundry facilities • Library, pool
table • Self-guided historical walking tours • Walk to tennis court,
public pool and museum • Canoe
rental • Drive to beach • Off-street
parking
RATES: *$40 (1), $50-$60 (2), $10
add'l person • Full breakfast • Open
year-round • NBBBA Member*

St. Stephen
The Tides Retreat ★★★
Polly Steele, Todd's Point,
St. Stephen, E3L 2W9
(506) 466-3040
Fax (506) 466-2143
Rte. 3 • Waterfront property • Four
o/n units, private B&S • Cable TV

in living room • Pets welcome •
Non-smoking only
FEATURES: Laundry facilities •
Licensed dining room with meals
included in rates • Hot tub • Walk
to beach • Off-street parking •
Vacation packages
*RATES: $65-$85 (1), $130-$170
(2)* • *Full breakfast* • *Open year-
round* • *Visa accepted* •

Sussex
Anderson's Holiday Farm Bed & Breakfast ★★
RR 2, Sussex, E0E 1P0
(506) 433-3786
Rte. 890, Exit 416 • Three o/n
units, one shared B&S • Cable
TV in lounge
FEATURES: Off-street parking
RATES: $35-$45 (2) • *Full
breakfast* • *Open year-round*

Sussex
Apohaqui Inn ★★★
Louise Cosman, 7 Foster Street,
Apohaqui, E0G 1A0
(506) 433-4149
Off Rte. 1 • Seven o/n units, four
private 1/2 B, one shared B&S •
Cable TV in living room • Non-
smoking only
FEATURES: Laundry facilities •
Meals on request • Air-condition-
ing • Off-street parking
*RATES: $35 (1), $45-$60 (2), $8
add'l person* • *Full breakfast* •
Open year-round • *MC, Visa
accepted* • *NBBBA; TIANB
Member*

Sussex
Dutch Valley Heritage Inn ★★★
Vickey S. Bell, RR 4, Waterford
Road, Sussex, E0E 1P0
(506) 433-1339
Fax (506) 433-4287
Off Rte. 1 or Rte. 2, Exit 416,
413, or 420 • Historic home
(c.1810) • Three o/n units, private
B&S • Cable TV in lounge • Non-
smoking only
FEATURES: Off-street parking
*RATES: $45 (1), $55 (2), $10
add'l person* • *Continental breakfast* • *Open May-Sept.* • *Visa
accepted* • *NBBBA Member*

Sussex
Stark's Hillside Bed & Breakfast "Inn-Style" ★★★ ½
Peter & Elizabeth Stark, RR 4
Waterford, Sussex, E0E 1P0
(506) 433-3764
Off Rte. 1, 2 or 111, Exit 416,
420 or 179, 3 km past Poley
Mountain • Three o/n units, pri-
vate B&S • Cable TV in lounge •
Non-smoking only
FEATURES: Meals on request •
Air-conditioning • Off-street
parking • Vacation packages
*RATES: $60 (1), $75 (2), $10
add'l person* • *Full breakfast* •
Open year-round • *Visa accepted*
• *Reservations required* •
NBBBA; TIANB Member

Whites Brook
Mom's
Bed & Breakfast ★★
Diane Bolduc, RR 3, Kedgwick,
E0K 1C0
(506) 284-2586
Rte. 17 • Three o/n units, one shared
B&S; one housekeeping suite •
Cable TV in living room •
FEATURES: Walk to beach • Off-
street parking • Vacation packages
*RATES: $30 (1), $40 (2) • Open
year-round*

Woodstock
Down Home
Bed 'n'Breakfast ★★★
Tracie Jones, 698 Main Street,
Woodstock, E0J 2B0
(506) 328-1819
Three o/n units, one shared B&S,
one private B&S • TV in rooms •
Pets welcome
FEATURES: French spoken •
Laundry facilities • Air-conditioning
• On- and off-street parking
*RATES: $36-$39 (1), $42-$59 (2),
$6-$10 add'l person • Open year-
round • Visa accepted • NBBBA
Member*

Woodstock
Edgewater Pines
Bed & Breakfast ★★ ¹/₂
Carolyn Drake, RR 1, Bulls Creek,
Woodstock, E0J 2B0
(506) 328-3285
Rte. 103, Exit 199 • One o/n unit,
private B&S • Cable TV in lounge •
Telephone in room • Non-smoking
only
FEATURES: On-street parking
*RATES: $60 (2) • Full breakfast •
Open July-Aug. • Off-season by
reservation*

Woodstock
The Foot of the Hill/
Au Pied de la Colline ★★★
Jean & Tom Bridgeo, 109
Sherwood Drive, Box 56,
Woodstock, E0J 2B0
(506) 328-3585
Fax (506) 325-2899
Toll free 1-888-354-4444
Exit 188 • Waterfront property •
Three o/n units, one private B&S,
one shared B&S • Cable TV and
telephone in rooms and lounge •
Non-smoking only
FEATURES: Laundry facilities •
Air-conditioning • Off-street parking
*RATES: $40 (1), $50 (2), $20 add'l
person • Continental or full break-
fast • Open year-round • MC, Visa
accepted*

Woodstock
Froehlich's Swiss Chalet
Bed & Breakfast ★★ ¹/₂
Edgar & Elfi Froehlich, RR 2,
Woodstock, E0J 2B0
(506) 328-6751
Rte. 105 • Waterfront property with
magnificent views • Two o/n units,
private B&S • Cable TV in living
room • Non-smoking rooms avail-
able
FEATURES: Laundry facilities •
Off-street parking
*RATES: $40 (1), $45 (2), $10 add'l
person • Full breakfast • Open May-
Oct. • NBBBA Member*

Woodstock
Lenten Rose
Bed & Breakfast
Experience ★★ ¹/₂
Marlene & Gary McCallum, 28
Mark Street, Grafton Heights,
Woodstock, E0J 2B0
(506) 328-8476

Rte. 105 or 585, Exit 188 •
Waterfront property in peaceful sur-
roundings, providing a safe haven
for travellers, especially women •
Two o/n units, one shared B&S •
Cable TV in sitting room • Non-
smoking only
FEATURES: Off-street parking
*RATES: $45.25 (1), $49.50-$52.50
(2), $10 add'l person • Full break-
fast • Open year-round • NBBBA
Member*

Woodstock
Shirley's
Bed & Breakfast ★★½
Shirley Reid, 116 Parkwood Drive,
Woodstock, E0J 2B0
(506) 325-2756
Rte. 188 • Two o/n units, private
B&S • Cable TV in sitting room •
No alcohol • Non-smoking only
FEATURES: Off-street parking •
Laundry facilities
*RATES: $40 (1), $50 (2), $10 add'l
person • Open year-round*

Woodstock
The Queen Victoria
Guest House B&B ★★★ ½
133 Chapel Street, Woodstock, E0J
2B0
(506) 328-8382
Fax (506) 328-4884
Rte. 188, off TransCanada Hwy. •
Turn-of-the-century house furnished
with antiques • Two o/n units, private B&S • Cable TV in sitting
room • Non-smoking only
FEATURES: Laundry facilities •
Off-street parking
*RATES: $55 (1-2), $20 add'l per-
son • Open May-Oct.*

Youngs Cove Road
Black Bear Lodge
Bed & Breakfast ★★ ½
Gilbert Pelletier, Youngs Cove
Road, Queen's County, E0E 1S0
(506) 488-2244
Fax (506) 488-2068
Rte. 2, exit at Grand Lake Drive •
Waterfront property • Two o/n units,
one shared B&S • Cable TV in
lounge • Telephone in rooms • Pets
welcome • Non-smoking rooms
available
FEATURES: Laundry facilities •
Walk to beach • Off-street parking
*RATES: $40 (1), $45 (2), $8 add'l
person • Full breakfast • Open year-
round • Visa accepted • NBBBA
Member*

Chapter 2

Newfoundland

Aquaforte
Hagan's Hospitality Home ★★★
Mrs. Rita Hagan, General Delivery, Aquaforte, A0A 1A0
(709) 363-2688/363-2213
Aquaforte Rte. 10 • Three o/n units, shared B&S • Cable TV and telephone in rooms • Children under 10 yrs free
FEATURES: Laundry facilities • Dining room featuring fresh seafood • Playground and fishing nearby • 9 km (5.4 mi) from archaeological dig in historic Ferryland
RATES: $38-$48 (1-2), $10 add'l person • Full breakfast • Open year-round • Major credit cards accepted

Avondale
Country Lane ★★ ½
Masons Road, Avondale, A0A 1B0
(709) 229-4413
Rte. 60 • Bright and airy modern home • Two o/n units, one shared B&S • Cable TV • No smoking in rooms, please
FEATURES: Quiet and peaceful • Laundry facilites • Whale- and iceberg-watching, fishing and hiking nearby
RATES: $35-$45 (1-2) • Continental breakfast • Open May 15-Oct. 15

Badger
Woodlands Kettle Bed & Breakfast ★★★
19 Church Street, Box 70, Badger, A0H 1A0
(709) 539-2588
Toll free 1-888-539-2588
Off-season (905) 333-4853
Fax (905) 549-2488
Badger Rte. 1, in central Newfoundland • Former convent (c. 1900) • Four o/n units, private B&S • Cable TV, telephone and radio in rooms • Non-smoking only
FEATURES: Wheelchair accessibility • Elegant dining room • Salmon fishing area • 30 km (18 mi) to Grand Falls, Windsor • Tea and crafts room • Meal packages
RATES: $45-$59 (1-2) • Full breakfast • Open May-Oct. • Visa accepted • HNL Member

Baie Verte
Bailey's Dorset Country Inn ★★ ½
Box 184, Baie Verte, A0K 1B0
Rte. 410 • Eight o/n units, private B&S • Cots available • No pets, please • No smoking in rooms, please
FEATURES: Near skiing • Laundry facilities
RATES: $46-$56 (1-2), $10 add'l person • Breakfast • Open year-round • Visa accepted

Baie Verte
Dorset Bed and Breakfast ★★ ½
56 Barn Hill, Box 606, Baie Verte, A0K 1B0
(709) 532-8031/4587
Fax (709) 532-4517
Rte. 410 • Three o/n units, private B&S • Cable TV in lounge • Radio

in rooms • Pets welcome • Non-
smoking only
FEATURES: Dining room •
Whale-, iceberg- and bird-watching
• Playground
*RATES: $40-$45 (1-2), $10 add'l
person, $5 children under 15 yrs •
Full breakfast • Open year-round •
Visa accepted*

Bay Bulls
Gatherall's Hospitality Home (B&B)
Northside Road, Bay Bulls,
A0A 1C0
(709) 334-2887
Fax (709) 334-2176
Toll free 1-800-41-WHALE
Bay Bulls Rte. 10, follow blue signs
for Gatherall's Boat Tours • Seaside
accommodations • Three o/n units,
one shared B&S • Telephone • Non-
smoking only
FEATURES: Dining room •
Interpretive boat tours to Witless
Bay Seabird Ecological Reserve
(puffins guaranteed) • Whale-
watching and hiking nearby
*RATES: $42-$52 (1-2) $14 add'l
person • Full breakfast • Open May-
Oct. • Major credit cards accepted •
HNL Member*

Bay Bulls
O'Brians B&B ★★ ¹/₂
North Side Road, Bay Bulls,
A0A 1C0
(709) 334-2007
Fax (709) 753-3140
E-mail obriens@netfx-inc.com
Seaside accommodation with beau-
tiful ocean view from balcony •
Two o/n units • Cable TV •
Newfoundland dog on premises •
Pets allowed • No smoking in
rooms, please
FEATURES: Laundry facilities •

Playground • Boat tours to
Ecological Reserve • Whale-, ice-
berg- and bird-watching nearby •
Fishing
*RATES: $40-$45 (1-2) •
Continental breakfast • Open May-
Oct. • Major credit cards accepted*

Bay L'Argent
Country Lodge ★ ¹/₂
Box 103, Bay L'Argent, A0E 1B0
(709) 461-2516/2388
Six o/n units, private B&S • TV •
Pets allowed
FEATURES: Laundry facilities •
En route to Rencontre East ferry,
with parking facilities • Dining
room with home-cooked meals •
Room service • Picnic area • Fishing
nearby
*RATES: $35-$45 (1-2), $5 add'l
person • Open May 1-Oct. 31 •
Major credit cards accepted • HNL
Member*

Bonavista
Abbott's Cape Shore B&B ★★ ¹/₂
Box 689, Bonavista, A0C 1B0
(709) 468-7103
Two o/n units, one shared B&S •
Cable TV and telephone in rooms •
No smoking in rooms, please
FEATURES: Dining room •
Playground • Fishing • Whale- and
iceberg-watching nearby
*RATES: $50 (1-2) • Full breakfast •
Open year-round*

Bonavista
Butler's By The Sea ★★ ½
15 Butler Crescent, Box 642,
Bonavista, A0C 1B0
(709) 468-2445
Bonavista Rte. 230 • Two o/n units,
private B&S • Cable TV • Cot available • Pets allowed • No smoking in
rooms, please
FEATURES: Laundry facilities •
Dining room • Barbecue • Picnic
area • Kitchenette available •
Whale-, iceberg- and bird-watching
nearby
*RATES: $50-$65 (1-2), $10 add'l
person • Full breakfast • Open year-
round*

Bonavista
Silver Linings Bed & Breakfast ★★ ½
Box 1497, Chapel Hill Road,
Bonavista, A0C 1B0
Tel & Fax (709) 468-1278
Bonavista Rte. 230 • Registered
Gothic-style heritage home, furnished with antiques • Three o/n
units, shared B&S • Cable TV • No
smoking in rooms, please
FEATURES: Laundry facilities •
Library • Three fireplaces • Whale-,
iceberg- and bird-watching •
National Historic Site nearby
*RATES: $60-$75 (1-2) • Full
breakfast • Open year-round • Visa
accepted*

Bonavista
White's Bed & Breakfast ★★ ½
21 Windlas Drive, Box 323,
Bonavista, A0C 1B0
(709) 468-7018
Bonavista Rte. 230 • Three o/n
units, one private 1/2 B, two shared
B&S • Cable TV and clock radio in

rooms • Children welcome • Non-
smoking only
FEATURES: Laundry facilities •
Dining room • Evening snack •
Bicycle rentals • Whale-, iceberg-
and bird-watching
*RATES: $40-$75 (2), $10 add'l
person • Full breakfast • Open year-
round • Major credit cards accepted
• HNL Member*

Botwood
Atlantic Hotel ★★
2 Air Base Road, Box 40, Botwood,
A0H 1E0
(709) 257-2242/2820
Fax (709) 257-3964
Ten o/n units, private B&S • Cable
TV/VCR and telephone in rooms •
Children under 12 yrs free • Cot
available • Pets permitted
FEATURES: Lounge • Private parties and Saturday night dances
*RATES: $47-$52 (1), $57 (2), $5
add'l person • Continental breakfast
• Open year-round • Major credit
cards accepted • HNL Member*

Boxey
Auntie's Inn Hospitality Home ★ ½
Box 10, Site 4A, Boxey, A0H 1M0
(709) 888-6581/5211/4221
Fax (709) 888-6581
Boxey Rte. 363 • Four o/n units,
one shared B&S • Non-smoking
rooms available
FEATURES: Meals on request •
Fishing and hiking nearby
*RATES: $29-$39 (1-2), $7 add'l
person • Full breakfast • Open May
1-Oct. 31 • Major credit cards
accepted*

Branch
Whalen's
Hospitality Home ★★ ½
Box 46, Branch, St. Mary's Bay,
A0B 1E0
Tel & Fax (709) 338-2506
Branch Rte. 100 • Four o/n units,
one shared B&S • Cable TV, radio
and telephone in rooms • No pets,
please • Non-smoking rooms available
FEATURES: Dining room featuring traditional home-cooked meals •
Whale-, bird-watching and fishing
nearby • Hiking tours • Thirty-
minute drive from Cape St. Mary's
Ecological Reserve
RATES: $42-$53 (1-2) •
Continental breakfast • Open year-round • MC, Visa accepted • HNL
Member

Brigus
Brittoner ★★ ½
12 Water Street, Box 163, Brigus,
Conception Bay, A0A 1K0
(709) 528-3412
Brigus off Rte. 70, near Hawthorne
Cottage and Olde Stone Barn •
Restored Victorian heritage home
on waterfront property • Three o/n
units, one private B, one shared
B&S, two suites • Pets permitted •
No smoking in rooms, please
FEATURES: Laundry facilities •
Picnic area • Playground • Fishing
and hiking nearby
RATES: $50-$55 (2-3) • Full
breakfast • Open year-round

Brigus
Brookdale Manor ★★ ½
Frank & Shirley Roberts, Farm
Road, Box 121, Brigus, A0A 1K0
(709) 528-4544
Brigus Rte. 60, 20 km from Rte. 1

on Rte. 70 • Quiet country setting •
Four o/n units, private B&S • Cable
TV and telephone in sitting room •
Cot available • Non-smoking only
FEATURES: Wheelchair accessibility • Tea room • Dining room •
Patio deck • Picnic tables • Whale-
and iceberg-watching nearby
RATES: $45-$55 (2), $10 add'l
person • Continental breakfast •
Open year-round • Visa accepted •
HNL Member

Brigus
The Cabot Inn
Bed & Breakfast ★★
Box 89, Brigus, Conception Bay,
A0A 1K0
(709) 528-4959
In Brigus centre, minutes away from
all historic sites • Colonial-style
interior • Six o/n units, private and
shared B&S • Cable TV and telephone in family room • Non-smoking only
FEATURES: Wheelchair accessibility • Room service • Whale-, iceberg- and bird-watching • Fishing
and hiking nearby
RATES: $40-$45 (1-2), $10 add'l
person • Full breakfast • Open
June-Oct.

Brigus
Riverhead Chalet
Bed & Breakfast ★★ ½
Antler Beach, Box 71, Brigus,
Conception Bay, A0A 1K0
(709) 528-3295
Brigus Rte. 60 • Waterfront property
with mature grounds andantique furnishings • Three o/n units, two
shared B&S • Cable TV and telephone in sitting room • Non-smoking only
FEATURES: Beautiful view •
Laundry facilities • Traditional
Newfoundland meals on request •
Banquet/meeting facilities • Tour
boat • Whale-, iceberg- and bird-
watching • Fishing and hiking nearby
*RATES: $50-$55 (1-2), $10 add'l
person • Full breakfast • Open May-
Oct.*

Brookfield
Yellow Teapot Inn ★★
54 Main Street, General Delivery,
Badger's Quay, A0G 1B0
(709) 536-5858
Brookfield off Rte. 320 • Four o/n
units, one shared B&S • Cable TV
in sitting room • Pets permitted,
usually on leash • Non-smoking
rooms available
FEATURES: Laundry facilities •
Restaurant • Craft shop • Provincial
Park nearby • Whale- and iceberg-
watching
*RATES: $35 (1), $40 (2), $5 add'l
person • Continental breakfast •
Open year-round • Visa accepted*

Burgeo
Burgeo Haven
Bed & Breakfast ★★ ½
63 Reach Road, Box 414, Burgeo,
A0M 1A0
Tel & Fax (709) 886-1282

Burgeo Rte.
480 •
Historic
home on
waterfront
property •
Four o/n units, one private B&S,
one shared B&S • Cable TV and
telephone in sitting room • Non-
smoking only
FEATURES: Laundry facilities •
Room service • Patio • Picnic area •
Sandy beaches, bird-watching and
hiking nearby • Ferry to Ramea-
Francois nearby
*RATES: $40-$60 (1-2), $10 add'l
person • Full breakfast • Open year-
round • Visa accepted • HNL Member*

Burin
Country Frills
Bed & Breakfast ★★ ½
Box 76, Winterland Road, Burin,
A0E 1G0
(709) 891-2897
Rte. 221 • Country home, close to
nature • Two o/n units, one shared
B&S (whirlpool) • Children wel-
come • Non-smoking only
FEATURES: Evening snack •
Tours available • Craft shop
*RATES: $48 (2), $8 add'l person •
Continental breakfast • Open May
15-Oct. 31 • MC, Visa accepted*

Burin
Evergreen House
& Crafts ★★ ½
7 Winterland Road, Box 386, Burin
Bay Arm, A0E 1G0
(709) 891-4177
Fax (709) 279-2857
Burin, Rte. 221 • Two o/n units, one
shared B&S • Cable big-screen TV
and telephone in rooms • Non-
smoking only
FEATURES: Country elegance sur-

rounded by woods • Laundry facilities • Evening snack • Fireplaces • Whirlpool • Bird-watching, fishing, golf and hiking nearby
RATES: Rates not available • Full breakfast • Open year-round • Major credit cards accepted

Burin
Sound of the Sea Bed & Breakfast ★ ½
11A Seaview Drive, Box 291, Burin, A0E 1E0
(709) 891-1760
Restored merchant's home in quiet setting, nestled in the hills overlooking the ocean • Four o/n units, one shared B&S • Cot available • No smoking in rooms, please
FEATURES: Fishing, golf and hiking nearby • Walk to Burin Heritage House • Laundry facilities
RATES: $40-$50 (1-2), $10-$15 add'l person • Continental breakfast • Open year-round • Major credit cards accepted

Campbellton
P.J.'s Bed and Breakfast ★★
Pauline and Joan Fudge, 33 Indian Arm Road, Box 179, Campbellton, A0G 1L0
(709) 261-2786
Campbellton Rte. 340 • Two o/n units, one shared B&S • Cable TV, radio and telephone in rooms
FEATURES: Laundry facilities • Meals on request • Two lounging areas • Fishing and mini-golf nearby
RATES: $35-$40 (1-2), $5 add'l person • Full breakfast • Open year-round

Cape Onion
Tickle Inn at Cape Onion ★★ ½
Box 62, RR 1, Cape Onion, A0K 4J0
Tel & Fax (709) 452-4321
Off-season (709) 739-5503
Cape Onion Rte. 437 • Century-old heritage home on beachfront property in pastoral setting • Four o/n units, two shared B&S • Telephone • Cot available • Non-smoking rooms available
FEATURES: Home-cooked Newfoundland meals on request • Dining room • Parlour • Picnic area • Nine acres of meadows and hills for hiking • Whale-, iceberg- and bird-watching nearby • Close to L'Anse aux Meadows and St. Anthony
RATES: $48 (1-2), $10 add'l person • Continental breakfast • Open June 1-Sept. 30 • MC, Visa accepted • HNL Member

Carbonear
Keneally Manor Heritage Inn ★★ ½
8 Patrick Street, Carbonear, Box 31001, Mount Pearl, A1N 4L5
(709) 596-1221
Fax (709) 596-0744
Rte. 70 • Award-winning historic property with antique furnishings • Four o/n units, private B&S
FEATURES: Meeting facilities • Picnic area • Gift shop • Whale-, iceberg-, bird-watching and fishing nearby
RATES: $45-$65 (1-2), $10 add'l person • Continental breakfast • Open June-Oct. • MC, Visa accepted • HNL Member

Carter's Cove
Highway Bed & Breakfast
Barbara Burt, Main Road, Box 11, Carter's Cove, A0G 1P0
(709) 629-3484
Virgin Arm Rte. 345 • Two o/n units, one shared B&S • Cable TV and telephone in rooms
FEATURES: Whale-, iceberg- and bird-watching, fishing and hiking nearby
RATES: $35-$40 (2) , $10 add'l person • Continental breakfast • Open June-Sept.

Cartyville
Hulan's Tourist Home ★★ ½
Box 13, Cartyville, A0N 1G0
(709) 645-2376
Cartyville Rte. 404 • Two o/n units, private B&S; one cottage • Cable TV in rooms • Cot available • Children free • Non-smoking only
FEATURES: Salmon fishing • Park nearby • Port aux Basques Ferry Terminal 110 km (66 mi)
RATES: $35-$40 (1-2), $40-$50 (cottage), $5 add'l person • Continental breakfast • Open May 1-Oct. 31 • Major credit cards accepted • HNL Member

Change Island
Seven Oakes Island Inn ★★★
Box 57, Change Island, A0G 1R0
Tel & Fax (709) 621-3256
Off-season Box 133, Deer Lake, A0K 2E0; (709) 635-2247
Twenty-minute car ferry to Change Islands • 100-year-old fish merchant's home • Eight o/n units, private B&S; three cottages • Cable TV in lounge • No pets, please •

Non-smoking only
FEATURES: Laundry facilities • Newfoundland meals on request • Dining room • Parlour with fireplace • Playground and picnic area • Whale-, iceberg-watching and hiking nearby
RATES: $49-$69 (1-2), $85 (cottage) • Off-season and weekly rates • Open May-Oct. 31 • HNL Member

Churchill Falls
Black Spruce Chalet
Box 238, Churchill Falls, A0R 1A0
(709) 925-3241
Fax (709) 925-3285
Six o/n units, shared B&S • Cable TV in common area
FEATURES: Banquet/meeting facilities • Dining room • Picnic area • Bird-watching and fishing nearby
RATES: $44 (1-2) • Continental breakfast • Open year-round

Clarenville
Island View Hospitality Home ★★ ½
128 Memorial Drive, Box 1465, Clarenville, A0E 1J0
(709) 466-2062
Stately home overlooking Random Sound • Four o/n units, one shared B&S • Cable TV and telephone in living room • No pets, please • Non-smoking only
FEATURES: Well-informed hostess • Evening snack • Fitness facilities • Hiking and National Park nearby • Twenty-five minutes to Twin Rivers Golf Course
RATES: $39 (1), $65 (2), $10 add'l person • Continental breakfast • Open year-round • Major credit cards accepted

Clarenville
Jane's Tourist Home ★★ ¹/₂

261 Marine Drive, Box 431,
Clarenville, A0E 1J0
(709) 466-1329
5 km (3 mi) from Rte. 1 •
Attractively restored century-old
heritage home with original slate
roof, in quiet location • Three o/n
units, private B&S • Cable TV and
telephone in rooms • Non-smoking
only
FEATURES: Laundry facilities •
Dining room • Golf and gourmet
restaurant nearby
*RATES: $35-$60 (1-2) •
Continental breakfast • Open June 1
-Sept. 30*

Clarenville
Patrick's Bed & Breakfast ★★

Box 271, Shoal Harbour, A0C 2L0
(709) 466-1906
Clarenville Rte. 1 • Three o/n units,
shared B&S • Cable TV/VCR and
clock radio in rooms
FEATURES: French spoken •
Laundry facilities • Meals on
request • Fishing, golfing and hiking
nearby • Off-street parking
*RATES: $30 (1), $35 (2) •
Continental breakfast • Open year-
round*

Clarenville
Sanctuary Country Inn ★★★

23 Balbo Drive, Box 1448,
Clarenville, A0E 1J0
Tel & Fax (709) 466-3103
Two o/n units, private B&S • Cable
TV, telephone and clock radio in
rooms • Non-smoking only
FEATURES: Laundry facilities •

Licensed • Living room with fireplace • Formal dining room (breakfast served only) • Central air conditioning • Overlooking the Shoal
Harbour Canada Goose Sanctuary,
near Trinity Pageant, and Hibernia
Project tours
*RATES: $49-$69 (1-2), $16 add'l
person • Full breakfast • Open year-
round • Visa accepted • HNL
Member*

Clarenville
The Squeeze-More Inn ★★ ¹/₂

147 Memorial Drive, Box 1527,
Clarenville, A0E 1J0
(709) 466-3719
Cozy rooms in a country atmos-
phere with heart-felt hospitality •
Two o/n units, one shared B&S •
Cot available • Non-smoking only
FEATURES: Picnic table and patio
• Downhill and cross-country skiing
nearby • Whale-, iceberg- and bird-
watching nearby • Close to golf,
hiking and National Park
*RATES: $39-$44 (1-2), $5 add'l
person • Continental breakfast •
Open year-round*

Clarenville
Whitehall
Country Inn ★★ ¹/₂
70 Memorial Dive, Clarenville,
A0E 1J0
Tel & Fax (709) 466-2413
E-mail
lfrich@turner.eastcoll.nf.ca
Modern conveniences in a restored
eighty-year-old home • Four o/n
units, shared B&S • Cable TV in
rooms • No smoking in rooms,
please
FEATURES: Banquet/meeting
facilities • Playground • Golf and
National Park nearby
*RATES: $65-$85 (1-2) • Full
breakfast • Open year-round •
Major credit cards accepted • HNL
Member*

Clarke's Beach
Country Manor
B&B ★★
Box 28192, St. John's, A1B 4J8
(709) 786-9000
Rte. 70, Clarke's Beach • Three o/n
units, one private B, one shared
B&S
FEATURES: Tennis court • Whale-,
iceberg-, bird-watching and fishing
nearby
*RATES: $45-$60 (1-2) •
Continental breakfast • Open June-
Sept.*

Clarke's Beach
Kaldory Inn
Bed and Breakfast ★★ ¹/₂
Cal & Doris Dory, Main Street, Box
361, Clarke's Beach, A0A 1W0
(709) 786-0900
Rte. 70, Clarke's Beach •
Waterfront property snuggled
beneath a mountain • Three o/n
units, private B&S; one suite • Cot

available •
Cable TV
• No
smoking
in rooms,
please
FEATURES: Sitting room and
library • Housekeeping services •
Large patio with gas barbecue •
Kitchenette available • Bird-watching, fishing and hiking nearby
*RATES: $45-$75 (1-2), $10 add'l
person • Full breakfast • Open year-
round • Visa accepted*

Conception Bay South
Sleep Inn
Bed & Breakfast ★★★
33 Ivimey Place, Box 4032,
Manuels, A1W 1G5
(709) 834-2905
Three o/n units, one shared B&S •
Cable TV • Cot available • Non-
smoking rooms available
FEATURES: Laundry facilities •
Playground • Heated outdoor swimming pool • Scenic river walking
trails • Whale-, iceberg- and bird-
watching • Fishing nearby
*RATES: $48-$55 (1-2), $10 add'l
person • Full breakfast • Open year-
round • HNL Member*

Conception Bay South
Villa Nova
Bed & Breakfast ★★
Box 5157, Long Pond, Conception
Bay South, A1W 1J9
(709) 834-1659
Rte. 60 • Three o/n units, one shared
B&S • Cable TV • No smoking in
rooms, please
FEATURES: Laundry facilities •
Meals on request • Scenic view
from living room • Patio deck with
barbecue • Whale-, iceberg-watch-
ing and hiking nearby • Ten minutes

to marina/yacht club
RATES: $45-$55(1-2) • *Full break-fast* • *Open May-Oct.* • *Major credit cards accepted*

Conception Harbour
Conception Tourist Inn ★★ ¹/₂
General Delivery, Conception Harbour, A0A 1Z0
(709) 229-3988
Rte. 60 • Country inn with bed & breakfast atmosphere • Seven o/n units, private B&S • Cable TV in rooms • Cot available
FEATURES: Laundry facilities • Dining room • Picnic area • Whale-, iceberg- and bird-watching • Fishing and hiking nearby • Diving site
RATES: $44-$49 (1-2), $5 add'l person • *Full breakfast* • *Open year-round* • *Major credit cards accepted* • *HNL Member*

Conche
Seashell Hospitality Home ★★
Box 86, Conche, A0K 1Y0
(709) 622-4151
Conche Rte. 434 • Quiet setting next to the sea, with scenic views • Three o/n units, shared B&S • Cable TV and telephone in rooms • Pets allowed • Non-smoking only
FEATURES: Laundry facilities • Whale- and iceberg-watching, fishing and hiking nearby
RATES: $35 (1), $40 (2) • *Continental breakfast* • *Open year-round*

Corner Brook
Bell's Bed & Breakfast ★★★
2 Fords Road, Corner Brook,
A2H 1S6
(709) 634-5736/1150
Corner Brook Rte. 1 • Exit via 450A, Lewis Pkwy • Located at the corner of St. Mark's Ave. and Fords Rd. • Four o/n units, private B&S • Cable TV in sitting room • Telephone and radio in rooms • Non-smoking only
FEATURES: Laundry facilities • Fireplaces • Propane barbecue • Recreational facilities and fishing nearby • Close to Terra Transport Bus Terminal
RATES: From $44 (2), $10 add'l person • *Full breakfast* • *Open year-round* • *Major credit cards accepted* • *HNL Member*

Corner Brook
Bide-A-Night Hospitality Home ★★ ¹/₂
11 Wellington Street, Corner Brook, A2H 5H3
(709) 634-7578
Corner Brook Rte. 1 • Two o/n units, one shared B&S • Cable TV and radio in rooms • No pets, please
FEATURES: Home baking • Picnic area • Fishing, golf, hiking and National Park nearby
RATES: $30 (1), $40 (2) • *Full breakfast* • *Open year-round*

Corner Brook
Goodyear Manor ★ ½
47 West Street, Corner Brook,
A2H 2Y6
(709) 634-4907
In town centre • Two o/n units, private B&S • Pets permitted • No smoking in rooms, please
FEATURES: Laundry facilities • On-street parking • Fishing and hiking nearby
RATES: $40-$45 (1-2) • Full breakfast • Open year-round

Cow Head
A & A Guest Home ★★
Box 147, Cow Head, A0K 2A0
(709) 243-2389
Cow Head Rte. 430 • Two o/n units, one shared B&S; one housekeeping suite • Cable TV in living room • Radio in rooms • Pets permitted, usually on leash
FEATURES: Barbecue • Beach, boat tours and nature walks nearby • Close to Gros Morne National Park
RATES: $40 (1), $45 (2), $55 (suite), $12 add'l person, $5 add'l child under 6 yrs • Full breakfast • Open June 25-Labour Day • HNL Member

Cow Head
J. & J.
Hospitality Home ★★
Box 107, Cow Head, A0K 2A0
(709) 243-2521
Cow Head Rte. 430 • Within boundaries of Gros Morne National Park • Four o/n units, two private B&S, two shared B&S • Cable TV • Cot available • Non-smoking only
FEATURES: Wheelchair accessibility • Laundry facilities • Barbecue • Outdoor swimming pool • Hiking trails and bird-watching nearby

RATES: $40 (1), $50 (2), $8 add'l person, $4 child under 12 yrs • Full breakfast • Open June 1-Oct. 31 • Major credit cards accepted

Cupids
Guyview Manor ★★ ½
General Delivery, Cupids, A0A 2B0
(709) 528-4248
Two o/n units, one shared B&S • Cable TV in sitting room • Non-smoking only
FEATURES: Picnic and playground area • Pony and hay rides • Whale- and iceberg-watching nearby
RATES: $45-$55 (1-2) • Continental breakfast • Open year-round

Cupids
Skipper Ben's
B&B ★★ ½
Box 76, Cupids, A0A 2B0
(709) 528-4436
Fax (709) 737-1901
Four o/n units, shared B&S • Cots available • Non-smoking only
FEATURES: Dining room • Whale- and iceberg-watching, fishing and hiking nearby • Walk to archaeological dig, site of Canada's first English settlement
RATES: $45-$55 (1-2), $10 add'l person • Full breakfast • Open year-round • Major credit cards accepted

Daniel's Harbour
Seaview
Bed & Breakfast ★★ ½
182 Main Street, Box 38, Daniel's Harbour, A0K 2C0
(709) 898-2581
Daniel's Harbour Rte. 430 • Three o/n units, one shared B&S • Cable TV and telephone in rooms • Cot available • Pets permitted, usually

on leash • Non-smoking only
FEATURES: Laundry facilities •
Picnic area, playground • Whale-,
iceberg- and bird-watching, fishing,
hiking and National Park nearby
RATES: *$36 (1), $40 (2), $8 add'l
person • Full breakfast • Open year-
round*

Doyles
Long Range
Bed & Breakfast ★★ ½
Box 823, RR 1, Doyles, A0N 1J0
(709) 955-2901
Upper Ferry, Rte. 406 • Beautiful
scenery in quiet surroundings • Two
o/n units, one shared B&S •
Telephone • Cot available • Non-
smoking only
FEATURES: Traditional
Newfoundland warmth and hospitality • Laundry facilities • Thirty minutes from ferry • Bird-watching,
fishing, golf and hiking nearby
RATES: *$35-$45 (2), $10 add'l
person • Continental breakfast •
Open June 1-Sept. 30*

Eastport
Pinsent's
Bed & Breakfast ★★ ½
17 Church Street, Box 85, Eastport,
A0G 1Z0
(709) 677-3021
Eastport Rte. 310 • Quaint salt-box
home surrounded by lilac trees,
roses and aspens • Two o/n units,
one shared B • Cable TV • Non-
smoking only
FEATURES: Laundry facilities •
Whale-, iceberg- and bird-watching
• Fishing, golfing and hiking nearby
RATES: *$35 (1), $45 (2), $10 add'l
person • Full breakfast • Open year-
round • HNL Member*

Eastport
Sharoz Inn ★★ ½
5 Burden's Road, Box 115,
Eastport, A0G 1Z0
(709) 677-3539
Eastport Rte. 310 • Country inn with
warm and personal atmosphere,
delicious food and immaculate lodg-
ings • Six o/n units, private B&S •
Cable TV in rooms • Non-smoking
only
FEATURES: Wheelchair accessibility • Dining room • Housekeeping
services • Whale- and iceberg-
watching, golf, hiking and National
Park nearby
RATES: *$44-$75 (1-2) •
Continental breakfast • Open May-
Nov. • MC accepted • HNL Member*

Englee
Reeves Ocean View
Bed & Breakfast ★★★
69 Church Road, Box 217, Englee,
A0K 2J0
(709) 866-2531
Englee Rte. 433 • Two o/n units,
private B • Cable TV, telephone and
clock radio in rooms
FEATURES: View of icebergs and
whales from balcony overlooking
the ocean • Laundry facilities •
Bird-watching, fishing and hiking
nearby
RATES: *$35-$50 (1-2), $5-$10
add'l person • Continental breakfast
• Open year-round • Visa accepted •
HNL Member*

English Harbour West
Olde Oven Inn ★★ ½
Main Road, Box 40, English
Harbour West, Fortune Bay,
A0H 1M0
(709) 888-3461/3251
Fax (709) 888-3441
English Harbour West Rte. 360 •
Traditional Newfoundland home
with view of harbour • Four o/n
units, shared B&S • Cable TV and
telephone in sitting room • Pets per-
mitted, usually on leash • Non-
smoking only
FEATURES: Laundry facilities •
Kitchenette • Bird-watching, fishing
and hiking nearby
*RATES: $40 (1), $50 (2), $15 add'l
person • Continental breakfast •
Open year-round • MC, Visa
accepted • HNL Member*

Exploits Island
Devon House ★★ ½
Box 430, Lewisporte, A0G 3A0
(709) 541-3230/535-2509
Fax (709) 535-0805
Heritage home on remote resettled
island • Four o/n units, shared B&S
• Telephone • Pets permitted • No
smoking in rooms, please
FEATURES: All meals included •
Boat transportation • Laundry facili-
ties • Dining room • Housekeeping
services • Outdoor hot tub • Whale-,
iceberg- and bird-watching
*RATES: $100 (1) • Open May 15-
Sept. 15 • MC, Visa accepted*

Ferryland
The Ark of Avalon
Bed & Breakfast ★★ ½
General Delivery, Ferryland,
A0A 2H0
(709) 432-2861
Ferryland Rte. 10 • Four o/n units,
two shared B • Satellite TV • No
smoking in rooms, please
FEATURES: Laundry facilities •
Home-cooked meals • Dining room
• Patio deck with barbecue •
Fishing, hiking and museum nearby
*RATES: $45-$50 (2) • Full break-
fast • Open year-round*

Flower's Cove
Labrador Vue
Bed & Breakfast ★ ½
Box 145, Flower's Cove, A0K 2N0
(709) 456-2396/2526
Flower's Cove off Rte. 430 • Three
o/n units, two shared B&S • Cable
TV in living room • No pets, please
FEATURES: Access to kitchen •
Hunting and fishing nearby •
Icebergs, whales and seals (watch
the running of seals in the spring) •
Close to Strait of Belle Isle ferry, St.
Anthony Airport, Sandy Cove
Airstrip, L'Anse aux Meadows
Viking site, and Port au Choix Point
Rich Indian Burial Grounds (all
within one hour by car)
*RATES: $40 (1), $45 (2) •
Continental breakfast • Open year-
round*

Fogo Island
Alma's
Bed and Breakfast ★★ ½
Alma Kinden, Box 90, Stag
Harbour, Fogo Island, A0G 4B0
(709) 627-3302/3225
Fogo Island Rte. 333 • Three o/n
units, one shared B&S • Cable TV
and radio in rooms • Cot available •
Non-smoking only
FEATURES: Laundry facilities •
Evening snack • Picnic area •
Hiking trails • Snowmobiling and
cross-country skiing in season •
Whale-, iceberg- and bird-watching
• Swimming and beaches nearby •

Craft shop and museums nearby •
Boat tours available
*RATES: $43.50 (1), $48.50 (2), $10
add'l person • Full breakfast • Open
May 15-Oct. 15*

Fogo Island
Payne's Hospitality Home ★ ½
Box 201, Fogo, A0G 2B0
(709) 266-2359
Fogo Island off Rte. 335 via ferry
from Farewell • Three o/n units, one
shared 1/2 B • Cable TV and telephone • No smoking in rooms,
please
FEATURES: Meals included •
Playground and picnic area • Close
to museum, craft shop and scenic
areas • Whale-, iceberg- and bird-
watching • Fishing and hiking nearby
*RATES: $28-$32 (1), $56 (2) •
Open year-round*

Forteau
Grenfell Louie A. Hall ★★ ½
3 Willow Avenue, Box 137,
Forteau, A0K 2P0
(709) 931-2916
Forteau Rte. 510 • Former home of
the International Grenfell Nursing
Association (c. 1946) • Five o/n
units, two shared B&S • Cable
TV/VCR in living room • No pets,
please • Non-smoking only
FEATURES: Laundry facilities •
Meals on request • Dining room and
living room with fireplace • Close to
playground • Whale-, iceberg-, bird-
watching and fishing nearby
*RATES: $35 (1), $40 (2), $7 add'l
person • Family rates available •
Open year-round • Continental
breakfast • Visa accepted • HNL
Member*

Fox Harbour
Last Chance Bed & Breakfast ★★
General Delivery, Fox Harbour,
A0B 1V0
(709) 227-7119
Located near Nova Scotia ferry •
Four o/n units, shared B&S • Pets
welcome • No smoking in rooms,
please
FEATURES: Near Castle Hill
National Historic Site, Atlantic
Charter Monument and Cape St.
Mary's Bird Sanctuary
*RATES: $50 (1-2), $ 10 add'l per-
son • Full breakfast • Open year-
round*

Gander
Cape Cod Inn B&B ★★★
66 Bennet Drive, Gander, A1V 1M9
Tel & Fax (709) 651-2269
Gander Rte. 1 • Three o/n units, private B&S; one suite • Cable TV and
telephone in rooms • Non-smoking
only
FEATURES: Maid service •
Fishing and golf nearby • Thirty-
minute drive to whale- and iceberg-
watching
*RATES: $45-$75 (1-2), $10 add'l
person • Continental breakfast •
Open year-round • MC, Visa
accepted*

Gander
Country Inn ★★ ½
315 Gander Bay Road, Box 154,
Gander, A1V 1W6
(709) 256-4005
Fax (709) 651-1004
Rte. 330, 4 km (2.4 mi) from Rte. 1
• Nine o/n units, private B&S •
Cable TV and telephone in rooms •
Cots available • Pets permitted, usually on leash
FEATURES: Wheelchair accessibility • Room service • Playground •
Golf and hiking nearby
*RATES: $42 (1), $48 (2), $5 add'l
person • Continental breakfast •
Open year-round • MC, Visa
accepted • HNL Member*

Gander
Traveller's Choice Inn
Bed & Breakfast ★★ ½
303 Gander Bay Road, Box 183,
A1V 2R3
(709) 256-7846
Rte. 330 off Rte. 1; three-minute
drive from Gander • Two o/n units,
one shared B&S • Cable TV and
telephone in sitting room • No
smoking in rooms, please
FEATURES: Laundry facilities •
Dining room • Spacious sundeck •
Hand-crafted items for sale
*RATES: $40 (1), $45 (2), $10 add'l
person • Continental breakfast •
Open June-Sept.*

Gaskiers
Tobin's Gaskiers Bay ★★ ½
Main Highway, Box 143, St.
Mary's, A0B 3B0
(709) 525-2463/2849
Gaskiers Rte. 90 • Overlooks St.
Mary's Bay • Two o/n units, one
shared B&S • Cable TV and telephone in rooms • No smoking in
rooms, please
FEATURES: Laundry facilities •
Home-cooked meals on request •
Whale-, iceberg- and bird-watching
• Hiking and caribou herd nearby
*RATES: $40-$60 (2), $10 add'l
person • Full breakfast • Open year-
round*

Gaultois
Gaultois Inn ★★★
Box 151, Gaultois, A0H 1N0
(709) 841-4141/3186
Rte. 364 via ferry from Hermitage-
Sandyville • Six o/n units, private
B&S • Cable TV and telephone in
rooms • Pets permitted
FEATURES: Laundry facilities •
Dining room featuring fresh seafood
• Lounge • Room service
*RATES: $50-$60 (2) • Continental
breakfast • Open year-round • Visa
accepted*

Glovertown
30 Main
Bed & Breakfast ★★ ½
30 Main Street South, Box 58,
Glovertown, A0G 2L0
(709) 533-2559
Fax (709) 533-2640
Glovertown Rte. 310 • Four o/n
units, shared B&S • Cable TV and
telephone in rooms • Cot available •
Non-smoking only
FEATURES: Modern home with
comfortable surroundings • Whale-,
iceberg- and bird-watching •
Fishing, golf and hiking nearby •
Close to Terra Nova National Park
*RATES: $40-$50 (2), $10 add'l
person • Continental breakfast •
Open May-Oct. • Major credit cards
accepted*

Glovertown
Ackerman's
Bed & Breakfast ★★ ½
Box 239, Glovertown, A0G 2L0
(709) 533-2811/2810
Glovertown Rte. 310, on the border
of Terra Nova National Park • Four
o/n units, private B&S • Pets per-
mitted
FEATURES: Golf and National
Park nearby
*RATES: $40 (1), $50 (2), $5 add'l
person • Continental breakfast •
Open year-round*

Glovertown
The Lilac Inn B&B ★★★
Pinetree Road, Box 221
Glovertown, A0G 2L0
(709) 533-6038
Enjoy true Newfoundland hospitality
and modern luxuries in our newly-
restored, Victorian-style home •
Three o/n units, private B&S • Cots
available • Pets permitted • Non-
smoking only
FEATURES: Bird-watching, fishing and National Park nearby •
Afternoon tea and evening snack
*RATES: $50-$60 (1-2), $10 add'l
person • Full breakfast • Visa
accepted • HNL Member*

Grand Bank
Thorndyke
Bed & Breakfast ★★ ½
33 Water Street, Box 39, Grand
Bank, A0E 1W0
(709) 832-0820/279-3384
Grand Bank Rte. 210 • Sea captain's
mansion (c. 1917), overlooking
Fortune Bay • Four o/n units, private B&S • Cot available • Pets welcome • Non-smoking only
FEATURES: Golf and hiking nearby
RATES: $35-$50 (2), $10 add'l

*person • Full breakfast • Open May-
Sept. • Visa accepted*

Grand Bruit
Dutch Inn ★★
Grand Bruit, A0M 1G0
(709) 492-2730/2665
Grand Bruit off Rte. 470 via coastal
boat from Rose Blanche • Cable TV
and telephone in rooms
FEATURES: Dining room •
Lounge • Guide services available
*RATES: $50 (1-2), $10 add'l per-
son • Open year-round*

Grand Falls-Windsor
Carriage House
Inn ★★★ ½
181 Grenfell Heights, Grand Falls-
Windsor, A2A 2J2
Tel & Fax (709) 489-7185
Toll free 1-800-563-7133
Grand Falls-Windsor Rte. 1 •
Country home in quiet setting on six
acres • Four o/n units, private B&S
• Cable TV and telephone in rooms
• Pets welcome, on leash • Non-
smoking only
FEATURES: Library • Spacious
sun deck • Full equestrian facility,
with stable tours • Newfoundland
dog and pony on premises • Golf
course nearby • Hiking on property
*RATES: $49-$79 (1-2), $10 add'l
person • Full breakfast • Open year-
round • Visa accepted • HNL Member*

Grand Falls-Windsor
Poplar Inn
Bed & Breakfast ★★ ½
Wayne & Beth Thorne, 22 Poplar
Road, Grand Falls-Windsor,
A2A 1V5
(709) 489-2546
Grand Falls-Windsor Rte. 1, Exit
19, keep right • Three o/n units, private B&S • Cable TV and clock
radio in rooms • Telephone • Non-
smoking only
FEATURES: Elegant and comfortable home in quiet surroundings •
Golf, fishing and playground nearby
• Centre-of-town location close to a
variety of services, restaurants and
shopping
*RATES: $40-$50 (2), $10 add'l
person • Continental or full breakfast • Open year-round • MC, Visa
accepted • HNL Member*

Gunners Cove
Valhalla
Bed & Breakfast ★★ ½
Box 10, Gunners Cove, L'Anse aux
Meadows, A0K 2X0
(709) 623-2018
Fax (709) 623-2144
Off-season (709) 896-5519
Gunners Cove Rte. 436 • Four o/n
units, private B&S • Telephone •
Radio • Pets permitted • Non-smok-
ing only
FEATURES: Wheelchair accessi-
bility • Author Annie Proulx (*The
Shipping News*) stayed here • Room
service • Kitchenette available
*RATES: $45 (1), $55 (2) •
Continental breakfast • Open June-
Oct. • Visa accepted*

Happy Valley-Goose Bay
Bradley's
Bed & Breakfast
13 MacKenzie Drive, Box 164,
Station C, Happy Valley-Goose
Bay, A0P 1C0
(709) 896-8006
Happy Valley-Goose Bay Rte. 500 •
Three o/n units, shared B&S • Cable
TV and telephone in rooms • Non-
smoking only
FEATURES: Homemade bread,
muffins and jams • Laundry facili-
ties • Lounge • Room service •
Picnic area • Walk to golf course,
local bars, restaurants and shops
*RATES: $40-$55 (1-2) •
Continental breakfast • Open year-
round • Visa accepted*

Happy Valley-Goose Bay
Davis Bed & Breakfast
14 Cabot Crescent, Box 811, Station
B, Happy Valley-Goose Bay,
A0P 1E0
(709) 896-5077
Happy Valley-Goose Bay Rte. 520 •
Four o/n units, private B&S • Cable
TV in sitting room • Telephone and
radio in rooms • Non-smoking only
FEATURES: Wheelchair accessi-
bility • Laundry facilities • Best
homemade bread and jams • Banks,
restaurants, Post Office and car
rentals nearby
*RATES: $40-$60 (2-3) •
Continental breakfast • Open year-
round • MC, Visa accepted • HNL
Member*

Happy Valley-Goose Bay
Royal Inn ★★ ½
3 Royal Avenue, Box 69, Station B,
Happy Valley-Goose Bay, A0P 1E0
(709) 896-2456
Fax (709) 896-5501

Newly renovated inn on quiet street in town centre • Nine o/n units, private B&S; nine housekeeping suites • Cable TV and telephone in rooms • No pets, please • No smoking in rooms, please
FEATURES: Picnic area • Barbecues on decks
RATES: $57-$99 (1-4), $10 add'l person • Continental breakfast • Open year-round • Major credit cards accepted • HNL member

Harbour Grace
Garrison House Inn
16 Water Street, Box 736, Harbour Grace, A0A 2M0
(709) 596-3658
Rte. 70 • 1811 heritage home furnished with antiques • Three o/n units, private B&S • Telephone • No smoking in rooms, please
FEATURES: Wheelchair accessibility • Laundry facilities • Dining room • Room service • Garden • Whale-, iceberg-watching and hiking nearby
RATES: $49-$63 (1-2) • Open year-round • Major credit cards accepted • HNL Member

Harbour Grace
Old Rothesay House ★★ ½
Box 943, Harbour Grace, A0A 2M0
(709) 596-2268
Rte. 70 • Queen Anne-style Victorian house in heritage district, on the ocean • Four o/n units, private B&S • Cable TV and telephone • Cot available • Non-smoking rooms
FEATURES: French spoken • Laundry facilities • Banquet/meeting facilities • Room service • Whale-, iceberg-, bird-watching and hiking nearby
RATES: $49-$59 (2), $10 add'l person • Open year-round • Major credit cards accepted

Harbour Main
Kennedy's Country Corner Bed & Breakfast ★★ ½
Box 74, Lakeview, Harbour Main, A0A 2P0
(709) 229-6568
Lakeview Rte. 60 • Two o/n units, private B&S (Jacuzzi) • Cable TV and telephone in rooms • Pets welcome • Non-smoking only
FEATURES: French spoken • Beautiful scenery overlooking pond • Laundry facilities • Room service • Propane barbecue on veranda • Whale-, iceberg-watching, fishing and hiking nearby
RATES: $40-$45 (2), $5 add'l person • Full breakfast • Open year-round

Harcourt
Hollingside Bed & Breakfast ★★
1 Luther Place, Mount Pearl, A1N 3E7
(709) 747-3663
Harcourt Rte. 232 • Clean, comfortable accommodation • Three o/n units, one shared B&S • Two cats and one dog on premises • No pets, please • Non-smoking only
RATES: $50-$60 (2) • Continental breakfast • Open year-round • Reservations required

Hawke's Bay
Baie View
Bed & Breakfast ★★ ½
Miranda Mouland, Box 54,
Hawke's Bay, A0K 3B0
(709) 248-5270
Toll free 1-800-354-5270
Hawke's Bay Rte. 430 • Three o/n
units, two shared B&S • Cable TV
in rooms • Pets permitted, usually
on leash • Designated smoking area
FEATURES: Wheelchair accessibility • Laundry facilities • Meals on
request • Evening snack • Barbecues
• Playground • Whale- and iceberg-
watching
*RATES: $35 (1), $40 (2), $5 add'l
person • Continental breakfast •
Open year-round • AE, MC, Visa
accepted •*

Hawke's Bay
Gloria's
Bed & Breakfast ★★ ½
27 Bayview Drive, Box 26,
Hawke's Bay, A0K 3B0
(709) 248-5131

Hawke's Bay
Rte. 430 •
Three o/n units,
shared B&S •
Cable TV and
telephone in rooms • No pets, please
• Non-smoking only
FEATURES: Clean, quiet, homey
atmosphere • Laundry facilities •
Beauty salon on premises • Picnic
area • Fishing and hiking nearby
*RATES: $35 (1), $40 (2), $7 add'l
person • Continental breakfast •
Open year-round*

Heart's Delight
Farm House
Hospitality Home ★★ ½
Box 72, Heart's Delight, Trinity

Bay, A0B 2A0
(709) 588-2393
Heart's Delight Rte. 80 • Three o/n
units, one private B, one shared
B&S • Cable TV and telephone in
family room • Non-smoking only
FEATURES: Playground • Fishing,
beach and swimming nearby •
Provincial Park and museum nearby
• Historic Trans-Atlantic Cable
Station and craft shop nearby
*RATES: $40-$50 (2), $10 add'l
person • Continental breakfast •
Open May 1-Nov. 30*

Hillgrade
Sunset
Bed & Breakfast ★★
General Delivery, Hillgrade,
A0G 2S0
(709) 628-5209/5312
Off Rte. 340 • Quiet, peaceful area
overlooking ocean • Three o/n units,
private B&S • Cable TV in rooms •
Pets welcome • Non-smoking only
FEATURES: Sun room with tele-
scope • Laundry facilities •
Homemade baked goods •
Kitchenette available • Whale- and
iceberg-watching nearby
*RATES: $45-$50 (2), $10 add'l
person • Continental breakfast •
Open May 1-Oct. 15*

Holyrood
Beach Cottage
Bed & Breakfast ★★ ½
Godson Road, Holyrood,
Conception Bay, A0A 2R0
(709) 229-4801
Holyrood Rte. 60 • Three o/n units,
private B&S • Cable TV in sitting
room • No pets, please • Non-smoking only
FEATURES: Ocean view • Dining
room • Picnic area • Outdoor swimming • Whale- and iceberg-watch-

ing nearby
RATES: $44-$49 (2) • Open June 15-Sept. 15 • HNL Member

Horwood
Bennings
Bed & Breakfast ★★
General Delivery, Stoneville, A0G 4C0
(709) 541-3091
Holyrood off Rte. 331 • Two o/n units, one shared B&S • No pets, please • Non-smoking only
FEATURES: Many rivers and ponds for trout and salmon fishing • Ice fishing and skidooing in season • Twenty minutes to Fogo and Change Islands Farewell Ferry
RATES: $40-$45 • Continental breakfast • Open May 1-Sept. 30 • Visa accepted

Jackson's Arm
Peggy's
Hospitality Home ★★
Box 39, Jackson's Arm, White Bay, A0K 3H0
(709) 459-3333/482-2628
Jackson's Arm Rte. 420 • Four o/n units, private B&S • Cable TV and telephone in rooms • Cot available • Pets permitted, usually on leash • Non-smoking only
FEATURES: French spoken
RATES: $40 (1-2), $15 add'l person • Continental breakfast • Open year-round

L'Anse-Amour
Davis
Bed & Breakfast ★★
Rita Davis, General Delivery, L'Anse-Amour, A0K 3L0
(709) 927-5690
L'Anse-Amour Rte. 510 • Three o/n units, two shared B&S • Cable TV

and telephone in sitting room • Non-smoking only
FEATURES: Laundry facilities • Barbecue and picnic table • Playground • Whale- and iceberg-watching nearby
RATES: $32 (1), $36 (2), $5 add'l person • Continental breakfast • Open year-round • MC, Visa accepted

L'Anse au Clair
Beachside
Hospitality Home ★★ ½
9 Lodge Road, General Delivery, L'Anse au Clair Rte. 510, L'Anse au Clair, A0K 3K0
(709) 931-2662
Toll free 1-800-563-8999
• Three o/n units, shared B&S • Telephone in rooms • Pets permitted • Non-smoking only
FEATURES: Laundry facilities • Whale- and iceberg-watching • Fishing and hiking nearby
RATES: $45 (1-2), $10 add'l person • Continental breakfast • Open year-round • MC, Visa accepted • HNL Member

L'Anse-Au-Loup
Barney's
Bed & Breakfast ★★
General Delivery, L'Anse-Au-Loup,
A0K 3L0
(709) 927-5634
L'Anse-au-Loup Rte. 510 • Clean,
comfortable accommodations •
Three o/n units, one shared B&S •
Telephone
FEATURES: Laundry facilities •
Home-cooked seafood meals •
Homemade bread and pies made
from bakeapples and partridge
berries • Picnic area • Indoor swim-
ming • Whale-, iceberg-, bird-
watching and fishing nearby
RATES: $30-$45 (1-2) •
Continental breakfast • Open year-
round • HNL Member

L'Anse aux Meadows
Marilyn's
Hospitality Home ★★ ½
Box 5, Hay Cove, L'Anse aux
Meadows, A0K 2X0
(709) 623-2811
Hay Cove Rte. 436 • Three o/n
units, shared B&S • Cable TV and
telephone • No smoking in rooms,
please
FEATURES: L'Anse aux Meadows
Viking site and straits view only 1
km (.6 mi) away • Meals on request
• Whale-, iceberg-, bird-watching
and hiking nearby
RATES: $35 (1), $40 (2), $5 add'l
person • Full breakfast • Open
April-Nov. • Visa accepted

L'Anse aux Meadows
Viking Nest ★★ ½
Box 127, Hay Cove, A0K 2X0
(709) 623-2238
Three o/n units, shared B&S • Cable
TV in rooms and sitting room •
Telephone in rooms
FEATURES: Use of kitchen and
barbecue • Meals on request •
Evening snack • Walk to L'Anse
aux Meadows National Historic Site
• Close to Viking boat tours
RATES: $30-$38 (1-2) • Full
breakfast • Open year-round • Visa
accepted

Lark Harbour
Mary's
Bed & Breakfast ★★ ½
127 Little Port Road, Lark Harbour ,
Box 231, Corner Brook, A2H 6C9
(709) 681-2210/789-3642
Large home, forty-five minutes
from Corner Brook on Rte. 450 •
Two o/n units, one shared B&S •
Cot available • Pets welcome
FEATURES: Hiking nearby •
Picnic area
RATES: $35-$45 (1-2), $5 add'l
person • Full breakfast • Open
June 1-Sept. 6

LaScie
Rogers'
Bed & Breakfast ★★★
6 Rogers' Lane, Box 203, LaScie,
A0K 3M0
(709) 675-2505
LaScie Rte. 414 • Four o/n units,
private B&S • Non-smoking only
FEATURES: Wheelchair accessibility • Meals on request • Whale-,
iceberg- and bird-watching nearby
RATES: $35 (1), $40 (2), $10 add'l
person • Continental breakfast •
Open year-round • HNL Member

Lewisporte
Northgate
Bed & Breakfast ★★ ½
June Leschied, 106 Main Street,
Box 358, Lewisporte, A0G 3A0
(709) 535-2258
Country-style home • Four o/n units,
private B&S • Cable TV/VCR and
telephone in lounge • Pets permitt-
ted, usually on leash • Non-smoking
only
FEATURES: Sitting rooms with
fireplace • Picnic area • Whale-, iceberg-watching, fishing, hiking and-
boat tours nearby • Near Labrador
ferry terminal • Laundry facilities
*RATES: $40-$50 (1-2), $10 add'l
person • Full breakfast • Open May 1
-Oct. • HNL Member*

Little Bay Islands
Sheltered
Harbour Inn ★★
Box 22, Little Bay Islands, A0J 1K0
(709) 626-5341/5476
Little Bay Islands off Rte. 392 via
ferry from Shoal Arm • Three o/n
units, shared B&S • Cable TV •
Cots available • Non-smoking only
FEATURES: Laundry facilities
nearby • Dining room • Evening
snack • Sun deck • Barbecue •
Picnic area • Gazebo
*RATES: $35-$45 (1-2) • Senior citi-
zens' 10% discount • Continental
breakfast • Open June-Oct. • Visa
accepted*

Little Rapids
Adams House
Bed & Breakfast
Roberts Drive, Box 283, Corner
Brook, A2H 6C9
Tel & Fax (709) 634-0064
E-mail adamsb&b@newcomm.net
Beautiful establishment in the mag-
nificent Humber Valley • Four o/n
units, private B&S • Cot available •
Telephone in rooms • Non-smoking
only
FEATURES: Dining room •
Fishing nearby • Close to Marble
Mountain Ski Resort
*RATES: $45-$55 (1-2), $10 add'l
person • Full breakfast • Open year-
round • Major credit cards accepted*

Little Rapids
Humber Valley
Hospitality Home ★★ ½
26 Roberts Drive, Box 15, Corner
Brook, A2H 6C3
(709) 634-2660
Rte. 1, Exit 10 • Excellent overnight
stop en route to Gros Morne Park •
Three o/n units, shared B&S • Cable
TV • Telephone • Cot available • No
pets, please • No smoking in rooms,
please
FEATURES: Near Marble
Mountain Ski Resort • Picnic area
*RATES: $39-$45 (1-2), $9 add'l
person • Senior citizens' 10% dis-
count • Continental breakfast •
Open June 15-Sept. 15; Feb. 1-
March 31 • Visa accepted • HNL
Member*

Makkovik
Adlavik Inn
Box 123, Makkovik, A0P 1J0
(709) 923-2389
Five o/n units, private B&S • Cable
TV and telephone in rooms • No pets,
please • No smoking in rooms, please
FEATURES: Dining room featuring char, caribou and homemade
jams • Laundry facilities • Room
and maid service • Fishing nearby
*RATES: $70 (1), $100 (2) • Open
year-round • Major credit cards
accepted*

Marystown
Bayside
Bed & Breakfast ★★ ½
31 Water Street West, Marystown,
A0E 2M0
(709) 279-3286
Beautiful location overlooking
Mortier Bay • Three o/n units •
Cable TV • Telephone • Non-smoking only
FEATURES: Craft store, museums
and shopping nearby • Close to
beaches and golf course • Evening
snack
*RATES: $45-$55 (1-2) • Full
breakfast • Open year-round •
Major credit cards accepted*

Marystown
Creston House
B&B ★★ ½
219 Creston Boulevard, Marystown,
A0E 1K0
(709) 279-3384
E-mail kmconrad@earthlink.net
Three o/n units, private B&S • Cot
available • Non-smoking only
FEATURES: Close to malls and
golf course • Hiking nearby
*RATES: $35-$45 (1-2), $10 add'l
person • Full breakfast • Open year-
round • Visa accepted*

Ming's Bight
M & M
Hospitality Home ★★ ½
14 Newtown Road, Ming's Bight,
A0K 3S0
(709) 254-8221
Ming's Bight Rte. 418 • New home
• Three o/n units, one private B&S,
one shared B&S • No pets, please •
No smoking in rooms, please
FEATURES: Laundry facilities •
Patio deck • Whale-, iceberg-
watching and fishing nearby

*RATES: $38 (1-2) • Full breakfast •
Open year-round*

Norris Point
Eileen's
Bed & Breakfast ★★ ½
Eileen James, Box 159, Norris
Point, A0K 3V0
(709) 458-2427
Norris Point Rte. 430 • Three o/n
units, one private 1/2 B, one shared
B&S • Cable TV and telephone in
rooms • Cots available • Non-smoking only
FEATURES: Located in the centre
of Gros Morne National Park, with
great views of Bonne Bay • Fishing,
golfing and hiking nearby
*RATES: $30 (1), $45 (2), $5 add'l
person • Continental breakfast •
Open year-round • HNL Member*

Norris Point
Sugar Hill Inn ★★★ ½
115-129 Rte. 431, Box 100, Norris
Point, A0K 3V0
Tel & Fax (709) 458-2147
Norris Point Rte. 430 • "Civilization
in the wilderness" • Four o/n units,
private B&S • Cable TV and tele-
phone in rooms • Pets permitted •
Non-smoking only
FEATURES: Gourmet cuisine and
fine wines available • Laundry facil-
ities • Licensed dining room • Room
service • Hot tub and sauna •
National Park nearby
*RATES: $76-$156 (2), $10 add'l
person • Open Jan. 15-Oct. 15 •
Major credit cards accepted • HNL
Member*

Norris Point
Terry's
Bed & Breakfast ★★
Box 167, Norris Point, Bonne Bay,
A0K 3V0
(709) 458-2373
Norris Point Rte. 430 • Five o/n
units, shared B&S • Cable TV and
telephone • Pets permitted, usually
on leash • Non-smoking only
FEATURES: In Gros Morne Park
with spectacular view of world-
famous tableland • Laundry facilities • Playground and picnic area •
Fishing and hiking nearby
*RATES: $40 (1), $45 (2), $15 add'l
person • Full breakfast • Open
June-Sept.* • HNL Member

North West River
Blake's
Bed & Breakfast ★★
Box 81, North West River,
A0P 1M0
(709) 497-8348
North West River Rte. 520 • Four
o/n units, one shared B&S • Cable
TV in living room
FEATURES: Large, old-fashioned
kitchen • Laundry facilities • Meals
on request
*RATES: $45 (2) • Continental
breakfast • Open year-round*

Old Perlican
The Captain's Inn ★★ ½
Box 48, Old Perlican, Trinity Bay,
A0A 3G0
(709) 587-2626
Fax (709) 587-2447
Rte. 70 • Restored home with hard-
wood floors • Four o/n units, private
B&S • Cable TV in rooms
FEATURES: Home cooking •
Laundry facilities • Dining room •
Meeting facilities • Group tours to

Baccalieu Island arranged
*RATES: $55 (1-2), $5 add'l person
• Open year-round • Major credit
cards accepted*

Petite Forte
Anchor's Down Inn ★★ ½
181 Middle Cove, Torbay,
A1K 1G1
(709) 428-4251
Off-season (709) 437-5481
Petite Forte Rte. 210 • Peaceful and
serene heritage property, located in
isolated fishing community now
linked by road to Burin Peninsula •
Three o/n units, one private B&S,
two private 1/2 B • Telephone • No
smoking in rooms, please
FEATURES: Laundry facilities •
Meals on request • Outdoor swimming • Bird-watching, golf and hiking nearby •
*RATES: $35-$55 (1-2) • Full
breakfast • Open May-Oct.* • MC,
Visa accepted • HNL Member

Petty Harbour
Orca Inn ★★ ½
Reg & Mildred Carter, Main Road,
Box 197, Petty Harbour, A0A 3H0
(709) 747-9676
Website
http://www.bbcanada.com/94.html
Petty Harbour Rte. 11 • Scenic fishing village • Four o/n units, two
shared B&S • Cable TV and telephone • No pets, please • Non-
smoking only
FEATURES: Room service •
Whale- and iceberg-watching nearby • Close to seabird sanctuary •
Fifteen-minute drive from downtown St. John's and Cape Spear
*RATES: $45-$50 (1-2), $5 add'l
person • Continental breakfast •
Open year-round • MC, Visa
accepted • HNL Member*

Placentia
Avalon
Bed & Breakfast ★★ ¹/₂
32 Fox Harbour Road, Dunville,
A0B 1S0
(709) 227-3896
FEATURES: Central to historic sites
*RATES: $45-$50 (1-2) • Full
breakfast • Open year-round*

Placentia
Linehan's
Hospitality Home ★★
Box 186, RR 1, Placentia, A0B 2Y0
(709) 227-5717/3333
Placentia Rte. 100 • Country setting
• Four o/n units, one shared B&S •
Cable TV • Pets permitted • Non-
smoking only
FEATURES: Good food in a
relaxed at-home atmosphere • Picnic
area • Nature walks • Trout and
salmon fishing in ocean behind
house • Bird-watching • Hair salon
on premises
*RATES: $45-$50 (1-2), $10 add'l
person • Full breakfast • Open year-
round*

Placentia
Rosedale Manor ★★ ¹/₂
Riverside Drive, Box 329, Placentia,
A0B 2Y0
(709) 227-3613
Placentia Rte. 100 • Heritage home
• Four o/n units, private B&S •
Cable TV • Telephone • Non-smok-
ing only
FEATURES: Picnic area • Bird-
watching, hiking and National
Historic Site nearby • Close to
Argentia ferry
*RATES: $50-$60 (1-2), $10 add'l
person • Continental breakfast •
Open year-round • Visa accepted*

Placentia
Trudon
Hospitality House ★★ ¹/₂
Highway Road, General Delivery,
Freshwater, A0B 1W0
(709) 227-2774
Fax (709) 227-5555
Freshwater Rte. 100, 2 km (1.2 mi)
from Nova Scotia ferry • Six o/n
units, private B&S • Cable TV/VCR
and telephone in sitting room
FEATURES: French spoken •
Laundry facilities • Lounge • Bird-
watching, hiking and fishing nearby
*RATES: $52-$57 (1-2), $10 add'l
person • Full breakfast • Open year-
round • Visa accepted*

Point Leamington
Ocean Side
Country Lodge ★★
General Delivery, Point
Leamington, A0H 1Z0
Tel & Fax (709) 483-2002
Six o/n units, private B&S; two cab-
ins • Pets welcome
FEATURES: Whale-, iceberg-, bird-
watching and fishing nearby • Laundry
facilities • Dining room • Room service
*RATES: $45 (1-2), $60-$70
(cabin), $10 add'l person •
Continental breakfast • Open year-
round • HNL Member*

Point Leamington
Skipper's View
Bed & Breakfast
and Cottage ★★ ¹/₂
259 Main Street, Box 154, Point
Leamington, A0H 1Z0
(709) 484-3415/3271
Point Leamington Rte. 350 • One
o/n unit (sleeps four), private B&S;
one cottage • Cable TV and telephone • Pets welcome • Non-smoking only

FEATURES: Traditional Newfoundland music • Piano • Picnic area • Visit Newfoundland pony sanctuary • Whale-, iceberg-, bird-watching, fishing, golf and hiking nearby • Close to playground *RATES: $50-$55 (1-2), $60 (cottage), $15 add'l person • Breakfast • Open year-round • HNL Member*

Plum Point
Storehouse
Bed & Breakfast ★ ½
General Delivery, Plum Point, A0K 4A0
(709) 247-2117
Off Rte. 430, opposite Post Office on road to Brig Bay • Conveniently located near Strait of Belle Isle ferry and historic sites • Three o/n units, one shared B&S • Pets welcome • Non-smoking only
FEATURES: Laundry facilities
RATES: $25-$40 • Continental breakfast • Open year-round

Pool's Cove
By the Bay
Hospitality Home
Box 84, Pool's Cove, Fortune Bay, A0H 2B0
Tel & Fax (709) 665-3176
Pool's Cove off Rte. 362 • Three o/n units, shared B&S • Cable TV and telephone in rooms • Cot available • Children under 12 yrs free • Pets permitted • Non-smoking only
FEATURES: Laundry facilities • Bird-watching, fishing and hiking nearby
RATES: $35-$40 (1-2), $5-$10 add'l person • Full breakfast • Open year-round • MC, Visa accepted • HNL Member

Port aux Basques
Caribou
Bed & Breakfast ★★ ½
30 Grand Bay Road, Box 53, Port aux Basques, A0N 1K0
(709) 695-3408
E-mail douglasg@nlnet.nf.ca
Website http://www.ccn.cs.dal.ca/-ae050/profile.html
2 km (1.2 mi) from ferry • Four o/n units, two private B&S, one shared B&S • Cots available • No pets, please • Non-smoking only
FEATURES: Room service • Bird-watching, fishing and hiking nearby • Craft shop • Evening tea
RATES: $43-$49 (1-2), $6-$10 add'l person • Continental breakfast • Open May 1-Oct. 31 • Major credit cards accepted • HNL Member

Port aux Basques
Four Seasons
Bed & Breakfast ★★ ½
82 High Street, Box 627, Port aux Basques, A0M 1C0
(709) 695-3826
1 km (.6 mi) to ferry • Three o/n units, one private 1/2 B, one shared B&S • Cable TV/VCR • Cot available • No pets, please • Non-smoking only
FEATURES: Snacks • Picnic area • Barbecue • Parking
RATES: $40-$55 (1-2), $10 add'l person • Off-season rates • Continental breakfast • Open year-round • Major credit cards accepted • HNL Member

Port aux Basques
Heritage Home ★★ ½
11 Caribou Road, Box 1187, Port
aux Basques, A0M 1C0
(709) 695-3240
Walking distance to ferry • Four o/n
units, one private B&S, one shared
B&S; one family suite • Telephone
in rooms • Cable TV in living room
• Cot available • No pets, please •
No smoking in rooms, please
FEATURES: Playground, shops,
museum and restaurants nearby
*RATES: $40-$55 (1-2), $10 add'l
person • Continental breakfast •
Open May-Oct. • MC, Visa accepted
• HNL Member*

Port au Choix
Jeannie's Sunrise
Bed & Breakfast ★★ ½
Fisher Street, Box 189, Port au Choix
(709) 861-3679
Three o/n units, private B&S •
Telephone in rooms • Cot available
• Non-smoking only
FEATURES: Picnic area • Whale-,
iceberg-watching and fishing nearby
*RATES: $35-$45 (1-2), $5 add'l per-
son • Continental breakfast • Open year-
round • Major credit cards accepted*

Port au Choix
Point Riche Inn ★★ ½
Box 334, Port au Choix, A0K 4C0
(709) 861-3773/2112
Private oceanfront property on road
to Interpretation Centre and Point
Riche Lighthouse • Three o/n units,
one private B&S, one shared B&S •
Cable TV/VCR • Radio and tele-
phone in rooms • Non-smoking only
FEATURES: Dining room •
Fishing, hiking and historic site nearby
*RATES: $40-$55 • Continental
breakfast • Open June 27-Aug. 30*

Point au Choix
R & N
Bed & Breakfast ★★ ½
General Delivery, Point au Choix,
A0K 4C0
(709) 861-3435
Fax (709) 861-3722
Two o/n units, shared B&S • Cable
TV in rooms • Non-smoking only
FEATURES: Fishing and hiking
nearby • Kitchenette available •
Laundry facilities
*RATES: $35-$40 (1-2), $7 add'l
person • Continental breakfast •
Open year-round*

Port au Port
Spruce Pine Acres ★★★ ½
Box 219, Port au Port, A0N 1T0
Tel & Fax (709) 648-9600
E-mail spacres@atcon.com
Four o/n units, private B&S; one
chalet • Cable TV and telephone •
Non-smoking only
FEATURES: Sauna and hot tub •
Fitness facilities • Dining room •
Banquet/meeting facilities • Valet
service • Campfire pit • Soft adven-
ture tourism packages with advance
notice
*RATES: $69 (1), $79 (2), $125-
$175 (chalet), $20 add'l person •
Open year-round • Major credit
cards accepted • HNL Member*

Port Blandford
Terra Nova
Hospitality Home ★★ ½
General Delivery, Port Blandford,
A0C 2G0
(709) 543-2260
Toll free 1-888-267-2333
Fax (709) 543-2241
Port Blandford Rte. 233 • Five o/n
units, private B&S; one suite; one
cottage • Cable TV in rooms • Non-

smoking only *FEATURES:* Partial wheelchair accessibility • Picturesque scenery and tasteful decor • Great food and activities galore • Banquet/meeting facilities • Whale-, iceberg-watching, golf course and National Park nearby • Close to Discovery Trail *RATES: $55 (1-2), $65 (suite), $8 add'l person • Full breakfast • Open year-round • Major credit cards accepted • HNL Member*

Port Rexton
Just Like Home ★ ½
Box 1, Site 6, Port Rexton,
A0C 2H0
(709) 464-3338
Ten-minute drive from historic Trinity • Four o/n units, shared B&S • Cable TV • Telephone • Non-smoking only
FEATURES: Whale-, iceberg-watching and fishing nearby *RATES: $45-$53 (1-2) • Continental breakfast • Open year-round • Major credit cards accepted*

Port Rexton
Parkside Inn
Box 132, Port Rexton, A0C 2H0
(709) 464-2151
Port Rexton, Rte. 230 • Six o/n units, private B&S • Cable TV
FEATURES: Dining room • Lounge • Close to historic Trinity, central to major tourist attractions • Whale-, iceberg- and bird-watching • Fishing and hiking nearby *RATES: $45-$55 (1-2), $10 add'l person • Full breakfast • Open year-round • Major credit cards accepted • HNL Member*

Portland Creek
Entente Cordiale ★★ ½
General Delivery, Portland Creek,
A0K 4G0
(709) 898-2288
Off season (709) 634-7407
Portland Creek Rte. 430 • Secluded property with historic decor • Four o/n units, private B&S • Cable TV in sitting room • Non-smoking only
FEATURES: Dining room • Swimming on sandy beach • Close to "Arches" scenic attraction • Fishing, hiking and National Park nearby
RATES: $50 (1-2) • Continental breakfast • Open July-Sept. • Major credit cards accepted

Portugal Cove
Beachy Cove Bed & Breakfast ★★
Box 159, Portugal Cove, A0A 3K0
(709) 895-2920
Two o/n units, shared B&S • Cable TV in rooms • Pets permitted
FEATURES: Beautiful view of Conception Bay • Whale-, iceberg-watching and hiking nearby • Ten minutes from St. John's Airport
RATES: $50-$55 (1-2) • Full breakfast • Open year-round • Visa accepted

St. Phillips
Country Loft ★★
Dogberry Hill Road, Box 441, RR 1,
St. Phillips, A1L 1C1
(709) 895-2615
E-mail
eghiscoc@calvin.stemnet.nf.ca
Rte. 40 or 41 • Two o/n units, one
shared B&S • Cable TV and tele-
phone in rooms • No pets, please •
Non-smoking only
FEATURES: Many festive occa-
sions celebrated • Newfoundland
library collection • Toothbrush,
bathrobe and slippers provided •
Whale- and iceberg-watching near-
by • Fifteen minutes to St. John's
Airport
RATES: $50-$55 (1-2) • *Breakfast* •
Open year-round • *HNL Member*

Raleigh
Taylor's
Bed & Breakfast ★★
Box 99, Raleigh, A0K 4J0
(709) 452-2112/2136
Raleigh Rte. 437 • Four o/n units,
shared B&S • Cable TV and telephone • Cots available • Non-smoking only
FEATURES: Laundry facilities •
Home-cooked meals on request •
Near L'Anse aux Meadows • Close
to Burnt Island Cape with two hundred species of wild and rare flowers
*RATES: $32 (1), $42 (2), $10 add'l
person* • *Full breakfast* • *Open
June-Sept.* • *Visa accepted*

Rigolet
Sivulik Country Inn ★★
Box 58, Rigolet, A0P 1P0
(709) 947-3444
Coastal Labrador (accessible by
coastal boat from St. Anthony or
Happy Valley-Goose Bay) • Seven

o/n units, private B&S • Cable TV
in rooms
FEATURES: Dining room • Room
service • Banquet/meeting facilities
• Whale-, iceberg-watching, fishing
and hiking nearby
RATES: $85-$95 (1-2) • *Open
year-round* • *Visa accepted*

Red Bay
Basinview
Bed & Breakfast ★★ ½
(709) 920-2002
Located in the sixteenth-century-
world whaling capital • Four o/n
units, shared B&S • Telephone •
Cot available • Non-smoking only
FEATURES: Whale-, iceberg-
watching and fishing nearby • Near
Red Bay/Basque Whaling Museum
and historic site • Home-cooked
meals
*RATES: $32-$45 (1-2), $5-$10
add'l person* • *Continental breakfast*
• *Open year-round*

Roberts Arm
Lake Crescent Inn ★★ ½
Evelyn & Bruce Warr, 2 Main
Street, Box 69, Roberts Arm,
A0J 1R0
(709) 652-3067/3568
Fax (709) 652-3056
Four o/n units, shared B&S
(whirlpool) • Cable TV and tele-
phone in rooms • Non-smoking only
FEATURES: Laundry facilities •
Room service • Beaches, boating
and hiking trails nearby • Whale-,
iceberg- and bird-watching •
Snowmobiling in season • Salmon
fishing • Located half-way between
Port aux Basques and St. John's
*RATES: $32 (1), $37 (2), $10 add'l
person* • *$99 (three-night stay)* •
Full breakfast • *Open year-round* •
MC, Visa accepted • *HNL Member*

Rocky Harbour
Betty's B&B ★★ ½
Box 112, Rocky Harbour, A0K 4N0
(709) 458-2850
Two o/n units, one shared B&S •
Cable TV and telephone • Non-
smoking only
FEATURES: Whale-, iceberg-
watching, fishing and hiking nearby
RATES: $35-$45 (1-2) •
Continental breakfast • Open year-
round

Rocky Harbour
Evergreen Bed & Breakfast ★★
Donald & Annie Shears, Evergreen
Lane, Box 141, Rocky Harbour,
A0K 4N0
(709) 458-2692
Rocky Harbour Rte. 430 • Four o/n
units, two shared B&S • Cable TV •
Telephone • Cot available • Non-
smoking only
FEATURES: Homemade bread and
a variety of Newfoundland jams •
Whale-, iceberg- and bird-watching
• Fishing, hiking and National Park
nearby • Close to swimming pool,
mini-golf and go-carts
RATES: $35 (1), $39 (2) • Full
breakfast • Open May 1-Sept. 30 •
MC, Visa accepted • HNL Member

Rocky Harbour
Violet Major's Hospitality Home ★★
Pond Road, Rocky Harbour,
A0K 4N0
(709) 458-2537
Toll free 1-800-999-2537
Rocky Harbour Rte. 430 • Four o/n
units, private B&S • Cable TV and
telephone in rooms • Cot available •
Pets permitted, usually on leash
FEATURES: Living room •

Laundry service • Picnic tables,
patio and barbecue • Swimming
pool • Close to Funland Resort
RATES: $25 (1), $45 (2) •
Breakfast • Open year-round • HNL
Member

Rocky Harbour
Ocean Acre Inn Bed and Breakfast ★★ ½
Main Street North, Rocky Harbour,
A0K 4N0
(709) 458-2272
Off-season 194 Kaye St., Lower
Sackville, NS, B4C 1N2;
(902) 865-5397
Rocky Harbour Rte. 430 •
Oceanfront accommodation located
in the heart of Gros Morne National
Park • Four o/n units, shared B&S •
Cable TV and telephone in living
room • Non-smoking only
FEATURES: Newfoundland library
• Bird-watching and hiking nearby •
Close to banks, restaurants and
laundromat
RATES: $35-$45 (1-2), $10 add'l
person • Full breakfast • Open
June-Sept. • MC, Visa accepted

Rocky Harbour
Wildflowers Bed & Breakfast ★★ ½
Main Street North, Rocky Harbour,
A0K 4N0
(709) 458-3000
Fax (709) 458-2625
Rocky Harbour Rte. 430 • Three o/n
units, shared B&S
FEATURES: Laundromat •
Evening meals on request •
Restaurant • Craft shop • Near
Lobster Cove Lighthouse
RATES: $40-$50 (1-2) •
Continental breakfast • Open year-
round

Roddickton
Betty's
Bed & Breakfast ★★
Box 194, Roddickton, A0K 4P0
(709) 457-2371
Roddickton Rte. 433 • Three o/n
units, shared B&S • Cable TV and
telephone in rooms • Pets permitted
• Non-smoking only
FEATURES: Laundry facilities •
View the cloud hills and watch the
whales in the bay • Whale-, iceberg-
watching and fishing nearby
RATES: $35-$40 (1-2) •
*Continental breakfast • Open year-
round • Visa accepted*

Southport
By The Pond
Bed & Breakfast ★★ ¹/₂
Box 502, RR 1, Southport,
A0E 2A0
(709) 548-2248
Fax (709) 548-2580
Southport Rte. 204 • Two o/n units,
one shared B&S • Cable TV and
telephone in rooms • No pets, please
• Non-smoking only
FEATURES: Fishing on location •
Laundry facilities • Whale-, iceberg-
and bird-watching nearby • Seventy
minutes from Terra Nova
RATES: $40-$45 (1-2) • *Full
breakfast • Open May-Oct.* • *Visa
accepted*

Spaniards Bay
Bay Ridge Cottage ★★ ¹/₂
Main Highway, Box 401, Bay
Roberts, Spaniards Bay, A0A 1G0
(709) 786-3006
Spaniards Bay Rte. 70 • Four o/n
units, shared B&S • Cable TV •
Telephone on each floor • Cot avail-
able • Children under 5 yrs free •
Non-smoking only

FEATURES: Laundry facilities •
Meals on request • Barbecue pits •
Walking trails • Art and craft shops
and historic sites nearby
*RATES: $37 (1), $47 (2), $10 add'l
person • Full breakfast • Open year-
round*

Springdale
Hull's Riverview
Bed & Breakfast ★★ ¹/₂
Box 729, Springdale, A0J 1T0
(709) 673-4518/3835
Fax (709) 673-3177
Springdale Rte. 390, 2 km (1.2 mi)
off Rte. 1 • Quiet location overlooking salmon river • Two o/n units,
one shared B&S • Cable TV and
telephone • Pets permitted, usually
on leash • Non-smoking only
FEATURES: Homemade bread and
jams • Picnic area • Whale-, ice-
berg-, bird-watching, fishing and
hiking nearby • Driving range on
premises
*RATES: $35-$45 (2), $10 add'l
person • Full breakfast • Open year-
round • Visa accepted • HNL Member*

Springdale
Indian River Brook
Bed & Breakfast ★★ ¹/₂
Box 664, Springdale, A0J 1T0
(709) 673-3886
2 km (1.2 mi) from Rte. 1 on Rte.
390; turn right before bridge at
Indian River Brook to second house
• Two o/n units, one shared B
FEATURES: Craft shop featuring
provincial tartans • Newfoundland
dog on premises
*RATES: $35 (1), $45 (2), $10 add'l
person • Full breakfast • Open year-
round • MC, Visa accepted • HNL
Member*

Square Pond
Southwell's Spruce Grove Resort ★ ½
Box 57, Gander, A1V 1W5
(709) 424-1216
Rte. 1, 30 km (18 mi) east of
Gander, on Square Pond • Four o/n
units; two housekeeping suites •
Cable TV in rooms • Cot available •
Pets permitted
FEATURES: Snowmobile trails •
Playground • Laundry facilities •
Room service • Dining room
*RATES: $33-$45 (1-2), $5 add'l
person • Open year-round • Major
credit cards accepted*

St. Anthony
Dogberry Cottage Bed & Breakfast ★★
15A Tuckers Lane, Box 702,
St. Anthony, A0K 4S0
(709) 454-3539
St. Anthony Rte. 430 • Two o/n
units, one shared B&S • Cable TV
in living room • Telephone in hall •
Non-smoking only
FEATURES: Peaceful and quiet
location • Whale-, iceberg-watching
and hiking nearby
*RATES: $32-$38 (1-2) •
Continental breakfast • Open mid-
June-Sept. 30*

St. Anthony
Fishing Point Bed & Breakfast
Box 726, St. Anthony, A0K 4S0
(709) 454-3117/2828
Four o/n units, shared B&S • Cable
TV and telephone • No smoking in
rooms, please
FEATURES: Whale-, iceberg-
watching, fishing and hiking nearby
• Close to Lightkeeper's Cafe
RATES: $35-$40 (1-2) • Breakfast

*extra • Open May-Oct. • Major
credit cards accepted*

St. Anthony
Howell's Tourist Home ★★ ½
1 Spruce Lane, Box 214,
St. Anthony, A0K 4S0
(709) 454-3402/8494
St. Anthony Rte. 430 • Four o/n
units, private B&S • Cable TV in
sitting room • Non-smoking only
FEATURES: Laundry facilities •
View of Anthony Harbour •
Newfoundland literature and maga-
zines available • Iceberg- and
whale-watching nearby
*RATES: $33-$39, $6 add'l person •
Open April-Nov. • Visa accepted*

St. Anthony
Trailsend Hospitality Home ★★ ½
1 Cormack Street, Box 392,
St. Anthony, A0K 4S0
(709) 454-2024/8477
St. Anthony Rte. 430 • Four o/n
units, two shared B&S • Cable TV
and telephone in rooms • Non-
smoking only
FEATURES: Wheelchair accessibility • Laundry facilities • Whale-,
iceberg-watching and National
Historic Site nearby
*RATES: $35-$45 (1-2), $6 add'l
person • Full breakfast • Open
June 1-Sept. 30 • Visa accepted*

St. Anthony
Villa Lemaire B&B ★★
21 Lemaire Road, Box 195, St.
Anthony, A0K 4T0
(709) 454-2590
Fax (709) 454-2010
E-mail drichard@nlnet.nf.ca
Three o/n units • Cot available •
Non-smoking only
FEATURES: Laundry facilities •
Whale-, iceberg-watching, hiking
and historic site nearby
*RATES: $40-$50 (1-2), $8 add'l
person • Full breakfast • Open year-
round • Major credit cards accepted*

St. Bride's
Atlantica Inn ★★
General Delivery, St. Bride's,
A0B 2Z0
(709) 337-2860
St. Bride's Rte. 100 • Five o/n units,
private B&S • Cable TV in rooms •
Cot available
FEATURES: Dining room • Room
service • Close to Cape St. Mary's
Bird Sanctuary • One hour from
Argentia ferry terminal • Whale-,
iceberg-, bird-watching, hiking and
fishing nearby
*RATES: $35-$40 (1-2), $5 add'l
person • Open year-round • Major
credit cards accepted*

St. John's
Avalon House
Bed & Breakfast ★★★
22 Holloway Street, St. John's,
A1C 3R6
Tel & Fax (709) 579-4393
E-mail
mwilson@sparky2.esd.mun.ca
Website
**http://.wordplay.com/tourism/aval
onhouse.html**
Comfortable Victorian home with
views, within walking distance of
restaurants and shops • Two o/n
units, private B&S • Cable TV •
Cats on premises • Not suitable for
children • Non-smoking only
FEATURES: Whale-, iceberg-
watching and hiking nearby • Fax
and e-mail facilities available • Off-
street parking
*RATES: $45-$60 (1-2), $10 add'l
person • Open year-round • Major
credit cards accepted*

St. John's
A Bonne Esperance
House ★★★
20 Gower Street, St. John's,
A1C 1N1
(709) 726-3835
Toll free 1-888-726-3835
Fax (709) 739-0496
Downtown St. John's • Spacious
Victorian house • Four o/n units,
private B&S • Clock radio in rooms
• Cable TV and telephone • Pets
permitted • Non-smoking only
FEATURES: Period furnishings •
Room service and laundry facilities
• Five-minute walk to downtown
and Provincial Archives; minutes
from Signal Hill • Off-street parking
*RATES: From $50 • Full breakfast
• Open year-round • MC, Visa
accepted • HNL Member*

St. John's
A Gower Street
House ★★★
Leonard Clarke, 180 Gower Street,
St. John's, A1C 1P9
Tel & Fax (709) 754-0047
Toll Free 1-800-563-3959
**E-mail mpasinok@public.com-
pusult.nf.ca**
Four o/n units, private B • Cable TV
and telephone in rooms • No smok-
ing in rooms, please

FEATURES: Heritage building, regional art displayed throughout • Laundry facilities • Kitchenette available • Room service • Five-minute walk to harbour, museum, cathedrals, tours, and archives • Off-street parking
RATES: $45-$100 (1-2), $20 add'l person • Continental breakfast • Open year-round • Major credit cards accepted • Cancellation policy

St. John's
Balmoral Inn ★★★
Maria Petrov, 38 Queen's Road, St. John's, A1C 2A5
(709) 754-5721
Fax (709) 722-8111
Toll free 1-888-270-8592
E-mail balmoral@public.com-pusult.nf.ca
Downtown heritage mansion • Three o/n units, private B&S • Cable TV and telephone in rooms • • Non-smoking only
FEATURES: Antique furnishings • Laundry facilities • Sitting room • Historical artwork • Afternoon tea • Air-conditioning • Five-minute walk to harbour, museum, cathedrals, courts, archives, galleries, live theatre and restaurants • Off-street parking
RATES: $40-$175 (1-2), $20 add'l person • Continental breakfast • Open year-round • Major credit cards accepted • HNL Member

St. John's
Bird Island Guest Home ★★ ¹⁄₂
150 Old Topsail Road, St. John's, A1E 2B1
(709) 753-4850/722-1675
Fax (709) 753-3140
E-mail obriens@netfx-inc.com
Older home with hardwood floors, fireplaces and balconies • Two o/n

units, shared B&S • Cable TV and telephone in rooms • No pets, please • Non-smoking only
FEATURES: Regional books and information available • Boat tours • Close to city centre • Day trips for bird- and whale-watching available with shuttle service
RATES: $50 (1), $60 (2) • Continental breakfast • Open May-Oct. • MC, Visa accepted • HNL Member

St. John's
Cantwell House ★★ ¹⁄₂
25 Queen's Road, St. John's, A1C 2A4
(709) 754-8439
Close to city centre • Three o/n units, private B&S • Cable TV and telephone in rooms • No pets, please • No smoking in rooms, please
FEATURES: Laundry facilities
RATES: $55 (1), $60 (2) • Full breakfast • Open year-round • Major credit cards accepted

St. John's
Compton House ★★★
26 Waterford Bridge Road, St. John's, A1E 1C6
(709) 739-5789
Website http://www.grtplaces.com

/ac/compton/ Elegant Victorian mansion • Five o/n units, private B&S; six suites • Cable TV and telephone in rooms • Not suitable for children • No pets, please • Non-smoking only
FEATURES: Period furnishings • Housekeeping services • Whale-, iceberg-watching, golfing and hiking nearby
RATES: $59-$199 (1-2), $15 add'l person • Full breakfast • Open year-round • AE, ER, MC, Visa accepted • HNL Member

St. John's
English Ryall House ★★ ½
6 Wood Street, St. John's, A1C 3K9
(709) 576-0363
Turn-of-the-century house in downtown with spectacular view of harbour • Four o/n units, private B&S • Clock radio in rooms • Cable TV • Non-smoking only
FEATURES: Laundry facilities • National Park nearby • Maid service
RATES: $50-$95 (1-2) • Full breakfast • Open year-round • Major credit cards accepted

St. John's
Fairmede Century Farm Bed & Breakfast ★★ ½
179 Brookfield Road, Box 7095, St. John's, A1E 3Y3
(709) 364-3980
Fax (709) 364-1696

Four o/n units, one shared B&S • Cable TV and telephone • Non-smoking only
FEATURES: Dining room • Playground and picnic area • Fishing, golfing and hiking nearby • Winter weekend packages include sleigh rides and cross-country skiing
RATES: $40-$60 (1-2) • Open year-round

St. John's
Fireside Bed & Breakfast ★★ ½
28 Wicklow Street, St. John's, A1B 3H2
(709) 726-0237
Two o/n units, one shared B&S • Cable TV and telephone • No pets, please • Non-smoking only
FEATURES: Laundry facilities • Whale-, iceberg-watching, golfing and hiking nearby
RATES: $45-$55 (1-2) • Full breakfast • Open year-round

St. John's
Fort William Bed & Breakfast ★★ ½
5 Gower Street, St. John's, A1C 1M9
(709) 726-3161
Fax (709) 739-0990
Heritage home near city centre • Three o/n unit, private B&S; one suite • Cable TV • Non-smoking only
FEATURES: Antique furnishings • Sitting room with fireplace • Kitchenette available • Whale- and iceberg-watching nearby
RATES: $45-$80 (1-2), $15 add'l person • Full breakfast • Open year-round • Major credit cards accepted

St. John's
Leaside Manor B&B ★★ ½
39 Old Topsail Road, St. John's,
A1E 2A6
(709) 722-0387
Fax (709) 722-4660
E-mail leaside@nfld.com
Tudor-style mansion (c. 1921) in
downtown location • Two o/n units,
one shared B&S; two suites • Cable
TV in rooms • No smoking in
rooms, please
FEATURES: Whale-, iceberg- and
bird-watching nearby • French and
German spoken • Internet service •
Holiday planning
*RATES: $69-$109 (1-2), $15 add'l
person • Full breakfast • Open year-
round • Major credit cards accepted
• HNL Member*

St. John's
Monkstown Manor ★★ ½
51 Monkstown Road, St. John's,
A1C 3T4
(709) 754-7324
Fax (709) 722-8557
**E-mail
tkearley@morgan.ucs.mun.ca**
Historic home (c. 1890) with rare
collection of Newfoundland memo-
rabilia • Two o/n units, one shared
B&S • Cot available • Pets welcome
FEATURES: Garden setting •
Laundry facilities • Whale-, iceberg-
watching and hiking nearby • Jacuzzi
*RATES: $45-$55 (1-2), $5 add'l
person • Continental breakfast •
Open year-round • Major credit
cards accepted*

St. John's
Monroe House
Bed & Breakfast ★★★
8a Forest Road, St. John's,
A1C 2B9

(709) 754-0610
E-mail monhouse@newcomm.net
Website
**http://www.wordplay.com-mon-
roe_house/**
Former Prime Minister's home •
Three o/n units, private B&S •
Cable TV and telephone in sitting
room • Clock radio in rooms
FEATURES: Furnished with
antiques • Laundry facilities •
Evening wine served • Separate
guest living room with fireplace
*RATES: $74 (1), $89 (2) • Full
breakfast • ER, MC, Visa accepted*

St. John's
Oh What A View ★★ ½
184 Signal Hill Road, St. John's,
A1A 1B3
(709) 576-7063
Spectacular view of old St. John's
and the harbour • Four o/n units,
private and shared B&S • Cable TV
• No pets, please • Non-smoking only
FEATURES: Plain old
Newfoundland hospitality • Whale-
iceberg- and bird-watching •
Fishing, golf and hiking nearby
*RATES: $65-$80 (1-2) •
Continental breakfast • Open May
15-Oct. 15 • Visa accepted • HNL
Member*

St. John's
Pleasant Mem'ries
Bed & Breakfast ★ ½
110 Pleasant Street, St. John's,
A1E 1L4
(709) 753-2378
Restored home (c. 1925) • Two o/n
units, one shared B&S • No pets,
please • Non-smoking only
FEATURES: Local drinks and a
song or two
*RATES: $35 (1), $50 (2) • Full
breakfast • Open May 1-Sept. 30*

St. John's
The Roses
Bed & Breakfast ★★ ½
9 Military Road, St. John's, A1C 2C3
(709) 726-3336
Fax (709) 726-3483
E-mail poneill@newcomm.net
Four o/n units, private B&S • Cable
TV in rooms • Cot available ($5) •
Non-smoking only
FEATURES: Furnished with
antiques • Housetop kitchen with
panoramic view of St. John's •
Whale-, iceberg- and bird-watching
• Hiking and National Historic Site
nearby
*RATES: $55-$70 (1-2), $10 add'l
person • Full breakfast • Open year-
round • AE, MC and Visa accepted
• HNL Member*

St. John's
Sebastian House ★★ ½
28 Gower Street, St. John's,
A1C 1N1
(709) 754-1326
Nineteenth-century home in historic
downtown • Three o/n units; one
suite • Non-smoking only
FEATURES: Private balconies •
Whale-, iceberg-, bird-watching and
hiking nearby
*RATES: $65-$75 (1-2), $10 add'l
person • Continental breakfast •
Open mid-May-Sept. • Major credit
cards accepted*

St. John's
Waterford Manor ★★★
185 Waterford Bridge Road,
St. John's, A1E 1C7
(709) 754-4139
Fax (709) 754-4155
Website
**http://www.grtplaces.com/ac/wate
rford**

Award-winning Victorian-style
B&B just minutes from town centre
and Bowring Park • Three o/n units,
private B&S; three suites (Jacuzzi) •
Cable TV and telephone in rooms •
Designated smoking area
FEATURES: Elegant living room
with fireplace • Room service •
Banquet and meeting facilities •
Whale-, iceberg- and bird-watching
nearby
*RATES: $85-$200 (1-2) • Breakfast
• Open year round • MC, Visa
accepted • HNL Member*

St. John's
Winterholme
Heritage Inn ★★★
79 Rennies Mill Road, St. John's,
A1C 3R1
(709) 739-7979
Toll free 1-800-599-7829
Fax (709) 753-9411
**E-mail winterholme@nf.sympati-
co.com**
Website
**http://www.mediatoush.com-win-
terholme**
National historic property located in
heritage district • Seven o/n units,
private B&S; four housekeeping suites
• Cable TV and telephone in rooms
FEATURES: French spoken •
Laundry facilities • Fireplaces •
Housekeeping services • Golf, hik-
ing and National Historic Site nearby
• Off-street parking
*RATES: $69-$179 (1-2), $10 add'l
person • Continental breakfast •
Open year-round • Major credit
cards accepted*

Steady Brook
Edgewater Inn ★★ ½
14 Forest Drive, Box 202, RR 1,
Steady Brook, A2H 2N2
(709) 634-3474

Steady Brook Rte. 1 • Located on beautiful Humber River, near Marble Mountain Ski Resort • Four o/n units, private B&S • Cable TV and telephone • Non-smoking only
FEATURES: Fishing nearby • Boat tours arranged
RATES: $35-$45 (1-2), $10 add'l person • Full breakfast • Open year-round • Visa accepted • HNL Member

Steady Brook
Huxter's
Bed & Breakfast ★★ ½
Ken & Cheryl Huxter, 2 Forest Drive, Box 170, Steady Brook, A2H 2N2
(709) 634-4999
Toll free 1-888-489-8377
Steady Brook Rte. 1 • Riverfront property • Three o/n units, one shared B&S • Cable TV and telephone in rooms • Non-smoking only
FEATURES: Salmon outfitting • Patio deck • Near Marble Mountain Ski Resort and Corner Brook • Golf, hiking, swimming and National Park nearby
RATES: $35 (1), $45 (2) • Continental breakfast • Open year-round • Major credit cards accepted • HNL Member

Steady Brook
Wilton's
Bed & Breakfast ★★ ½
57 Marble Drive, Box 160, Steady Brook, A2H 2N2
Tel & Fax (709) 634-5796

Exit 8 at Steady Brook • Three o/n units, shared B&S • Cable TV and telephone • No pets, please • Non-smoking only

FEATURES: Playground and picnic area • Bird-watching, salmon and trout fishing • Hiking and National Park nearby • Two minutes from Marble Mountain Ski Resort; five minutes from Corner Brook
RATES: $33-$40 (1-2), $10 add'l person • Continental breakfast • Open year-round

Stephenville
Harmon House-Billard's
Bed & Breakfast ★★ ½
George & Myra Billard, 144 New Mexico Drive, Box 656, Stephenville, A2N 3B5
Tel & Fax (709) 643-4673
Toll free 1-800-644-4673

Cape Cod-style home located on former U.S. Airforce Base • Four o/n units, shared B&S • Cable TV in rooms • Children under 5 yrs free • No pets, please • Non-smoking only
FEATURES: "Newfoundlandia" and local knowledge • Laundry facilities • Room service • Fishing, golf and National Park nearby
RATES: $42-$69 (1-2), $10 add'l person • Continental breakfast • Open year-round • Major credit cards accepted

Sunnyside
Brookside Hospitality Home ★★ ¹/₂
Main Road, Box 104, Sunnyside, A0B 3J0
(709) 472-4515
Sunnyside, 2 km (1.2 mi) off Rte. 1 • Two o/n units, one shared B&S • Cable TV and telephone in living room • Radio in rooms • Children under 6 yrs free • Pets permitted • Non-smoking only
FEATURES: Wheelchair accessibility • Laundry facilities • Evening snack • Hiking nearby • Close to Hibernia project
RATES: $35-$45 (1-2), $10 add'l person • Open year-round

Torbay
See the Sea Bed & Breakfast ★★ ¹/₂
102 Marine Drive, Torbay, A1K 1A7
(709) 437-1915
Torbay Rte. 20 • Three o/n units, one shared B&S • Cable TV in rooms • No smoking in rooms, please
FEATURES: Host Mickey Michael will entertain you with romantic songs • French spoken • View of ocean and whales • Minutes from St. John's Airport
RATES: $55-$60 (1-2) • Continental breakfast • Open year-round

Traytown
Janes' Tourist Home ★★★
Waterfront Road, General Delivery, Traytown, A0G 4K0
(709) 533-2221
Traytown Rte. 310 • Borders on Terra Nova National Park • Three o/n units, private B&S; one suite •

No pets, please • Non-smoking only
FEATURES: Health-conscious people will appreciate ocean and mountain views, clean fresh air and drinking water • Laundry facilities • Whale-, iceberg- and bird-watching • Fishing, golf and hiking nearby
RATES: $40-$60 (1-2), $10 add'l person • Continental breakfast • Open June 1-Oct. 1

Trepassey
Northwest Bed & Breakfast ★★ ¹/₂
Harold and Marie Pennell, Box 5, Site 14, Trepassey, A0A 4B0
(709) 438-2888
Trepassey Rte. 10 • Four o/n units, shared B&S • Cable TV and telephone in rooms • Cot available
FEATURES: Picnic area and playground • Outdoor swimming • Can arrange lighthouse tour, seabird-sanctuary tour, and whale- and bird-watching boat tours
RATES: $40-$45 (1-2), $10 add'l person • Continental breakfast • Open year-round • Visa accepted

Trinity
Barb's Bed & Breakfast ★★ ¹/₂
Site 6, Box 5, Trinity, A0C 2S0
(709) 464-3748
2.5 km (1.5 mi) Rte. 230 • Modern split-level home • Three o/n units, one shared B&S • Cable TV and telephone in rooms • Cot available • Pets welcome • No smoking in rooms, please
FEATURES: Dining room • Off-street parking
RATES: $45-$55 (1-2), $5 add'l person • Full breakfast • Open year-round • Major credit cards accepted

Trinity
Campbell House
Bed & Breakfast ★★★
Trinity Bay, A0C 2S0
Tel & Fax (709) 464-3377
E-mail heritage@voyager.new-comm.net
Website
http://www.newcomm.net/campbell
Off-season 24 Circular Road, St. John's, A1C 2Z1; (709) 753-8945

TransCanada Hwy to Clarenville, Exit Rte. 230, 70 km (42 mi) towards Bonavista on Discovery Trail, Rte. 239 to Trinity Bay • Award-winning restored historic property (c. 1840) by the sea • Four o/n units, private B&S • Cable TV and telephone in rooms • Children over 7 yrs welcome • No pets, please • Non-smoking only
FEATURES: Antique furnishings • Gardens • Parlour with fireplace • Room service • Fax on premises • Hiking trails • Whale- and iceberg-watching nearby • Restaurants nearby
RATES: $70-$85 (1-2), $10 add'l person • Full breakfast • Open May-Oct. • Major credit cards accepted • HNL Member

Trinity
Eriksen Premises
General Delivery, Trinity, A0C 2S0
(709) 464-3698/2151
Fax (709) 464-2104
Trinity Rte. 239 • Victorian building with fantastic view of historic Trinity • Four o/n units, private B&S • Cot available • No smoking in rooms, please
FEATURES: Dining room (recommended in *Where to Eat in Canada*)

• Whale-, iceberg- and bird-watching • Fishing and hiking nearby
RATES: $70-$90 (1-2), $15 add'l person • Full breakfast • Open May-Oct. • Major credit cards accepted • HNL Member

Trinity
The Village Inn ★★ ½
Box 10, Trinity, Trinity Bay, A0C 2S0
(709) 464-3269
Fax (709) 464-3700
Trinity Rte. 239 • Historic inn (c.1910) • Twelve o/n units, private B&S • No pets, please • Non-smoking only
FEATURES: Resident world-renowned whale scientist • Dining room • Lounge • Whale-, iceberg- and bird-watching • Fishing and hiking nearby
RATES: $39-$89 (1-2), $10 add'l person • Open year-round • Major credit cards accepted • HNL Member

Trinity East
Peace Cove Inn ★★ ½
Art & Louise Andrews, Box 48, Paradise, A1L 1C4
(709) 781-2255/464-3738
Trinity East off Rte. 230 at Port Rexton • Award-winning turn-of-the-century former sea captain's home • Five o/n units, private B&S • Cable TV • Telephone • Non-smoking only
FEATURES: Located in scenic fishing village in Trinity Harbour • Whale-, iceberg- and bird-watching nearby • Hiking on country and coastal trails; abandoned villages to explore
RATES: $49-$65 (1-2), $10 add'l person • Open May-Oct. • Full breakfast • Major credit cards accepted • HNL Member

Triton
Bridger's
Bed & Breakfast ★★ ½
Sylvia & Eugene Bridger, 4 Mount
Tan Heights, Box 69, Triton,
A0J 1V0
(709) 263-7324
Off TransCanada Hwy at South
Brook, Halls Bay, 41 km (24.6 mi)
on Rte 380 • Three o/n units, one
shared B&S • Cable TV and tele-
phone in rooms • Non-smoking only
FEATURES: Laundry facilities •
Home-cooked meals on request •
Evening snack • Patio and backyard
• Homemade jams and jellies available
• "Craft Corner"
RATES: $30 (1), $35 (2) •
Breakfast • Open year-round • HNL
Member

Trout River
Crocker's
Bed & Breakfast ★★
Main Street, Box 10, Trout River,
A0K 5P0
(709) 451-5220/3141
Trout River Rte. 431 • Near ocean,
in Gros Morne National Park •
Three o/n units, shared B&S • Cable
TV and telephone in rooms • No
smoking in rooms, please
FEATURES: Friendly, relaxing
atmosphere • Dining room •
Kitchenette available • Whale-, ice-
berg-watching, fishing and hiking
nearby
RATES: $30 (1-2) • Continental
breakfast • Open May 15-Sept. 15 •
Major credit cards accepted • HNL
Member

Trouty
Riverside Lodge
(Tourist Home) ★★
Box 9, Site 3, Trouty, A0C 2S0

Tel & Fax (709) 464-3780
Trouty Rte. 239 • Ten o/n units • No
smoking in rooms, please
FEATURES: Wheelchair accessibility • Dining room • Picnic area •
Housekeeping unit available • Close
to Historic Trinity • Whale-, ice-
berg- and bird-watching • Fishing
and hiking nearby
RATES: $39-$60 (1-2), $5 add'l
person • Open April-Oct. • HNL
Member

Twillingate
Beach Rock
Bed & Breakfast ★★
Box 350, RR 1, Little Harbour,
Twillingate, A0G 4M0
(709) 884-2292
Twillingate Rte. 340 • Traditional
Newfoundland home (c. 1904),
overlooking the bay • Two o/n units,
one shared B&S • Cable TV and
telephone • Non-smoking only
FEATURES: Tea room • Whale-,
iceberg-watching and hiking nearby
RATES: $35 (1), $40 (2), $5 add'l
person • Open year-round •
Continental breakfast • HNL
Member

Twillingate
Harbour Lights
Inn ★★ ½
189 Main Street, Twillingate,
A0G 4M0
(709) 884-2763
Fax (709) 884-2701
Twillingate Rte. 340 • Lovingly
restored nineteenth-century house •
Five o/n units, private B&S • Cable
TV and telephone in rooms • Non-
smoking only
FEATURES: Wheelchair accessi-
bility • Laundry facilities • Kitchen
available • Meals on request •
Jacuzzi • Whale-, iceberg-,bird-

watching and hiking nearby
RATES: $55-$85 (1-2), $10 add'l
person • Full breakfast • Open year-
round • MC, Visa accepted • HNL
Member

Twillingate
Hillside
Bed & Breakfast ★★ ½
5 Young's Lane, Box 4,
Twillingate, A0G 4M0
(709) 884-5761
Twillingate Rte. 340 • House built
in 1874 • Four o/n units, private
B&S • Cable TV and telephone in
rooms • Non-smoking only
FEATURES: View of icebergs •
Laundry facilities • Trails to hilltop
lookout • Homemade bread and
jams are our specialty • Whale-,
bird-watching and hiking nearby
RATES: $40 (1), $45-$48 (2), $10
add'l person • Continental breakfast
• Open June 1-Sept. 30 • HNL
Member

Twillingate
Mariner's Rest
Bed & Breakfast
63 Toulinquet Street, Box 326,
Twillingate, A0G 4M0
(709) 884-2677
Four o/n units, shared B&S
FEATURES: Homemade breads,
muffins and jams • Picnic area •
Whale-, iceberg-watching, fishing
and hiking nearby
RATES: $40-$50 (1-2) •
Continental or full breakfast • Open
June-Sept. • Major credit cards
accepted

Twillingate
Ocean Breeze
Bed & Breakfast
41 Main Street, Box 152,
Twillingate, A0G 4M0
(709) 884-2866
Located up the street from the
Iceberg shop • Three o/n units, one
shared B&S
FEATURES: Homemade breads
and jams • Whale- and iceberg-
watching nearby
RATES: $35-$45 (1-2) •
Continental breakfast • Open May-
Sept. • Visa accepted

Twillingate
Toulinquet Inn
Bed & Breakfast ★★★
Cecile Mast & Hazel Young, 56
Main Street, Box 610,Twillingate,
A0G 4M0
(709) 884-2080/2028
Fax (709) 884-2936
Twillingate Rte. 340 • Traditional
Newfoundland home on waterfront •
Three o/n units, private B • Cable
TV in living room • Cot available •
Pets permitted, usually on leash •
Non-smoking only
FEATURES: Ocean view •
Laundry facilities • Room service •
Dining room • Whale-, iceberg-
watching and hiking nearby
RATES: $40 (1), $45 (2), $10 add'l
person • Continental breakfast •
Open June-Sept. • Visa accepted •

Witless Bay
Armstrong's
Bed & Breakfast ★★
Main Street, Box 39, Witless Bay,
A0A 4K0
(709) 334-2201
E-mail anita@avalon.nf.ca
Rte. 10 • Two o/n units, one shared
B&S • Cable TV and telephone •
No smoking in rooms, please
FEATURES: Whale-, iceberg-,
bird-watching and fishing nearby •
Close to Witless Bay Ecological
Reserve and boat tours
*RATES: $40-$45 (1-2) • Full
breakfast • Open May-Sept.*

Witless Bay
Elaine's Seaside
Bed & Breakfast ★★
Box 125, Lower Loop Place,
Witless Bay, A0A 4K0
(709) 334-2722
Witless Bay Rte. 10 • Modern home
wiith spectacular ocean view •
Three o/n units, one shared B&S •
Cable TV in rooms • Non-smoking
only
FEATURES: Bonfires on beach •
Kitchenette available • Close to
caribou herd and archaeological dig
• Whale-, iceberg- and bird-watch-
ing nearby
*RATES: $40-$58 (1-2), $5 add'l
person • Full breakfast • Open year-
round*

Witless Bay
Jean's
Bed & Breakfast ★★
1 Lundrigan's Road, General
Delivery, Witless Bay, A0A 4K0
(709) 334-2075
Witless Bay Rte. 10 • Two o/n
units, one shared B&S • Cable TV
in living room • Non-smoking only

FEATURES: Ocean views and
scenic seashore walks • Sun room
and gazebo • Whale-, iceberg- and
bird-watching • Hiking, fishing and
National Park nearby • Close to
laundry facilities, restaurant, ocean
tours and craft shops • Thirty minutes from St. John's
*RATES: $40 (1), $50 (2) • Full
breakfast*

Woody Point
Victorian Manor★★ ½
Stan & Jenny Parsons, Gros Morne
National Park, Box 165, Woody
Point, A0K 1P0
Tel & Fax (709) 453-2485

 Fourth-gener-
ation
Victorian fam-
ily home •
Three o/n
units, one pri-
vate B&S, one shared B&S; three
housekeeping suites; one guest
house • Cable TV and telephone •
Cot available • No pets, please •
Non-smoking only
FEATURES: Dining room •
Housekeeping services • Barbecue •
Cross-country skiing and sea kayaking in season • Whale-, iceberg-
watching and hiking nearby
*RATES: $50-$125 (1-2), $7 add'l
person • Continental breakfast •
Open year-round • Major credit
cards accepted • HNL Member*

Chapter 3

Nova Scotia

Advocate Harbour
Reid's Century Farm Bed & Breakfast
Donna Reid, 1391 West Advocate Road (West Advocate), RR 3, Parrsboro, B0M 1S0
(902) 392-2592
Rte. 209 • Working beef farm • Three o/n units, private B&S • TV in two rooms and family room • No pets, please
FEATURES: Near West Advocate entrance to Cape Chignecto Park
RATES: $30 (1), $40 (2), $10 add'l person (STC) • Family rates available • Full breakfast 7-9 • Open June 1-Sept. 30 • Off-season by reservation • NSFC Member

Advocate Harbour
Land's End Retreat B&B
Lillian Ward, 1219 West Advocate Road, RR 3, Parrsboro, B0M 1S0
(902) 392-2835
Hwy. 104, Exit 4, Rte. 302 to Rte. 242, through Joggins to W. Advocate; or Hwy. 104, Exit 11, Rte. 2 through Parrsboro • Two o/n units, one shared S • TV/VCR and piano in living room • Cot available • Children welcome • No smoking in rooms, please
RATES: $25 (1), $40 (2), $10 add'l person • Full breakfast 7-10 • Open May 15-Nov. 15

Afton
Chestnut Corner Bed & Breakfast ★★★
Gordon & Joan Randall, RR 1, Afton Station, B0H 1A0
(902) 386-2403
Hwy. 104, 20 km (12.5 mi) east of Antigonish, Exit 36A, 3 km (2 mi) • Three o/n units, one shared B&S • TV/VCR in living room • Non-smoking only
FEATURES: Barbecue • Hiking trail
RATES: $30-$35 (1), $35-$40 (2), $5-$10 add'l person • Full breakfast 7-9:30 • Open May 15-Oct. 15 • Visa accepted • IGNS; NSRS Member

Albert Bridge
Sunlit Valley Farm B&B
Hazel Ferguson, 821 Brickyard Road, RR 2 Albert Bridge, Marion Bridge, B0A 1P0
(902) 562-7663
Fax (902) 562-2222
From Port Hawkesbury, Rte. 4 or Hwy 105 to Sydney area, then Rte. 22 towards Louisbourg, cross Mira River, turn left on Brickyard Rd. • Four o/n units, two shared B&S • Cable TV in lounge • Non-smoking only
RATES: $40-$60 (1-2) • Off-season rates • Full breakfast 7:30-9:30 • Open May 1-Oct. 31 • Off-season by reservation • MC, Visa accepted • NSRS Member

Alma
Pine Hedge
Bed & Breakfast
Theresa & John Patton, RR 1,
Westville, B0K 2A0
(902) 396-5726
Hwy 104, exit at Granton, turn at
Irving garage; or Hwy 106, Exit 2
(from Pictou Rotary) • Three o/n
units, one shared B&S • Cable TV
and radio in rooms • No pets, please
• Non-smoking only
FEATURES: Laundry facilities •
Screened patio • Barbecue • Air-
conditioning • Close to beaches, golf
course and family amusement park
*RATES: $35 (1), $40 (2), $10 add'l
person • Full breakfast 7:30-10:00 •
Open May 1-Oct. 30 • Off-season by
reservation • Visa accepted • NSRS
Member*

Alma
Stoneycombe Lodge ★★★
Keith & Edith Selwyn-Smith, RR 3,
Westville, B0K 2A0
Tel & Fax (902) 396-3954
Toll free 1-800-461-5999
North off Hwy 104 on Alma Rd. at
Alma • Three o/n units, private B&S
• Cable TV and radio in lounge • No
pets, please • Non-smoking only
FEATURES: Heated swimming
pool
*RATES: $30-$50 (1), $45-$65 (2),
$10 add'l person (STC) • Off-season
rates Oct. 1-June 1 by reservation •
Continental or full breakfast 7:30-9
• Open year-round • MC, Visa
accepted • NSRS Member*

Amherst
Bonnvie
Bed & Breakfast ★★★
Barb Clarke, 54 Albion Street,
Amherst, B4H 2V8

Tel & Fax (902) 667-7430
Hwy 104, Exit 4, approx. 2.5 km
(1.5 mi) towards Amherst, on the
corner of Albion and Queen St. •
Restored Victorian home • Three
o/n units, one shared B&S • Cable
TV in games room • No pets, please
• Smoking area
FEATURES: Laundry facilities •
Screened deck • Fax machine and
photocopier available
*RATES: $40 (1), $55 (2), $10 add'l
person • Off-season rates Nov. 1-
April 30 • Full breakfast 8-9 • Open
year-round • MC accepted*

Amherst
Breeze In
Bed & Breakfast
Gerald & Lu Freeman, Box 153,
Amherst, B4H 3Z2
(902) 667-5518
Fax (902) 667-4998

Hwy 104, Exit
3, turn right
towards
Amherst on
Rte. 6E, first
driveway on
the left with long lane and white
fence • Renovated former farmhouse (c. 1890) • Two o/n units, private B&S; one housekeeping suite •
Cot available • Non-smoking only
FEATURES: Housekeeping unit is
fully equipped
*RATES: $45-$55 (1-2), $70 (house-
keeping suite), $10 add'l person •
$360 (weekly) • Breakfast • Open
June 1-Oct. 1 CNTA; NSRS Member*

Amherst
Brown's Guest Home
Deane & Nancy Allen, 158 Victoria
Street East, Amherst, B4H 1Y5
(902) 667-9769
Three o/n units, two shared B •

Cable TV in lounge • No pets, please
RATES: $28-$30 (1), $30-$38 (2) (STC) • *Open May 1-Oct. 31* • *MC, Visa accepted*

Amherst
MacKay's Guest Home B&B
Carol & Edward MacKay, 149 East Victoria Street, Amherst, B4H 1Y2
(902) 667-9935
Three o/n units, one shared B&S • Non-smoking only
FEATURES: Music room featuring large collection of Broadway musicals • Theatre packages arranged
RATES: $35 (1), $40-$45 (2) • *Continental breakfast 7:30-9:30* • *Open May 1-Nov. 1* • *Off-season by reservation*

Amherst
Seven Gables Bed & Breakfast ★★★ ½
Lorne & Hazel McMullin, Tidnish Crossroads, RR 2, Amherst, B4H 3X9
(902) 661-2377

26 km (16 mi) from Amherst on Rte. 366 (Northumberland Strait) •
Tastefully restored Victorian-style home with period furnishings • Four o/n units, private B&S (one whirlpool) • No pets, please • Non-smoking only
FEATURES: Furnished with antiques • Meals on request • Afternoon and evening refreshments • Spacious lawns and gardens
RATES: $55-$70 (1-2) • *Full breakfast 7:30-9* • *Open May 15-Oct. 15* • *Off-season by reservation* • *MC, Visa accepted* • *NSRS Member*

Amherst
Treen Mansion Bed & Breakfast
Marilyn Boss, 113 Spring Street, Amherst, B4H 1T2
(902) 667-2146
Hwy 104, Exit 3 (Victoria Street) turn right on Regent St., left on Spring St. • Three o/n units, one private B&S, one shared B&S • Cable TV in living room • No smoking in rooms, please
FEATURES: Laundry facilities
RATES: $30 (1), $45-$48 (2) (STC) • *Continental breakfast 7-9* • *Open year-round* • *Visa accepted* • *NSRS Member*

Amherst
Victoria Garden Bed & Breakfast (c. 1903) ★★★ ½
Carl & Beatrice Brander, 196 Victoria Street East, Amherst, B4H 1Y9
(902) 667-2278

Hwy 104, Exit 3.4 km (2.5 mi) • Three o/n units, one private B&S, one shared B&S • Cable TV in living room • Smoking outdoors only
FEATURES: Evening tea and sweets • Pleased to cater to special diets (with prior notice) • Various tours arranged
RATES: $40 (1), $50-$60 (2), $10 add'l person (STC) • *Full breakfast 7:30-9:30* • *Open May 1-Sept. 30* • *Off-season by arrangements* • *MC, Visa accepted* • *IGNS; NSRS Member*

Annapolis Royal

Bread and Roses Country Inn

Richard & Monica Cobb, 82
Victoria Street, Box 177, Annapolis
Royal, B0S1A0
(902) 532-5727
Toll free 1-800-906-5727
Registered heritage property
(c. 1882) • Nine o/n units, private B
• Not suitable for children under 12
yrs • Small dog on premises • No
pets, please • Non-smoking only
FEATURES: Antique furnishings,
Nova Scotia folk art, contemporary
Canadian and Inuit art • Evening tea
RATES: $60-$85 (1), $70-$95 (2),
$20 add'l person • 10% discount for
three-night stay • Continental
breakfast • Open Mar.1-Oct. 30 •
MC, Visa accepted • NSRS Member

Annapolis Royal

English Oaks B&B

Fran & Gordon Atwell, Box 233,
Annapolis Royal, B0S 1A0
(902) 532-2066
Off Rte. 201, east end of Annapolis
Royal at Alden Hubley Dr. •
Spacious park-like setting with
panoramic view • Three o/n units,
private B&S; two suites • Clock-
radio in rooms • Cable TV in lounge
• Children under 3 yrs free
FEATURES: Screened veranda, •
Picnic table and barbecue • Trout
pond
RATES: $45-$50 (1-2), $15 add'l
person, $10 add'l person under 12
yrs • Full breakfast 7-9 • Open April
1-Oct. 31 • NSRS Member

Annapolis Royal

Garrison House Inn

Patrick Redgrave, 350 St. George
Street, Box 108, Annapolis Royal,

B0S 1A0
(902) 532-5750
Fax (902) 532-5501
Registered historic property
(c. 1854) • Seven o/n units, private
B; one suite
FEATURES: Licensed dining room
RATES: $45-$72 (1), $55-$78 (2-
3), $10 add'l person • Breakfast 8-
9:30 • Open April-Dec. • AE, MC,
Visa accepted • CAA; NSRS
Member

Annapolis Royal

Grange Cottage Bed & Breakfast

Ray & Maude Marshall, 102 Ritchie
Street, Box 536, Annapolis Royal,
B0S 1A0
(902) 532-7993
St. George St. at Grange St., turn
left to Ritchie St. • Three o/n units,
one shared B • Cable TV/VCR in
lounge
FEATURES: Sunporch
RATES: $38 (1), $46 (2), $8 add'l
person • Full breakfast 7:30-9 •
Open year-round • MC, Visa
accepted • NSRS Member

Annapolis Royal

Hillsdale House

Leslie Langille, 519 St. George
Street, Box 148, Annapolis Royal,
B0S 1A0
(902) 532-2345
Fax (902) 532-7850
Registered heritage property (c.
1849) • Ten o/n units, private B •
Cable TV in lounge • Non-smoking
only
FEATURES: Patio • Historic gar-
dens next door • Walk to Fort Anne,
museums, art galleries and restau-
rants • Close to theme park, Tidal
Hydro Electric Plant and the
Habitation

RATES: $65-$90, $10 add'l person
• *Full breakfast 8-10* • *Open May
15-Oct. 15* • *MC, Visa accepted*

Annapolis Royal
Joy Qua Lodging B&B
Giselle Beauchamp, 3602 Hwy 1,
RR 2, Annapolis Royal, B0S 1A0
Tel & Fax (902) 532-2209
E-mail aq367!@ccn.c.s.dal.ca
4 km (2.5 mi) west of town •
Between two brooks overlooking
Annapolis Basin • Two o/n units,
one shared B&S • Cable TV in liv-
ing room • Clock radio in rooms •
Cot available • Dog on premises •
No smoking in rooms, please
FEATURES: Artwork for sale • French
spoken • Barbecue and picnic area
RATES: $35 (1), $45 (2), add'l per-
son $5-$10 • *Continental breakfast
7:30-8:45* • *Open June 1-Oct. 15* •
NSRS member

Annapolis Royal
King George Inn
Donna & Michael Susnick and Faye
McStravick, 548 Upper St. George
Street, Box 34, Annapolis Royal,
B0S 1A0
(902) 532-5286
Off-season (902) 425-5656
Registered heritage property (c.1868)
and former sea captain's home •
Four o/n units, two shared B&S;
one two-room suite • Cable TV in
parlour • Pay telephone • Crib avail-
able • Non-smoking only
FEATURES: French spoken •
Evening tea and coffee • Library •
Classic movies in parlour • Piano •
Board and lawn games • Bicycles
RATES: $44 (1), $49 (2), $56 (3),
$88 (suite), $7 add'l person • *Full
breakfast 7-9* • *Open May 17-Sept.
30* • *MC, Visa accepted* • *NSRS
Member*

Annapolis Royal
Poplars
Bed & Breakfast
Syd & Iris Williams, 124 Victoria
Street, Box 277, Annapolis Royal,
B0S 1A0
(902) 532-7936
Rte. 1, one block east of traffic light
• Nine o/n units, six private B, two
powder room, one shared B • Cable
TV in lounge • Baby bed and cot
available • No pets, please • Non-
smoking only
FEATURES: Wheelchair accessi-
bilty • Fireplace in lounge
RATES: $33-$55 (1-2), $8 add'l
person (STC) • *Continental break-
fast 7:30-8:45* • *Open year-round* •
Visa accepted • *NSRS Member*

Annapolis Royal
Queen Anne Inn
Leslie J. Langille, 494 Upper St.
George Street, Annapolis Royal,
B0S 1A0
(902) 532-7850
Registered heritage property (c.
1865) • Ten o/n units, private B •
Cable TV in sitting room • Non-
smoking only
RATES: $50-$95 (2), $10 add'l
person • *Full breakfast* • *Open year-
round* • *MC, Visa accepted*

Annapolis Royal
Turret Bed & Breakfast
Barb & George Dunlop, 372 St. George Street, Annapolis Royal, B0S 1A0
(902) 532-5770
Registered historic property • Three o/n units, one shared B, one shared 1/2 B • TV in lounge
RATES: $35 (1), $45 (2-3) • Full breakfast 7:30-9:30 • Open year-round

Antigonish
Antigonish Victorian Inn
Lois & Jack Lilly, 149 Main Street, Antigonish, B2G 2B6
Tel & Fax (902) 863-1103
Toll free 1-800-706-5558
Magnificent turreted Victorian mansion on five acres • Eight o/n units, private B or B&S; two housekeeping suites • Cable TV in rooms • Children over 12 yrs welcome • No pets, please • Non-smoking only
RATES: From $50 (2), $60 (suite), $10 add'l person (STC) • Breakfast 7:30-9:30 • Open June 25-Aug. 31 • Off-season by reservation

Antigonish
Bekkers Bed & Breakfast ★★★
Sisca Bekkers, RR 2, Antigonish, B2G 2K9
(902) 863-3194/1713
 Hwy 104, Exit 32 to Rte. 245, 3 km (1.5 mi) to Clydesdale Rd., turn left 1.5 km (1 mi) on the left • Two o/n units, two B&S • Cable TV in living room • No pets, please • Non-smoking only

RATES: $40-$50 (2) • Full breakfast 7-9 • Open June 1-Oct. 31

Antigonish
Green Haven Bed & Breakfast
Al & Martha Balawyder, 27 Greening Drive, Antigonish, B2G 1R1
(902) 863-2884/5059
Toll free 1-888-863-2884
Hwy 104, Exit 31, first left • Three o/n units, one private B, one shared B • Cable TV, radio and telephone in lounge • No pets, please • Non-smoking only
FEATURES: Bilingual • Stereo and piano in lounge
RATES: $44.40-$61.05 (2) (tax incl.) • Full breakfast 7-9 • Open year-round

Antigonish
MacIsaac's Bed & Breakfast ★★★
Hugh & Bev MacIsaac, 18 Hillcrest Street, Antigonish, B2G 1Z3
(902) 863-2947
Hwy 104, Exit 32 at traffic lights to West St.; bear right at St. Ninian St., take second street past St. Ninian's Cathedral and turn right at Hillcrest St. to second house on right • Quiet residential area • Three o/n units, one shared B&S, one shared 1/2 B • Cable TV and clock radio in rooms • Cot available
FEATURES: One block from city centre • Picnic table • Off-street parking
RATES: $35 (1), $45-$50 (2) • Off-season rates • Full breakfast 7:30-8:30 • Open May 1-Oct. 15 • Off-season by reservation • MC, Visa accepted • IGNS; NSRS Member

Antigonish
Shebby's
Bed & Breakfast
(c. 1854) ★★★ ¹/₂
Mary MacDonald, 135 Main Street,
Antigonish, B2G 2B6
(902) 863-1858
Toll free 1-800-863-1858
Three o/n units, one private B
(whirlpool), one shared B&S •
Cable TV in rooms and living room
• Non-smoking only
FEATURES: Handmade quilts •
Downtown location
*RATES: $37.50-$55 (1), $45-$60
(2) (STC) • Weekly and off-season
rates • Full breakfast 7:30-9 • Open
May 15-Oct.15 • Off-season by
reservation • NSRS Member*

Antigonish
White Lights
Bed & Breakfast
Anne Wowk, 77 Hawthorne Street,
Antigonish, B2G 1A6
(902) 863-9374
Off-season (403) 432-1810
Hwy 104, Exit 32 to Rte. 245 (left
at lights to Hawthorne St.) • Three
o/n units, one shared B&S • Cable
TV in lounge • Small pets permitted
• Non-smoking only
*RATES: $40 (1), $45-$50 (2) (STC)
• Full breakfast 7:30-9:30 • Open
May 15-Sept. 4 • NSRS Member*

Ardoise
Eastwood Farm
Bed & Breakfast
Anne Soper, Ardoise, RR 1,
Ellershouse, B0N 1L0
(902) 757-2702
Hwy 101, Exit 4, Rte. 1E approx.
8.5 km (5.5 mi) • Dutch colonial-
style house furnished with antiques
and collectibles • Two o/n units, one

shared B&S • Cable TV/VCR •
Clock radio in rooms • Not suitable
for children under 10 yrs • No
smoking in rooms, please
FEATURES: Swimming pool •
Walking trails
*RATES: $45 (1), $50 (2) • Full
breakfast 7:30-9:30 • Open May 15-
Oct. 15 • NSRS Member*

Arichat
L'Auberge Acadienne
Beverly Boudreau, High Road, Box
59, Arichat, B0E 1A0
(902) 226-2200/2150
Fax (902) 226-1424
On Isle Madame, Exit 46 off Hwy
104, Rte. 206 • New 19th-century-
style Acadian country inn • Eight
o/n units, private B&S
FEATURES: Licensed dining room
and lounge
*RATES: $60-$125 (1-2), $10 add'l
person (STC) • Open May-Oct. •
AE, MC, Visa accepted • NSRS
Member*

Auld's Cove
Bluefin
Bed & Breakfast ★★ ¹/₂
Gardiner & Linda Burton, Box 119,
Port Hastings, B0E 2T0
Tel & Fax (902) 747-2010
In Auld's Cove at Canso Causeway;
enter at Cove Motel • Four o/n
units, two shared B&S • Satellite
TV • No pets, please
FEATURES: Licensed dining room
at Cove Motel • Ocean swimming •
Canoes and fishing charters avail-
able • Lake and gift shop nearby
*RATES: $46 (1), $51-$56 (2), $10
add'l person • Full breakfast • Open
May-Nov. • AE, MC, Visa accepted
• NSRS Member*

Aylesford
Back Inn Tyme
Bed & Breakfast
Marlene & Alfred Bezanson, 3069
Highway 1, RR 1, Aylesford, B0P
1C0
(902) 847-9661
Hwy 101, Exit 16 towards town;
turn left at stop sign onto Rte. 1 •
Farm-style home (c. 1890) • Two
o/n units, one shared B • Clock
radio in rooms • Cable TV in sitting
room • Non-smoking only
*RATES: $45 (1), $55 (2), $10 add'l
person • Full breakfast 7-9 • Open
May 15-Oct. 15 • NSRS Member*

Aylesford
Reborn Farm
Bed & Breakfast
Eleanor Witter
(902) 847-3689
Hwy 101, Exit 16N, turn left at first
crossroad, 1.8 km (1 mi) on right •
Working hobby farm with small
animals • Three o/n units, one private B&S, one shared B&S; one
suite • Non-smoking only
*RATES: $32 (1), $37 (2), $55
(suite) • Full breakfast 9 • Open
year-round*

Baddeck
The Bay Tourist Home
Bed & Breakfast
Patricia & Harold Edwards, Box 24,
Baddeck, B0E 1B0
(902) 295-2046
Hwy 105, Exit 10 to Rte. 205, 1.5
km (1 mi) west of Baddeck • Three
o/n units, one shared B • Cable TV
in lounge • No pets, please • Non-
smoking only
FEATURES: Complimentary
evening tea/coffee • Very quiet
location

*RATES: $34 (1), $39 (2) •
Continental breakfast 7:30-9 • Open
May 1-Oct. 31*

Baddeck
Breezy Brae
Bed & Breakfast
Michael & Patricia Woodford, 1163
Baddeck Bay Road, Box 566,
Baddeck, B0E 1B0
(902) 295-2618
Fax (902) 295-1700
Hwy 105, Exit 9 or 10, Rte. 205, 3
km (2 mi) east of village • One hun-
dred-year-old summer estate with
long veranda overlooking Bras d'Or
Lakes • Four o/n units, two shared
B&S; one cottage • No pets, please
• Non-smoking only
*RATES: $45 (1), $50-$55 (2) (taxes
incl) (STC) • Continental breakfast
7:30-9 • Open June 15-Sept. 15 •
TIANS Member*

Baddeck
Broad Water
Inn & Cottages (c. 1794)
Gail Holdner, Box 702, Baddeck,
B0E 1B0
(902) 295-1101
2.2 km (1.3 mi) east of town on Bay
Road (Rte. 205) • Overlooking Bras
d'Or Lakes • Three o/n units, private B&S; four housekeeping cottages • No pets, please • Non-smoking only
FEATURES: Manicured gardens •
Local art and craft gallery/shop
*RATES: $65-$98 (1-2), $90-$150
(cottage), $10 add'l person (STC) •
Off-season rates • Continental
breakfast • Open year-round • Dis,
MC, Visa accepted • Cancellation
policy*

Baddeck
Duffus House Inn
(c. 1830)
John & Judy Langley, Water Street,
Box 427, Baddeck, B0E 1B0
(902) 295-2172
Off-season (902) 928-2878
Quiet waterside inn • Four o/n units.
private B&S; three suites • Not suit-
able for children • No pets, please •
Non-smoking only
FEATURES: Furnished with
antiques • English-style gardens •
Extensive library • Private dock •
Close to hiking trails
*RATES: $65-$95 (1), $75-$95 (2),
$115-$125 (suite), $15 add'l person
(STC) • Continental breakfast •
Open May-Oct. • Visa accepted •
Cancellation policy • UCI Member*

Baddeck
Dunlop Guest House ★★ ½
Pat Dunlop, 552 Chebucto Street,
Baddeck, B0E 1B0
(902) 295-1100
Register at the Telegraph House:
479 Chebucto St. • Historic
Victorian home on shore of Bras
d'Or Lakes • Four o/n units, one pri-
vate B&S, one shared B&S • Cable
TV/VCR in living room • Non-
smoking only
FEATURES: Kitchen facilities •
Private beach
*RATES: $69 (1), $79-$85 (2) (STC)
• Open year-round • Please call
Telegraph House for information
and reservations*

Baddeck
Eagle's Perch
Bed & Breakfast
Gail Holdner, Box 425, Baddeck,
B0E 1B0
(902) 295-2640

Hwy 105, Exit 9; turn north at stop
sign away from Baddeck and follow
Margaree Rd. to Baddeck Bridge 4
km (2.5 mi); cross bridge and turn
left (west) 1 km (.6 mi) from bridge
on left • Log home on Baddeck
River • Three o/n units, one private
B, one shared B&S • No pets,
please • Non-smoking only
FEATURES: Canoe rentals
*RATES: $32-$47 (1), $40-$55 (2),
$10 add'l person (STC) • Full
breakfast 7:30-9 • Open May 1-Oct.
31 • Off-season by reservation •
MC, Visa accepted • Cancellation
policy • CBBBA; NSRS Member*

Baddeck
Flying Squirrel
Bed & Breakfast
Linda Murphy, Box 185, Baddeck,
B0E 1B0
(902) 295-2904
Hwy 105, Exit 9N to Baddeck
Bridge 4 km (2.5 mi), turn left
towards Hunter's Mountain 2 km
(1.5 mi) • Log house with mountain
view • One o/n unit, private B&S •
TV in living room • No pets, please
• No smoking indoors, please
*RATES: $40 (1), $50 (2) • Full
breakfast • Open May 15-Oct. 31*

Baddeck
Kerr's Bed & Breakfast
Shirley Kerr, Hillcrest Drive, Box
731, Baddeck, B0E 1B0
(902) 295-3476
Hwy 105E, left on Exit 9, follow
signs to Hillcrest Dr. • Two o/n
units, one shared B&S; one cottage
• Cable TV/VCR in living room
*RATES: $30 (1), $35 (2), $50 (cot-
tage), $10 add'l person (STC) •
Continental breakfast • Visa accepted • NSRS Member*

Baddeck
Lynwood
Country Inn ★★★
Daryl MacDonnell & Louise
DesRochers, 23 Shore Road,
Baddeck, B0E 1B0
(902) 295-1995
Fax (902) 295-3084
Century-old home located in the
heart of town • Three o/n units, private B&S • Non-smoking only
FEATURES: Wheelchair accessibilty • Licensed dining room overlooking Bras d'Or Lakes • Large
deck • Whirlpools
*RATES: $60-$110 (1-2) (STC)•
Off-season rates • Continental
breakfast 7-10 • Dis, MC, Visa
accepted • Open year-round • NSRS
Member*

Baddeck
M and V
Bed & Breakfast
Mack & Viola Garland, Box 284,
Baddeck, B0E 1B0
(902) 295-2668
Hwy 105, Exit 9 to Baddeck Bridge
Rd. • Three o/n units, one private
B&S, one shared B&S, one private
1/2 B • No pets, please • Non-smoking only
*RATES: $35-$45 (1), $40-$50 (2)
(tax incl.) (STC) • Continental
breakfast 7-8:30 • Open May 1-Oct.
31 • Visa accepted*

Baddeck
MacNeil House ★★★
Gregg Ross, Box 399, Baddeck,
B0E 1B0
(902) 295-2340
Fax (902) 295-2484
Toll free 1-800-565-VIEW (8439)
Website
http://www.morandan.com/moran

dan/silverdart/home.html
Hwy 105, Exit 8, Rte. 205 to Shore
Rd. • Six o/n units (suites), private
B&S • Cable TV, radio and telephone in rooms
FEATURES: Suites have living
room, fireplace, kitchen, Jacuzzi and
balcony • Live Scottish entertainment • Licensed dining room •
Picnic lunches • Playground • Airconditioning • Outdoor heated
swimming pool • Lakeside beach •
Walking trails • Chip-and-putt area •
Bicycle rentals • Craft and gift shop
• Vacation packages
*RATES: $125-$225 • Off-season
rates • Open May 15-Oct. 31 • AE,
DC, MC, Visa accepted • IGNS;
NSRS Member*

Baddeck
Restawyle
Bed & Breakfast
Peter & Patti MacAulay, 321 Shore
Road, RR 3, Baddeck, B0E 1B0
(902) 295-3253
Hwy 105, Exit 8 • Four o/n units,
two shared B&S • Cable TV in living room • Non-smoking only
*RATES: $40-$55 (2) (STC)•
Continental breakfast 7:30-9 •
Open May 15-Dec. 15 • Visa
accepted*

Baddeck
Sarah Jean's
Bed & Breakfast
Mary Lou MacDonald, 18 High
Street, Box 241, Baddeck, B0E 1B0
(902) 295-3162
Two o/n units, one shared B&S •
Cable TV • Non-smoking only
FEATURES: Walking distance into
town
*RATES: $40 (1), $50 (2) • Full
breakfast 7:30-9:30 • Open yearround • NSRS Member*

Baddeck
Sealladh Aluinn
Bed & Breakfast
Shelagh Roberts, 251 Shore Road,
Box 59, Baddeck, B0E 1B0
(902) 295-1160
Hwy 105, Exit 8 • Overlooking Bras
d'Or Lakes • Three o/n units, one
shared B&S • Cable TV • Non-
smoking only
*RATES: $35 (1), $45 (2) (STC) •
Continental breakfast 7:30-9 • Open
May 15-Oct. 31 • MC, Visa accepted*

Baddeck
Tree Seat
Bed & Breakfast
Barb & Ken MacLeod, 555
Chebucto Street, Box 648, Baddeck,
B0E 1B0
(902) 295-1996
Hwy 105, Exit 8 • Three o/n units,
one shared B&S • Non-smoking only
*RATES: $42 (1), $50 (2) • Full
breakfast 7:30-9 • Open June 1-Oct.
31 • Visa accepted • NSRS Member*

Baddeck
The Village Manse
Bed & Breakfast
Jack & Gennie Twigg, Chebucto
Street, Baddeck, B0E 1B0
(902) 295-1224
Off-season (305) 252-6477
Hwy 105, Exit 8 to town centre •
Former Presbyterian Manse (c.
1902) • Three o/n units, one shared
B&S • Cable TV in living room •
Clock radio in rooms • Non-smok-
ing only
*RATES: $50-$60 (1), $60-$70 (2),
$10 add'l person • Continental
breakfast 7:30-9:30 • Open July 1-
Oct. 31 • Visa accepted*

Barrington
MacMullen House
Bed & Breakfast
(c. 1882) ★★★
Margaret Doane, 2456 Hwy 3,
Barrington, B0W 1E0
(902) 637-3892
Site of oilskin factory in early 1900s
• Three o/n units, two shared B&S;
one cottage • Cable TV in lounge •
Families welcome • Crib available •
Non-smoking only
FEATURES: Three-storey barn is
designated as a provincial heritage
property • Barbecue and picnic table
*RATES: $40 (1), $50 (2), $10 add'l
person (STC) • Full breakfast 7-9 •
Open year-round (cottage available
July-Aug.) • NSRS Member*

Barrington Passage
Old School House
Inn & Cottages
Nellie Goreham, Highway 3, Box
303, Barrington Passage, B0W 1G0
(902) 637-3770
Fax (902) 637-3711
Rte. 3, Barrington Passage • Six o/n
units, two shared S • No smoking in
rooms, please
FEATURES: Licensed dining room
and lounge • Cottages available
*RATES: $35-$45 (1-2) • Open
year-round • AE, MC, Visa accepted
• NSRS Member*

Barss Corner
(near Mahone Bay and
Lunenburg)
100 Acres and an Ox
Country Inn ★★★ ½
Ardythe Wildsmith, RR 2, Barss
Corner, B0R 1A0
(902) 644-3444
E-mail bwildsmi@is.dal.ca

 Hwy 103, Exit
11, 19 km (12
mi) inland
towards Barss
Corner • Large
acreage with lake and river frontage
• Three o/n units, private B • No
pets, please • Non-smoking only
FEATURES: Traditional Gothic
Revival reproduction home filled
with antiques • Meals and box
lunches on request • Rural retreat
with hiking, salmon and trout fishing, canoeing, swimming and camp-
fires • Close to Mahone Bay and
Lunenburg
RATES: $55-$75 (1-2) (STC) • Full
breakfast • Open June 1-Oct. 31 •
Off-season by reservation • Visa
accepted • Reservations preferred •
NSRS Member

Barton
Barton House B&B
Laurette Deschênes, RR 1, Box 33,
Barton, B0W 1H0
(902) 245-6695
Two o/n units, one private B, one
shared B; one suite
FEATURES: Outdoor hot tub •
Raspberry picking • French spoken
RATES: $40 (1), $45 (2), $75
(suite) • Full breakfast until 10 •
Open May 1-Oct. 31 • NSRS
Member

Bass River
King's Rest Beach
Bed & Breakfast
George & Clarice Fulton, 300 Birch
Hill Road, Bass River, B0M 1B0
(902) 647-2672
Recently renovated home situated
on Cobequid Bay • Three o/n units,
private B&S • Not suitable for small
children • Non-smoking only
FEATURES: Three sitting rooms
and viewing decks overlooking the
bay • World's highest tides: explore
the ocean floor before the tide
comes in • Clam-digging, bass fishing and bird-watching • Steps to
beach for swimming and beachcombing
RATES: $48-$55 (1-2), $70 (suite),
$10 add'l person (STC) • Full
breakfast 7-9 • Open year-round

Bay St. Lawrence
Buck's
Bed & Breakfast ★★ ½
Wilma Buchanan, Box 17,
St. Margaret's Village, B0C 1R0
(902) 383-2075/2597
Fax (902) 383-2995
Turn off Cabot Trail at Cape North,
16 km (10 mi) to Bay St. Lawrence
• Two o/n units, one shared B •
TV/VCR in lounge • Clock radio in
rooms • No pets, please • No smok-
ing in rooms, please
RATES: $32 (1), $40 (2) (STC)•
Breakfast 7:30-9 • Open May-Oct. •
Off-season by reservation

Bay St. Lawrence
Carol's
Bed & Breakfast
Carol MacKinnon, St. Margaret's
Village, B0C 1R0
(902) 383-2631
On the Capstick Hwy • New home

in quiet highland setting • Three o/n units, one private S, one shared B&S • TV in living room • Non-smoking only
RATES: $40-$45 (1), $45-$50 (2), $10 add'l person • Full breakfast 7:30-9:30 • Open year-round • Visa accepted

Bay St. Lawrence
Highlands By the Sea B&B
Susanne & Reginald MacDonald, St. Margaret's Village, B0C 1R0
(902) 383-2537
Turn off Cabot Trail at Cape North, 13 km (8 mi) on Bay St. Lawrence Rd. • Century-old rectory house, surrounded by mountains • Three o/n units, two shared B&S • TV/VCR in lounge • Clock radio in rooms • No pets, please • No smoking in rooms, please
FEATURES: Hiking trails • Horseshoe pit • Whale-watching and deep-sea fishing arranged
RATES: $35 (1), $40 (2), $8 add'l person (STC) • Full breakfast 7:30-9 • Visa accepted

Bayfield
Sea 'Scape Bed & Breakfast and Cottages ★★★
Frank & Lelia (O Rourke) Machnik, Box 94, Heatherton, B0H 1R0
(902) 386-2825
Website http://destination-ns.com/sunrise/seascape
Hwy 104, Exit 36, north 7 km (4.5 mi). 26 km (16 mi) east of Antigonish • 150-acre coastal property with panoramic views • One o/n unit
FEATURES: Laundromat • Barbecue • Playground • Cottages

available • Sandy beach and dunes, walking trails, bird-watching, and fishing • Boat tours, boats and canoes available • Babysitting
RATES: $50 (2), $5 add'l person • Off-season rates May, June and Oct. • Breakfast • Open May 1-Oct. 31 • Visa accepted • CAA; NSRS Member

Bayside
Anchors Gate Bed & Breakfast
George & Nancy Pike, 4281 Prospect Road, Bayside, B3Z 1L4
(902) 852-3906
Rte. 333, 14 km (9 mi) from Peggy's Cove on scenic Shad Bay • Two o/n units, one shared S; one housekeeping suite • TV, clock radio and ceiling fan in rooms • Cable TV in lounge • No pets, please • Non-smoking only
FEATURES: Renovated in nautical theme • Walk-through flower garden • Laundry facilities
RATES: $50 (1-2), $75 (suite), $12 add'l person • $475 (weekly) • Full breakfast 7:30-9:30 • Open May 15-Oct. 15 • Off-season by reservation • MC, Visa accepted

Bear River
By The Brook
Bed & Breakfast
Anita & Edwin Chisholm, 1894
Clementsvale Road, Box 179, Bear
River, B0S 1B0
Tel & Fax (902) 467-3612
E-mail
edwin.chisholm@ns.sympatico.ca
Hwy 101, Exit 24 • Recently reno-
vated home (c. 1870) with cozy sun-
porch and spacious patio • Three o/n
units, private B&S • Cable TV/VCR
in sitting room • Cat on premises •
No smoking in rooms, please
FEATURES: French spoken •
Mountain bikes available •
Barbecue
*RATES: $45 (1), $50 (2), $8 add'l
person • Full breakfast 8-9 • Open
May 1-Oct. 31 • Off-season by
reservation • Visa accepted •
Cancellation policy • NSRS Member*

Bear River
Inn Bear River B&B
Doug Dockrill & Zoë Onysko, Box
142, Bear River, B0S 1B0
(902) 467-3809
E-mail
innbear@clan.tartennet.ns.ca
Hwy 101, Exit 24, Upper River Rd.
• Gothic Revival (1860) known
locally as the Millionaire's House •
Three o/n units, one private B, one
shared B • Reading room with
TV/VCR • Cats on premises • Non-
smoking only
FEATURES: Collections of
antiques, vintage quilts, hats, period
clothing, hooked rugs and original
art • Piano and fireplace in lounge •
Stained glass windows • Verandas
*RATES: $34 (1), $36 (2), $8 add'l
person • Full breakfast • Open Jan.-
Nov. • MC, Visa accepted • NSRS
Member*

Bear River
Lovett Lodge Inn B&B
Adrian Potter, Main Street, Box
119, Bear River, B0S 1B0
(902) 467-3917
Hwy 101, Exit 24 or 25, 10 min.
east of Digby • Victorian doctor's
residence (c. 1892) • Four o/n units,
two private B, one shared B; one
family suite • Cable TV/VCR and
radio in lounge • Pets welcome •
Smoking area
FEATURES: Antiques • Art and
music • Historic medical library •
Laundromat • Evening tea • Located
on tidal river in the "Switzerland of
Nova Scotia" • Alpine tea garden •
Hiking trails • Whale-watching
arranged
*RATES: $37-$43 (1), $45-$55 (2),
$9 add'l person • Full breakfast •
Open May 20-Oct. 31 • Visa accepted • NSRS Member*

Beaverbrook
Stewart House
Bed & Breakfast
Michael Stewart, 2468 Highway
236, RR 1, Truro, B2N 5A9
(902) 895-1659
E-mail nstn5793@fox.nstn.ns.ca
Hwy 102, Exit 14 • New home furnished with antiques • Two o/n
units, private B&S; two suites •
Clock radio in rooms • Cable TV in
living room • No pets, please • Non-
smoking only
FEATURES: Swimming pool •
Library and music area
*RATES: $50 (1-2), $75 (suite), $10
add'l person • Weekly rates • Full
breakfast 7:30-9 • Open April 1-
Nov. 30 • AE, Visa accepted*

Berwick
Berwick Inn
Bruce & Anne Drummond, 160 Commercial Street, Berwick, B0P 1E0
(902) 538-8532
Victorian century home • Five o/n units, two shared B&S • TV in lounge
FEATURES: Kitchen facilities • Air-conditioning
RATES: $43 (1), $53 (2) • Full breakfast 8-10 • Open May 1-Dec. 31 • Off-season by reservation • MC, Visa accepted • IGNS; NSRS Member

Berwick
Fundy Trail Farms B&B
Marie & Derill Armstrong, 2986 McNally Road (Burlington), RR 5, Berwick, B0P 1E0
(902) 538-9481
Fax (902) 538-7934
Hwy 101, Exit 15, north on Rte. 360 to stop sign, Hwy 221, left to Viewmont sign, right 6.5 km (4 mi) to four-way intersection, left 1.3 km (0.8 mi) • Century-home overlooking Bay of Fundy • Three o/n units, one shared B&S, one shared 1/2 B
RATES: $35 (1), $40 (2), $8 add'l person • Full breakfast 8-8:30 • Open year-round • NSRS Member

Berwick
North Haven Bed & Breakfast
Jennie Mahar, RR 5, Berwick, B0P 1E0
(902) 538-8441
Hwy 101, Exit 15 to Rte. 360N, approx. 8 km (5 mi) over North Mountain towards Harbourville, second house on left on Garland •

Georgian-style home • Three o/n units, one private 1/2 B, one shared B&S (whirlpool) • No pets, please • Non-smoking only
FEATURES: Evening tea • Patio overlooking formal gardens
RATES: $45 (1), $50 (2) • Full breakfast 7:30-8:30 • Open May 15-Oct. 15 • Off-season by reservation • NSFCV; NSRS Member

Bible Hill
At the Organery
Akke Van der Leest, 53 Farnham Road, Bible Hill, B2N 2X6
(902) 895-6653
Hwy 102, Exit 14A • Three o/n units, one private B, one shared B&S • Cable TV/VCR in family room • Clock radio and ceiling fan in rooms • Pets on premises • Non-smoking only
FEATURES: Private collection of over one hundred antique reed organs for viewing or playing • Piano in family room
RATES: $50-$60 (2), $10 add'l person • Full breakfast 8-9 • Open May 1-Oct. 31 • Off-season by reservation • Visa accepted • NSFC; NSRS Member

Bickerton West
By the Sea
Bed & Breakfast
Bruce & Dolores Kaiser, Box 39,
Port Bickerton West, B0J 1A0
(902) 364-2575
Rte. 7 to Sherbrooke to Rte. 211,
east for 26 km (16 mi) • Three o/n
units, one private B&S, one shared
B&S • Cable TV in lounge • Cot
and crib available • No pets, please •
Non-smoking only
FEATURES: Harbour, ocean and
lighthouse views from deck •
Private road to scenic shore
*RATES: $30-$55 (1-2), $10 add'l
person (STC) • Full breakfast 7:30-
9:30 • Open May 15-Oct. 15 • Off-
season by reservation • Visa accepted • ESTA; NSFC; NSRS Member*

Bickerton West
Nautical Watch
Bed & Breakfast
Joyce Mills, 31 Harbourview Drive,
Box 112, Bickerton West, B0J 1A0
(902) 364-2052
Rte. 7 to Rte. 211 at Stillwater, 25.5
km (16 mi), follow signs • Former
hotel (1895-1945) situated on isth-
mus • Two o/n units, one shared
B&S • Cable TV in living room •
Cot available • No pets, please •
Non-smoking only
*RATES: $40 (1), $45 (2), $15 add'l
person • Full breakfast 7-10:30 •
Open May 1-Oct. 31 • MC, Visa
accepted • NSRS Member*

Big Harbour
The Roost B&B
Lal Coleman, 727 Big Harbour
Road, RR 2, Baddeck, B0E 1B0
(902) 295-2722
E-mail roost@morandan.com
3 km (2 mi) off Hwy 105, on Big

Harbour Rd. • Quiet location •
Three o/n units, one shared B&S,
one shared 1/2 B • Clock radio in
rooms • Adults only • Non-smoking
only
FEATURES: Picnic table and patio
deck • Garden • Bird-watching
*RATES: $45-$65 (1-2) • Open June
15-Oct. 15 • Check-in after 4 p.m. •
MC, Visa accepted • NSRS Member*

Big Pond
Big Pond
Bed & Breakfast
Keith & Pat Nelder, RR 1, East
Bay, B0A 1H0
(902) 828-2476
Fax (902) 828-3065
Three o/n units, one private B&S,
one shared B&S
FEATURES: Lake swimming •
Walking trail • Charter boats avail-
able • Vacation packages
*RATES: $36-$40 (1), $46-$50 (2) •
Full breakfast 7-10 • Open May 1-
Nov. 1 • NSRS Member*

Big Pond
MacIntyre's
Bed & Breakfast
Ed & Ann MacIntyre, 7903
Highway 4, Big Pond, RR 1, East
Bay, B0A 1H0
(902) 828-2184
Three o/n units, one private S, one
shared B&S • Clock radio in rooms
• Non-smoking only
FEATURES: Saltwater frontage •
Walking trails
*RATES: $35-$45 (1), $42-$50 (2) •
Open May-Oct. • Off-season by
reservation • NSRS Member*

Blandford
Blownaway
Bed & Breakfast
Michelle & Paul Cordeiro, 5206
Highway 329, Blandford, B0J 1C0
(902) 228-2041
Cellular (902) 275-7401
Hwy 103, Exit 6 or 7 • Three o/n
units, one shared B • Cable
TV/VCR, stereo, and telephone in
lounge • Children welcome • No
smoking in rooms, please
FEATURES: Piano in library
RATES: $50 (1-2), $10 add'l person • Full breakfast 7-9 • Open May 1-Oct. 31 • Off-season by reservation • Visa accepted • Cancellation policy

Blockhouse
By-Way Guest House
B&B
Bill & Shirley Murphy, RR 3,
Blockhouse, Mahone Bay, B0J 2E0
(902) 624-9636
Hwy 103, Exit 11, 1.5 km (1 mi)
towards New Cornwall • Three o/n
units, one shared B • TV and radio
in lounge
RATES: $35 (1), $45 (2) $10 add'l person • Full breakfast • Open July 1-Sept. 30 • Visa accepted • NSRS Member

Boisdale
Lakeview
Bed & Breakfast
Leona O'Handley, Boisdale, RR 2,
Christmas Island, B0A 1K0
(902) 871-2808
Cellular (902) 565-7290
Hwy 105, Exit 6, at Little Narrows,
follow Rte. 223 to Boisdale • Two
o/n units, one shared B&S • Cable
TV in living room • Non-smoking
only

RATES: $40 (1), $45 (2) • Full breakfast 8 • Open year-round • NSRS Member

Bras d'Or
Annfield Manor
Country Inn (c. 1893)
Denise & Bill Mulley, Church
Road, Bras d'Or, B0C 1B0
(902) 736-8770
1.5 km (1 mi) off Hwy 105, Exit
18W • Historic mansion • Seven o/n
units, private and shared B&S
FEATURES: Gardens • Lunch and
dinner served on request
RATES: $45-$70 (1-2), $15 add'l person • Full breakfast • Open year-round • MC accepted • Reservations required • NSRS Member

Bras d'Or
Dreamland
Bed & Breakfast
Melena & Alan Rea, Box 619, RR
1, Bras d'Or, B0K 1B0
(902) 674-2083
Fax (902) 674-2991
Hwy. 105, Exit 13 at Brass d'Or, 16
km (10 mi) on Ross Ferry-Kempt
Head Rd. • Three o/n units, one private S, one shared B&S • Cable TV
in family room • Cot available •
Children welcome • No pets, please
• Non-smoking only
FEATURES: Great views • Private
swimming • Fishing • Use of canoes
RATES: $46-$52 (1-2) • Weekly and off-season rates • Full breakfast 7-8:30 • Open May 1-Oct. 31 • NSRS Member

Bras d'Or

Gilead Bed & Breakfast

Aileen & Eugene Devoe, Box 809, RR 1, Bras d'Or, B0C 1B0

Tel & Fax (902) 674-2412

Hwy 105, Exit 14 at Bras d'Or, first driveway on left • Two o/n units, private B • Non-smoking only
FEATURES: View of Kelly's Mountain and Great Bras d'Or Channel from veranda • Sitting room with stone fireplace • Barbecue • Bird-watching • Fifteen minutes to Nfld. ferry; twenty minutes to Cabot Trail
RATES: $45-$50 (1), $55-$60 (2), $8 add'l person • Full breakfast 7-9 • Open year-round • Visa accepted • NSRS Member

Bridgetown

Bush's by the Bay Bed & Breakfast

Cora & Bill Bush, 8724 Shore Road East, RR 2, Hampton, B0S 1L0

(902) 665-2048

Hwy 101, Exit 20 to Church St. in Bridgetown (becomes Hampton Mountain Rd.) to Hampton, head east on Shore Rd. 1.6 km (1 mi) • Two o/n units, one shared B • Cable TV/VCR in lounge • Radio in rooms
FEATURES: Walking trails • Horseshoe pit
RATES: $35 (1), $45 (2) (tax incl.) • Breakfast 7-9:30 • Open May-Oct.

Bridgetown

Stichers' Cottage Bed & Breakfast

377 Granville Street, Box 362, Bridgetown, B0S 1C0

(902) 665-4009

Hwy 101, Exit 20 • Comfortable older home (c. 1921) decorated

throughout with cross-stitch • Three o/n units, two shared B&S • Families welcome • Cat on premises • Non-smoking only
RATES: $45 (1-2), $5-$10 add'l person • Full breakfast 7:30-8:30 • Open March 1-Oct. 31

Broad Cove

South Shore Country Inn ★★★ ½

Avril Betts, Route 331, Broad Cove, B0J 2H0

Tel & Fax (902) 677-2042
Toll free 1-800-565-8183
E-mail abtoursm@fox.nstn.ca

Hwy 103, Exit 15 from Halifax or Exit 17 from Yarmouth, follow signs • Nineteenth-century inn • Four o/n units (suites), private B • Cable TV, clock radio and telephone in rooms • Not suitable for small children • Non-smoking only
FEATURES: Licensed dining room • Kitchenette available • Two-minute walk to ocean beach • Retreat programs and vacation packages
RATES: $69-$135 (1-2), $15 add'l person (STC) • Breakfast • Open Easter-Oct. • Off-season by reservation • AE, MC, Visa accepted • IGNS; NSRS; TNS Member

Brookfield

Anglers Arm Bed & Breakfast

Verlie Grant, 13 Crystal Lake Road, Brookfield, B0N 1C0

Tel & Fax (902) 673-2590

Hwy 102, Exit 12, Rte. 289E over railroad track through flashing lights, first left past two schools (Brookfield Rd.) to Crystal Lake Rd. • Landscaped country property • Three o/n units, two shared B&S • Cable TV in sitting room • Non-

smoking only
FEATURES: Partial wheelchair accessibility • Lawn games • Private trout pond for fly fishing
RATES: $35 (1), $45 (2), $10 add'l person (STC) • Full breakfast 7-9 • Open May 1-Oct. 31 • Visa accepted • Check-out 10 a.m. • NSRS Member

Brookfield
Mrs. Densmore's Bed & Breakfast
Helen & Garth Densmore, 82 Highway 289, RR 2, Brookfield, B0N 1C0
(902) 673-2365
Hwy 102, Exit 12, right to flashing light at Brookfield, then Rte. 289, first farm on right • Nursery sod farm (c. 1830), home to six generations of same family • Two o/n units, one shared B&S • Cable TV/VCR in den • No pets, please • Non-smoking only
RATES: $35 (1), $40 (2) • Full breakfast 7-9 • Open May 1-Nov. 1

Brookfield
Past and Presents Bed & Breakfast
Johanna Benning, 519 Highway 2, RR 2, Brookfield, B0N 1C0
Tel & Fax (902) 673-3082
Hwy 102, Exit 12 to Brookfield, left at light • Three o/n units, one private S, one shared B&S • Cable TV/VCR in living room • Children over 12 yrs welcome • Smoking outside only
RATES: $35-$40 (1), $45-$50 (2) • Full breakfast 8-9 • Open year-round • Visa accepted • NSRS Member

Brookfield
Pleasant Valley Bed & Breakfast
Susan Peterson, 5 Pleasant Valley Road, RR 2, Brookfield, B0N 1C0
(902) 673-2742/3295
Hwy 102, Exit 12, turn left and take first road on left • Three o/n units, one shared B&S • Clock radio in rooms • Cable TV in living room • Non-smoking only
RATES: $30 (1), $35-$40 (2) • Full breakfast 7-9 • Open year-round • Visa accepted • NSRS Member

Brooklyn
Come From Away Bed & Breakfast
Sharon & Lionel Boomer, 50 Chambers Road, RR 1, Newport, B0N 2A0
(902) 757-2162
Hwy 101, Exit 5, Rte. 14 through village, stay left of monument, uphill to flashing light, turn left, go over bridge and turn left again • Two o/n units, one shared B&S • Cable TV/VCR in sitting room • Children under 8 yrs free • No pets, please • Non-smoking only
RATES: $45 (1), $60 (2), $10 add'l person • Full breakfast 7:30-9:30 • Open year-round • NSRS Member

Bucklaw
Castle Moffett ★★★★
Mr. & Mrs. Desmond Moffett, Box 678, Baddeck, B0E 1B0
(902) 756-9070
Fax (902) 756-3399
Website http://www.destination-ns.com/cabot/castle
Hwy 105, Bucklaw, 19 km (12 mi) west of Baddeck • Castle on 185-acres of wooded mountainside • Centrally located on the Bras d'Or Lakes • Three o/n units (suites), private B&S (Jacuzzi) • Not suitable for children • Non-smoking only
FEATURES: Views of lakes • Living area with fireplace • Art gallery in Great Hall • Grand piano • Air-conditioning • Honeymoon packages
RATES: $150-$225 (2) (STC) • Breakfast • Open year-round • MC, Visa accepted • IGNS; NSRS; TIANS Member

Caledonia
Forest Farm
Bed & Breakfast
Velda & Ronnie Forrest, 813 New Grafton Road, RR 2, Caledonia, B0T 1B0
(902) 682-2459
Rte. 8 to New Grafton Rd, 5 km (3 mi) • Older home on hobby farm in quiet rural setting • Three o/n units, one shared S • Cable TV in living room • No smoking in rooms, please
RATES: $40 (1), $45 (2), $10 add'l person • Full breakfast 7:30-9 • Open year-round • Visa accepted

Caledonia
Whitman Inn ★★★
Bruce & Nancy Gurnham, 12389 Highway 8, Kempt, B0T 1B0
(902) 682-2226

Fax (902) 682-3171
E-mail whitman@ro.isisnet.com
Website
http://www.isisnet/com/whitmaninn
4 km (2.5 mi) south of Kejimkujik National Park • Ten o/n units, private B; one suite (Jacuzzi); one housekeeping suite • No pets, please • Non-smoking rooms available
FEATURES: Licensed dining room (by reservation) • Picnic lunches • Lounge area • Indoor heated pool, sauna and whirlpool • Vacation packages
RATES: $50-$55 (1), $55-$65 (2), $85 (suite), $110 (housekeeping suite), $5 add'l person, $25 (MAP) • Breakfast 8-9:30 • Open year-round • MC, Visa accepted • CAA; NSRS; TNS; UCI Member

Canning
Farmhouse Inn
B&B ★★★★
Ellen & Doug Bray, 1057 Main Street, Box 38, Canning, B0P 1H0
Tel & Fax (902) 582-7900
Toll free 1-800-928-4346
E-mail
farmhous@ns.sympatico.ca
Website
http://www.valleyweb.com/farmhouseinn/
Hwy 101, Exit 11; or Rte. 1N to Rte. 358 • Six o/n units, private B&S; one luxury suite • Cable TV/VCR • Crib available • No pets, please • Non-smoking only
FEATURES: Two parlours with fireplaces • Library • Afternoon tea • Antiques and handmade quilts• Exercise room • Sleigh rides in season
RATES: $39-$89 (1), $49-$99 (2), $10 add'l person • Full breakfast • Open year-round • MC, Visa

accepted • CAA; IGNS; NSRS; TIANS Member

Canning
Tree Tops
Bed & Breakfast

Eleanor & Bernard Mason, 2340 Gospel Road, RR 3, Canning, B0P 1H0
(902) 582-7470
Hwy 101, Exit 11 to Rte. 1, then Rte. 358 at Irving station; follow road for 16.1 km (10 mi) towards Look Off, turn left 1.2 km (0.8 mi) on left • View of Annapolis Valley • Two o/n units, one shared S • Cot available • Not suitable for children under 5 yrs • No pets, please • Non-smoking only
FEATURES: View of world's highest tides
RATES: $40-$45 (1), $45-$50 (2), $5-$12 add'l person • Full breakfast • Open May 15-Oct. 15 • Off-season by reservation

Canso
Pendletons'
Bed & Breakfast

Vera Rhynold, 1228 Union Street, Box 371, Canso, B0H 1H0
(902) 366-2875
Hwy 104, Exit 37 to Rte. 16; or from Sherbrooke, take Marine Drive • Three o/n units, one shared S • Cable TV/VCR in lounge • No pets, please • Non-smoking only
RATES: $40 (1), $50 (2) (STC) • Breakfast 7:30-9 • Open May-Nov.

Canso
Whale's Tail
Bed & Breakfast

Myrna Livingston, 37 Sterling Street, Canso, B0H 1H0
(902) 366-2271

Hwy 104, Exit 37; or from Sherbrooke, take Marine Drive • Three o/n units, two shared B&S • Cable TV in living room • No pets, please • Non-smoking only
FEATURES: French spoken • Collection of Elvis memorabilia
RATES: $40 (1), $50 (2) • Open year-round • NSRS Member

Cape d'Or
Cape d'Or Lightkeepers
Guest House

David Austin, Cape d'Or, Advocate Harbour, B0M 1A0
(902) 664-2108
5.5 km (3.5 mi) from Advocate, follow signs • Lighthouse site on Minas Channel • Two o/n units, one shared B&S; one suite • TV in common room • Non-smoking only
FEATURES: Large decks • Hiking trails • Bird-watching and rare plant life • International biological program site • Boat tours (Aug.-Sept.) • Full-service restaurant • Outdoor fire pits and barbecue • Vacation packages
RATES: $40 (1), $50 (2), $80 (suite), $125 (whole house), $10 add'l person • Open June 1-Oct. 15 • Visa accepted

Cape North
Oakwood Manor ★★★
Sharon McEvoy, Box 1, Comp 9,
Cape North, B0C 1G0
Tel & Fax (902) 383-2317
1.5 km (1 mi) on Bay St. Lawrence
Rd.; 1.5 km (1 mi) on North Side
Rd. • Two-hundred-acre country
estate • Three o/n units, two shared
B (sink in rooms) • TV/VCR and
movies in lounge • Pay telephone •
No pets, please • Non-smoking only
*RATES: $35 (1), $45-$52 (2), $7
add'l person (STC) • Full breakfast
7:30-9:30 • Open May 1-Oct. 31 •
Visa accepted • IGNS; NSRS
Member*

Cape North
The Ridge Guest House
Bonita Wilkie, 29024 Cabot Trail,
RR 1, Dingwall, B0C 1G0
(902) 383-2152
Quiet setting surrounded by high-
lands • Two o/n units, one shared S
• No smoking in rooms, please
FEATURES: Kitchen facilities
*RATES: $35 (1), $40 (2) •
Breakfast on request • Open June 1-
Oct. 15*

Cape Sable Island
Penney Estate Bed & Breakfast Ltd.
Lois & Herbert Atkinson, 4 Penney
Beach Road, North East Point, Box
57, Barrington Passage, B0W 1G0
Tel & Fax (902) 745-1516
On Rte. 330 (Cape Sable Island), off
Rte. 3 • Three o/n units, two shared
B&S • Cable TV
*RATES: $40 (1), $50 (2), $10 add'l
person • Full breakfast 7-9 • Open
year-round • MC, Visa accepted*

Catalone
Camilla Peck's Tourist Home Bed & Breakfast
Mrs. Camilla Peck, 5353 Highway
22, Louisbourg, B0A 1M0
(902) 733-2649
On Rte. 22 at Catalone, 8 km (5 mi)
from Louisbourg; 22.5 km (14 mi)
from Sydney, Exit 8 to Rte. 22 •
Farmhouse (c. 1902) on scenic hilltop away from traffic • Three o/n
units, one shared B • TV and radio
in lounge • Children under 5 yrs free
FEATURES: Complimentary cof-
fee/tea • Variety of animals to view
*RATES: $35 (1), $40-$42 (2), $10-
$12 add'l person (STC) • Full
breakfast 7:30-9:30 • Open June 1-
Oct. 30 • NSRS Member*

Catalone
MacLeod's Bed & Breakfast
Ramona MacLeod, 5247 Highway
22, Louisbourg, B0A 1M0
(902) 733-2456
Hwy 125, Exit 8 on Rte. 22, 10 km
(6 mi) to Louisbourg • Three o/n
units, one private B, one shared
B&S • TV and radio in lounge • No
pets, please • Non-smoking only
*RATES: $30-$35 (1), $45-$50 (2),
$10-$20 add'l person (STC) • Full
breakfast 7-9 • Open May 1-Sept. 30
• Visa accepted • NSRS Member*

Centreville
Browning's Bed & Breakfast
Orval & Gerri Browning, 8358
Highway 221, RR 2, Centreville,
B0P 1J0
(902) 582-7062
Hwy 101, Exit 12 to Rte. 359 to
Rte. 221E • Large park-like setting
with duck ponds • Three o/n units,

one shared B&S • TV, clock radio and ceiling fan in rooms • Cable TV in sitting room • Children welcome • No smoking in rooms, please
RATES: $45 (1), $55 (2), $10 add'l person • Full breakfast 8-10 • Open May 1-Sept. 30 • NSRS Member

Charlos Cove
Seawind Landing Country Inn ★★★ ½
Lorraine & Jim Colvin, Charlos Cove, B0H 1T0
(902) 525-2188
Toll free 1-800-563-INNS (4667)
Award-winning inn on secluded twenty-acre coastal property • Twelve o/n units, private B&S or S (six whirlpools) • Non-smoking only
FEATURES: Ocean beaches, sheltered coves and nature trails • Licensed seaside dining room • Antique furnishings • Barbecue, picnic tables and lawn games • Sailing, motor boating, canoeing and mountain biking, • Ocean swimming, seal-watching and clam-digging • Vacation packages
RATES: $60-$90 (1), $70-$100 (2), $210 (suite) (STC) • Breakfast 7-9 • Open May 1-Oct. 30 • DD, MC, Visa accepted • CAA; IGNS; NSRS; UCI Member

Chegoggin
Gateway Farms Bed & Breakfast
Lloyd & Joy Sweeney, RR 3, Box 2020, Yarmouth, B5A 4A7
(902) 742-9786
Cellular (902) 749-7309
From Rte. 1, Chegoggin Rd. 4 km (2.5 mi) to yield sign, turn right to fourth house on left • Three o/n units, one shared B, one shared B&S • TV in lounge • Infants free •

Non-smoking only
RATES: $30-$40 (1-2), $5 add'l person • Full breakfast 7-8:30 • Open May 1-Nov. 1

Chester
Captain's House Inn
Nicki Butler & Jane McLoughlin, 29 Central Street, Chester, B0J 1J0
(902) 275-3501
Fax (902) 275-3502
Early Victorian home (c. 1822) • Four o/n units, private B&S
FEATURES: Large waterfront decks • Licensed dining room and lounge
RATES: $70 (1), $75 (2) (STC) • Continental breakfast • Open year-round • AE, DC, MC, Visa accepted

Chester
Gray Gables Bed & Breakfast
David & Jeanette Tomsett, 19 Graves Island Road, RR 1, Chester, B0J 1J0
(902) 275-3983
Website http://www.destination-ns.com/lighthouse/graygables/
Hwy 103, Exit 7 or 8, off Rte. 3 in East Chester • Three o/n units, private B&S • Cable TV/VCR in sitting room • Not suitable for children under 12 yrs • No pets, please • Non-smoking only
FEATURES: View of Mahone Bay and Graves Island Park • Dutch spoken • Afternoon or evening refreshments • Whirlpool • Bicycles available
RATES: $75-$85 (1-2), $20 add'l person • Full breakfast 7-9 • Open May 15-Oct. 31 • Off-season by reservation • MC, Visa accepted • IGNS Member

Chester
Haddon Hall
Inn ★★★★ ½
Cynthia O'Connell, 67 Haddon Hill
Road, Box 640, Chester, B0J 1J0
(902) 275-3577
Fax (902) 275-5159
Eighty-five-acre hilltop country
estate with ocean view • Nine o/n
units (suites), private B&S (Jacuzzi)
• Cable TV and telephone in rooms
• No pets, please • No smoking in
rooms, please
FEATURES: Wheelchair accessibility • Professionally designed inte-
riors • Licensed restaurant with
gourmet dining • Life-size chess
game • Heated outdoor swimming
pool • Tennis court • Boat rentals
and charter service • Recreational
private island
*RATES: From $150 (2), $15 add'l
person (STC) • Continental breakfast • Open April 1-Jan. 1 • AE, DC,
MC, Visa accepted • Cancellation
48 hours in advance • CAA; IGNS;
NSRS; TIANS Member*

Chester
Hemlock House
Bed & Breakfast
Bobby Young & Peter Fitch, 71
Central Street, Box 592, Chester,
B0J 1J0
(902) 275-3854
In town centre at Union St. •
Originally annexed to Hackmatack
Hotel (c. 1903), on one acre of
beautifully landscaped property in
quiet area • Three o/n units, one
shared B, one shared B&S • No
pets, please
*RATES: $75 (1-2) • Full breakfast
8-10 • Open May 1-Oct. 31 • Visa
accepted*

Chester
Mecklenburgh Inn ★★★
Suzi Fraser, 78 Queen Street, Box
350, Chester, B0J 1J0
Tel & Fax (902) 275-4638
Website http://destination-
ns.com/lighthouse/mecklenburgh
Located in the heart of the village
next to the Post Office • Four o/n
units, two shared B&S • Clock radio
in rooms • TV/VCR in living room •
Children over 10 yrs welcome •
Smoking on balcony only
FEATURES: Registered heritage
property • Living and dining rooms
with fireplaces
*RATES: $50 (1), $59-$65 (2), $20
add'l person • Full breakfast 8-9:30
• Open May 24-Oct. 31 • Visa
accepted • CAA; IGNS; NSRS;
SSTA Member*

Chester
Stoney Brook
Bed & Breakfast ★★★
Jeanne & Ned Nash, Box 716,
Chester, B0J 1J0
(902) 275-2342
Website http://www.destination-
ns.com/lighthouse/stoneybrook

On Rte. 3 at
Chester •
Registered
heritage
property •
Four o/n
units, one shared S, one shared B&S
• Children over 10 yrs welcome •
No pets, please • Non-smoking only
FEATURES: French spoken •
Fireplace • Gardens
*RATES: $50-$60 (1-2) • Breakfast
8-9 • Open May 1-Oct. 15 • Visa
accepted • NSRS; SSBBA; SSTA
Member*

Chester Basin
The Sword & Anchor
Arthur & Jane McLaughlin and
Nicki Butler, 5306 Route 3, Chester
Basin, B0J 1K0
(902) 275-2478/3501
Sister inn to The Captain's House,
Chester • Waterfront property with
large deck • Nine o/n units, private
B&S
RATES: $70 (1), $75 (2) (STC) •
Continental breakfast • *Open year-
round*

Cheticamp
Auberge
déjeuner de soleil Inn
Anne & Armand St. Jean, Box 974,
Cheticamp, B0E 1H0
(902) 224-1373
Turn at Post Office on Belle March
Rd., follow signs • Seven o/n units,
three shared B&S, one shared S •
Cable TV in living room • No
smoking in rooms, please
FEATURES: Wheelchair accessi-
bility • Peaceful countryside with
view • French spoken • Berry-pick-
ing in season
RATES: $40 (1), $45-$70 (2) • *Full
breakfast 7-10* • *Open year-round* •
MC, Visa accepted • *IGNS; NSRS
Member*

Cheticamp
Blue Island
Bed & Breakfast
Betty Gunther, 107 Cheticamp
Island Road, Box 675, Cheticamp,
B0E 1H0
(902) 224-3077
Log house with views of town and
harbour • Two o/n units, one shared
B&S • TV in living room • Children
under 7 yrs free
RATES: $40 (1), $45 (2), $15 add'l

person (STC) • *Continental breakfast 7:30-9:30* • *Open June 15-
Oct. 15*

Cheticamp
Cheticamp Outfitters
Bed & Breakfast
Veronica & Gilles Hache, Point
Cross, Box 448, Cheticamp,
B0E 1H0
(902) 224-2776
Fax (902) 224-2382
Three o/n units, one shared S •
Clock radio in rooms • TV/VCR in
living room • No smoking in rooms,
please
FEATURES: Guest decks and bar-
becue • Great ocean view •
Complete licensed outfitting/guiding
service • French spoken
RATES: $40 (1), $45 (2) (STC) •
Full breakfast until 10 • *Open April
1-Dec. 15* • *Off-season by reserva-
tion* • *AE, MC, Visa accepted* •
NSRS Member

Cheticamp
Germaine's Bed & Breakfast ★★ ½

Germaine & Roland Doucet, Route 19, Point Cross, Box 275, Cheticamp, B0E 1H0
Tel & Fax (902) 224-3459

Located in Point Cross, 8 km (5 mi) south of Cheticamp • Three o/n units, one private B, one shared B&S • Cable TV in living room • Children over 5 yrs welcome • No pets, please
FEATURES: Bilingual Acadian family • Panoramic view of sunsets • Walking trail to ocean
RATES: $38 (1), $42-$45 (2), $14 add'l person (STC) • Full breakfast 7-9:30 • Open April 1-Oct. 30 • MC, Visa accepted • CBBBA; IGNS; NSFC; NSRS Member

Cheticamp
L'Auberge Doucet Inn ★★★

Adele & Ronnie Doucet, Box 776, Cheticamp, B0E 1H0
(902) 224-3438
Fax (902) 224-2792
Toll free 1-800-646-8668
Eight o/n units, private B&S • Cable TV in rooms and lounge • Children under 12 yrs free
FEATURES: Wheelchair accessibility • Whale-watching crusies
RATES: $55-$70 (1), $60-$75 (2), $8 add'l person (STC) • Continental breakfast 7:30-10 • Open May 1-Nov. 15 • AE, MC, Visa accepted • IGNS; NSRS Member

Cheticamp
Laurence Guest House B&B (c. 1879)

Judy Wakefield & Sylvia LeLievre, 15408 Main Street, Cheticamp, B0E 1H0
(902) 224-2184
In centre of town • Four o/n units, two shared B&S • Clock radio in rooms • Not suitable for children • No pets, please • Non-smoking only
FEATURES: French spoken
RATES: $40 (1), $48 (2), $8 add'l person • Full breakfast 7-9 • Open May 15-Oct. 15 • Off-season by reservation • MC, Visa accepted

Cheticamp
Les Créations Carole Bed & Breakfast

Wallace & Carole Aucoin, 15068 Cabot Trail, Box 790, Cheticamp, B0E 1H0
Tel & Fax (902) 224-2035
In village centre • Two o/n units, one shared S • Cable TV in living room • No pets, please
FEATURES: French spoken • Craft shop on premises
RATES: $45 (1-2) • Continental breakfast 7-9 • Open June 1-Oct. 15 • MC, Visa accepted

Cheticamp
Overnight Country Log Home B&B

Adrienne Deveaux, Belle Marche Road, Box 337, Cheticamp, B0E 1H0
(902) 224-2816
Turn at post office, 1.4 km (0.9 mi) on right • Rustic log home in quiet countryside • Two o/n units, one shared B • Cable TV in living room • No smoking in rooms, please
RATES: $40 (1), $45 (2) •

Continental breakfast 8-9:30 • *Open June 1-Sept. 30* • *NSRS Member*

Cheverie
Studio Vista
Bed & Breakfast
Karen & Ted Casselman, 2018 New Cheverie Road, Cheverie, B0N 1G0
(902) 633-2837
Fax (902) 633-2850
Hwy 101, Exit 4 or 5 to Brooklyn, Rte. 215 to Cheverie, follow signs • One o/n unit, private B&S • TV and telephone in room • No pets, please • No smoking inside, please
FEATURES: 40 km (25 mi) view overlooking three beaches and world's highest tides • Gardens • Safe walking • Bird-watching • Fossils • Handwoven blankets for sale
RATES: $45 (1), $58 (2) • *Full breakfast* • *Open May-Oct.* • *Off-season by reservation* • *Visa accepted* • *NSRS Member*

Clark's Harbour
Cape Island
Bed & Breakfast
Sheila Evans, Box 9, Clark's Harbour, B0W 1P0
(902) 745-1356
Hwy 103 to Barrington Passage to Rte. 3 to Rte. 330, 13 km (8 mi) • Three o/n units, one shared S • Cable TV in living room
RATES: $35 (1), $45 (2), $10 add'l person (STC) • *Full breakfast 7-10* • *Open year-round* • *Off-season by reservation* • *NSRS Member*

Clementsport
Olde Port of Clements (c. 1827)
Bed & Breakfast
James & Christine Povah, 8 Clementsport Road, Clementsport, B0S 1E0
(902) 638-8120
Hwy 101, Exit 23, 5 km (3 mi) east on Rte. 1 to Clementsport • Colonial-style home • Two o/n units, private B&S • TV in rooms • Non-smoking only
FEATURES: Situated on mouth of Moose River • French spoken • Canoeing • Art gallery and antiques
RATES: $40-$45 (1-2), $5 add'l person (no GST) (STC) • *Full breakfast 7-9* • *Open June-Sept.* • *NSRS Member*

Clyde River
Clyde River Inn ★★★
Michael Nickerson & Patricia Atwood, 10525 Highway 103, Box 2, Clyde River, B0W 1R0
(902) 637-3267
Hwy 103, Exit 28 • Restored stage-coach inn (c. 1880), furnished with antiques and collectibles • Two o/n units, private B&S; one suite • Clock radio in rooms • Cable TV in parlour • No smoking in rooms, please
RATES: $45 (1), $55 (2), $80 (suite), $10 add'l person • *Continental breakfast* • *Open May 1-Oct. 31* • *Off-season by reservation* • *Visa accepted* • *NSRS Member*

Cole Harbour

Cole Harbour

Cole Harbour Bed & Breakfast

Doug & Audrey Uloth, Cole Harbour, RR 2, Larry's River, B0H 1T0

(902) 358-2889

Toll free 1-800-565-9144

On Rte. 316, 30 km (18 mi) west of Canso; 42 km (26 mi) from Guysborough • Two o/n units, one shared B&S

FEATURES: View of harbour and sunsets • Evening snack • Host is a lobster fisherman with boat to view seals

RATES: $30 (1), $45 (2) (STC) • Full breakfast 8 • Open year-round

Coxheath (near Sydney)

Edna's Bed & Breakfast

Edna Ponée, 17 Andrews Avenue, Sydney, B1R 2G8

(902) 567-2239

Quiet residential setting • Three o/n units, two shared B&S • Cable TV in rooms and living room • No pets, please • Non-smoking only

RATES: $32 (1), $40 (2) (STC) • Full breakfast 7-8:30 • Open year-round • Please call for reservations • NSRS Member

Creignish

Creignish Bed & Breakfast

Sandra Kuzminski, Creignish, Port Hastings, B0E 2T0

(902) 625-3336

Rte. 19, 10 km (6 mi) north of Canso Causeway • Three o/n units, one private B&S, two shared B

FEATURES: Ocean swimming, fishing, hiking trails, geological tours • Sea cliffs, canoeing and kayaking • Children's activities and

workshops

RATES: $35 (1), $40-$50 (2) • Full breakfast • Open May 1-Oct. 31

Cribbons Point

Cribbons Cottages and Bed & Breakfast

Paul & Laureen Boyd, Cribbons Point, B2G 2L2

(902) 863-6320/2936

Off season 3 Bantry Lane, Antigonish, B2G 2W3

20 km (12.5 mi) from Antigonish on Rte. 337N • Two o/n units, one shared B&S; four cottages • No pets, please

FEATURES: Ocean view • Playground, horseshoe pit and picnic tables • Bicycles • Ocean swimming at sandy beach • Walking trails • Hunting and deep-sea fishing arranged • Boats available

RATES: $30 (1), $40 (2), $80 (cottage), $10 add'l person • Off-season and weekly rates • Open May-Nov. • Visa accepted

Darling Lake

Churchill Mansion Country Inn

Bob Benson, RR 1, Yarmouth, B5A 4A5

(902) 649-2818

Off-season (902) 467-3549

Rte. 1, 14.5 km (9 mi) northeast of Yarmouth at Darling Lake • Heritage property with widow's walk • Eight o/n units, private B • Cable TV in lounge • Children under 6 yrs free

FEATURES: Meals on request • Lake swimming • Canoeing

RATES: $35-$49 (1), $44-$59 (2-3), $10 add'l person (STC) • Off-season rates • Breakfast 7-10 • Open May 1-Nov. 15 • MC, Visa accepted • IGNS; NSRS Member

Debert
Berry Farm
Bed & Breakfast
John & Sophie Esau, 433 Plains
Road, Debert, B0M 1G0
Tel & Fax (902) 662-2389
2 km (1.5 mi) from Hwy 104,
Debert/Belmont intersection •
Operating family farm surrounded
by hardwood forest • One o/n unit,
private B • Children welcome • No
pets, please • Non-smoking only
FEATURES: Evening snack •
French and German spoken
*RATES: $25 (1), $40 (2), $10 add'l
person • Full breakfast • Open
June 1-Oct. 15*

D'Escousse
D'Escousse
Bed & Breakfast
Sara & Al McDonald, RR 1,
D'Escousse, B0E 1K0
(902) 226-2936
Hwy 104, Exit 46, Rte. 320E
towards Arichat to Rte. 320S •
Three o/n units, one shared B&S •
TV in lounge • Crib available •
Non-smoking only
FEATURES: Ocean swimming
*RATES: $32 (1), $42 (2), $12 add'l
person • Full breakfast • Open May
15-Oct. 15*

Digby
Bayside
Bed & Breakfast
Bob & Theresa Marshall, 115
Montague Row, Box 459, Digby,
B0V 1A0
(902) 245-2247
Beautiful waterfront view • Ten o/n
units, four private B, two shared B •
Cable TV • No pets, please
FEATURES: Kitchen facilities
RATES: $40-$45 (1), $45-$50 (2),

*$7 add'l person (STC) • Off-season
rates • Continental breakfast 8-10 •
Open year-round • AE, MC, Visa
accepted • IGNS; NSRS Member*

Digby
Mary's Waterview
Bed & Breakfast
Mary Harvieux, 34 Carleton Street,
Box 1314, Digby, B0V 1A0
(902) 245-4949
Two o/n units, one shared B&S •
Cable TV in living room • No
smoking in rooms, please
FEATURES: View of Fundy tides
from deck • Whale-watching
arranged
*RATES: $35 (1), $50 (2), $10 add'l
person • Full breakfast 8-9 • Open
year-round • Visa accepted • NSRS
Member*

Digby
Ocean Hillside
Bed & Breakfast
Maria & Bob Cabana, RR 3, Shore
Road, Digby, B0V 1A0
(902) 245-5932

Minutes
from Digby
ferry •
Overlooks
Annapolis
Basin • Four
o/n units, one private B&S, one private B, one shared S • Non-smoking
only
FEATURES: Laundry facilities •
Afternoon tea • Victorian antiques,
handmade quilts and crafts • Flower
gardens • Whale-watching arranged
*RATES: $50-$65 • Full breakfast •
Open May 1-Oct. 31 • Off-season by
reservation • Visa accepted • NSRS
Member*

Digby
Salt & Light
Bed & Breakfast
John & Jill Bonham, 189 King
Street, Box 493, Digby, B0V 1A0
(902) 245-4562
Fax (902) 245-1919
Hwy 101, Exit 26, Rte. 303 to
Warwick St., second street on the
left past Victoria St. • Victorian
home (c. 1870) with veranda, over-
looking Annapolis Basin • Four o/n
units, one shared B&S, one shared S
• No pets, please • No alcohol •
Non-smoking only
FEATURES: Our mandate: Joshua:
24:15
*RATES: $35-$40 (1), $45-$50 (2)
(STC) • Full breakfast 7:30-8:30 •
Open year-round • Visa accepted •
ETTA Member*

Digby
Summer's Country Inn
B&B ★★★
Herbert & Gloria Robicheau,
16 Warwick Street, Digby,
B0V 1A0
(902) 245-2250
Fax (902) 245-6694
Centrally located restored 1800s
country inn • Seven o/n units, pri-
vate B; one housekeeping suite •
Cable TV/VCR in lounge
FEATURES: Maritime home-
cooked dinners on request • Evening
coffee or tea • High poster and brass
beds • Barbecue • Bicycle rentals •
Whale-watching arranged
*RATES: $50-$65, $99 (suite), $10
add'l person (STC) • Off-season
rates • Full breakfast • Open May 1-
Oct. 31 • MC, Visa accepted • NSRS
Member*

Digby
Thistle Down
Country Inn ★★★ ½
Ed Reid & Lester Bartson,
98 Montague Row, Box 508, Digby,
B0V 1A0
(902) 245-4490
Fax (902) 245-6717
Toll free 1-800-565-8081
Historic 1904 home on Digby
Harbour with view of fishing fleet
and Annapolis Basin • Twelve o/n
units, private B • Cable TV/VCR in
lounge • Public telephone in lobby •
Non-smoking only
FEATURES: French spoken •
Candlelight dinners in Queen
Alexandra dining room on request •
Bicycle rentals
*RATES: $55-$65 (1), $65-$95 (2),
$15 add'l person (STC) • Off-season
rates • Full breakfast 7:30-9 • Open
May 1-Oct. 31 • AE, DC, MC, Visa
accepted • NSRS Member*

Digby
Westway House B&B
Keith & Evelyn Burnham, 6
Carleton Street, Box 1576, Digby,
B0V 1A0
Tel & Fax (902) 245-5071
Heritage property (c. 1839) • Four
o/n units, one private B, two shared
B • Cable TV/VCR in rooms and
lounge • Cot and crib available •
Children under 5 yrs free
FEATURES: Panoramic view of
8.5 m (28 ft.) tides • Evening tea •
Library • Antiques and handcrafted
quilts • Barbecue and picnic table •
Golf and whale-watching arranged
*RATES: $30-$36 (1), $37-$46 (2-
3), $8 add'l person • Full breakfast
8-9:30 • Open May 15-Oct. 15 •
Off-season by reservation • MC,
Visa accepted • NSRS Member*

Dingwall
Inlet Bed & Breakfast
Brian Fitzgerald, Box 18, Dingwall, B0C 1G0
(902) 383-2112
2.5 km (1.5 mi) from Cabot Trail on Dingwall Harbour • Three o/n units, two shared B&S • TV in living room • No pets, please • Non-smoking only
RATES: $35 (1), $42-$45 (2), $9 add'l person (STC) • Full breakfast 7:30-9 • Open May 1-Oct. 31 • Off-season by reservation • CBBBA; NSRS Member

Durham
Rose Cottage Bed & Breakfast (c. 1814) ★★★
Judy & Sonny Campbell, RR 2, Pictou, B0K 1H0
(902) 485-6733
Hwy 104, Exit 20 to Rte. 376, 4.5 km (3 mi) east from Exit 20; or Rte. 376, 12.5 km (8 mi) west from Pictou Rotary on the West River • 18 km (11 mi) from PEI ferry • Three o/n units, one shared B&S • Cable TV/VCR in lounge • Non-smoking only
FEATURES: Fireplace, games, and piano in lounge • Gift shop • Picnic and playground area • Laundry facilities
RATES: $35 (1), $45-$55 (2) • Continental or full breakfast 7:30-9:30 • Open year-round • MC, Visa accepted • NSRS Member

East Chester
East Chester Inn B&B
Jess & Ross Davis, 3280 Highway 3, East Chester, B0J 1J0
(902) 275-3017/4790
On Rte. 3, 1.5 km (1 mi) east of Chester • Six o/n units, one shared B&S, one shared B • Cable TV and radio in lounge
RATES: $34 (1), $44-$59 (2) (STC)• Full breakfast 8 • Open May-Oct. • NSRS Member

East LaHave
Ferry View Bed & Breakfast
Henk & Judith Smits, 4392 Route 332, East LaHave, RR 3, Bridgewater, B4V 2W2
(902) 766-4716
Just past the ferry towards Riverport • Beautiful scenic view of LaHave Islands • Two o/n units, private S • TV in lounge • No pets, please • Non-smoking only
RATES: $45 (1), $55 (2) • Full breakfast • Open May-Oct. • MC, Visa accepted

East LaHave
Tradewinds Bed & Breakfast
Walter & Edna Lomertin, 4952 East LaHave, RR 3, Bridgewater, B4V 2W2
(902) 766-4020
On Rte. 332, 3 km (2 mi) upriver from LaHave Ferry • Three o/n units, private B&S • Clock radio and ceiling fan in rooms • TV and telephone in lounge • Cat on premises • No pets, please • Non-smoking only
FEATURES: German spoken • Upper sun deck overlooking river • Bicycles • Fifteen minutes to Lunenburg and Bridgewater
RATES: $47-$55 (1), $52-$60 (2), $10 add'l person (STC) • Full breakfast until 9 • Open May-Oct. • Off-season by reservation • MC, Visa accepted • NSRS Member

East Margaree
Margaree Inn
Bed & Breakfast

Julia & Dianne LeBlanc, Box 19,
Margaree Harbour, B0E 2B0
(902) 235-2524/2935
1 km (0.5 mi) off Cabot Trail • Four
o/n units, private B&S • TV in
rooms
*RATES: $40 (1), $50 (2), $10 add'l
person • Full breakfast 7-8:30 •
Open May-Oct. 31 • Off-season by
reservation • MC, Visa accepted •
NSRS Member*

Economy
Silver House
Bed & Breakfast

Carole & Ray Dibbon, 3289
Highway 2, Economy, B0M 1J0
(902) 647-2022
33 km (20 mi) east of Parrsboro •
Lovingly renovated home • Three
o/n units, one private B&S, one
shared B&S • TV/VCR in living
room • Not suitable for children
under 12 yrs • No pets, please •
Smoking outside only
FEATURES: Sunporch • Evening
snacks; cakes for special occasions
*RATES: $44-$49 (1-2) (STC) • Full
breakfast • Open May-Dec.*

Economy
Thompson's
Bed and Breakfast

Kathleen Thompson, Lower
Economy, B0M 1J0
(902) 647-2777
On Rte. 2, 29 km (18 mi) east of
Parrsboro • Three o/n units, one
shared B&S • TV, radio and piano
in lounge
FEATURES: Overlooking world's
highest tides
RATES: $40 (1-2) (tax incl.) (STC)

*• Full breakfast 7-10 • Open May-
Dec.*

Elmsdale
Forevergreen House
B&B

Joanna Howell, 18 Garden Road,
Elmsdale, B0N 1M0
(902) 883-4445
Fax (902) 883-1456
Hwy 102, Exit 8, 2.5 km (1.5 mi)
towards Windsor • Country home
on five acres of grounds and gardens • Three o/n units, private B&S
• Cable TV/VCR and stereo in guest
sitting room • Horse and dog on
premises • Smoking on deck only
FEATURES: Evening snack •
Brass beds • Furnished with
antiques
*RATES: $45 (1), $55 (2), $65
(suite), $10 add'l person (STC) •
Full breakfast 7:30-9:30 • Open
year-round • Visa accepted*

Fall River
The Arbour
Bed and Breakfast

Evangeline Brown, 1303 Fall River
Road, Fall River, B2T 1E6
Tel & Fax (902) 861-2324
Hwy 102, Exit 5 to Rte. 2, north to
Fall River Rd. • One o/n unit, pri-
vate B&S • Cable TV/VCR in guest
lounge • Children over 13 yrs wel-
come • Non-smoking only
FEATURES: Guest lounge with
mini-fridge • Sunroom
*RATES: $50 (1), $55 (2), $10 add'l
person • Full breakfast 7-9 • Open
May-Oct. • Off-season by reserva-
tion • Visa accepted • NSRS
Member*

Fall River
An Olde Manor House B&B (c. 1847)

Launa Lunn, 1380 Rocky Lake Drive, P.O. Box 323, Waverley, B0N 2S0

(902) 861-1800 (collect calls accepted)

Hwy 102, Exit 5; or Rte. 118, Exit 14, across from Post Office

• Victorian house (c. 1847) • Two o/n units, one shared B&S; one suite • TV/VCR in lounge • Cot and crib available • Non-smoking only
FEATURES: Furnished with antiques • Library of regional books • Music parlour • Two fireplaces • Barbecue • Indoor hot tub in sunroom • Swimming and canoeing in Lake William • Ten minutes from airport; twenty minutes from downtown Halifax
RATES: $39-$59 (1-2), $99 (suite), $10 add'l person • Full breakfast 7-9 • Open May 1-Nov. 9 • Off-season by reservation • Visa accepted • NSFBBA; NSRS Member

Fall River
Avril's Place B&B ★★★

Avril Betts, 23 Scout Camp Road, Fall River, Box 44208, Bedford, B4A 3Z8

Tel & Fax (902) 861-1066
Toll free 1-800-565-8183
E-mail abtoursm@fox.nstn.ca

Hwy 102, Exit 5, towards Hwy 118 (Dartmouth); follow signs • One o/n unit, private B • TV, clock radio and coffee machine in room • Non-smoking only
FEATURES: View of Miller Lake • Laundry facilities • Fridge available

• Fax/photocopier available • Pedal boat
RATES: $45 (1), $49.95 (2) (STC) • Continental breakfast • Open year-round • AE, MC, Visa accepted • NSRS Member

Fall River
Milligan Home Bed & Breakfast ★★ ½

Charles & Hester Milligan, 2093 Portobello Road,Waverley, B0N 2S0

(902) 861-1142
Toll free 1-800-749-8881

Hwy 102, Exit 5, Rte. 318 to Waverley, 4 km (2.5 mi) on the right • Three o/n units, one shared B&S • No pets, please • Non-smoking only
FEATURES: Lake swimming
RATES: $50 (1-2) • Continental or full breakfast 7-9 • Open April-Dec. • NSRS Member

Fall River
Nap 'n' Nibble Bed & Breakfast ★★★

Judith Church, 20 Beaverbank Road, Lower Sackville, B4E 1G5

(902) 865-9100

Rte. 102, Exit 4B then Exit 2 to Beaverbank Rd. • Three o/n units, two shared B&S • TV/VCR, radio and telephone in lounge • No pets, please • Non-smoking only
FEATURES: Laundry facilities • Close to major highways and Halifax Airport
RATES: $35 (1), $40-$45 (2) • Family and weekly rates • Breakfast 8-9 • Open year-round • MATA; NSRS Member

Falmouth
Apple Valley Inn
B&B ★★ ½
Mary Dinner, 98 Town Road, Box 3, Falmouth, B0P 1L0
(902) 798-8169
Hwy 101, Exit 7, left on Rte. 1, take first right on Town Rd. • Renovated older home • Three o/n units, two shared B&S • Cable TV in sunroom • Not suitable for younger children • Non-smoking only
RATES: $50 (1), $60 (2) (STC) • Full breakfast 8-10 • Open May 24-Sept. 30 • Visa accepted • NSRS Member

Folly Lake
Winnet House B&B
Angela L. Younger, RR 1, Londonderry, B0M 1M0
(902) 662-4197
On Hwy 104 at Folly Lake • Three o/n units, one shared B&S • TV/VCR in living room • Non-smoking only
FEATURES: Piano in living room • Evening snack • Deck with view of lake and mountain • Lake swimming, canoeing and fishing • Bird-watching • Walking trails • Packages available
RATES: $35-$45 (1-2) • Full breakfast 7:30-10 • Open year-round • NSRS Member

Forks Baddeck
Auld Manse B&B
Marj Theriault, RR 1, Forks Baddeck, B0E 1B0
(902) 295-2362
Toll free 1-800-254-7982
Hwy 105E, Exit 9, turn left then right to Baddeck Forks; stay on paved road, take second laneway on right after second iron bridge • 11

km (7 mi) north of village • Three o/n units, one private B, one shared B&S • TV in lounge • Non-smoking only
RATES: $35 (1), $45-$50 (2), $55 (private bath), $7-$10 add'l person (STC) • Full breakfast 6:30-8:30 • Open March 1-Nov. 30

Garden of Eden
Edein Gardens
Bed & Breakfast
Ron & Glenda Fraser, 3595 Kerrogare Road, Garden of Eden, RR 5, New Glasgow, B2H 5C8
(902) 922-2739
Hwy 104, Exit 26 to Rte. 347S (between New Glasgow and Sherbrooke Village); or from Rte 7, at Aspen, Rte. 347N • Family blueberry farm • Three o/n units, one shared B&S • Clock radio and fan in rooms • TV/VCR in living room • Cot available • Children under 5 yrs free • Non-smoking only
FEATURES: Evening tea
RATES: $35 (1), $45 (2), $10 add'l person • Full breakfast 7:30-9:30 • Open June 15-Sept. 30 • Visa accepted • NSRS Member

Glendale
Apple Tree Farm
Bed & Breakfast
Bruno & Liliane Spieser, MacInnis Road, RR 1, Glendale, B0E 3L0
(902) 625-5516
Hwy 105, Exit at MacInnis Rd; 15 minutes from Port Hastings • Working farm with purebred Icelandic horses and registered Scottish Highland cattle • Two o/n units, one shared S, one shared B&S (whirlpool) • Non-smoking only
FEATURES: Riding lessons available • German spoken • Sauna
RATES: $40 (1), $50 (2), $10 add'l

person • Continental breakfast •
Open June 1-Oct. 31 • Off-season
by reservation • NSRS Member

Glace Bay
Blossoms & Lace
Bed & Breakfast
Linda Aucoin, 127 Haulage Road,
Reserve Mines, B0A 1V0
(902) 849-3550/6351
From Reserve St. turn onto Haulage
Rd. just before the "Welcome to
Glace Bay" sign • Modern, ranch-
style home • Three o/n units, two
shared B&S • Cable TV, radio,
stereo and telephone in lounge •
Non-smoking only
RATES: $40 (1), $50 (2), $15 add'l
person (STC) • Full breakfast 8-10 •
Open year-round • MC, Visa
accepted • CBBBA; CBTA; NSFC;
NSRS; TIANS Member

Glace Bay
Innkeepers
Bed & Breakfast
Sharon Brewer, 16 York Street,
Glace Bay, B1A 6B4
(902) 849-0886
Former Knox United Church Manse
(c. 1905) • Three o/n units, one
shared B&S • Cable TV in one
room and sitting room • Non-smoking only
RATES: $45-$55 (1-2) • Full
breakfast 7:30-9:30 • Open May 1-
Oct. 31

Glace Bay
Justamere
Bed & Breakfast
Angus & Brenda MacDonald, 2489
Tower Road, RR 1, Glace Bay,
B1A 5T9
(902) 849-0218
Just off Marconi Trail, at end of

Brookside St. • Three o/n units, two
private B&S, one shared B&S •
Clock radio in rooms • Cable
TV/VCR in lounge
RATES: $40-$45 (1), $46-$50 (2),
$15 add'l person • Full breakfast 7-
9 • Open May-Oct. • NSRS Member

Glace Bay
Wight House
Bed & Breakfast
Margaret Wight, 2 Hillier Street,
Glace Bay, B1A 1A4
(902) 842-0788
Hwy 105 to Rte. 4 through Reserve
Mines • Ocean views from bed-
rooms and deck • Three o/n units,
one shared B&S • No pets, please •
No smoking in rooms, please
RATES: $40 (1), $50 (2) • Full
breakfast 8-9:30 • Open year-round

Glace Bay
Will-Bridg House
B&B ★★★
Eileen Curry, 322 King Edward
Street, Glace Bay, B1A 3W3
(902) 849-6585
Turn left off Rte. 4E, 4 km (2.5 mi)
from Sydney • Victorian-style home
• Four o/n units, one private B&S,
one shared B&S; one housekeeping
suite • Cable TV in lounge • Cot
and crib available • No smoking in
rooms, please
RATES: $40-$50 (1), $45-$55 (2),
$60-$65 (suite), $10 add'l person •
Full breakfast 7:30-9 • Open year-
round • Visa accepted • NSRS
Member

Glen Margaret
Shore Gardens Bed & Breakfast

Pat & Paul Freake, 10502 Peggy's Cove Road, Glen Margaret, Box 989, RR 1, Tantallon, B0J 3J0
Tel & Fax (902) 823-3093
Hwy 103, Exit 5 on Rte. 333 • 2.3 acres of organic gardens overlooking St. Margaret's Bay • Two o/n units, one shared B&S • TV in living room • Non-smoking only
FEATURES: Campfire area and picnic table on beach
RATES: $45-$50 (1-2), $10 add'l person • Discount for longer stay • Continental breakfast 7:30-9 • Open July 1-Aug. 30

Gold River
Pictor's Place Bed & Breakfast

Nell Schilder, 5950 Highway 3, Gold River, B0J 1K0
(902) 627-2989
Fax (902) 627-1252
Two o/n units, one shared B&S • Children welcome • Cat on premises • Non-smoking only
FEATURES: French and Dutch spoken • Coffee room and garden
RATES: $45 (1-2) (STC) • Full breakfast • Open year-round

Grand Narrows
Bras d'Or Lakes Hideaway Bed & Breakfast ★★★

Jane & John Worton, 601 Derby Point Road, RR 1, Grand Narrows, Christmas Island, B0A 1C0
(902) 622-2009
Fax (902) 622-2365
Hwy 105, Exit 6, Rte. 223E, 29 km (18 mi); or Hwy 125, Exit 3 to Rte. 223W, 51.5 km (32 mi) • Centrally located with panoramic lake view • Three o/n units, one private B&S, one shared B&S • TV/VCR in lounge • Not suitable for children • Non-smoking only
FEATURES: Fridge and stone fireplace in lounge • Fishing • Cycling • Patio • Air-conditioning • Garden • Access to beach and hiking trails
RATES: $44-$55 (1), $50-$60 (2) (STC) • Full breakfast 7:30-10 • Open May 1-Oct. 31 • Off-season by reservation • Visa accepted • NSRS Member

Grand Pré
Grand Pré House B&B (Gowan Brae c. 1770)

June Robertson, Box 42, Grand Pré, B0P 1M0
(902) 542-4277
Hwy 101, Exit 10 to Hwy 1, turn right on Grand Pré Road, turn right again, 0.3 km (0.2 mi) to 273 Old Post Rd. • Registered eighteenth-century heritage home • Three o/n units, two shared B&S • Non-smoking only
FEATURES: Fresh fruit in season and home-baked bread • Piano • Furnished with antiques • Shaded lawns and orchards • Lawn games and picnic table • Spacious grounds with beautiful view
RATES: $40 (1), $50-$60 (2), $15 add'l person • Full breakfast • Open June-Sept. • Visa accepted • NSRS Member

Grand Pré
Inn the Vineyard B&B (c. 1779) ★★★ ½

John Halbrook & Cally Jordan, 264 Old Post Road, Box 106, Grand Pré, B0P 1M0
(902) 542-9554
Fax (902) 542-1248

E-mail 101610.2263@com-puserve.com
Exit 10 off Hwy 101 to Grand Pré, follow signs • Restored provincial heritage home in owners' family since 1779 • Three o/n units, private B • Cable TV/VCR in common room • Pets welcome • Non-smoking only
FEATURES: French spoken • Furnished with antiques • Games in common room • Nova Scotia art displayed • Barbecue • Bicycles • Bay of Fundy view • Babysitting
RATES: $67-$75 (1-2) (STC) • Full breakfast • Open June 1-Sept. 30 • Visa accepted • NSRS Member

Grand River
Bonnach and Molasses Inn
Donna Morrison, 1826 Grand River, B0E 1M0
Tel & Fax (902) 587-2554
Rte. 247, 25 km (16 mi) from St. Peter's • Three o/n units, private B&S; one housekeeping suite • TV and clock radio in rooms • Children under 12 yrs free • No pets, please
FEATURES: Licensed dining room
RATES: $40 (1), $50 (2), $60 (suite), $10 add'l person • Open year-round • Visa accepted

Granville Centre
Mount Nod Bed & Breakfast
Clare J. Burrow, Box 1079A, 6047 Highway 1, Granville Centre, RR 1, Granville Ferry, B0S 1K0
(902) 532-7461
On Hwy 1 in Granville Centre • Three o/n units, one shared B&S • Cable TV/VCR in living room • Crib available • Pets on premises • Non-smoking only
RATES: $50-$75 (1-2), $10 add'l

person • Full breakfast 7:30-9 • Open June 30-Sept. 30 • Off-season by reservation • NSRS Member

Granville Ferry
Moorings Bed & Breakfast
Susan & Nathaniel Tileston, 5287 Granville Street, Box 118, Granville Ferry, B0S 1K0
Tel & Fax (902) 532-2146
From Rte. 1, 1.5 km (1 mi) on road to Port Royal Habitation • Built in 1881 by Capt. Joseph Hall • Three o/n units, one private S, two shared B&S
FEATURES: Furnished with antiques and contemporary art • Unique tin ceilings • Bicycles • Waterfront picnic area • Rooms overlook historic Fort Anne and the Annapolis Basin
RATES: $38-$42 (1), $44-$50 (2), $10 add'l person • Full breakfast 8-9:30 • Open May-Oct. • Off-season by reservation • Visa accepted • NSRS Member

Granville Ferry
Nightingale's Landing Bed & Breakfast

Sandra & Jim Nightingale, Box 30, Granville Ferry, B0S 1K0
Tel & Fax (902) 532-7615
From Rte. 1, 1.5 km (1 mi) in village of Granville Ferry • Historic Victorian house (c. 1870) with gingerbread trim and large veranda overlooking Annapolis River and Fort Anne • Three o/n units, one shared B; one suite • Non-smoking only
FEATURES: Furnished with antiques • German spoken • Fireplace • Gardens • Antique and-craft shop on premises
RATES: $40 (1), $45-$60 (2-3), $10 add'l person • Full breakfast 8-9:30 • Open May-Oct. • Off-season by reservation • Visa accepted • NSRS Member

Granville Ferry
White Raven Inn

Hans & Jeanne Denee, 5345 Granville Street, Granville Ferry, B0S 1K0
(902) 532-5595
E-mail ak760@ccn.cs.dal.ca
On road to Port Royal Habitation • Registered heritage property (early 1800s) • Two o/n units, private B&S or S • Children over 10 yrs welcome • No pets, please • Non-smoking only
FEATURES: Dutch, German and French spoken • Licensed restaurant with Cordon Bleu chef
RATES: $50-$65 (1), $65-$80 (2) • Breakfast 8-9 • Open April 1-Jan. 1 • AE, MC, Visa accepted • NSRS Member

Great Village
Windflower Coach House Bed & Breakfast ★★★

Richard Michaud, RR 1, Great Village, B0M 1L0
(902) 668-2780
Hwy 104, Exit 11, 5 km (3 mi), turn left on Balamore Loop and continue left • Original stagecoach stop (late 1700s) • Two o/n units, one shared B&S; one suite • TV in den • Non-smoking only
FEATURES: Tea or lemonade on arrival • Heated swimming pool • Cross-country skiing and walking trails
RATES: $45-$55 (1-2), $70 (suite) (STC) • Full breakfast 7-9 • Open year-round • Visa accepted • Please call for reservations • NSRS Member

Guysborough
Carritt House Bed & Breakfast (c. 1842)

Buster & Sharon Jarvis, 20 Pleasant Street, Box 297, Guysborough, B0H 1N0
(902) 533-3855
On Rte. 16 • Three o/n units, one shared B&S • Cable TV/VCR in common area • No smoking in rooms, please
RATES: $40 (1), $50 (2), $10 add'l person • Continental or full breakfast 7-9:30 • Visa accepted • Open year-round • NSRS Member

Guysborough
Morgan's Point Bed & Breakfast

Charlotte Morgan, Box 201, Guysborough, B0H 1N0
(902) 533-3813
Fax (902) 533-2895
Hwy 104, Exit 37 to Rte. 16 to

Guysborough • Two o/n units, one shared B&S • TV/VCR in lounge • Non-smoking only
FEATURES: Private saltwater beach • Kennels
RATES: $50 (1-2) • Breakfast 8-9:30 • Open year-round • Visa accepted

Hackett's Cove
Havenside
Bed & Breakfast
Shelley & Karl Webb,
225 Boutilier's Cove Road,
Hackett's Cove, B0J 3J0
Tel & Fax (902) 823-9322
Toll free 1-800-641-8272
E-mail webbk@atcon.com
Hwy 103, Exit 5, Rte. 333 to Hackett's Cove, then turn right on Boutilier's Cove Rd. • Luxury accommodation in spacious new home on scenic cove • Three o/n units, private B&S • Cable TV/VCR in sitting room • No pets, please • Non-smoking only
FEATURES: Games room with Brunswick pool table • Picnic site and barbecue • Salt water swimming • Canoe for guests' use • Sailing yacht for charter • Special "Land & Sea" package available
RATES: $55-$85, $15 add'l person (STC) • Full breakfast 9 • Open year-round • MC, Visa accepted • IGNS; MATA; NSRS; SMBBA; TIANS Member

Halifax, Dartmouth, Bedford
Autumn Leaves
Bed & Breakfast
Audrey J. Brown, 12 Evans Court, Dartmouth, B2X 2T5
902) 435-3980
Rte. 111, Exit 6, Rte. 318N (Braemar, Waverley Rd.), 1 km (0.5 mi), then turn right onto Evans

Court • Three o/n units, one shared B&S • Clock radio in rooms • Cable TV/VCR in living room • Designated smoking area
RATES: $43-$52 (1-2) • Full breakfast 8:30-9:30 (earlier on request) • Open April 1-Oct. 31 • NSRS Member

Halifax, Dartmouth, Bedford
Beautiful Bedford
Bed & Breakfast ★★★
Lynda & Richard Downing,
512 Basinview Drive, Bedford,
B4A 1T4
(902) 835-2110
Toll free 1-800-320-3340
Hwy 102, Exit 3, turn right on Rte. 213, third street on the left • Three o/n units, private B&S; two suites • Pets on premises • No pets, please • Non-smoking only
RATES: $65-$70 (1-2), $110-$135 (suite), $15 add'l person (STC) • Full breakfast 7-9 • Open May 1-Oct. 31 • Off-season by reservation • NSRS Member

Halifax, Dartmouth, Bedford
Bobs' Bed & Breakfast
Robert Grandfield & Robert Woods,
2715 Windsor Street, Halifax,
B3K 5E1
(902) 454-4374
Old-home charm • Three o/n units, one private B, two shared B • Not suitable for children • No pets, please • Non-smoking only
FEATURES: Original Nova Scotian art throughout • Outdoor hot tub • Patio and garden
RATES: $60-$85 (2) • Full breakfast • Open May 1-Oct. 31 • MC accepted • NSRS Member

Halifax, Dartmouth, Bedford
Caribou Lodge
B&B ★★★
Bruce & Anna Ellis, 6 Armada
Drive, Halifax, B3M 1R7
(902) 445-5013
E-mail museum@atcon.com
Quiet Victorian charm • Three o/n
units, private B&S • Cable TV •
Telephone • Cot available • Non-
smoking only
FEATURES: Working art studio
and gallery with wildlife studies by
A.J. Scanlan-Ellis
*RATES: $55-$65 (2), $10 add'l
person • Continental breakfast 7-9 •
Open year-round • AE, Visa accept-
ed • NSRS Member*

Halifax, Dartmouth, Bedford
Caroline's
Bed & Breakfast ★★ ¹/₂
Caroline McCully, 134 Victoria
Road, Dartmouth, B3A 1V6
(902) 469-4665

Uphill from
the Angus L.
Macdonald
bridge •
Three o/n
units, two
shared B • Cable TV in lounge •
Non-smoking only
*RATES: $33-$40 (1-2) •
Continental breakfast 8-9:30 • Open
May 1-Oct. 31 • NSRS Member*

Halifax, Dartmouth, Bedford
Do Duck In ★★★ ¹/₂
Jeanette Romkey, 14 Cathy Cross
Drive, Dartmouth, B2W 2R5
Tel & Fax (902) 434-4358
Off-season (813) 532-0242
Hwy 111 in Dartmouth, Exit 7E
(Cole Harbour/Woodlawn Rd), turn
left on Woodlawn through two sets

of lights, right on Day St. to stop
sign, right on Clifford St. to Cathy
Cross Dr. • Three o/n units, one private B&S, one shared B&S; one
suite (Jacuzzi) • TV and clock radio
in rooms • Cable TV/VCR in lounge
• Cot and crib available • Children
under 12 yrs $5 (under 5 yrs free) •
Non-smoking only
FEATURES: Outdoor swimming
pool
*RATES: $35-$45 (1), $50-$60 (2),
$75 (suite), $10 add'l person • Full
breakfast 7:30-9:30 • Open May 15-
Oct. 15 • MC accepted • NSRS
Member*

Halifax, Dartmouth, Bedford
Fountain View
Guest House ★★
Helen Vickery, 2138 Robie Street,
Halifax, B3K 4M5
(902) 422-4169
**Toll free 1-800-565-4877 (evenings
& weekends)**
E-mail ap599@cnn.cs.dal.ca

Opposite
Halifax
Commons,
near the
Citadel •
Seven o/n
units, four shared B • Cable TV,
clock radio and ceiling fan in rooms
• No pets, please • Non-smoking
rooms available
FEATURES: City tours arranged
*RATES: $24-$28 (1), $30-$40 (2-4)
• Off-season rates • Continental
breakfast (extra) on request • Open
year-round •*

Halifax, Dartmouth, Bedford
Four Marks
Bed & Breakfast
Mrs. Emma K. Creese, 306 Portland
Street, Dartmouth, B2Y 1K4
(902) 466-6929
Exit 7W off Hwy 111 to Rte. 207
(Portland St.) • Three o/n units, two
shared B&S • Cable TV and clock
radio in rooms • No pets, please
FEATURES: Basketball hoop and
lawn games in backyard
*RATES: $36 (1), $45 (2), $9.add'l
person (STC) • Full breakfast 7:30-
9 • Open year-round*

Halifax, Dartmouth, Bedford
Fresh Start
Bed & Breakfast
Innis & Sheila MacDonald, 2720
Gottingen Street, Halifax, B3K 3C7
(902) 453-6616
Fax (902) 453-6617
Toll free 1-888-453-6616
Modest Victorian mansion • Eight
o/n units, two private B&S, three
shared B&S • Clock radio in rooms
• Cable TV and telephone in lounge
• Non-smoking only
FEATURES: Laundry facilities •
Off-street parking
*RATES: $50-$70 (1), $55-$70 (2),
$10 add'l person (STC) • Full
breakfast at guests' convenience •
Open year-round • AE, DC, MC,
Visa accepted • IGNS; NSRS
Member*

Halifax, Dartmouth, Bedford
Galloway
Bed & Breakfast
Margaret Galloway, 1760 Vernon
Street, Halifax, B3H 3N2
(902) 422-1110
Central location • Three o/n units,
one shared B&S • Cable TV in liv-
ing room • Non-smoking only
*RATES: $40-$49 (1), $49-$54 (2) •
Continental breakfast 8-9 • Open
June 1-Oct. 7 • NSRS Member*

Halifax, Dartmouth, Bedford
Garden Inn B&B
Karen Jamieson, 1263 South Park
Street, Halifax, B3J 2K8
(902) 492-8577
Conveniently located in downtown
Halifax off Spring Garden Rd. •
Registered heritage home • Nine o/n
units, one private B, one private 1/2
B, two shared B • Cable TV
*RATES: $50-$70 (1-2), $10 add'l
person (STC) • Continental break-
fast • Open year-round • Visa
accepted • NSRS Member*

Halifax, Dartmouth, Bedford
Halliburton House
Inn ★★★★
Robert Pretty, 5184 Morris Street,
Halifax, B3J 1B3
(902) 420-0658
Fax (902) 423-2324
E-mail halhouse@newedge.net
Registered heritage property near
the waterfront and farmers' market •
Twenty-eight o/n units, private B&S
or S; three suites • Cable TV, radio
and telephone in rooms • Children
under 16 yrs free
FEATURES: Antique furnishings •
Full-service dining room and garden
cafe • Air-conditioning • Cozy
library • Free parking
*RATES: From $110 (2), $15 add'l
person (STC) • Continental break-
fast • Open year-round • AE, DC,
MC, Visa accepted • CAA; IGNS,
NSRS; TNS Member*

Halifax, Dartmouth, Bedford
Marie's
Bed & Breakfast
Marie Wilson, 3440 Windsor Street, Halifax, B3K 5G4
(902) 453-4987
Three o/n units, one shared B&S • Cable TV in lounge • No pets, please • Non-smoking only
RATES: $30 (1), $40 (2) • Breakfast 8-9 • Open May 15-Oct. 31 • NSRS Member

Halifax, Dartmouth, Bedford
Martin House
Bed & Breakfast
Helmuth & Medlinda Wiegert, 62 Pleasant Street, Dartmouth, B2Y 3P5
(902) 463-7338
Fax (902) 466-2857
Overlooking Halifax/Dartmouth Harbour • Three o/n units, one shared B&S • No pets, please • Non-smoking only
FEATURES: Furnished with antiques
RATES: $55 (1), $55-$65 (2) • Continental breakfast 8-9 • Open May 15-Oct. 31 • NSRS Member

Halifax, Dartmouth, Bedford
Nova's Place
Bed & Breakfast ★★★
Nova Rochford, 27 Portland Estates Boulevard, Dartmouth, B2W 6A1
(902) 435-2935
Fax (902) 434-4221
Hwy 111, Exit 7E to Rte. 207 (Portland St.) to Portland Estates • Modern home • Three o/n units, one private B&S (Jacuzzi), one shared B&S • Cable TV/VCR in lounge • Clock radio and telephone in rooms • No pets, please • Non-smoking only

RATES: $45-$55 (1), $55-$70 (2), $10 add'l person • Full breakfast 7:30-9:30 • Open May 1-Oct. 15 • Off-season by reservation • Visa accepted • NSRS Member

Halifax, Dartmouth, Bedford
Queen Street Inn
Alfred J. Saulnier, 1266 Queen Street, Halifax, B3J 2H4
(902) 422-9828
Registered heritage property • Six o/n units, shared B • Not suitable for children • No pets, please • Non-smoking only
FEATURES: Decorated with Nova Scotia antiques and paintings • Off-street parking
RATES: $40-$45 (1), $45-$50 (2) (STC) • Open year-round • NSRS Member

Halifax, Dartmouth, Bedford
Rankin
Bed & Breakfast ★★ ½
Harvey & Linda Pardy, 45 Rankin Drive, Lower Sackville, B4C 3A7
(902) 865-3151
E-mail pardylg@atcon.com
Hwy 101, Exit 1K, turn right on Cobequid Rd., left on Glendale, then first street on right past three sets of lights • Two o/n units, one-shared S, one shared B (Jacuzzi) • Cable TV/VCR, stereo and telephone in lounge • Crib and highchair available • Children under 12 yrs free • Small pets permitted • Smoking in lounge area
FEATURES: Kitchen facilities • Barbecue • Shuttle service to Halifax airport
RATES: $45 (1-2), $12 add'l person • Continental breakfast • Open year-round

Halifax, Dartmouth, Bedford
Rebecca's
Bed & Breakfast
Rebecca Lampshire, 2719 Windsor
Street, Halifax, B3K 5E1
(902) 455-5802
Charming older home, centrally
located • Three o/n units, one shared
B&S
FEATURES: Fireplace in living
room • Tea and biscuits on arrival •
Canopy bed • Formal dining room •
Patios off one room and in backyard
*RATES: $45-$50 (1-2), $10 add'l
person • Full breakfast • Open year-
round • NSRS Member*

Halifax, Dartmouth, Bedford
Seawatch
Bed & Breakfast
Elaine E. Hatfield, 139 Ferguson's
Cove Road, Box 135, Site 14, RR 5,
Armdale, B3L 4J5
(902) 477-1506
On Halifax Harbour, near York
Redoubt • One o/n unit, private
B&S • Cable TV/VCR in lounge •
Radio in room • No pets, please •
Non-smoking only
FEATURES: Light housekeeping
facilities
*RATES: $55 (1), $65 (2) (STC) •
Continental breakfast 7:30-9:30 •
Open year-round • NSRS Member*

Halifax, Dartmouth, Bedford
Sterns Mansion
Inn ★★★ ½
Bill de Molitor, 17 Tulip Street,
Dartmouth, B3A 2S5
(902) 465-7414
Fax (902) 466-2152
Toll free 1-800-565-3885
South on Victoria Rd, turn left onto
Tulip • Restored century home •
Five o/n units, private B (two

Jacuzzi) • Cable TV/VCR and telephone in sitting room • No pets,
please • Non-smoking only
FEATURES: Evening tea and
sweets • Player piano in sitting
room • Air-conditioning •
Honeymoon packages
*RATES: $55-$110 (1), $65-$130
(2) (STC) • Full breakfast • Open
year-round • AE, MC, Visa accepted
• IGNS; MATA; NSRS; TIANS
Member*

Halifax, Dartmouth, Bedford
Top Floor
Bed & Breakfast ★★★
Ina Kelson & Vikki Sweeney, 1379
St. Margaret's Bay Road, Lakeside,
B3T 1A8
(902) 876-7587
At Halifax city limits, Hwy 103,
Exit 4 through Timberlea to corner
of Raines Mill Rd.; Hwy 102, Exit
2A through Beechville, second
house on right after Lakeside sign •
One o/n unit, private B; one suite •
Cable TV/VCR • Clock radio in
rooms
FEATURES: Evening snack • Patio
and picnic table • Barbecue • Lawn
games • Locked bicycle garage
*RATES: $55 (1), $65 (2), $110
(suite) (STC) • Full breakfast •
Open June 1-Oct. 15 • NSRS
Member*

Halifax, Dartmouth, Bedford
Virginia Kinfolks ★★★
Lucy & Dick Russell, 1722 Robie
Street, Halifax, B3H 3E8
Tel & Fax (902) 423-6687
Toll free 1-800-668-STAY (7829)
One block from Public Gardens •
Three o/n units, private S (B&S
available) • Cable TV • Not suitable
for children • Non-smoking only
FEATURES: Antique furnishings •
Library
*RATES: $48 (1), $72 (2), $12 add'l
person (STC) • Discount for three-
night stay and senior citizens • Full
breakfast • Open year-round • IGNS
Member*

Harbourville
Fundy Tide
Bed & Breakfast
Lynne & George Spicer, 385 Russia
Road, Harbourville, RR 5, Berwick,
B0P 1E0
(902) 538-3922
Hwy 101, Exit 15, Rte. 360N, 12
km (7.5 mi) to Russia Rd. • View of
the Bay of Fundy with access to
rocky shoreline • Two o/n units, one
shared B&S • TV in living room •
Non-smoking only
*RATES: $35 (1), $40 (2) • Full
breakfast 7-9 • Open May 15-Oct.
15 • Off-season by reservation •
NSRS Member*

Hatchet Lake
Tanner's
Bed & Breakfast
Gerald & Sheena Tanner, 265 Club
Road, Hatchet Lake, B3T 1R3
(902) 852-4964
From Hwy 103, 10 km (6 mi) on
Rte. 333 to Club Rd. • Two o/n
units, one shared B&S • Cable TV
in den • Non-smoking only

FEATURES: Swimming pool •
Rowboat for guests' use
*RATES: $50 (1), $60 (2), $10 add'l
person • Full breakfast 7:30-9 •
Open May 15-Oct. 15*

Hebron
Eaton's Cottages, Motel
& Tourist Home
Kelvin & Brenda French, Box 40,
Hebron, B0W 1X0
Tel & Fax (902) 742-2007
Hwy 101, Exit 34, Rte. 1.• On
Doctor's Lake, 4 km (2.5 mi) north-
east of Yarmouth • Three o/n units,
one shared B&S, one shared B; four
cottages; three motel units • Cable
TV • Pay phone • No pets, please
FEATURES: Picnic area • Private
beach • Lake swimming • Boating
and fishing
*RATES: $30-$60 (1-2), $5 add'l
person • Off-season rates • Open
March 15-Nov. 1 • MC, Visa
accepted • NSRS Member*

Hilden
Ann's Farmhouse
Bed & Breakfast ★★★
Ann & David Pullen, 2627 Irwin
Lake Road, Hilden, RR 1,
Brookfield, B0N 1C0
(902) 897-0300
Toll free 1-800-603-7887
From Truro, take Hwy 2 to Hilden,
turn right at flashing light for 4 km
(2.5 mi); or from Hwy 102, Exit 12
to Brookfield and Hilden and turn
left at flashing light • Old farmhouse in pastoral setting • Three o/n
units, two shared B&S • Cable TV,
radio and telephone in lounge •
Non-smoking only
*RATES: $35 (1), $50 (2) • Full
breakfast 7:30-9 • Open April 1-
Oct. 31 • Visa accepted • NSRS
Member*

Hilden
Julaine's Tourist Home B&B
Judith Castell, 31 Edwards Road, Hilden, B0N 1C0
(902) 897-4450
Hwy 102, Exit 12 or 13, follow signs to Hilden • Three o/n units, two shared B • Dog and cat on premises • Non-smoking only
FEATURES: Evening snack
RATES: $30 (1), $35-$40 (2), $7 add'l person • Breakfast • Open May 1-Oct. 31 • NSRS Member

Horne's Road
Jennifer's Country Bed & Breakfast
Jennifer Thomas, 33 Wilford Place, Horne's Road, Mira, B0A 1P0
(902) 564-0589/737-5189
Horne's Road off Sydney-Louisbourg Hwy • Three o/n units, one shared B&S • TV in living room • Families welcome • Non-smoking only
FEATURES: Evening tea • Horse stables on property (children may ride in paddock, but no trail riding)
RATES: $35 (1), $45 (2) (STC) • Full breakfast 7-9 • Open May 15-Oct. 15 • CBBBA; NSRS Member

Hubbards
Dauphinee Inn
Rhys & Kim Harnish, 167 Shore Club Road, Hubbards, B0J 1T0
(902) 857-1790
Toll free 1-800-567-1790
Off-season fax (902) 857-9555
Hwy 103, Exit 6 • On the shore of Hubbards Cove • Six o/n units, private B&S; two suites (Jacuzzi) • Cable TV in lounge • No pets, please • Designated smoking area
FEATURES: Licensed dining room and sun deck • Herb garden • Wharf • Row boat, canoe, fishing rods and bicycles available • Bird-watching and deep-sea fishing
RATES: $76-$117 (1-2) • Breakfast • Open May 1-Oct. 30 • AE, DC, Dis, MC, Visa accepted • CAA; IGNS; NSRS; TNS; UCI Member

Hubbards
Just Inn Tyme Bed & Breakfast
Gary & Julia Dorey, 1538 Highway 329, RR 1, Hubbards, B0J 1T0
(902) 857-3298
Hwy 103, Exit 6, Rte. 329S, five minutes from village • Secluded country inn overlooking St. Margaret's Bay • Three o/n units, one shared B&S • Non-smoking only
FEATURES: Recreation area with fireplace, stereo and pool table
RATES: $55 (1), $65 (2) • Full breakfast • Open June 15-Nov. 15 • NSRS Member

Hubbards
Wyndecrest Bed & Breakfast
Terry June Harnish, 247 Shore Club Road, Hubbards, B0J 1T0
(902) 857-3191
Hwy 103, Exit 6 • Traditional country home on the shore of Hubbards Cove • Three o/n units, one shared B&S • No pets, please • Non-smoking only
FEATURES: Rooms have cove view • Library • Local land and sea tours arranged • "Storytelling, Tea and Tales," on first Saturday of every month
RATES: $50 (1), $60 (2), $85 (3) (STC) • Full breakfast 8-9:30 • Open year-round • Reservations preferred

Hubley
Mourning Dove Bed & Breakfast
Susan & Heinz Gaube, 11 Hawkins Drive, Hubley, B3Z 1B6
(902) 876-2590
Hwy 103, Exit 4, Rte. 3W, first left into Lake of the Woods, first right onto Five Island Rd., 1.5 km (1 mi) to Kenley Rd., turn left twice • Peaceful setting with abundant wildlife • One o/n unit, private B&S • Cable TV/VCR in living room • No pets, please • Non-smoking only *RATES: $50 (1), $60 (2)* • *Full breakfast 7:30-9* • *Open June 15-Sept. 15*

Indian Brook
Piper's Guest House
James & Lucy Piché, Indian Brook, RR 1, Englishtown, B0C 1H0
(902) 929-2339
Fax (902) 929-2067
Five o/n units, two shared B (Jacuzzi) • TV in lounge *RATES: $30 (1), $36 (2), $5.50 add'l person (STC)* • *Open June 1-Nov. 15*

Indian Point
Bayview Pines Country Inn
Adolf & Elisabeth Sturany, Indian Point, RR 2, Mahone Bay, B0J 2E0
(902) 624-9970
Hwy 103, Exit 10 towards Mahone Bay, left at Indian Point sign for 6 km (3.5 mi) • Six o/n units, private B&S; two suites (Jacuzzi) • Cable TV • Pay phone • Children under 3 yrs free
FEATURES: Licensed Viennese-style restaurant serving breakfast and dinner
RATES: $58 (1), $68 (2), $100 (suite), $15 add'l person (STC) • *Weekly rates* • *Continental breakfast 8-10* • *Open May 1-Oct. 31* • *MC, Visa accepted* • *CAA; IGNS; NSRS Member*

Indian Point
Marline Spike Guest House B&B
Tricia Barr, RR 2, Indian Point, Mahone Bay, B0J 2E0
(902) 624-8664
Hwy 103, Exit 10 to Indian Pt., 6.5 km (4 mi) • Sea captain's house overlooking ocean and islands • Three o/n units, two shared B, one shared 1/2 B • Cable TV, radio and telephone in lounge • Children under 5 yrs free • No pets, please • Non-smoking only
FEATURES: Afternoon tea • Canoe
RATES: $40-$55 (1-2), $10 add'l person • *Continental breakfast 7:30-9* • *Open June 25-Oct. 1* • *NSRS Member*

Ingonish
Bear Cove Bed & Breakfast
Gerald Brown, Box 41, North Ingonish, B0C 1K0
(902) 285-2699/564-0019
Beautiful view of Cape Smokey from balcony • Two o/n units, one shared S • No pets, please • Non-smoking only
RATES: $40 (1), $45 (2), $10 add'l person (STC) • *Full breakfast 7-8:30* • *Open June 1-Nov. 15* • *IGNS Member*

Ingonish Beach
Island Inn B&B
Paula & Perry MacKinnon, Box 116, Ingonish Beach, B0C 1L0
(902) 285-2402
Fax (902) 285-2684
Toll free 1-800-533-7015
Website
http://www.morandan.com/moran dan/ingonish/island/inn.html
On Cabot Trail • Eleven o/n units, eight private B, three shared B • Cable TV in lounge • Pay telephone • Children under 5 yrs free • Pets welcome, with prior permission
FEATURES: Ocean and lake views • Licensed dining room • Fireplace in lounge • Sailing tours available • Craft shop
RATES: $42-$59 (1-2), $10 add'l person • Full breakfast 8-10 • Open year-round • MC, Visa accepted • NSRS Member

Inverness
MacLeod Inn ★★★
Alistair MacLeod, Broad Cove Road, RR 1, Inverness, B0E 1N0
(902) 258-3360
Off Rte. 19, 5 km (3 mi) north of Inverness • Panoramic view of Northumberland Strait & Mabou Highlands • Five o/n units, private B&S (three Jacuzzi) • TV in rooms • Non-smoking only
FEATURES: Local art • Reading and sitting room • Bicycle rentals • Boat tours • Horseback riding • Small gift shop
RATES: $60-$90 (STC) • Off-season rates • Continental breakfast 7:30-9:30 • Open May 1-Oct. 31 • MC, Visa accepted • NSRS Member

Judique
Rachel By The Sea Bed & Breakfast
Rachel Scarano, 1524 Shore Road, Box 181, Judique North, B0E 1P0
(902) 787-2741
Rte. 19, turn left on Shore Road • Three o/n units, one shared B&S • TV/VCR in living room • No pets, please • Non-smoking only
RATES: $35 (1), $45 (2) • Full breakfast 8-9 • Open year-round • AE, MC, Visa accepted

Kentville
Grand Street Inn
Richard & Sandra Snow, 160 Main Street, Kentville, B4N 1J8
(902) 679-1991
Beautiful century home with fine examples of carpentry and oak • Six o/n units, private B • Non-smoking only
FEATURES: Front and back deck • Outdoor swimming pool (chemical-free)
RATES: $65-$105 (1-3) • Full breakfast 8:30-10 • Open year-round • MC, Visa accepted • ETTA; IGNS; NSRS; TIANS Member

Kentville
Wickwire House
Bed & Breakfast (c.1895)
Darlene & Jim Peerless, 183 Main
Street, Kentville, B4N 1J6
(902) 679-1188
Fax (902) 679-5196
Website
http://www.bbcanada.com
Award-winning restored Victorian
home close to downtown • Two o/n
units, one private B, one private
B&S • TV and telephone in lounge •
Not suitable for children • Non-
smoking only
FEATURES: Furnished with
antiques • Princess grand piano •
Veranda and gazebo • View of
Cornwallis River
*RATES: $73-$78 (2), $15 add'l
person • Full breakfast 8-9:30 •
Open May 1-Oct. 31 • Off-season by
reservation • MC, Visa accepted •
ETTA; NSRS Member*

Lakeville
Hutten Family Farm
B&B
Anne van Arragon Hutten, 161
Thorpe Road, Lakeville, B4N 3V7
(902) 678-7088
Rte. 359 to Centreville, west on Rte.
221 for 6.5 km (4 mi), turn right on
Lamont Rd. to T, then left on
Thorpe to first farm • Working farm
under the North Mountain • One o/n
unit, private B • No pets, please •
Non-smoking only
*RATES: $44 (1), $49 (2), $10 add'l
person • Full breakfast • Open
April-Oct. • Off-season by reserva-
tion • Reservations preferred*

LaHave
Court Yard Garden
Bed & Breakfast
Jean & James Campbell, 3562
Highway 331, Box 51, LaHave,
B0R 1C0
(902) 688-1926
Century-old house with Victorian-
style decor • Three o/n units, two
shared B&S • Pets on premises • No
smoking in rooms, please
FEATURES: Veranda overlooking
LaHave River • Courtyard garden
*RATES: $40 (1), $50 (2) (STC) •
Full breakfast 8-10 • Open year-
round • NSRS Member*

LaHave
Hove-To Inn B&B
Patricia Hamilton, RR 1,
Pleasantville, B0R 1G0
(902) 688-1025
Fifteen minutes from Bridgewater
on Rte. 331, west side of LaHave
River • Historic sea captain's house
on the banks of the LaHave • Two
o/n units, one shared B&S • Cot and
crib available • Children welcome •
Pets welcome
*RATES: $40 (1), $50 (2) (STC) •
Full breakfast 7-9 • Open June 15-
Oct. 15*

LaHave
Keeper's
Bed & Breakfast
Phil & Carol Kenny, 38 Fort Point
Road, LaHave, B0R 1C0
(902) 688-2399
E-mail keepers@isisnet.con
Peaceful, secluded property on his-
toric Fort Point on LaHave River •
Three o/n units, one private B, one
shared B&S • TV in lounge • Pets
on premises • No pets, please
FEATURES: Beautiful view and

gardens
*RATES: $45-$50 (1), $50-$55 (2),
$10 add'l person (STC) • Full
breakfast 7-9 • Open May 1-Oct. 31
• Reservations preferred • NSRS
Member*

Lawrencetown
Alberta's Place
Bed & Breakfast (c. 1858)
Alberta Dumas, 670 Main Street
West, RR 1, Lawrencetown, B0S
1M0
(902) 584-7222
Hwy 101, Exit 19, Rte. 1W,
between Bridgetown and Middleton
• Three o/n units, two shared B&S;
one family suite • TV and clock
radio in rooms • Cot or crib $5 •
Smoking area
FEATURES: Outdoor swimming
pool • Family suite has two connect-
ing rooms
*RATES: $30-35 (1), $40-$45 (2),
$55 (suite), $7 add'l person (STC) •
Full breakfast 8-9 • Open May 18-
Aug. 31 • NSRS Member*

Lawrencetown
Cricket's Harp Inn
Ingrid Jahn & Michel Jodoin, 7165
Highway 201, RR 1, Lawrencetown,
B0S 1M0
Fax (902) 584-3389
Toll free 1-800-732-0057
Hwy 101, Exit 19 to Rte. 1, towards
Lawrencetown; turn right on
Lawrencetown Lane, left on Rte.
201E, 2.5 km (1.5 mi) • Renovated
homestead (c. 1867) on ninety-three
acres with apple and fruit orchards •
Three o/n units, one shared B&S •
Cable TV/VCR in sitting room • No
pets, please • Non-smoking only
FEATURES: Wrap-around porch
with valley view • French, German,
Spanish and Portuguese spoken •

Dinner on request • Play area •
Farm animals • Babysitting
*RATES: $50 (1), $55 (2), $10 add'l
person • Full breakfast 8:30 • Open
year-round • AE, Visa accepted •
NSRS Member*

Lawrencetown Beach
Moonlight Beach Inn
Calvin & Jane Dominie,
Lawrencetown Beach, B0J 2S0
(902) 827-2712
**Toll free 1-800-SEA-0191 (732-
0191)**
Hwy 7 or 107 to Rte. 207 to
Lawrencetown Beach, 16 km (10
mi) east of Dartmouth •
Overlooking ocean, beach and sand
dunes • Three o/n units, private
B&S; two suites (whirlpool B); one
housekeeping suite • Cable TV and
clock radio in rooms
FEATURES: Seaside lounge •
Fireplace • Pool table • Exercise
equipment • Telephone, fax and
VCR available • Hot tub • Walking
and cycling trails • Ocean and lake
swimming, surfing, windsurfing,
boating, fishing, cross-county skiing, sledding, and skating in season
*RATES: $85-$125 (1-2), $15 add'l
person • Breakfast • Open year-
round • MC, Visa accepted • IGNS;
NSRS Member*

Lawrencetown Beach
Seaboard
Bed & Breakfast ★★★
Sheila & Barrie Jackson, 2629
Crowell Road, RR 2, Porter's Lake,
B0J 2S0
(902) 827-3747
Toll free 1-800-732-6566
Hwy 107 to Rte. 207 (Marine
Drive) at foot of Porter's Lake •
Three o/n units, one shared B&S,
one shared S • Cot available • Cable
TV/VCR in lounge • Non-smoking
only
FEATURES: Evening snack •
Barbecue and picnic table • Porch
with sea and lake view • Walking
trails to beach • Surfing and skiing •
Canoe and bicycles available
*RATES: $40 (1), $50-$55 (2), $15
add'l person (STC) • Full breakfast
7:30-9 • Open year-round • Nov. -
May by reservation • Visa accepted
• ESTA; NSFC; NSRS Member*

Little Harbour
Chestnut Lane
Bed & Breakfast
Joye Taylor-Ross, Little Harbour,
RR 1, New Glasgow, B2H 5C4
(902) 755-4202
Hwy 104, Exit 22 to Hwy 106, Exit
1A towards Trenton, 11 km (7 mi),
left on Rte. 289, 4 km (2 1/2 mi);
from Pictou Rotary, Hwy 106, Exit
1A • Three o/n units, one shared
B&S • Non-smoking only
FEATURES: Evening tea
*RATES: $42 (1), $52 (2) • Off-sea-
son rates • Full breakfast 7:30-9:30
• Open year-round • NSRS Member*

Little Harbour
Three Flags
Bed & Breakfast
Carolyn Duncan, Black Point Road,
Little Harbour, RR 1, Trenton,
B0K 1X0
(902) 755-6289
Hwy 104W, Exit 22 to Hwy 106,
Exit 1A, Rte. 348, turn left, 17 km
(10 mi) to Black Point Rd.; Hwy
104E, Exit 27A, Melmerby Beach, 8
km (4.8 mi) to stop sign, turn left, 5
km (3 mi) to Black Point Rd. •
Great water view • Three o/n units,
one private B, one shared B&S •
Clock radio in rooms • Cable TV in
common room • Non-smoking only
*RATES: $50-$60 (1-2) (STC) • Full
breakfast 7-9:30 • Open year-round
• MC, Visa accepted • Reservations
preferred • NSRS Member*

Liverpool
Geranium House
Bed & Breakfast
Peter & Joan Bray, 87 Milton Road
East, Box 59, Liverpool, B0T 1K0
(902) 354-4484
Hwy 103, Exit 19 towards
Liverpool, first house on right •
Two o/n units, one shared B&S •
Cable TV in living room • Children
and cyclists welcome • No smoking
in rooms, please
*RATES: $30 (1), $40 (2) • Full
breakfast 7-9 • Open June 1-Oct. 31*

Liverpool
Hopkins House
Bed & Breakfast
Michiline & Don Hines, 120 Main
Street, Liverpool, B0T 1K0
(902) 354-5484
Across from Perkins Museum •
Loyalist home, pre-1812 • Three o/n
units, two shared B&S • TV in

lounge • Cots available • Children under 2 yrs free
FEATURES: Ten years in business • French spoken
RATES: *$40 (1), $50 (2), $10 add'l person (tax incl.) • Full breakfast at guests' convenience • Open year-round • Cash only*

Liverpool
Lane's Privateer Bed & Breakfast ★★★
Ron & Carol Lane, 33 Bristol Avenue, Box 509, Liverpool, B0T 1K0
(902) 354-3456
Fax (902) 354-7220
Toll free 1-800-794-3332
On Rte. 3 in Liverpool, on Mersey River • Annex to Lane's Privateer Inn • Three o/n units, two shared B&S • Cable TV, radio and telephone in rooms • No pets, please • Non-smoking only
FEATURES: Full use of Inn's facilities • Canoe rentals • Bookstore • Coffee shop
RATES: *$40 (1), $45 (2) (STC) • Continental breakfast • Open year-round • AE, CB, DC, MC, Visa accepted • NSRS; TIANS Member*

Liverpool
MacPherson House Bed & Breakfast
Leona Farrow, 41 MacPherson Street, Box 223, Liverpool, B0T 1K0
(902) 354-2565
Restored two-hundred-year-old home • Two o/n units, one shared B&S • Cable TV in living room • Radio in rooms • Non-smoking only
FEATURES: Hand-hooked wool mats available
RATES: *$35 (1), $45 (2) • Full breakfast 7-9 • Open May 15-Oct. 31*

Liverpool
Royal Bed & Breakfast
Reg & Carole Thompson, Box 285, Liverpool, B0T 1K0
(902) 354-5368
Hwy 103, Exit 18 or 19 • Three o/n units, one shared B • Families welcome • Non-smoking only
FEATURES: Outdoor swimming pool
RATES: *From $40 (2) (STC) • Open May-Oct. • NSRS Member*

Liverpool
Taigh Na Mara Bed & Breakfast
Rita Collins & Chris Donaldson, 58 Main Street, Liverpool, B0T 1K0
(902) 354-7194
On Liverpool Bay • Three o/n units, private B&S • Clock radio in rooms • Cable TV in lounge • No pets, please • Non-smoking only
RATES: *$50-$65 (2), $10 add'l person (STC) • Full breakfast 8-9 • Open year-round • NSRS Member*

Lochiel Lake (Aspen)
Lochiel Lake Bed & Breakfast
Lainie & Maggie Jo Landry, RR 5, Antigonish, B2G 2L3
(902) 783-2309
Website
http://www.bbcanada.com/817.html
At Lochiel Lake, 26 km (15.5 mi) from historic Sherbrooke Village on Rte. 7; or 35 km (22 mi) from Antigonish; or 3.2 km (2 mi) from Aspen on Rte. 7 • Three o/n units, one private B&S, one shared B&S • TV in lounge • Non-smoking only
FEATURES: Sun deck overlooking lake • Lake swimming • Boating and private dock for guests' use
RATES: $40 (1), $45-$55 (2) (STC) • Full breakfast • Open July-Sept. 1 • Off-season weekends by reservation • NSRS Member

Lockeport
Hillcrest Bed & Breakfast ★★ ½
Pam Decker, 5 Crest Street, Lockeport, B0T 1L0
(902) 656-3300/2404
Fax (902) 656-2006
Three o/n units, one shared B&S • Cable TV/VCR in living room • Clock radio in rooms • No smoking in rooms, please
FEATURES: Registered heritage property, operating as an hotel from late 1800s • Five-minute walk to Crescent Beach
RATES: $40 (1), $50 (2), $7 add'l person • Full breakfast 7:30-9:30 • Open year-round • Visa accepted

Lockeport
Seventeen South Bed & Breakfast
Margaret Mitchell, 17 South Street, Lockeport, B0T 1L0
(902) 656-2512
Cape Cod-style house by the sea • Three o/n units, one private S, one shared B&S • Cable TV/VCR in living room • Children welcome • No pets, please • Non-smoking only
FEATURES: Ocean view • Cyclists welcome and workshops available • Ocean swimming
RATES: $45 (1), $55 (2), $7 add'l person • Full breakfast 8-9 • Open year-round • Visa accepted

Lorneville
Amherst Shore Country Inn ★★★★
Donna Laceby, RR 2, Amherst, B4H 3X9
(902) 661-4800
Toll free 1-800-661-ASCI (2724)
Off-season Box 839, Wolfville, B0P 1X0
At Lorneville, 32 km (20 mi) from Amherst on Rte. 366, on Northumberland Strait • Four o/n units, private B; four suites (Jacuzzi); one cottage (seasonal) • No pets, please • Non-smoking only
FEATURES: Licensed gourmet dining room, by reservation • Private beach swimming
RATES: $79-99 (2), $129 (suite), $99 (cottage), $7 add'l person • Off-season rates • Full breakfast 8-9 • Open May 1-Oct. 15 • MC, Visa accepted • Cancellation policy • CAA; TNS Member

Lorneville
Goodwin's Chat & Chew Bed & Breakfast ★★ ½
Fraser & Arleen Goodwin, RR 2, Amherst, B4H 3X9
(902) 661-0282
At Lorneville, about 32 km (20 mi) from Amherst on Rte. 366, on Northumberland Strait • Three o/n units, one shared B&S • TV in living room • No pets, please • Non-smoking only
FEATURES: Piano and organ in living room • Orchard with variety of fruit trees • Horseshoe pit, tether ball and badminton • Access to beach, swimming and walking trail
RATES: $40 (1), $45 (2), $7 add'l person • Full breakfast 7:30-9:30 • Open May 15-Oct. 15 • NSRS Member

Louisbourg
Ashley Manor Bed & Breakfast ★★ ½
Stacy Simpson, Main Street, Louisbourg, B0A 1M0
(902) 733-3268
Three o/n units, two shared S • Cable TV in lounge • Adults only • No pets, please
FEATURES: Walking distance to Fortress Louisbourg
RATES: $35 (1), $45-$49 (2) (STC) • Full breakfast at guests' convenience • Open year-round • NSRS Member

Louisbourg
Cranberry Cove Inn
Carole Swander, 17 Wolfe Street, Louisbourg, B0A 1M0
(902) 733-2171
Fax (902) 733-2449
Renovated turn-of-the-century home close to Fortress Louisbourg

entrance • Seven o/n units, private B&S (some Jacuzzi) • Children 10 yrs and older welcome • Non-smoking only
FEATURES: Licensed dining • Walking distance from town
RATES: $85-$130 (1-2) • Full breakfast • Open year-round • AE, MC, Visa accepted • IGNS; NSRS Member

Louisbourg
Evensong Bed & Breakfast
Margaret Marshall, 30 Upper Warren Street, Box 272, Louisbourg, B0A 1M0
Tel & Fax (902) 733-3691
Turn up at post office • Restored Victorian home • Two o/n units, one shared B&S • Cable TV in living room • Crib available • Non-smoking only
RATES: $40 (1), $45 (2) (STC) • Full breakfast 7:30-9 • Open May 1-Oct. 31

Louisbourg
Grandmother's Place Bed & Breakfast
Jennifer Pope, 6 Brittanic Street, Box 301, Louisbourg, B0A 1M0
(902) 733-2375
Fax (902) 539-3529
Off-season (902) 562-1130
Off Main St. • Three o/n units, one shared B&S • Cable TV in lounge
RATES: $40 (1-2), $10 add'l person • Breakfast 7:30-10 • Open May-Sept. • MC, Visa accepted • NSRS Member

Louisbourg
Greta Cross
Bed and Breakfast
Greta Cross, 81 Pepperell Street,
Box 153, Louisbourg, B0A 1M0
(902) 733-2833
Three o/n units, two shared B&S •
Cable TV and radio in lounge •
Telephone and clock radio in rooms
• Children under 5 yrs free • Non-
smoking only
FEATURES: Scenic view •
Laundry facilities • Kitchen privi-
leges • Electric organ in lounge
RATES: $32 (1), $40 (2) (STC) •
Full breakfast at guests' conve-
nience • Open May 1-Nov. 1 • NSRS
Member

Louisbourg
Kathy's
Bed & Breakfast
Larry & Kathy Rudderham, 18
Upper Warren Street, Box 133,
Louisbourg, B0A 1M0
(902) 733-2264
Town centre, turn right at post
office • Three o/n units, one shared
B&S • Cable TV in one room and
sitting room
RATES: $40 (1), $45 (2) • Full
breakfast 7:30-10 • Open year-
round (Sept. 1-May 1 by reserva-
tion)

Louisbourg
Levy's Bed & Breakfast
Annie Levy, 7 Marvin Street, Box
175, Louisbourg, B0A 1M0
(902) 733-2793
Three o/n units, one shared B&S,
one shared 1/2 B • Cable TV and
radio in lounge • Non-smoking only
RATES: $32 (1), $45 (2) (STC) •
Full breakfast 7:30-8:30 • Open
May-Oct.

Louisbourg
Louisbourg
Harbour Inn ★★★ ½
Parker & Suzanne Bagnell, 9
Warren Street, Louisbourg, B0A
1M0
(902) 733-3222
Toll free 1-888-888-8INN (8466)
Century-old sea captain's house •
Eight o/n units, private B (five
Jacuzzi) • Not suitable for children •
No pets, please • Non-smoking only
FEATURES: Balconies overlook
harbour and Fortress • Honeymoon
suite available • Licensed dining
room
RATES: $85-$95 (2), $125 (suite) •
Breakfast • Open May 1-Oct. 31 •
AE, MC, Visa accepted • NSRS
Member

Louisbourg
Stacey House
Bed & Breakfast
Geraldine Beaver, 7418 Main
Street, Louisbourg, B0A 1M0
(902) 733-2317/564-1011
Town centre • Four o/n units, one
private S, one shared B&S • TV in
den • No pets, please • No smoking
in rooms, please
RATES: $40-$45 (1), $45-$50 (2),
$16 add'l person, $10 add'l child
under 16 yrs • Full breakfast • Open
May 1-Oct. 31 • MC, Visa accepted
• NSRS Member

Louisbourg
The Manse
Bed & Breakfast ★★ ½
Dorothy Brooks, 10 Strathcona
Street, Louisbourg, B0A 1M0
(902) 733-3155
Victorian home overlooking harbour
• Three o/n units, two shared B&S •
Children over 12 yrs welcome

RATES: $35 (1), $45 (2) (STC) •
Full breakfast • Open April 1-Oct.
31 • Off-season by reservation •
NSRS Member

Louisbourg
Wilson's
Bed & Breakfast
Harold & Jessie Wilson, 75 Wolfe
Street, Box 13, Louisbourg,
B0A 1M0
(902) 733-2659
Overlooking harbour and fortress •
Two rooms, private B&S • Cable
TV in living room • Non-smoking
only
RATES: $35 (1), $45 (2), $10 add'l
person • Full breakfast 7:30-8:30 •
Open June 1-Sept. 30

Louisdale
Seal Cove
Bed & Breakfast
Vivian Sampson, 341 Main Street,
RR 1, Louisdale, B0E 1V0
(902) 345-2155
From Hwy 104, Exit 46, turn left at
caution light, 1.5 km (1 mi) • Three
o/n units, one shared B&S
FEATURES: Ocean view from
decks • Evening lunch and snacks
on request • Dining room
RATES: $32 (1), $40 (2) (STC) •
Full breakfast 6-9 • Open May-
Oct. 31 • CBBBA; NSRS Member

Lower Argyle
Ye Olde Argyler
Lodge and Ocean View
Restaurant
Allan & Ginger MacKenzie, Lower
Argyle, RR 1, Glenwood,
B0W 1W0
(902) 643-2500
Fax (902) 643-2312
Toll free 1-800-504-1114

E-mail argyler@atcon.com
Website http://www.at-
data.ns.ca/argyle/lodge/lodge.html
Hwy 103, Exit 32 to Rte. 3, 7.5 km
(4.5 mi) • Twenty-five minutes from
Yarmouth and Maine ferries • New
cedar lodge on ocean's edge with
spectacular sunsets and views • Six
o/n units, private B&S; one cabin •
Cable TV and telephone in rooms •
Smoking outdoors only
FEATURES: Licensed restaurant
with gourmet dining • Swimming,
fishing, sea kayaking and beachcombing • Boat rentals and charters
• Three private islands to explore
RATES: $89-$149 (1-2), $12 add'l
person • Continental breakfast •
Open year-round • MC, Visa
accepted • NSRS Member

Lunenburg
Arbor View Inn
Daniel & Rose Orovec,
216 Dufferin Street, Lunenburg,
B0J 2C0
Tel & Fax (902) 634-3658
Toll free 1-800-890-6650
Turn-of-the-century home (c. 1907)
on large estate • Four o/n units, pri-
vate B; two suites • Non-smoking
only
FEATURES: Private dining rooms
• Library • Garden paths • Gourmet
weekend packages and cooking
classes available
RATES: $75-$105 (2)• Full break-
fast at guests' convenience • Open
year-round • AE, MC, Visa accepted
• IGNS; NSRS Member

Lunenburg
Blue Rocks Road Bed and Breakfast
Merrill & Al Heubach, 579 Blue Rocks Road, RR 1, Lunenburg, B0J 2C0
Tel & Fax (902) 634-8033
Toll free 1-800-818-3426
2 km (1.2 mi) from town centre; just past flashing light on road to Blue Rocks • On Lunenburg Bay • Three o/n units, one private B, one shared S • No pets, please • Non-smoking only
FEATURES: German spoken • Library • Veranda • Full-service bicycle shop with quality rentals on premises
RATES: $45-$55 (1), $55-$65 (2), $15 add'l person • Full breakfast • Open May 15-Oct. 15 • Off-season by reservation • MC, Visa accepted • IGNS; NSFC; NSRS; SSBBA Member

Lunenburg
Blue Nose Lodge
Ron & Grace Swan, Falkland Avenue and Dufferin Street, Box 399, Lunenburg, B0J 2C0
Tel & Fax (902) 634-8851
Toll free 1-800-565-8851
Three buildings, including two restored Victorian homes (c. 1860 and 1890) • Eleven o/n units, private S or B&S; two suites; one family suite • Cable TV in parlours • Children under 10 yrs free • Smoking in designated areas only
FEATURES: Walk to town centre, harbour, heritage district
RATES: $55-$90 (1-2), $125-$165 (family suite), $15 add'l person • Breakfast • Open year-round • AE, Dis, MC, Visa accepted • CAA; NSRS Member

Lunenburg
Boscawen Inn & McLachlan House
★★★ ¹/₂
Michael & Ann O'Dowd, 150 Cumberland Street, Box 1343, Lunenburg, B0J 2C0
(902) 634-3325
Fax (902) 634-9293
Toll free 1-800-354-5009
Two registered heritage properties (c. 1888 and 1905), overlooking the harbour • Twenty o/n units, private B
FEATURES: Licensed dining room • Meeting rooms • Sun deck
RATES: $85-$120 (2) • MAP available • Open Easter-Dec.• Off-season by reservation • AE, DC, MC, Visa accepted • CAA; IGNS; NSRS; TNS Member

Lunenburg
Brigantine Inn ★★ ¹/₂
Karyn Tannahill & Alan Creaser, 82 Montague Street, Box 195, Lunenburg, B0J 2C0
(902) 634-3300
Toll free 1-800-360-1181
Harbourside location in the heart of Lunenburg • Seven o/n units, private B&S • Cable TV, clock radio, telephone and balcony in rooms
FEATURES: Licensed restaurant and terrace
RATES: $45-$59 (1), $59-$79 (2), $10 add'l person • Off-season rates • Continental breakfast • Open year-round • AE, DC, Dis, MC, Visa accepted • IGNS; NSRS Member

Lunenburg
Commander's
Bed & Breakfast ★★★ ½
Tom & Judy Jennings, 56 Victoria
Road, Box 864, Lunenburg,
B0J 2C0
Tel & Fax (902) 634-3151
Located at intersection of Hwy 3
(Victoria Road) and Hwy 324
(Green St.) • Turn-of-the-century
home • Three o/n units, private B&S
• Cable TV/VCR in lounge • Clock
radio in rooms • Children over 12
yrs welcome
FEATURES: Three lounges with
books and games • Sun deck and
patio • Interesting naval memorabil-
ia, ship and train models and a
unique collection of pigs
*RATES: $50-$80 (1-2), $15 add'l
person • Full breakfast 8-9 • Open
year-round • AE, MC, Visa accepted
• NSRS; SSTA Member*

Lunenburg
Compass Rose Inn ★★★
Rodger & Suzanne Pike, 15 King
Street, Box 1267, Lunenburg,
B0J 2C0
Toll free 1-800-565-8509
Historic sea captain's house (c.
1825) • Four o/n units, private B&S
• Children under 2 yrs free
FEATURES: Licensed dining room
• Guest lounge • Garden patio • Gift
shop • Packages available
*RATES: $60-$75 (1-2) • Off-season
rates • Continental or full breakfast
8:30-9:30 • Open mid Feb.-Dec. •
AE, DC, MC, Visa accepted • NSRS;
UCI Member*

Lunenburg
Daniel Rudolf House
Bed & Breakfast ★★★
Jane & Jack Rowberry, 325 Lincoln
Street, Box 1208, Lunenburg,
B0J 2C0
Tel & Fax (902) 634-4110
Website
http://fox.nstn.ca/~trodgers/rudolf
Historic home (c. 1886) • Two o/n
units, private B&S • Cable TV/VCR
in lounge • Cats on premises • No
pets, please • Non-smoking only
*RATES: $75 (1-2), $15 add'l per-
son (STC) • Full breakfast • Open
May-Oct. • MC, Visa accepted •
NSRS Member*

Lunenburg
Greybeard's
Bed & Breakfast
Bob & Rosanna Higgins, 201
Pelham Street, Box 1576,
Lunenburg, B0J 2C0
(902) 634-9696
Restored home (c. 1888) close to
harbour and town centre • Three o/n
units, private B&S • Clock radio in
rooms • Cable TV/VCR in den •
Not suitable for children • No pets,
please
FEATURES: Reading room •
French spoken
*RATES: $50-$55 (2) • Full break-
fast • Open May-Dec. 15 • Off-sea-
son by reservation*

Lunenburg
Hillcroft Café and Guest House
Peter Fleischmann & Rafel Albo, 53 Montague Street, Box 1665, Lunenburg, B0J 2C0
(902) 634-8031
Restored 1850s home, furnished throughout with antiques, oriental carpets and curios from around the world • Three o/n units, one shared B&S • Library and piano in parlour • Not suitable for children • No pets, please • Non-smoking only
FEATURES: Licensed dining room • Garden sitting area
RATES: $45 (1), $60 (2) • Continental breakfast • Open May 1-Dec. 31 • MC, Visa accepted • NSRS Member

Lunenburg
Kaulbach House Historic Inn ★★★ ½
Enzo & Karen Padovani, 75 Pelham Street, Box 1348, Lunenburg, B0J 2C0
Fax (902) 634-8818
Toll free 1-800-568-8818
Award-winning registered heritage inn (c. 1880), overlooking water • Eight o/n units, private B&S or S • Cable TV in rooms • No pets, please • Non-smoking only
FEATURES: Antique furnishings • Licensed dining for guests • Off-street parking
RATES: $55-$85 (1), $60-$90 (2) (STC) • Full breakfast 8-9:15 • Open March 15-Dec. 15 • AE, MC, Visa accepted • CAA; NSRS; UCI Member

Lunenburg
Lamb & Lobster Bed and Breakfast
William & Hilary Flower, 619 Blue Rocks Road, RR 1, Lunenburg, B0J 2C0
(902) 634-4833
From Lunenburg, 1.3 km (.75 mi) on Blue Rocks Rd., 0.5 km (0.3 mi) beyond flashing light • Working sheep farm with beautiful ocean view • Three o/n units, one shared B, one shared1/2 B • Cable TV and telephone in lounge • Not suitable for small children • Non-smoking only
FEATURES: Border Collie demonstrations on request • Fishing and scuba diving charters
RATES: $40 (1), $50 (2) • Full breakfast 7:30-9:30 • Open June-Oct. 31 • Visa accepted

Lunenburg
Lennox Inn B&B
Robert Cram, 69 Fox Street, Box 254, Lunenburg, B0J 2C0
(902) 634-4043
Canada's oldest intact stagecoach inn (1791), decorated with period furnishings • Three o/n units, one private S, one shared B&S • Cable TV in living room • No pets, please • Non-smoking only
RATES: $45-$65 (1-2) • Full breakfast 8-9:30 • Open May 15-Oct. 15 • Visa accepted

Lunenburg
Lincoln House Bed & Breakfast
Tony & Georgia Morris, 130 Lincoln Street, Box 322, Lunenburg, B0J 2C0
(902) 634-7179
E-mail lincoln@fox.nstn.ca

Restored Victorian home (c. 1860) located in historic "old town" overlooking the harbour • Three o/n units, one private S, one shared B&S (sinks in rooms) • Cable TV/VCR in lounge • No pets, please • Non-smoking only
FEATURES: Victorian tea room on premises • Art workshop packages available
RATES: $50-$70 (1-2), $10 add'l person (STC) • Full breakfast 8-9:30 • Open year-round • MC, Visa accepted

Lunenburg
Lion Inn
Bed & Breakfast
George, Lois & Mindi Morin,
33 Cornwallis Street, Box 487,
Lunenburg,
B0J 2C0
(902) 634-8988
Georgian-style home (c. 1835) located in National Historic district • Three o/n units, private B&S • No pets, please
FEATURES: Two separate licensed dining rooms (one non-smoking), recommended by *Where to Eat in Canada*
RATES: $65 (1), $70-$75 (2), $15 add'l person • Off-season rates • Full breakfast • Open year-round • AE, MC, Visa accepted • NSRS Member

Lunenburg
Lunenburg Inn ★★★ ½
Gail & Don Wallace,
26 Dufferin Street, Box 1407,
Lunenburg, B0J 2C0
(902) 634-3963
Fax (902) 634-9419
Toll free 1-800-565-3963
Website
http://www.grtplaces.com/ac/luninn/

Registered heritage inn (c. 1893) • Seven o/n units, private B&S; two suites (whirlpool) • Cable TV in rooms • Cot available • Designated smoking area
FEATURES: Sun deck and covered veranda
RATES: $65-$115 (1-2), $15 add'l person • Off-season rates • Full breakfast 8-9:30 • Open year-round • AE, DC, MC, Visa accepted • IGNS; NSRS; UCI Member

Lunenburg
Mainstay
Country Inn ★★★
Elisabeth & Hubert Gieringer, 167 Victoria Road, Box 1510,
Lunenburg, B0J 2C0
(902) 634-8234
Fax (902) 634-7100
Toll free 1-800-616-4411
Three o/n units, private B (whirlpool)
FEATURES: Laundry facilities
RATES: $60-$70 (1-2) (STC) • Full breakfast 8-10:30 • Open June 15-Oct. 15 • AE, DC, Dis, MC, Visa accepted

Lunenburg
1826 Maplebird House B&B
Dean & Gail Westbrook,
36 Pelham Street, Box 493,
Lunenburg, B0J 2C0
(902) 634-3863
Fax (902) 634-9415
Central location • Three o/n units,
one shared B&S • Cable TV in living room • Cat on premises • Nonsmoking only
FEATURES: Swimming pool •
Parking
RATES: *$45 (1), $50 (2)* •
Continental breakfast 8-9:30 • *Open June 1-Sept. 30* • *Visa accepted* •
NSRS Member

Lunenburg
Old Hammett Hotel (c. 1790)
Wayne & Carolyn Bowser,
120 Montague Street, Box 220,
Lunenburg, B0J 2C0
(902) 634-8165/9965
Harbourside location • Seven o/n
units (suites), private B&S • Cable
TV, clock radio, ceiling fan and
sofa-bed in rooms • Not recommended for small children • No
pets, please • Designated smoking
area
FEATURES: Housekeeping units
available
RATES: *$75-$90 (1-2), $15 add'l
person (STC)* • *$450-$540 (weekly)*
• *Open June 1-Sept. 30* • *Off-season
by reservation* • *MC, Visa accepted*
• *NSRS Member*

Lunenburg
Pelham House Bed & Breakfast ★★★
Geraldine Pauley, 224 Pelham
Street, Box 358, Lunenburg,
B0J 2C0
(902) 634-7113
Fax (902) 634-7114
Toll free 1-800-508-0446
Century sea captain's home (c.
1906), decorated in period style •
Four o/n units, private B&S • Cable
TV/VCR in parlour • Clock radio,
hair dryer and fan on request • Not
recommended for small children •
Cats on premises • No pets, please •
Vented smoking room
FEATURES: Large library of
books and periodicals about the sea,
sailing and wooden boats • Laundry
facilities • Kitchen facilities •
Afternoon tea and picnic lunches
available • Sitting room with books
and games • Veranda overlooking
harbour • Close to restaurants, town
centre and harbour • Telephone and
fax available
RATES: *$65-$120 (1-2) (STC)* •
Off-season rates • *Full breakfast
7:30-10* • *Open April-Nov.* • *Off-season by reservation* • *MC, Visa
accepted* • *IGNS; NSRS Member*

Lunenburg
Rum Runner's Inn B&B ★★ ½
Gene & Yvonne Tanner,
66 Montague Street, Box 1090,
Lunenburg, B0J 2C0
(902) 634-9200/3881
Fax (902) 634-4822
Outstanding views of Lunenburg
Harbour • Nine o/n units, private
B&S • Cable TV, radio and telephone in rooms
FEATURES: Licensed dining room
RATES: *$56-$125 (1-3)* • *Off-sea-*

son rates • *Open year-round* • *AE,*
MC, Visa accepted • *IGNS; NSRS*
Member

Lunenburg
Sailor's Rest
Bed & Breakfast
Diane Stewart, 311 Pelham Street,
General Delivery, Lunenburg,
B0J 2C0
Tel & Fax (902) 634-8444
Elegant sea captain's home with
veranda and view of Lunenburg
Harbour • Three o/n units, two
shared B&S • Cable TV/VCR and
stereo in parlour • No pets, please •
Non-smoking only
RATES: $55 (1), $65 (2), $10 add'l
person • *Full breakfast 8-9:30* •
Open year-round • *MC, Visa*
accepted • *Check-in 3 pm*

Lunenburg
Seaside Tourist Home
Brenda Tanner, 24 Hopson Street,
Lunenburg, B0J 2C0
(902) 634-8256/3996
One o/n unit, private B • Cable TV
in guest sitting rooom • Non-smoking only
RATES: $50 (STC) • *Continental*
breakfast • *Open June 15-Sept. 15*

Lunenburg
Smuggler's Cove
Inn ★★ ½
Yvonne Tanner, 139 Montague
Street, Box 1090, Lunenburg,
B0J 2C0
(902) 634-9200
Fax (902) 634-4822
Check in at Rum Runner's Inn,
66-70 Montague Street • Four o/n
units, private B&S • Cable TV,
clock radio and telephone in rooms
FEATURES: Licensed dining room

• Elevator • Patio off three units
RATES: $100-$125 (2), $5 add'l
person • *Off-season rates* • *Open*
year-round • *AE, DC, MC, Visa*
accepted

Lunenburg
Westhaver Haus
Bed & Breakfast
Barbara Eisenhauer, 102 Dufferin
Street, Lunenburg, B0J 2C0
(902) 634-4937
Three o/n units, one shared B&S •
Cable TV in one room and living
room • Non-smoking only
RATES: $45 (1), $55-$60 (2) • *Full*
breakfast 8 • *Open June 1-Oct. 31* •
NSRS Member

Mabou
Beaton's
Bed & Breakfast
Mrs. Anne Beaton, Box 78, Mabou,
B0E 1X0
(902) 945-2806
On Rte. 19, just south of Mabou •
Three o/n units, one shared B&S •
Cable TV in sitting room • No pets,
please • Non-smoking only
RATES: $40 (1), $50-$55 (2), $20
add'l person (STC) • *Full breakfast*
8-9 • *Open year-round* • *NSRS*
Member

Mabou
Clayton Farm Bed & Breakfast
Isaac & Bernadette Smith, Box 33, Mabou, B0E 1X0
Tel & Fax (902) 945-2719

On Rte. 19 just south of Mabou • Large old-fashioned farmhouse and working farm on 185-acre peninsula • Four o/n units, one shared B&S • Non-smoking only
FEATURES: Municipal registered heritage property (c. 1835), furnished with antiques • Close to sandy beach and hiking trails
RATES: $40 (1), $50-$55 (2), $25 add'l person • Full breakfast • Open May 1-Oct. 31 • NSFC Member

Mabou
Duncreigan Country Inn ★★★ ½
Eleanor & Charles Mullendore, Box 59, Mabou, B0E 1X0
(902) 945-2207
Toll free 1-800-840-2207
New inn on harbour, featuring antique furnishings • Six o/n rooms, private B&S; one suite (whirlpool) • Cable TV in rooms • Non-smoking only
FEATURES: Licensed dining room (wheelchair accessible) • Canoe and bike available • Eagle-watching • Gift shop and gallery
RATES: $75-$110 (1-2), $15 add'l person (STC) • Off-season rates • Open year-round • MC, Visa accepted • NSRS; TNS; UCI Member

Mabou
Glendyer Mills Bed & Breakfast
Kathy McIntyre, RR 4, Mabou, B0E 1X0
(902) 945-2455
Follow signs from Mabou Village • Comfortable heritage property home (c. 1848), filled with antiques • Three o/n units, one shared B, one shared S; one suite
FEATURES: Sun deck with great view of gardens • Donkeys, geese and brook on property
RATES: $40-$50 (1), $50-$60 (2), $20 add'l person • Full breakfast • Open year-round • NSRS Member

Mabou
Rankins Bed & Breakfast
Donald & Mary Rankin, RR 3, Mabou Harbour, B0E 1X0
(902) 945-2375
Rte. 19 to Mabou Village, turn onto Mabou Harbour Road, 5.5 km (3.5 mi) from St. Mary's Church • Three o/n units, two shared B&S • Non-smoking only
FEATURES: Magnificent sunrises and sunsets
RATES: $35 (1), $40 (2) (STC) • Full breakfast • Open May 15-Oct. 31 • NSRS Member

Mahone Bay
Abundance Inn B&B
Mimi Findlay, 403 West Main Street, Mahone Bay, B0J 2E0
(902) 624-9943

Award-winning historic property decorated with

antiques and folk art • Two o/n units, private B • Clock radio in rooms
FEATURES: Fruit, flowers, chocolates, and toiletries provided
RATES: *$80 (1-2)* • *Full breakfast at guests' convenience* • *Open year-round (by chance or reservation)* • *NSRS Member*

Mahone Bay
Amber Rose Inn
Faith & John Piccolo, 319 West Main Street, Box 397, Mahone Bay, B0J 2E0
Tel & Fax (902) 624-1060
Hwy 103, Exit 11, turn left at four-way stop, 2 km (1.5 mi) from Mahone Bay Harbour, straight up from monument at main intersection, 1 km (0.5 mi) • Restored heritage house (c. 1875), originally J.E. Lantz General Store • Three o/n units (suites), private B&S (whirlpool) • Cable TV, clock radio, hairdryer, robes, fridge and coffee maker in rooms • Telephone on request • No pets, please • No smoking in rooms, please
FEATURES: Lawns and gardens • Air-conditioning • Local crafts
RATES: *$75-$95 (1-2), $15 add'l person* • *Full breakfast* • *Open May-Oct.* • *Major credit cards accepted* • *IGNS; NSRS Member*

Mahone Bay
Bay Abode
Bed and Breakfast
& Gallery ★★★
Gerry & Chris Nolan, 1486 Oakland Road, RR 2, Mahone Bay, B0J 2E0
(902) 624-1439
In Mahone Bay, 1.7 km (1 mi) from intersection of Hwy 3 and Oakland Rd. • Restored farmhouse (c. 1898), on twenty-acre landscaped and forested property • Three o/n units, one shared B&S • Cable TV/VCR and telephone in living room • Playpen and cot available • Children under 6 yrs free • No pets, please • Designated smoking area
FEATURES: Furnished with country antiques • Extensive library • Large screened porch • Horseshoe pit and croquet • Walking and ungroomed cross-country ski trails • Vistas of Mahone Bay and harbour • Small art gallery (oils)
RATES: *$45-$60 (1-2), $10 add'l person* • *Full breakfast 8-9* • *Open year-round* • *Visa accepted* • *Reservations preferred* • *MBBA; NSRS; SSTA Member*

Mahone Bay
Dory Inn
Bed & Breakfast
Tillie & John Biebesheimer, 404 Main Street, Box 130, Mahone Bay, B0J 2E0
(902) 624-6460
E-mail amyb@ra.isisnet.com
Restored Victorian home • Two o/n units, one shared B&S • Cable TV/VCR in parlour • Designated smoking area
FEATURES: Furnished with country antiques and early Nova Scotian collectibles • Books and games available • Rowboat at government wharf
RATES: *$45 (1), $50 (2)* • *Full breakfast until 9:30* • *Open year-round*

Mahone Bay
Echo Bay House
Irmtraut Schoen, 35 Sunnybrook Road, RR 1, Mahone Bay, B0J 2E0
(902) 624-4853/3735
Located on an inlet between Mahone Bay and Lunenburg: please call for directions • Two o/n units, private B • Cable TV in rooms • Cot available
FEATURES: Large private garden • German spoken • Kitchen facilities • Barbecue • Housekeeping units • Swimming, and sailing • Private wharf • Boat tours
RATES: $45-$65 (1-2), $10 add'l person (STC) • Open May-Oct • Visa accepted

Mahone Bay
Edgewater
Bed & Breakfast ★★★
Betty & Dave Hess, 44 Mader's Cove Road, Mahone Bay, B0J 2E0
(902) 624-9382
Fax (902) 624-8733

Just off Rte. 3, enroute to Lunenburg • Restored century home with waterfront view • Three o/n units, one shared B&S; one suite • TV in lounge • Clock radio and ceiling fan in rooms • Cots available • Children under 10 yrs free • No pets, please • Non-smoking only
RATES: $45 (1), $60-$65 (2), $10 add'l person • Off-season rates available • Full breakfast 8-9 • Open year-round • MC, Visa accepted • IGNS; MBBA; NSRS; SSBBA; SSTA Member

Mahone Bay
Fairmont House B&B
Thomas Hill & Michael McNair, 654 Main Street, Mahone Bay, B0J 2E0
(902) 624-6173
Toll free 1-800-565-5971
Victorian home (c. 1857) • Three o/n units, private B&S • Cable TV/VCR and games in parlour • Smoking area
RATES: $55 (1), $75 (2) (STC) • Full breakfast 8-9:30 • Open May 15-Oct. 10 • MC, Visa accepted

Mahone Bay
Heart's Desire
Bed & Breakfast
John & Rosalie Laughlin, 686 Main Street, Mahone Bay, B0J 2E0
(902) 624-8470
Victorian home • Two o/n units, private B&S; one suite, one housekeeping suite • Cable TV • Ceiling fan in rooms • No pets, please • Non-smoking only
FEATURES: Veranda overlooking bay • Piano, books and games in lounge
RATES: $68-$80 (1-2) • Full breakfast • Open May 1-Oct. 31 • MC, Visa accepted • NSRS Member

Mahone Bay
MacDonald's
Bed & Breakfast
Huguette MacDonald, 397 Main Street, Mahone Bay, B0J 2E0
(902) 624-9365
Hwy 103, Exit 10 or 11 • Three o/n units, one shared B • Cable TV in rooms and sitting room • Telephone and radio in lounge • No pets, please • Non-smoking only
RATES: $35 (1), $50 (2), $10 add'l person • Breakfast 8-9 • Open June 1-Nov. 30 • MC, Visa accepted

Mahone Bay
Manse at Mahone Bay Country Inn

Rose & Allan O'Brian, 88 Orchard Street, Box 475, Mahone Bay, B0J 2E0
(902) 624-1121
Fax (902) 624-1182
Restored 1860s manse with wonderful view of Mahone Bay • Four o/n units, private S and B&S • Cable TV, fax and telephone in rooms
FEATURES: Lunch and dinner on request • Library of books and music
RATES: $85 (1-2), $20 add'l person • Full breakfast • Open year-round • MC, Visa accepted • NSRS Member

Mahone Bay
Once Upon a Time B&B ★★★ ½

Lise & Denis Corcoran, 40 Pleasant Street, Mahone Bay, B0J 2E0
(902) 624-6383

Elegant, secluded Victorian home • Four o/n units, private B • Cable TV in sitting room • Children 16 yrs and under $14
FEATURES: French spoken • Parlour with piano and games • Five-minute walk to shore or downtown
RATES: $55-$75 (1-2) (STC) • Full breakfast • Open year-round • MC, Visa accepted • MBBA; NSRS; SSTA Member

Mahone Bay
Sou'Wester Inn ★★★ ½

Ron & Mabel Redden, 788 Main Street, Box 146, Mahone Bay, B0J 2E0
(902) 624-9296

Victorian shipbuilder's home • Four o/n units, private B&S • No pets, please • Non-smoking only
FEATURES: Furnished with antiques • Evening tea • Parlour with piano and games • Veranda overlooking waterfront • Picnic table • Touring and hiking maps
RATES: $75 (1-2), $15 add'l person • Full breakfast • Open May 1-Oct. 15 • MC, Visa accepted • CAA; NSRS Member

Mahone Bay
Threadneedle
Bed & Breakfast ★★★★
Donald Gillies, Indian Point Road,
Mahone Bay, B0J 2E0
(902) 624-8310
Fax (902) 624-1203
Toll free 1-888-763-3353
Hwy 103, Exit 10, 5 km (3 mi) from
Rte. 3 • Three o/n units, private B •
Cable TV/VCR in lounge • Radio in
rooms • No pets, please
FEATURES: Laundry facilities •
Kitchenette • Sauna • Private beach
• Needlepoint shop
*RATES: $72 (1-2), $15 add'l person (STC) • Breakfast 8:30-9:30 •
Open year-round • MC, Visa
accepted • IGNS; NSRS Member*

Mahone Bay
Walnut Tree Inn B&B
Olga Warren, FHCIMA,
35 Claremont Street, Box 138,
Mahone Bay, B0J 2E0
(902) 624-8039
At Pond St. • Two o/n units, one
shared B&S • Cable TV in living
room • Cat on premises • No smoking in rooms, please
*RATES: $40 (1), $50 (2) (STC) (tax
incl.) • Full breakfast • Open May
1-Sept. 30*

Mahone Bay
Westhavers Beach
Bed & Breakfast
Dorothy & Milton Dorey, 268
Mader's Cove Road, Box 436,
Mahone Bay, B0J 2E0
(902) 624-9261/9211
Three o/n units, one shared B&S;
one suite (whirlpool) • Cable TV
and clock radio in rooms • Smoking
outdoors only
FEATURES: View of Mahone

Bay's outer harbour and some hundreds of islands, from indoors and
from the decks
*RATES: $45 (1), $55 (2), $75-$85
(suite) • Full breakfast 7:30-9 •
Open May 15-Oct. 30 • Visa accepted • NSRS Member*

Mahone Bay
Zwickerwood
Bed & Breakfast
Lei-Valli Dunham Thompson, 906
South Main Street, Mahone Bay,
B0J 2E0
(902) 624-6249
180-year-old home on secluded
property overlooking Mahone Bay •
Three o/n units, two shared B&S •
Cable TV/VCR in library
FEATURES: Furnished with
antiques and Persian rugs •
Swimming pool and sun deck
*RATES: $60 (1), $70 (2) • Full
breakfast • Open year-round*

Maitland
Capt. Douglas House
Bed & Breakfast
Calvin Crowe, 8843 Highway 215,
Box 37, Maitland, B0N 1T0
(902) 261-2289
Hwy 102, Exit 14, Rte. 236 to Rte.
215, 32 km (20 mi) from exit •
Municipal heritage property (c.
1860) • Three o/n units, one shared
B&S • Cable TV in living room
FEATURES: Babysitting services •
Vacation packages
*RATES: $35 (1), $45 (2) • Full
breakfast 7:30-9:30 • Open May 1-
Oct. 31*

Maitland
Foley House Inn B&B
Lucy Maidment, Box 86, Maitland,
B0N 1T0
(902) 261-2844
From Halifax, take Hwy 102, Exit
10 to Rte. 215; from Truro, take
Hwy 102, Exit 14 to Rte. 236 to
Rte. 215 • Three o/n units, one private B, one shared B&S • Cable TV
in lounge
FEATURES: Licensed dining room
*RATES: $40-$45 (1), $50-$55 (2),
$12 add'l person (STC) • Full
breakfast • Open May 1-Oct. 31 •
Visa accepted • NSRS Member*

Malagash
Lavender Rose
Bed & Breakfast
Ida Young & Jerry Leger, 98 Purdy
Loop, Malagash, B0K 1E0
(902) 257-2300
Rte. 6, towards Malagash on
Sunrise Trial Scenic Diversion, 6.5
km (4 mi) to Purdy Loop, turn left,
second house on right • Three o/n
units, one shared B&S • TV in living room • Cot and crib available •
Cat on premises • Non-smoking
only
*RATES: $40 (1), $50 (2), $10 add'l
person • Full breakfast 7-9 • Open
June 1-Sept. 30 • NSRS Member*

Margaree Centre
Browns' Bruaich na
H' Aibhne
Bed & Breakfast ★★★
Alice Brown, Box 88, Margaree
Valley, B0E 2C0
(902) 248-2935
Toll free 1-800-575-2935
Off Cabot Trail 6.5 km (4 mi) on
the banks of the Margaree River •
Four o/n units, private B; one cottage • Children under 5 yrs free •
Cable TV in lounge
FEATURES: Laundry facilities •
Salmon and trout fishing • River
swimming • Walking trail to eagles'
nest • Cross-country skiing and
snowmobiling in season
*RATES: $40-$50 (1-2), $10 add'l
person (STC) • Full breakfast 7-9 •
Open year-round • MC, Visa
accepted • NSRS Member*

Margaree Centre
Treuten's
Bed & Breakfast ★★ ½
Waltraut & Werner Treuten,
161 Cranton Crossroads, Box 76,
Margaree Centre, B0E 1Z0
Tel & Fax (902) 248-2286
Just off Cabot Trail, follow signs •
Country setting perfect for regeneration • Three o/n units, two shared
B&S; one housekeeping suite • TV
in living room • Non-smoking only
FEATURES: Bicycles available •
German spoken
*RATES: $40-$52 (1-2), $90-$95
(suite), $5 add'l person • Full
breakfast 7-9 • Open year-round •
NSRS Member*

Margaree Forks
Fisherman's Paradise
Bed & Breakfast
W.G. MacConnell, 8358 General
Delivery, Margaree Forks, B0E 2A0
(902) 248-2890
Four o/n units, two shared B&S •
Clock radio in rooms • TV in living
room
*RATES: $40-$50 (1), $45-$55 (2) •
Full breakfast 7-9 • Open May 1-
Oct. 31 • NSRS Member*

Margaree Forks
Harrison Hill
Bed & Breakfast
Robin & Marilyn Harrison, Box
561, Margaree Forks, B0E 2A0
(902) 248-2226
Three o/n units, two shared B&S •
Cable TV/VCR in lounge • No pets,
please • Non-smoking only
FEATURES: Music room soirées •
Live theatre • Gift corner
RATES: $55 (1-2) (STC) •
Breakfast 8-9:30 • Open May24-
Oct. 31 • NSRS Member

Margaree Forks
McDaniel
Bed & Breakfast
Eleanor & Neil McDaniel, Box 532,
Margaree Forks, B0E 2A0
(902) 248-2734
1.5 km (1 mi) north of Margaree
Forks, on the Cabot Trail • Century-
old home on two-hundred-acre
property with river and mountain
walks • Two o/n units, one shared S
• Cable TV/VCR in living room •
No pets, please • Non-smoking only
FEATURES: Salmon pools
RATES: $34 (1), $42 (2) (STC) •
Full breakfast 7-9 • Open May 1-
Oct. 31 • Reservations preferred •
NSRS Member

Margaree Forks
Old Miller Trout Farm
B&B
Pat & John Stinson, 402 Doyles
Road, Margaree Forks, B0E 1A0
(902) 248-2080
2 km (1.2 mi) off the Cabot Trail •
250-acre property • Two o/n units,
private B&S • TV in lounge • No
pets, please • Non-smoking only
FEATURES: Trout fishing • Nature
trails

RATES: $50 (1-2) (STC) • Full
breakfast • Open May 24-Oct. 15

Margaree Harbour
Chimney Corner
Bed & Breakfast ★★★
Jan & Bob Wheeler, Box 6,
Margaree Harbour, B0E 2B0
Tel & Fax (902) 235-2104
On Shore Rd.; Rte. 219, 7 km (4.2
mi) south of Margaree Harbour •
Three o/n units, one private B&S,
one shared B&S; two cottages •
Cable TV in sitting room • Not suit-
able for children • No pets, please •
Non-smoking only
FEATURES: Evening snack •
Barbecue • Ocean swimming at pri-
vate beach • Fax available
RATES: $45 (1), $55 (2), $75-$90
(cottage) • Weekly rates • Full
breakfast at 9 • Open May 15-Oct.
15 • MC, Visa accepted •
Cancellation policy • IGNS; NSFC;
NSRS; TIANS Member

Margaree Harbour
Harbour View Inn B&B
Connie Jennex, Box 52, Margaree
Harbour, B0E 2B0
(902) 235-2314
At junction of Cabot and Ceilidh
Trails • Three o/n units, one shared
B, one shared 1/2 B; one chalet •
Cable TV in lounge
FEATURES: Fantastic views •
Ocean swimming
RATES: $34 (1), $42-$67 (2), $12
add'l person (STC) • Full breakfast
• Open year-round • Off-season by
reservation • MC accepted • NSRS
Member

Margaree Harbour
Mill Valley Farm
Bed & Breakfast ★★★ ½

Stu & Slawa Lamont, Margaree Harbour, B0E 2B0
Tel & Fax (902) 235-2834
From Cabot Trail, turn off at Scotch Hill, Mill Valley Hwy sign and keep right • One o/n unit, private B (Jacuzzi); two cabins • Cable TV in living room • Non-smoking only
FEATURES: Mountain view from acres of softwood and apple trees • French, German, Russian and Polish spoken • Olympic gym • Walking and hiking trails • Entire property is smoke-free • Vacation packages
RATES: *$85 (1-2), $68-$75 (cabin), $8 add'l person • Full breakfast 7-10 • Open year-round • MC, Visa accepted • Call for reservations • IGNS; NSRS; TIANS Member*

Margaree Harbour
Ocean Haven
Bed & Breakfast

Joan & Peter Sheehan, Box 54, Margaree Harbour, B0E 2B0
(902) 235-2329
Website
http://www.bbproton.com OR www.bb/582.html
Off-season (613) 837-4954
1 km (.6 mi) north of Margaree Harbour in Belle Cote • Three o/n units, two shared B&S; one cottage • Cable TV in lounge • No pets, please • Non-smoking only
FEATURES: Overlooking ocean with unobstructed view • Beaches nearby
RATES: *$45-$57 (1-2), $15 add'l person • $525 (weekly, cottage) • Full breakfast 7:30-8:30 • Open June 15-Oct. 15 • AE, MC, Visa accepted • Cancellation policy •*

Reservations recommended • NSRS Member

Margaree Harbour
Taylor's
Bed & Breakfast

Francis & Mary Taylor, RR 1, Margaree Harbour, B0E 2B0
(902) 235-2652
Approx. 1.6 km (1 mi) south of Margaree Harbour Bridge • Century-old house overlooking Margaree River and Gulf of St. Lawrence • Three o/n units, one shared B&S • TV in living room
RATES: *$32 (1), $40 (2) (STC) • Full breakfast 8-9 • Open May 1-Oct. 31*

Margaree Valley
Normaway Inn

David MacDonald, Box 101, Margaree Valley, B0E 2C0
(902) 248-2987
Fax (902) 248-2600
Toll free 1-800-565-9463
E-mail normaway@atcon.com
On Egypt Rd., 3 km (2 mi) off Cabot Trail • Tranquil 1920s inn on 250 acres • Nine o/n units, private B&S; nineteen cabins
FEATURES: Gourmet country dining room serving breakfast and dinner • Traditional films or music nightly • Barn concerts • Hiking trails • Tennis court • Mountain bike rentals • Licensed paved landing strip • Salmon and trout guides and equipment • Whale-watching tours arranged
RATES: *$45 (1), $85-$145 (2) (MAP) • Off-season and late check-in rates • Breakfast 7:30-10 • Open May-Nov. • Off-season by reservation • Dis, MC, Visa accepted • IGNS; NSRS; TNS; UCI Member*

Margaree Valley
Valley Bed & Breakfast
Angela Stepaniak, Margaree Valley, B0E 2C0
(902) 248-2651
2 km (1.2 mi) off Cabot Trail; 1 km from Margaree Airport • Three o/n units, one shared B&S • TV in living room • Non-smoking only
RATES: $35 (1), $40 (2) (STC) • Full breakfast at guests' convenience • Open May 15-Oct. 15 • Off-season by reservation • MC, Visa accepted

Margaretsville
Talisman
Bed & Breakfast
Jane Wills, 6 Seaman Street, General Delivery, Margaretsville, B0S 1N0
(902) 825-2531
Hwy 101, Exit 18 or 18A, Rte. 362 • Registered heritage property (c. 1861), with panoramic view of Bay of Fundy • Three o/n units, one shared B&S • Cable TV/VCR in living room • Not suitable for children • No pets, please • Non-smoking only
FEATURES: French spoken • Scent-free environment • Grand piano
RATES: $30-$40 (1), $42-$46 (2) • Open May 1-Oct. 31 • Off-season by reservation • MC accepted • NSRS Member

Marion Bridge
Li'l Bit of Heaven
Bed & Breakfast
Bruce & Carol Butts, 371 Trout Brook Road, Marion Bridge, B0A 1P0
(902) 727-2936
Hwy 125, Exit 7 to Marion Bridge, turn left 2.5 km (1.5 mi) on Trout Brook Rd. • Two o/n units, one private B&S, one shared B&S • TV and clock radio in rooms • Non-smoking only
FEATURES: Barbecue • Bonfires • River swimming, boating and fishing
RATES: $40-$55 (1), $55 (2), $10 add'l person (tax incl.) • Full breakfast 7-9 • Open May-Oct. • Off-season by reservation

Marion Bridge
Riverside
Bed & Breakfast
Lorraine Ferguson, 1818 Hillside Road, Box 140, Marion Bridge, B0A 1P0
(902) 727-2615
Hwy 125, Exit 7 to Rte. 327, 14 km (9 mi) to Marion Bridge, left on Hillside Rd., 4.5 km (3 mi) • Three o/n units, one shared B • No pets, please • Non-smoking only
FEATURES: Swimming, boating and fishing
RATES: $35 (1), $45 (2), $16 add'l person (STC) • Full breakfast 7-9 • Open May 1-Oct. 31 • Visa accepted • NSRS Member

Masstown
Shady Maple
Bed & Breakfast ★★★
James & Ellen Eisses, RR 1, Masstown, B0M 1G0
(902) 662-3565
Toll free 1-800-493-5844

Hwy 104, Exit 12, 3 km (2 mi) on Rte. 2; or Hwy 102, Exit 14A, 12 km (7 mi) • Operating farm with century-old home • Three o/n units, two shared B&S; one suite (whirlpool) •

Cable TV in lounge • Cots and crib available • Children under 3 yrs free • Non-smoking only
FEATURES: Fireplace in lounge • Evening snack • Heated swimming pool • View of bay from balcony • Vacation packages
RATES: $32 (1), $40-$65 (2), $5-$10 add'l person • Full breakfast • Open May 1-Oct. 31 • Visa accepted • NSFC; NSRS Member

Meteghan
Anchor Inn B&B

Marie & Hans deMan, 8755 Route 1, Box 19, Meteghan Centre, B0W 2K0
(902) 645-3390
On Rte. 1, 2 km (1.5 mi) north of Meteghan • Three o/n units, one shared S • Cable TV in lounge • Non-smoking only
RATES: $22.20 (1), $33.30-$38.50 (2), $11.10 add'l person (tax incl.) • Open May 15-Oct. 15

Middle Musquodoboit
Bruce Fulton's Bed & Breakfast

Bruce Fulton, 12408 Highway 224, Box 64, Middle Musquodoboit, B0N 1X0
(902) 384-2301
Hwy 102, Exit 10, 27 km (17 mi) on Rte. 224E • Four o/n units, one shared B&S • TV in living room • No smoking in rooms, please
FEATURES: Picnic table • Horseshoe pit
RATES: $35 (1), $40 (2) • Continental breakfast 7-9 • Open May 1-Oct. 31 • Off-season by reservation • NSRS Member

Middle Ohio
Five Acres Bed & Breakfast

Linda & David Ferretti, Middle Ohio, RR 1, Shelburne, B0T 1W0
(902) 875-4175
Hwy 103, Exit 26 to Rte. 203, 18.5 km (11.5 mi) • Pastoral setting on MacKay's Lake • Two o/n units, one shared S • No pets, please • No smoking in rooms, please
FEATURES: Outdoor swimming pool • Bird-watching
RATES: $40 (1), $45 (2) • Full breakfast 6-9 • Open year-round • Visa accepted • NSRS Member

Middle River
Seven Springs Farm Bed & Breakfast

Kevin & Linda Scherzinger, RR 3, Baddeck, B0E 1B0
Tel & Fax (902) 295-2094
From Margaree turn right at first Middle River West sign, 1.6 km (1 mi); from Baddeck take Cabot Trail Exit 7, 13.8 km (8.6 mi) and turn left at MacLennan's Cross, turn right after crossing river, 3.5 km (2.2 mi) to fourth farm on left • Restored farmhouse (c. 1839) nestled against green hills • One o/n unit, private B&S; two suites • Pets permitted outside only • Non-smoking only
FEATURES: Icelandic horses and working cattle farm • Gas fireplaces • Trail riding Sept. 15-Oct. 31 • Summer riding at Cheticamp Island
RATES: $55-$65 (1-2), $10 add'l person • Full breakfast • Open July 1-Oct. 31 • NSRS Member

Middleton
Fairfield Farm Inn (c. 1886) ★★★ ½
Richard & Shae Griffith, 10 Main Street, Box 1287, Middleton, B0S 1P0
Tel & Fax (902) 825-6989
Toll free 1-800-237-9896
Rte. 1W • Restored century-old farmhouse on working fruit and vegetable farm • Five o/n units, private B&S • Cable TV/VCR in parlour • Not suitable for children under 16 yrs • No pets, please • Non-smoking only
FEATURES: 110 acres bordered by Annapolis River • Laundry facilities • Kitchen facilities • Air-conditioning • Nature trails • Putting green • Car rentals
RATES: $45-$55 (1), $50-$65 (2) • Full breakfast • Open year-round • Oct. 15-April 30 by reservation • AE, Dis, MC, Visa accepted • CAA; IGNS; NSRS; UCI Member

Middleton
Falcourt Inn (c. 1920) ★★★ ½
LeGard family, 8979 Highway 201, Nictaux, RR 3, Middleton, B0S 1P0
(902) 825-3399
Fax (902) 825-3422
Toll free 1-800-464-8979
Hwy 101, Exit 18 or 18A, Rte. 1 to Rte. 10 to Rte. 201 (Nictaux) • Restored 1920s fishing lodge on the Nictaux River with mountain views • Six o/n units, private B; one suite (whirlpool) • TV and clock radio in rooms • No pets, please • Non-smoking rooms available
FEATURES: Wheelchair accessibility • Veranda • Laundry facilities • Licensed dining room • Common area • River fishing on property • Vacation packages

RATES: $70 (1), $75 (2), suite extra • Continental breakfast • Open year-round • AE, DC, MC, Visa accepted • IGNS; NSRS; TNS Member

Middleton
Mount Hanley Austria Inn ★★★
Astrid & Ambrose Schnetzer, Mount Hanley Road, RR 1, Middleton, B0S 1P0
Tel & Fax (902) 825-3744
E-mail austria@istar.ca
Website
http://www.valleyweb.com/austri-ainn
Hwy 101, Exit 18 to Mount Hanley • Six o/n units, private B&S; three suites (one Jacuzzi); one chalet (whirlpool and sauna) • TV in rooms • No pets, please
FEATURES: Wheelchair accessibility • Licensed dining room serving Austrian- and German-style meals • Private balconies • Deer farm on property
RATES: $49 (1), $59 (2), suite and chalet extra (tax incl.) • Open April 1-Oct. 31 • MC, Visa accepted • CAA; IGNS Member

Middleton
Victorian Inn B&B
Gary & Charlene Hannam, 145 Commercial Street, Box 1065, Middleton, B0S 1P0
(902) 825-6464
Restored century home, furnished with antiques • Four o/n units, one shared B&S • Cable TV in lounge • Children under 5 yrs free
FEATURES: Gardens • Outdoor swimming pool • Craft shop
RATES: $36 (1), $40-$44 (2), $4 add'l person • Continental and full-breakfast 8-9:30 • Open year-round • Visa accepted • NSRS Member

Milton
Morton House Inn
B&B ★★★
Valerie & Jay Blondahl, 147 Main
Street, Box 351, Milton, B0T 1P0
(902) 354-2908
Two minutes north of Liverpool on
Rte. 8; 1 km (0.5 mi) from Hwy
103, Exit 19 • Empire-style mansion
(c. 1864) • Six o/n units, private
B&S • Cable TV, radio and tele-
phone in lounge • No pets, please
FEATURES: Award-winning gar-
dens • Hiking • Canoeing • Marina •
Bicycles • River swimming •
Veranda overlooking Mersey River
• Internet access
*RATES: $59-$69 (1-2) (STC) • Off-
season rates Oct 16-May 15 • Full
breakfast 7:30-9 • Open year-round
• MC, Visa accepted • NSRS
Member*

Milton
Second Home
Bed & Breakfast
Sally Kaulback, 380 Main Street,
Milton, B0T 1P0
(902) 354-3573
E-mail stacyk@atcon.com
Hwy 103, Exit 19 to Rte. 8, 10 min-
utes from Liverpool • Bordered by
the Mersey River • Three o/n units,
one shared B&S • No pets, please •
Non-smoking only
*RATES: $30 (1), $35-$40 (2), $10
add'l person (STC) • Continental
breakfast • Open May 1-Nov. 1 •
Off-season by reservation • NSRS
Member*

Musquodoboit Harbour
Camelot Inn
Ms. P.M. "Charlie" Holgate,
Highway 7E, Box 31,
Musquodoboit Harbour, B0J 2L0
Tel & Fax (902) 889-2198
On Hwy 7E • Five acres of wood-
land overlooking river rapids and
salmon pool • Five o/n units, one
shared B&S, two shared S • No
pets, please • Non-smoking only
FEATURES: Lounge with fireplace
and library • River swimming
*RATES: $34-$45 (1), $52-$60 (2),
$70-$80 (3-4) • Breakfast 7:30-9 •
Open year-round • MC, Visa
accepted • NSRS Member*

Musquodoboit Harbour
Murphy's
Bed & Breakfast
Ralph & Judith Murphy, 30 Ostrea
Lake Road, RR 1, Musquodoboit
Harbour, B0J 2L0
Tel & Fax (902) 889-2779
On Ostrea Lake Rd., 200 m off Hwy
7 • Three o/n units, two shared B •
Non-smoking only
*RATES: $30 (1), $39 (2), $5 add'l
person (STC) • Open May 1-Oct. 31
• Off-season by reservation • NSRS
Member*

Musquodoboit Harbour
Seaview Fisherman's Home B&B

Mildred & Ivan Kent, Pleasant Point, RR 1, Musquodoboit Harbour, B0J 2L0
(902) 889-2561
Off Rte. 7, take Ostrea Lake-Pleasant Point Rd. to Kent Rd., 13 km (8 mi.) • Secluded house (c. 1861) on twenty-acre island (causeway) with lighthouse • Three o/n units, two shared B&S, one shared 1/2 B; one cottage • TV in lounge • No pets, please • Non-smoking only
FEATURES: Ocean view and beach area • Walking trails • Fishing boats nearby
RATES: $35 (1), $40-$45 (2), $50 (cottage), $10 add'l person • $250 (weekly, cottage) • Full breakfast 7-9 • Open April 1-Oct. 31 • Visa accepted • Off-season by reservation • NSFC; NSRS; Pantel Member

Musquodoboit Harbour
Tea & Treats Café & Inn

Jens & Renate Ziemsen, Musquodoboit Harbour, B0J 2L0
(902) 889-2880
Toll free 1-800-565-0828
Three o/n units, private B&S • Cable TV in rooms • No smoking in rooms, please
FEATURES: Licensed restaurant featuring Canadian- and German-style cuisine, recommended by *Where to Eat in Canada* • Sun deck • Playground • Outdoor aboveground swimming pool • Hiking and biking • Babysitting
RATES: $45 (1), $55-$65 (2), $10 add'l person (STC) • Continental breakfast 8-10:30 • Open May 15-Oct. 15 • AE, DC, Visa accepted • NSRS Member

Musquodoboit Harbour
Wayward Goose Inn ★★★

Judy & Randy Skaling, 343 West Petpeswick Road, Musquodoboit Harbour, B0J 2L0
Tel & Fax (902) 889-3654
Toll free 1-888-790-1777
Off Rte. 7, take road to West Petpeswick, 1.7 km (1 mi) on left
Three o/n units, private B (one whirlpool) • Cable TV/VCR in lounge • No pets, please • Non-smoking only
FEATURES: Stereo, pool table and fireplace in lounge • Fishing • Barbecue • Canoe, sailboat and row boat free for guests • Swimming • Walking and cross-country ski trails • Small boat docking and deep-water anchorage • Painting instruction available • Honeymoon packages
RATES: $49-$73 (1-2) (STC) • Full breakfast 7:30-9 • Open year-round • Oct. 15-April by reservation • MC, Visa accepted • ESTA; NSFC; NSRS Member

Neil's Harbour
Little Cove Bed & Breakfast

Reid & Norma Warren, 449 Neil's Harbour, Box 118, Neil's Harbour, B0C 1N0
(902) 336-2484
Take alternate scenic route at Neil's Harbour • Great ocean views and spectacular sunrise • Two o/n units, one shared B&S • Cable TV in living room • No smoking in rooms, please
RATES: $45 (1-2) • Full breakfast 8 • Open year-round • Visa accepted

Newburn
Country Homestead B&B
Karsa Veinotte, 126 Veinotte Road, Newburn, RR 1, Barss Corner, B0R 1A0
(902) 644-2196/2654
Hwy 103, Exit 11, Rte. 324N, 25 km (15.5 mi) • Three o/n units, one shared B&S • Cable TV and radio in living room • Cats on premises • Pets permitted, usually on leash • Designated smoking area
FEATURES: French spoken
RATES: $40 (1), $45 (2) • Full breakfast 7:30-9 • Open May 1-Oct. 31 • Off-season by reservation • NSRS Member

Newburn
Hackmatack Farm Bed & Breakfast
Heather Sanft & Janet Southwell, RR 3, Mahone Bay, B0J 2E0
(902) 644-2415
Fax (902) 644-3614
From Hwy 103, Exit 11, 24 km (15 mi) inland through the Cornwalls to Newburne, turn right on Walburne Rd. • Two o/n units, one shared B; one cottage • No smoking in rooms, please
RATES: $35 (1), $40 (2), $10 add'l person (STC) • Full breakfast 7-9 • Open May-Oct. • Off-season by reservation • Visa accepted • NSRS Member

New Germany
Oakwood Inn B&B
Rosemary & David Furlong, 5175 Highway 10, RR 2, New Germany, B0R 1E0
Tel & Fax (902) 644-1291
E-mail oakwood@ns.sympatico.ca
Hwy 103, Exit 12, 23 km (14.5 mi)

on Rte. 10 • Three o/n units, one shared B&S • Cable TV in living room • Designated smoking area
RATES: $40 (1), $50 (2), $10 add'l person • Continental breakfast 7-9 • Open year-round • Visa accepted • NSRS Member

New Glasgow
MacKay's Bed & Breakfast
Mrs. Evelyn MacKay, 44 High Street, New Glasgow, B2H 2W6
(902) 752-5889

Hwy 104, Exit 25 • Three o/n units, one shared B • Radio in rooms • Cable TV in lounge
RATES: $35 (1), $45-$50 (2), $10 add'l person • Breakfast 7:30-9 • Open June 15-Sept. 15 • Off-season by reservation • NSRS Member

New Glasgow
Wynward Inn B&B
Dorothy Leahy Walsh, 71 Stellarton Road, New Glasgow, B2H 1L7
(902) 752-4527
Hwy 106, Exit 2 to Abercrombie; Hwy 104, Exit 23 or 24 • Six o/n units, three shared B&S, one private B&S • Cable TV and radio in lounge
FEATURES: Picnic table and play area • Swimming pool
RATES: $38-$50 (1-2), $6 add'l person • Continental breakfast 5-11 • Open year-round • MC, Visa accepted

Newport Station
Wavertree Inn ★★★
Jane Reid Stevens, 5178 Highway
1, Newport Station, B0N 2B0
(902) 798-5864
On Rte. 1 between St. Croix and
Windsor • Victorian country home
furnished with antiques • Three o/n
units, one shared B • Cable TV in
lounge • Children under 5 yrs free
FEATURES: French and Dutch
spoken • Den with woodstove and
games • Library • Sun room •
Barbecue • Three acres of landscaped gardens • Vacation packages
*RATES: $40 (1), $50 (2), $8 add'l
person • Full breakfast 7:30-9:30 •
Open year-round • Visa accepted •
NSRS Member*

New Ross
Gold River Estate Bed & Breakfast
Donald McCleary, 183 Windsor
Road, RR 2, New Ross, B0J 2M0
(902) 689-2468
Hwy 103, Exit 9, 15 minutes from
Chester Basin, turn right at flashing
light towards Windsor • Private
estate with four acres of parkland •
Three o/n units, one shared B&S
(whirlpool) • Cable TV in games
room • No pets inside, please • No
smoking in rooms, please
FEATURES: Large stone patio •
Screened gazebo • Trout and salmon
rivers • Winter packages
*RATES: $55 (1), $65 (2) • Full
breakfast 7-9:30 • Open June 15-
Dec. 15 • Off-season by reservation
• MC, Visa accepted • NSRS
Member*

Nictaux Falls
Country Charm and Comfort Bed & Breakfast (c. 1890) ★★★ ½
Ilene Orr, 2305 Bloomington Road,
Nictaux Falls, Box 101, Middleton,
B0S 1P0
(902) 825-2566
Five minutes from junction of Rte. 1
and Hwy 10 near Middleton; ten
minutes from Greenwood • Restored
Queen Anne Revival-style century
home • Two o/n units, private B&S;
two suites • Cable TV and telephone
• Cot available • No pets, please •
Not suitable for children under 10
yrs • Non-smoking only
FEATURES: Views of picturesque
village and private parkland •
Evening tea and coffee • Herb and
vegetable gardens • Hiking, cycling,
tubing, nature trails, bird-watching
and cross-country skiing in season
*RATES: $55-$65 (1-2), $90-$105
(suite) (STC) • Full breakfast •
Open year-round • Reservations
preferred •*

Nictaux Falls
Country Lane Bed & Breakfast
Karen York, 8855 Highway 10,
RR 3, Middleton, B0S 1P0
(902) 825-6333
Hwy 101, Exit 18A through
Middleton to Rte. 10, 5 km (3 mi) on
right • Three o/n units, one shared S •
Clock radio in rooms • Cable TV in
sitting room • Smoking on sunporch only
FEATURES: Craft shop • Walking
trails • Barbecue • Kennels •
Evening tea served
*RATES: $35 (1), $40 (2), $8 add'l
person • Full breakfast 7:30-9 •
Open year-round*

North Brookfield
Big Oak Tree
Bed & Breakfast
Les & Emma Harlow, 293 Harlow
Road, RR 1, South Brookfield,
B0T 1X0
Tel & Fax (902) 682-2783
Hwy 103, Exit 13 to Rte. 325N, left
on Rte. 208; turn right on Rosette
Rd. at N. Brookfield and follow
signs • Restored century-old farmhouse on quiet peninsula between
two lakes • Three o/n units, one
shared S • Cable TV/VCR in sitting
room • No pets, please • Non-smoking only
FEATURES: Three-hole golf
course • Nature trails • Canoeing,
boating, fishing and swimming •
Large hardwood trees
*RATES: $35-$40 (1), $45-$60 (2),
$10 add'l person • Full breakfast 7-
9 • Open May 1-Oct. 31 • Visa
accepted • NSRS Member*

North East Margaree
Heart of Harts ★★★
Brooks Hart & Ethna Gillis, Box 21,
North East Margaree, B0E 2H0
(902) 248-2765
Fax (902) 248-2606
Minutes off Cabot Trail • 1880s
farmhouse furnished with antiques
and coloured glass collection • Five
o/n units, two shared B; four cottages • Satellite TV • Pets permitted
in cottages only • Non-smoking
only
FEATURES: Landscaped grounds,
including annuals and Heritage
Farm perennials • Salmon and trout
fishing • Cross-country skiing in
season • Dinner on request ($30 per
person)
*RATES: $40-$45 (1), $50-$70 (2),
$15 add'l person • Full breakfast
7:30-9 • Open year-round • MC,*

*Visa accepted • IGNS; NSRS
Member*

North River Bridge
Stephen's
Bed & Breakfast
Murdena & Bob Stephen, 279
Murray Road, North River Bridge
RR 4, Baddeck, B0E 1B0
Tel & Fax (902) 929-2860
Hwy 105, Exit 11, 19 km (12 mi)
north on Cabot Trail • Restored
country home, overlooking North
River • Three o/n units, two shared
B&S • Cable TV/VCR in living
room • Non-smoking only
*RATES: $50 • Full breakfast 7:30-9
• Open May 1-Oct. 31 • Off-season
by reservation • MC, Visa accepted
NSRS Member*

North Sydney
Alexandra Shebib's
Bed & Breakfast
Mrs. Alexandra Shebib, 88 Queen
Street, North Sydney, B2A 1A6
(902) 794-4876
2 km (1.5 mi) west of
Newfoundland ferry terminal • Four
o/n units, two shared B, one shared
1/2 B (sinks in rooms) • TV in
lounge • Children under 5 yrs free •
No smoking in rooms, please
*RATES: $35 (1), $45-$50 (2), $10
add'l person (STC) • Off-season
rates Oct. 15-April 15 • Full breakfast 7:30-9 • Open year-round •
Visa accepted • NSRS Member*

North Sydney
Dove House
Bed & Breakfast

Helene Reashore, 108 Queen Street, North Sydney, B2A 1A6
(902) 794-1055
Hwy 125, Exit 2 • Three o/n units, one private B, two shared B; one housekeeping suite • TV in sitting room • Non-smoking only
FEATURES: View of Sydney Harbour from large veranda and upper sun deck • Near Newfoundland ferry
RATES: $50 -$60 (1-2), $10 add'l person • Off-season rates • Full breakfast 6:30-9:30 • Open May 1-Oct. 31 • MC, Visa accepted • Off-season by reservation • NSRS Member

North Sydney
Heritage Home
Bed & Breakfast ★★★

Juana Moreland, 110 Queen Street, North Sydney, B2A 1A6
(902) 794-4815
Hwy 125, Exit 2 • Victorian home (c. 1860) with commanding view of harbour from all rooms • Four o/n units, one private B&S, two shared B&S; one housekeeping suite • Cable TV in family room
FEATURES: Furnished with antiques and local art • Library • Two minutes from Newfoundland ferry
RATES: $45 (1), $50-$70 (2), $65 (suite), $12 add'l person (STC) • Full breakfast 7-9 • Open year-round • Off-season by reservation • MC, Visa accepted • Check-out 10:30 a.m. • IGNS; TIANS Member

North Sydney
Lawlor House Inn

Sheilagh Burchell, 63 Pleasant Street, North Sydney, B2A 1L3
(902) 794-1145
Fax (902) 794-1074
Hwy 105, North Syndey exit, centre lane through lights, turn left • Beautiful historic property, furnished with antiques • Eight o/n units, private B&S • TV, telephone and fax available • Smoking outside only
FEATURES: Garden, gazebo and wrap-around veranda • Two minutes from Newfoundland ferry • Low-fat meals on request (breakfast and dinner)
RATES: $70 (1), $80 (2) • Breakfast • Open year-round • DC, MC, Visa accepted

North Sydney
Scottland Farm
Bed & Breakfast

Scott & Pamela Andrews, 2189 Shore Road, Point Edward, RR 1, North Sydney, B2A 3L7
(902) 564-0074
Hwy 125, Exit 4 or 5 to Rte. 239, 10 km (6 mi) • Working dairy farm • Two o/n units, one shared B&S • Cable TV/VCR in lounge • Children welcome • Pets welcome • No smoking in rooms, please
RATES: $38.35 (1), $44.40 (2) (tax incl.) • Breakfast 7-9 • Open May-Oct.

Nyanza
Don-El-Mar
Bed & Breakfast

Brian Plant, Nyanza, RR 3, Baddeck, B0E 1B0
(902) 295-1142/2564
Hwy 105, 17 km (10.5 mi) west off

Exit 8 • Edwardian home (c. 1904), with view of Indian Bay • Three o/n units, one shared B&S
RATES: $30 (1), $40 (2) (STC) • Full breakfast 7:30-9:30 • Open May 15-Oct.31

Oxford
Lea Side
Bed & Breakfast ★★★
Jean Wallace, 177 Water Street, Oxford, B0M 1P0
Tel & Fax (902) 447-3039
Hwy 104, Exit 6, turn north into town • Comfortable, restored turn-of-the-century home furnished with antiques and art • Three o/n units, one shared B&S, one shared 1/2 B • Cable TV in lounge • Designated smoking areas
FEATURES: Five-course, candle-light dinner on request • Evening snack • Electronic organ and stereo in lounge • Picnic tables, barbecue and play area
RATES: $40-$45 (1), $45-$50 (2), $10 add'l person (no GST) • Full breakfast • Open year-round • MC, Visa accepted • IGNS; NSRS Member

Paradise
Paradise Inn B&B
Claude & Kim Grimard, 116 Paradise Lane, Box 24, Paradise, B0S 1R0
(902) 584-3934
Website
http://www.valleyweb.com/paradiseinn
Hwy 101, Exit 19, just off Rte. 1 • Former Paradise Hotel (c. 1896) • Three o/n units, one private S, one shared S • Not suitable for children • No pets, please • Non-smoking only
FEATURES: Evening refreshments

• Outdoor seating • Lawn games
RATES: $40-$50 (1), $45-$55 (2), $10 add'l person (STC) • Full breakfast 8-9 • Open year-round • Visa accepted • IGNS; NSRS Member

Parrsboro
Gillespie House
Bed & Breakfast
Shirley Cormier, 358 Main Street, Box 464, Parrsboro, B0M 1S0
(902) 254-3196
Three o/n units, two shared B&S, one shared 1/2 B • Cable TV and telephone in lounge • Radio in rooms
RATES: $45 (2), $10 add'l person (STC) • Breakfast 7-10 • Open May-Oct. • Off-season by reservation

Parrsboro
Knowlton House
Bed & Breakfast
Keith & Joyce Knowlton, 21 Western Avenue, Parrsboro, B0M 1S0
(902) 254-2773
Three o/n units, three shared B&S • Cable TV in lounge • No pets, please • Non-smoking only
FEATURES: Bird-watching
RATES: $40 (1), $45-$50 (2), $15 add'l person (STC) • Full breakfast 7:30-8:30 • Open June 20-Sept. 15 • NSRS Member

Parrsboro
Maple Inn
Trevor & Anne McNelly, 17 Western Avenue, Box 457, Parrsboro, B0M 1S0
Tel & Fax (902) 254-3735
Historic property (c. 1893) • Eight o/n units, six private B, two shared B; one suite (Jacuzzi) • Cable TV in lounge • Radio in rooms • Pay telephone • Infants free • No pets, please • Non-smoking only
RATES: $45-$75 (1-2), $90 (suite), $10 add'l person • Full breakfast 7:30-8:30 • Open March 1-Nov. 30 • AE, MC, Visa accepted • CAA; NSRS Member

Parrsboro
Parrsboro Mansion B&B ★★★
Anita & Wolfgang Mueller, 15 Eastern Avenue, Box 579, Parrsboro, B0M 1S0
(902) 254-3339
Fax (902) 254-2585
Decorated with original European modern art • Three o/n units, one shared B&S • Cable TV and clock radio in rooms • No pets, please • Smoking on veranda only
FEATURES: Laundry facilities • Itinerary planning • Bicycles available • Afternoon coffee and sweets
RATES: $59-$64 (1), $64-$69 (2) • Full breakfast 8-10 • Open May 15-Oct. 15 • Off-season by reservation • MC, Visa accepted • NSRS Member

Parrsboro
White House
Muriel McWhinnie, Upper Main Street, Box 96, Parrsboro, B0M 1S0
(902) 254-2387
Five o/n units, one shared B&S, one shared 1/2 B • Cable TV and radio in rooms and sitting room • Children under 12 yrs free
RATES: $30 (1), $45 (2), $5 add'l person • Open July 1-Sept. 1 • Off-season by reservation

Peggy's Cove
Breakwater Inn Bed & Breakfast
Crystal Crooks, Peggy's Cove, B0J 2N0
(902) 823-2440/1755/3350
Fully renovated fisherman's home in Peggy's Cove • Three o/n units, private B&S (whirlpool) • Cable TV/VCR in rooms • No pets, please • Non-smoking only
RATES: $85 (2), $15 add'l person (STC) • Continental breakfast 8-9 • Open May-Nov. • Off-season by reservation • MC, Visa accepted

Peggy's Cove
Peggy's Cove Bed & Breakfast ★ ½
Audrey O'Leary, 19 Church Road, Peggy's Cove, B0J 2N0
(902) 823-2265
Spectacular views from large front and rear decks • Three o/n units, two shared B&S • Cable TV/VCR in lounge • Non-smoking only
RATES: $60 (2) • $350 (weekly) • Full breakfast • Open May 1-Oct. 31 • Off-season by chance or reservation • AE, MC, Visa accepted • NSRS Member

Pentz
The Old Manse Bed & Breakfast
Helen Murdock, 184 Pentz Road, RR 1, Pleasantville, B0R 1G0
(902) 688-2985
Off Rte. 331, 15 km (9 mi) south

from Bridgewater, opposite Pentz Pottery • Overlooking LaHave River • Two o/n units, one shared B • TV in games room • Non-smoking only
RATES: $45 (1-2) (STC) • Full breakfast • Open June 1-Oct. 31

Petite Riviere
Little River Bed & Breakfast

Joan C. Patterson, 5666 Route 331, Petite Riviere, B0J 2P0
(902) 688-1339
Hwy 103, Exit 15 to Italy Cross, to Rte. 331 • Three o/n units, one private B&S (Jacuzzi), one shared S • Non-smoking only
FEATURES: Large deck • Barbecue • Nature walks and bird-watching • Ocean swimming
RATES: $40 (1), $50-$65 (2), $15 add'l person • Full breakfast • Open year-round • NSRS Member

Pictou
Braeside Inn ★★★ ½

Michael & Anne Emmett, 126 Front Street, Box 1810, Pictou, B0K 1H0
(902) 485-5046
Fax (902) 485-1701
Toll free 1-800-613-7701
Hwy 104, Exit 22 to traffic circle, Pictou exit, turn right at end of Water St., left onto Front St. • Twenty o/n units, mostly private B • Cable TV and telephone in rooms • Children under 2 yrs free
FEATURES: Licensed dining rooms overlooking harbour • Summer deck dining • Casual dress code • Conference and banquet facilities • Packages available
RATES: $55-$95 (1), $55-$100 (2), $6 add'l person (STC) • Open year-round • AE, DC, MC, Visa accepted • CAA; IGNS, NSRS; TNS Member

Pictou
Consulate Inn ★★★

Floyd & Claudette Brine, 157 Water Street, Box 1642, Pictou, B0K 1H0
(902) 485-4554
Fax (902) 485-1532
Toll free 1-800-424-8283
On Pictou waterfront, fifteen minutes from PEI ferry • Registered heritage property (c. 1810) • Former American Consulate • Three o/n units, private B&S; five suites, whirlpool • Cable TV in all rooms
FEATURES: Licensed dining room overlooking harbour
RATES: $54-$115 (2) (STC) • Continental breakfast 7:30-9 • Open year-round • AE, MC, Visa accepted • CAA; IGNS; NSRS Member

Pictou
Customs House Inn

David & Douglas DesBarres, **38 Depot Street, Box 1542, Pictou, B0K 1H0**
(902) 485-4546
Brick and sandstone building (c. 1870), furnished with antiques • Nine o/n units, private B&S • Cable TV and telephone in rooms • Non-smoking rooms available
FEATURES: On Pictou waterfront with view of harbour • Licensed restaurant and lounge • Air-conditioning • Kitchenette available • Walking distance to all attractions
RATES: $69-$129 (STC) • Off-season rates • Continental breakfast • Open year-round • MC, Visa accepted •

Pictou
Jardine's Bed & Breakfast

Debbie Jardine, 202 Faulkland Street, Box 1642, Pictou, B0K 1H0
(902) 485-8580
Fax (902) 485-1532
In historic Pictou, just a five-minute walk to town centre or five-minute drive to PEI ferry • Heritage property (c. 1850) • One o/n unit (suite), private B • Cable TV and stereo in room • Cats on premises
FEATURES: Afternoon tea • Beautiful gardens
RATES: $65 (1-2) (tax incl.) • Continental breakfast 8-9 • Open July 1-Sept. 30 • Visa accepted • NSRS Member

Pictou
Linden Arms Bed & Breakfast ★★ ½

Earle & Nadine Maskell, 62 Martha Street, Pictou, B0K 1H0
(902) 485-6565
Three o/n units, one shared B&S • Cable TV and radio in rooms • Crib and cot available • Non-smoking only
RATES: $30 (1), $40 (2), $10 add'l person • Continental breakfast 7-9 • Open June 1-Sept. 30 • Off-season by reservation • NSRS Member

Pictou
Ship to Shore Inn

Wanda Arnold, 106 Front Street, Box 519, Pictou, B0K 1H0
(902) 485-9222
Former Old Pictou Iron Foundry (est. 1855), overlooking historic Pictou Harbour • Eight o/n units, three shared B; one family suite • Cable TV in lounge • Non-smoking only

FEATURES: Laundry facilities • Barbecue • Fax/photocopier available
RATES: $35 (1), $45 (2) • Continental breakfast 7:30-10 • Open year-round • AE, Visa accepted • NSRS Member

Pictou
Strathyre House Bed & Breakfast

Jean & Hugh McCrome, 2713 West River Road, Lyons Brook, Pictou, B0K 1H0
(902) 485-3495
On Rte. 376, 8 km (4 mi) from PEI ferry • Two o/n units, one shared B&S • Non-smoking only
FEATURES: Walking trails on forty-five acres
RATES: $40 (1), $50-$55 (2), $10 add'l person (STC) • Continental breakfast • Open May 24-Oct. 31 • Visa accepted

Pictou
W.H. Davies House Bed & Breakfast (c. 1855) ★★ ½

Cathy & Brian MacKinnon, 90 Front Street, Pictou, B0K 1H0
(902) 485-4864
Large Victorian home on waterfront, furnished in period style • Three o/n units, one private S, one shared S; one housekeeping suite • Cable TV in three rooms • No pets, please • Children welcome • Designated smoking area
RATES: $35-$60 (1), $40-$65 (2), $5-$10 add'l person • Continental breakfast 8-10 • Open year-round • Visa accepted • NSRS Member

Pictou
Walker Inn
(c. 1865) ★★★
Felix & Theresa Walker,
34 Coleraine Street, Pictou, B0K
1H0
(902) 485-1433
Toll free 1-800-370-5553
Registered heritage property in historic Pictou • Ten o/n units, private
B • Cable TV in rooms • No smoking in rooms, please
FEATURES: Licensed dining room
• Meeting room and library
*RATES: $60 (1), $70-$82 (2), $12
add'l person (STC) • Open year-round • Continental breakfast 7:30-
9 • AE, MC, Visa accepted • CAA;
HIAC; NSRS; UCI Member*

Pictou
Willow House Inn
(c. 1840)
Robert & Arvell Cormier,
11 Willow Street, Pictou, B0K 1H0
(902) 485-5740
Toll free 1-800-478-7789
Registered historic property in downtown area • Eight o/n units, six private B, two shared B • Cable TV in
rooms • No smoking in rooms, please
*RATES: $50-$70 (1), $55-$75 (2),
$10 add'l person • Full breakfast
7:30-9 • Open year-round • MC,
Visa accepted • CAA; NSRS
Member*

Pleasant Bay
Pleasant Bay Bed & Breakfast
Donald Bishop, Pleasant Bay,
B0E 2P0
(902) 224-2076
Three o/n units, one shared B&S •
TV and radio in rooms • Pets with
permission

FEATURES: French spoken • Gas
barbecue
*RATES: $40 (1-2) • Continental
breakfast 7:30-9 • Open year-round
• MC, Visa accepted*

Pleasant Bay
Windswept
Bed & Breakfast
Tanya Thompson, Pleasant Bay,
B0E 2P0
(902) 224-1424
Breathtaking seclusion between
ocean and mountains • Four o/n
units, one shared B&S, one shared S
• Non-smoking only
FEATURES: Whale-watching from
front porch
*RATES: $35 (1), $45 (2) (STC) •
Full breakfast 7:30-9 • Open year-round • NSRS Member*

Pleasantville
Blue Waters
Bed & Breakfast
Joyce & Don Goodspeed, 178 Pentz
Road, RR 1, Pleasantville, B0R 1G0
(902) 688-1007
Rte. 33, 15 km (9 mi) south from
Bridgewater, on LaHave River •
Newly renovated • One o/n unit (cottage), private S • Cable TV, radio
and telephone • Non-smoking only
*RATES: $65 (2), $10 add'l person •
Full breakfast • Open June 1-
Sept. 30*

Pleasantville
Harrises' Bed & Breakfast
Bob & May Harris, 1056 Mount Pleasant Road, RR 1, Pleasantville, B0R 1G0
(902) 688-2234
Hwy 103, Exit 15 to Petite Riviere, turn left to West Dublin, then left again on Mt. Pleasant Rd.; Hwy 103, Exit 12 to Rte. 331 in Bridgewater, left to West LaHave, turn right on Mt. Pleasant Rd. • Renovated 1910s house overlooking Huey Lake • Two o/n units, one shared B&S • Clock radio, fan and hair dryer in rooms • Non-smoking only
RATES: $35-$40 (1), $43-$45 (2) • Full breakfast 7-8:30 • Open May 15-Oct. 15 • Reservations preferred • NSFC; NSRS; SSTA Member

Plympton
Stagecoach Inn B&B
Alma & Frank Havenga, Highway 101, Plympton, B0W 2R0
(902) 837-4520
Registered heritage property (c. 1798) • Five o/n units, one private B, one shared B&S, one shared 1/2 B • Cable TV/ VCR in lounge
FEATURES: Library overlooking St. Mary's Bay
RATES: $29 (1), $36-$40 (2), $7 add'l person • Full breakfast 7:30-9:30 • Open June 1-Oct. 30 • Off-season by reservation • Visa accepted • NSRS Member

Pomquet
Porter's Bed and Breakfast ★★
George & Margaret Porter, 32 Pomquet Point Road, RR 7, Upper Pomquet, Antigonish,

B2G 2L4
(902) 386-2196

Hwy 104, 16 km (10 mi) east of Antigonish; from Pomquet/St. Andrew's intersection, north 3 km (2 mi) to Pomquet Point Rd. • Large farmhouse on twelve acres, surrounded by tidal waters • Four o/n units, two shared B • TV in lounge
FEATURES: Separate guest lounge
RATES: $30 (1), $40 (2) • Full breakfast at guests' convenience • Open May 1-Oct. 30 • Off-season by reservation • NSFC Member

Port Hastings
Marg's Bed & Breakfast
Margaret Laidlaw-Ashford, 1142 Highway 19, RR 1, Port Hastings, B0E 2T0
(902) 625-2401
6.5 km (4 mi) north of Causeway • Two o/n units, one shared B&S • TV/VCR in living room • Crib available • No smoking in rooms, please
RATES: $40 (1), $48 (2) • Full breakfast 7:30-9 • Open May 15-Oct. 15 • Visa accepted • NSRS Member

Port Clyde
MacLaren Inn B&B
Mrs. Eva Haeghaert, Port Clyde, Shelburne, B0W 2S0
(902) 637-3296
Hwy 103, Exit 28 • Victorian house on the waterfront with great views • Three o/n units, one shared B
RATES: $35 (1), $45 (2) (STC) • Full breakfast • Open June 1-Oct. 31

Port Hawkesbury
Harbourview Bed & Breakfast

Marlene Pase, 209 Granville Street, Box 378, Port Hawkesbury, B0E 2V0
(902) 625-3224
5 km (3 mi) from Causeway on Rte. 4 to Port Hawkesbury, take Granville St. exit • Ferry captain James Embree House (c. 1880) • Restored provincial heritage property on the waterfront • Three o/n units, one private B, one shared B&S • Not suitable for children • No pets, please • Non-smoking only
FEATURES: Evening tea and conversation in parlour • Off-street parking
RATES: $48-$53 (2) (STC) • Full breakfast at guests' convenience • Open June 1-Sept. 15 • Off-season by reservation • Visa accepted • NSRS Member

Port Hood
E.O.'s Hillcrest Inn

Mary Claire & Charles MacDonald, Box 149, Port Hood, B0E 2W0
(902) 787-3214
Excellent view of harbour and beach • Eleven o/n units, private B&S • Cable TV and clock radio in rooms • Designated smoking area
FEATURES: Partial wheelchair accessibility • Licensed dining room and lounge • Boat tours available
RATES: $60-$100 (1-2), $8 add'l person • Open year-round • MC, Visa accepted

Port Hood
Haus Treuburg Country Inn & Cottages ★★★ ½

Georg Kargoll, Central Avenue, Box 92, Port Hood, B0E 2W0
(902) 787-2116
Fax (902) 787-3216
Historic house with private beach • Two o/n units, private B; one suite; three cottages • Cable TV, radio and telephone in rooms and lounge • No pets, please • No smoking in rooms, please
FEATURES: Licensed gourmet dining room with French-Italian cuisine and German-style breakfast • Fishing tours available • Bicycles and lawn games for rent • Gift shop • Barbecue • Private sandy beach
RATES: $70-$90 (1-2), $95 (cottage), $10 add'l person (STC) • $550 (weekly, cottage) • Open May 15-Oct. 31 • MC, Visa accepted

Port Hood
Sunset Bed & Breakfast

Teresa Marie van Zutphen, 8518 Highway 19, Box 130, Port Hood, B0E 2W0
(902) 787-3120
43 km (27 1/2 mi) from Canso Causeway • Breathtaking view of Port Hood Island and St. George's Bay; magnificent sunsets • Four o/n units, two shared B&S • TV in solarium • Children under 10 yrs free • Non-smoking only
FEATURES: Tennis court • Sandy beach nearby • Cabot Trail day trips
RATES: $40 (1), $50 (2), $10 add'l person • Full breakfast 7-9 • Open year-round • NSRS Member

Port Howe
Apple Inn B&B
Edward & Linda Benoit,
7675 Route 6 (Sunrise Trail), Box
28, Port Howe, B0K 1K0
(902) 243-2814
Off-season (508) 627-5493
Restored historic farmhouse (c.
1885) • Three o/n units, two shared
B&S, one shared B; one family
suite • Cable TV/VCR in lounge •
No pets, please • Children welcome
• Non-smoking only
FEATURES: Overlooks forty-five
scenic acres and saltwater inlet •
Prize-winning breads and muffins at
breakfast • Library with stereo •
Picnic table, barbecue and play area
• Nightly films (over three hundred
to choose from, including many
children's favourites)
*RATES: $40 (1), $50 (2), $70
(suite) • Full breakfast 7:30-9 •
Open June 26-Aug. 29 • NSRS
Member*

Port Howe
Eagle Roost B&B
Ed & Diane Hanlon, 8903 Highway
321, Port Howe, Rockley, B0K 1K0
(902) 447-3359
42 km (26 mi) from New Brunswick
border: Rte. 6E to Rte. 321, 2 km
(1.2 mi) south • Thirty-five-acre
property on tidal river • Two o/n
units, two shared B&S • Cot available • Pets permitted • Designated
smoking area
FEATURES: Evening snack •
Laundry facilities • Lawns and gardens • Fish pond • Walking trails •
Hunting and fishing packages in
season
*RATES: $35 (1), $45 (2), $10 add'l
person (STC) • Full breakfast •
Open May 15-Oct. 15 • Visa accepted • NSRS Member*

Port Mouton
Apple Pie
Bed & Breakfast
John & Judy Adams, Box 32,
Central Port Mouton, B0T 1T0
Tel & Fax (902) 683-2217
**Toll free 1-888-72APPLE (722-
7753)**
Hwy 103, Exit 21 • Victorian-style
home overlooking ocean • Three o/n
units, one shared B&S • Cable TV
in lounge • Non-smoking only•
*RATES: $40 (1), $50 (2), $10 add'l
person • Full breakfast • Open year-
round • MC, Visa accepted • NSRS
Member*

Port Royal
Auberge Sieur de Monts
Inne
Leona & Stefan Straka, Port Royal,
Box 2055, RR 2, Granville Ferry,
B0S 1K0
(902) 532-5852
Two-hundred-year-old inn, coach-
house and mill • Four o/n units, private and shared B&S; one housekeeping suite • Children under 8 yrs
free
FEATURES: Kitchen facilities •
*RATES: $50-$55 (2), $10 add'l
person (STC) • Breakfast on request
• Open May-Oct. • MC, Visa accepted • NSRS Member*

Port Wade
Captain Snow's House
Bed & Breakfast
Len & Bev Sydenham, 1759
Granville Road, RR 2, Granville
Ferry, B0S 1K0
(902) 532-5588
Twenty-minute drive along north
side of basin, past Port Royal •
Unique century-old home built by
Capt. John Snow • Three o/n units,

one shared B&S • Cable TV/VCR in parlour • Cot available • Children under 6 yrs free • Non-smoking only
FEATURES: Lovely gardens with goldfish pond • Walking trail to sea • Craft and antique shop on premises
RATES: $35 (1), $45 (2), $10 add'l person • Full breakfast 7:30-9:30 • Open year-round • NSRS Member

Port Williams
Carwarden Bed & Breakfast ★★★
M. McMahon, 640 Church Street, RR 1, Port Williams, B0P 1T0
(902) 678-7827
Fax (902) 678-0029
Toll free 1-888-763-3320
Hwy 101, Exit 11 to Rte. 1, turn right on Rte. 358, left 4.4 km (2.6 mi) to Church St. • Registered heritage property with sweeping view of dykelands from veranda • Three o/n units, one private B, one shared B&S • No pets, please • Non-smoking only
FEATURES: Furnished with antiques • Drawing room for guest use • Evening tea • Shady lawns
RATES: $45-$60 (1-2), $15 add'l person • Full breakfast 8-9 • Open May 1-Oct. 31 • Visa accepted • IGNS; NSFC; NSRS; TIANS Member

Port Williams
Country Squire Bed and Breakfast
J. Earl & Rose Doyle, 990 Main Street, Port Williams, B0P 1T0
(902) 542-9125
Fax (902) 542-1522
Rte. 358 • Victorian home furnished with antiques • Four o/n units, two shared B • TV in living room
FEATURES: Piano in living room • Library • Swimming pool • Sauna
RATES: $40 (1), $45 (2), $15 add'l person • Full breakfast 7-9 • Open

May 27-Nov. 30 • Visa accepted • NSRS Member

Port Williams
Newcomb House Bed & Breakfast (c. 1881)
John Newcombe, 997 Main Street, Highway 341, Upper Dyke, B0P 1J0
(902) 678-7486
Hwy 101, Exit 11 to Rte. 358N, 5 km (3 mi) through Port Williams, turn left at Jawbone Corner (Rte. 341), 4.5 km (2 mi) on the right • Working farm with Georgian-style home overlooking Canard (Wellington) dykeland • Three o/n units, one shared B&S • Cable TV/VCR in living room • Non-smoking only
RATES: $40-$45 (1), $45-$55 (2) (STC) • Full breakfast at guests' convenience • Open May 1-Oct. 31 • Off-season by reservation • Visa accepted • NSFC; NSRS Member

Port Williams
Old Rectory Bed and Breakfast ★★★
Ron & Carol Buckley, 1519 Highway 358, RR 1, Port Williams, B0P 1T0
(902) 542-1815
Fax (902) 542-2346
E-mail orectory@fox.nstn.ca
Hwy 101, Exit 11 to Rte. 1, to Rte. 358, 3 km (2 mi) beyond Port Williams • Recently renovated century-old home • Three o/n units, one private B, one shared B&S • Cable TV in living room • Cot available • No pets, please • Non-smoking only
FEATURES: Evening tea • Gardens and orchard • U-Pick and cider-making in season • Geological field trips available
RATES: $45-$60 (1-2), $15 add'l person • $5 discount for second night • Full breakfast 7:30-9 • Open May 1-Oct. 31 • Off-season by reservation • ETTA; IGNS; NSFC; NSRS Member

Port Williams

Planters' (Barracks) Country Inn ★★★★

Allen & Jennie Sheito, 1464-1468 Starr's Point Road, Port Williams, B0P 1T0

(902) 542-7879

Fax (902) 542-4442

Toll free 1-800-661-7879

Hwy 101, Exit 11, Rte. 358, turn right at flashing lights in Port Williams • Oldest building in Nova Scotia to be restored as a country inn • Nine o/n units, private B&S; two suites • Cable TV in parlour • No pets, please • Non-smoking only *FEATURES:* French spoken • Licensed • Acacia Croft Tearoom serves lunch and afternoon tea • Heritage gardens and patios • Bicycles available • Tennis court *RATES: $59-$89 (1), $69-$109 (2) • Breakfast 7:30-9 • Open May 1-Oct. 31 • AE, MC, Visa accepted • Cancellation policy • CAA; NSRS; UCI Member*

Port Williams

Valley Rose Bed & Breakfast

Jim & Elaine Spencer, 1330 Belcher Street, RR1, Port Williams, B0P 1T0

(902) 542-0400

Fax (902) 542-0013

Hwy 101, Exit 11, follow signs to Port Williams, take first street on left over bridge, 1 km (.6 mi) on right • Magnificent home (c. 1893) on two acres of gardens, with terraced lawns and mature trees • Three o/n units, one private S, one shared B&S • Cable TV/VCR in living room • Cot, crib and highchair available • Pets on premises • No pets, please • Non-smoking only *FEATURES:* Screened Victorian

porch • Babysitting *RATES: $52-$64 (1), $62-$74 (2), $10 add'l person • Full breakfast 8-9 • Open year-round • MC, Visa accepted • NSRS Member*

Portapique

Teacups & Flowers Bed & Breakfast

Cliff & Emily Lane, Portapique, RR 1, Bass River, B0M 1B0

(902) 668-2235

Hwy 104, Exit 11, 13.5 km (8.5 mi) • Renovated farmhouse (c. 1847) • Three o/n units, one shared B&S • Clock radio in rooms • Pets on premises • Non-smoking only *FEATURES:* Evening snack • Reading room • Close to beaches *RATES: $30 (1), $40 (2) (STC) • $180-$240 (weekly) • Full breakfast 7:30-9:30 • Open May 1-Oct.31 • NSRS Member*

Prospect

Prospect Bed & Breakfast ★★★

Helena Prsala, 1758 Prospect Bay Road, Prospect, B3T 2B3

Tel & Fax (902) 852-4493

Toll free 1-800-SALTSEA (725-8732)

Hwy 333, Prospect exit (halfway between Halifax and Peggy's Cove) • Restored historic convent • Five o/n units, private B&S • Cable TV (with movie channel) in rooms • Children under 10 yrs free • Non-smoking only *FEATURES:* Ocean swimming • Sandy beach • Canoe • Walking trail • Eco-adventure tour packages *RATES: From $60 (1-2), $15 add'l person (STC) • Continental break-*

fast • *Open year-round • MC, Visa
accepted • IGNS; NSRS Member*

Pubnico
Chez Marie
Bed and Breakfast
Marie d'Entremont, Box 66, West
Pubnico, B0W 3S0
Tel & Fax (902) 762-2107
Rte. 335, 4 km (2.5 mi) off Rte. 3;
5.5 km (3.5 mi) off Hwy 103, Exit
31 • Quiet rural setting, half-hour
drive from Yarmouth • Three o/n
units, one shared B&S • Children
under 8 yrs free • Non-smoking
only
FEATURES: French spoken •
Barbecue • Bicycle shelter • Large
lawn • View of harbour
*RATES: $35 (1), $40 (2), $10 add'l
person • Continental breakfast •
Open May 15-Oct. 15 • Off-season
by reservation • MC, Visa accepted
• NSRS Member*

Pubnico
Yesteryear's
Bed & Breakfast ★★★
Richard & Deborah Donaldson,
Box 16, Pubnico, B0W 2W0
Tel & Fax (902) 762-2969
E-mail yesteryr@atcon.com

Hwy 103, Exit
31 to intersec-
tion of Rte. 335
and Rte. 3 •
Majestic
Victorian home
with antique
furnishings •
Three o/n units,
one private B, one shared S • Clock
radio and telephone in rooms •
Cable TV in sitting room • Non-
smoking only
FEATURES: Owner is captain of a
lobster fishing vessel • Bicycle shel-

ter • Walking trails
*RATES: $35 (1), $45 (2), $10 add'l
person • Continental breakfast 7-9 •
Open year-round • MC, Visa
accepted • NSRS Member*

Pugwash
Blue Heron Inn
B&B ★★★
David & Anne Gouldson, 10340
Durham Street, Box 405, Pugwash,
B0K 1L0
Tel & Fax (902) 243-2900
Four o/n units, three private B, one
shared 1/2 B; one housekeeping
suite • Cable TV/VCR in lounge •
Children under 10 yrs free
FEATURES: Licensed Italian
restaurant • Piano in lounge •
Bilingual • Picnic table
*RATES: $45-$60 (2), $8 add'l per-
son (STC) • Continental breakfast •
Open year-round • Visa accepted •
Cancellation policy • NSRS Member*

Pugwash
Maple Leaf Inn B&B
Sheila Ley, 10363 Durham Street,
Box 245, Pugwash, B0K 1L0
Tel & Fax (902) 243-2560
Directly off Rte. 6 (Sunrise Trail) •
Stately turn-of-the-century home
nestled on three acres in the heart of
Pugwash • Two o/n units, one
shared B&S; one family suite • TV
and radio in lounge • Cot available •
No pets, please • Non-smoking only
FEATURES: Close to beaches and
golf
*RATES: $45 (1), $50 (2), $60
(suite), $10 add'l person • Full
breakfast 8 • Open May 1-Oct. 31 •
Visa accepted • NSRS Member*

Queensland
Surfside Inn B&B ★★★ ½
Michelle & Bill Batcules, 9609 St. Margaret's Bay Road, RR 2, Hubbards, B0J 1T0
(902) 857-2417
Fax (902) 857-2107
Toll free 1-800-373-2417
Hwy 103, Exit 5 or 6 to Rte. 3, access from Queensland beach • Late 1800s sea captain's home with magnificent views • Four o/n units, private B (three whirlpools) • Cable TV/VCR, radio and hairdryer in rooms • Non-smoking only
FEATURES: Swimming pool • Craft and antique shop
RATES: $67-$100 (1), $72-$105 (2), $15 add'l person • Continental breakfast 8-9:30 • Open year-round • AE, Dis, MC, Visa accepted • Cancellation policy • CAA; IGNS; NSRS Member

Queensport
Queensport House Bed & Breakfast
Joyce Conrad, RR 2, Guysborough, B0H 1N0
(902) 358-2402
Off-season (902) 454-5020
Rte. 16 • Quiet setting with view of Chedabucto Bay • Three o/n units, private B&S • No pets, please • Non-smoking only
RATES: $45 (1), $55 (2), $10 add'l person • Full breakfast 7:30-9:30 • Open July 1-Labour Day (weekends only until Oct. 31) • Visa accepted

Reserve Mines
Becky's Bed & Breakfast
Lou & Rebecca Oliver, 208 Main Street, Reserve Mines, B0A 1V0
(902) 849-2974

Located between Sydney and Glace Bay • Hwy 105 to Rte. 4, 3 km (1.8 mi) from Sydney Airport, turn left on Main St., across from Reserve Mines Fire Hall • Three o/n units, one shared B&S, one shared B • Clock radio in rooms • Cable TV in two living rooms • No smoking in rooms, please
FEATURES: Kitchen facilities • Apartment available for extended stay
RATES: $40 (1) $50 (2), $20 add'l person (STC) • Full breakfast 7:30-9:30 • Open year-round • NSRS Member

Reserve Mines
MacGillivray House Bed & Breakfast
Maureen Morrissey, 2230 Sydney Road, Box 8, Reserve Mines, B0A 1V0
(902) 849-8056
Hwy 125, Rte. 4, 8 km (5 mi) towards Glace Bay • Three o/n units, private B or B&S • Cable TV in one room • Not suitable for children • No pets, please • Smoking outside only
RATES: $45-$55 (1-2) • Full breakfast 7-10 • Open May 15-Oct. 15 • Visa accepted • NSRS Member

River Bourgeois
Grandma's House Bed & Breakfast
Rose & Tom Scott, RR 1, River Bourgeois, B0E 2X0
(902) 535-2512
Fax (902) 535-3717
Hwy 104, Exit 47 to Rte. 4, turn right, 1 km (0.6 mi) • Victorian house with antique furnishings • Three o/n units, one shared S • Children over 12 yrs welcome • No

pets, please • No smoking in rooms, please
FEATURES: Dining room over-looking river • Gift and antique shop on premises
RATES: $35 (1), $45 (2) (STC) • Full breakfast 7-9 • Open May 15-Oct. 15 • MC, Visa accepted • NSRS Member

River Denys
Fernhaven Country Inn
Ferne MacLennan, Box 2, River Denys, B0E 2Y0
Tel & Fax (902) 756-3332
Hwy 105, Exit 3, 10 km (6 mi) towards River Denys • Fully restored heritage property • Three o/n units, private B&S • Clock radio in rooms • Cable TV and telephone in living room • Non-smoking rooms available
FEATURES: Dinner and evening snack served • Fax available • Weekend packages
RATES: $85 (1-2) • Full breakfast • Open year-round • Visa accepted

River Denys
Fiddler's Farm
Bed & Breakfast
Marilyn Ellis, RR 1, River Denys, B0E 2Y0
Tel & Fax (902) 756-2163
Hwy 105, Exit 3, 3.5 km (2 mi) towards River Denys • Three o/n units, one private S, one shared B&S • Clock radio in rooms • Cable TV in living room
FEATURES: Boarding for horses • Fax and meeting room available • Evening snack
RATES: $35 (1), $40-$45 (2) • Full breakfast • Open year-round • Visa accepted

River John
Mountain Farm
Bed & Breakfast ★★ ½
John & Margaret Minney, RR 2, River John, B0K 1N0
(902) 351-2821
Rte. 6 or 326 • Working farm with abundant wildlife • Three o/n units, one shared B&S • TV/VCR in living room • No pets, please • Non-smoking only
FEATURES: Evening snack
RATES: $35 (1), $50 (2), $10-$15 (children under 12 yrs) • Full breakfast at guests' convenience • Open May 1-Oct. 15 • NSFC; NSRS Member

Riverport
(near Lunenburg)
Barrett's
Bed & Breakfast ★★★
Bill & Sheila Barrett, 723 Feltzen South, Rose Bay, Riverport, B0J 2W0
Tel & Fax (902) 766-4655
Fifteen minutes from Lunenburg, next to Ovens Park • Quiet ocean-front former captain's house with view of Lunenburg town and harbour • Four o/n units, two shared B&S
FEATURES: Hooking and braiding artisans • Furnished with antiques • Reading room • Fishing • Bicycles • Ocean swimming • Hiking • Boats
RATES: $45 (1), $55 (2) • Full breakfast • Open year-round • MC, Visa accepted • NSRS Member

Salmon River Bridge
Salmon River House Country Inn
Adrien & Norma Blanchette, 9931 Highway 7, Salmon River Bridge, B0J 1P0
(902) 889-3353
Fax (902) 889-3653
Toll free 1-800-565-3353
Historic inn (c. 1855) • Six o/n units, private B&S; one family suite; one honeymoon suite (Jacuzzi) • Cable TV in four rooms and lounge • No pets, please • Non-smoking only
FEATURES: Wheelchair accessibility • Licensed dining room • Sun deck overlooking water • Lawn games • Bicycles • Saltwater fishing, boating and swimming • Hiking • Thirty-five minutes from Halifax Airport
RATES: $52.50-$65 (1), $68.25-$99.75 (2), $12.50 add'l person (STC) • Off-season rates Jan-April • Breakfast 7:30-9 • Open year-round • Off-season by reservation • DC, MC, Visa accepted • CAA; IGNS; NSRS; UCI Member

Sandy Cove
Olde (1890) Village Inn ★★★ ½
Dixie & Bob Van, Sandy Cove, Digby Neck, B0V 1E0
(902) 834-2202
Fax (902) 834-2927
Toll free 1-800-834-2206
Rte. 217W • Restored buildings (c. 1830-1890) with ocean view • Sixteen o/n units, private B&S; three cottages • Cable TV and pay telephone in lounges • No pets, please • Non-smoking only
FEATURES: French spoken • Licensed dining room, by reservation • Wicker sunroom • Lawn

games and chip-and-putt • Lake and ocean beach swimming • Hiking trails • Craft and art shop • Vacation packages
RATES: $60-$95 (2), $70-$100 (cottage), $10 add'l person • Off-season rates • Breakfast 8-9:30 • Open May 15-Oct. 15 • DC, Dis, MC, Visa accepted • Cancellation policy • CAA; NSRS; UCI Member

Sandy Cove
Sandy Cove Bed & Breakfast
Joyce & Louis Morin, 6363 Route. 217, Sandy Cove, B0V 1E0
(902) 834-2031
Three o/n units, two shared B&S • Cable TV in lounge • Children under 3 yrs free
FEATURES: French spoken • Kitchen facilities • Separate entrance for guests • Lake and ocean swimming • Whale-watching arranged
RATES: $33 (1), $45 (2), $8 add'l person, $5 children (STC) • Weekly rates • Full breakfast 8-10 • Open June 1-Oct. 1 • Visa accepted

Saulnierville
Bayshore Bed and Breakfast
Ted & Connie Murphy, Box 176, Saulnierville, B0W 2Z0
(902) 769-3671
On Rte. 1 at Saulnierville-Comeauville line • Farmhouse (c. 1830) with bay frontage • Three o/n units, one shared B&S; one suite • Cable TV in lounge • Cats on premises • Designated smoking area
RATES: $30 (1), $35-$40 (2), $50 (suite) • Full breakfast • Open year-round • NSRS Member

Seabright
The Mermaid's Garden Bed & Breakfast ★★★
Sara Ellis, 139 McDonald Point Road, Box 695, RR 1, Seabright, B0J 3J0
(902) 823-2227
E-mail elliss@is.dal.ca
Hwy 103, Exit 5 to Rte. 333, 9 km (5.5 mi) • Century-old home in quiet setting • Three o/n units, one shared B • Cable TV/VCR and stereo in lounge • Pets with permission • Non-smoking only
FEATURES: Library • Croquet • Puffin- and whale-watching
RATES: $55-$60 (1-2) (STC) • Full breakfast • Open June-Oct. • Off-season by reservation • IGNS; NSRS Member

Selma
The Cobequid Inn B&B ★★ ½
Les & Elaine Wright, RR 1, Maitland, B0N 1T0
(902) 261-2841
From Halifax: Hwy 102, Exit 10, Rte. 215W to Selma; from Truro: Exit 14 to Rte. 236 to Rte. 215W • Three o/n units, two shared B • Cable TV in lounge
FEATURES: Licensed dining room • Board games • Lawn chess and horseshoe pit • Outdoor swimming pool • Bicycles
RATES: $45-$55 (1-2), $20 add'l person, $10 children under 12 yrs (STC) • Full breakfast • Open May-Oct. • MC, Visa accepted • NSRS Member

Selma
Terranita Bed & Breakfast
Terry & Anita Duckenfield, 8098 Highway 215, RR 1, Maitland, B0N 1T0
Tel & Fax (902) 261-2102
From Truro: Hwy 102, Exit 14 to Rte. 236, then Rte. 215W to Selma; from Windsor: Hwy 101, Exit 5 to Rte. 14, then Rte. 215E to Selma • Restored country heritage home (c. 1825) on five-acre property overlooking Cobequid Bay • Two o/n units, one shared S • No pets, please • Non-smoking only
RATES: $40 (1), $50-$55 (2) • Full breakfast 7:30-9 • Open May 1-Oct. 31 • Visa accepted • NSRS Member

Sheet Harbour
Black Duck Seaside Inn B&B
Al & Gloria Horne, 25245 Highway 7, Port Dufferin.
Mailing address Box 26, Sheet Harbour, B0J 3B0
Tel & Fax (902) 885-2813

Large home with panoramic coastal views • One o/n unit, private B (whirlpool); two suites • Cable TV in lounge • Non-smoking only
FEATURES: Evening meal on request • Observatory • Bird-watching • Dock • Small boat rental • Day trips planned
RATES: $75 (1-2), $15 add'l person • Full breakfast 8-9:30 • Open year-round • Off-season by reservation • Visa accepted • ESTA; NSRS Member

Sheet Harbour
Elderberry Lane B&B
Gloria V. Walsh-Horne, 21 Behie Road, Box 26, Sheet Harbour, B0J 3B0
Tel & Fax (902) 885-2813
Three o/n units, one private B (whirlpool), one shared B&S; one cottage • Cable TV in one room and lounge • Smoking on deck only
RATES: $40 (1), $50-$55 (2), $60 (cottage), $10 add'l person • Full breakfast 8-9:30 • Open May 1-Oct. 31 • Off-season by reservation • Visa accepted • IGNS Member

Shelburne
Bear's Den
Elizabeth J. Atkinson, Box 883, Shelburne, B0T 1W0 .
(902) 875-3234
Corner of Water and Glasgow • Three o/n units, one shared B • Cable TV in one room and lounge • Pets welcome
FEATURES: Upstairs patio • Bicycle shed • Collector bears available
RATES: $35 (1), $45 (2) • Full breakfast 7:30-9:30 • Open year-round • Visa accepted

Shelburne
Cooper's Inn & Restaurant ★★★
Allan & Joan Redmond, 36 Dock Street, Box 959, Shelburne, B0T 1W0
(902) 875-4656
Toll free 1-800-688-2011
Award-winning heritage property (c. 1785) on historic Dock St. • Six o/n units; one suite • Non-smoking only
FEATURES: Fine dining in relaxed atmosphere, reservations recommended • Selected as a "Frommer's

Favourite" and recommended by *Where to Eat in Canada*, AAA/CAA and 3 Diamond
RATES: $65-$130 (1-2) (STC) • Breakfast • Open April-Oct. 6 • AE, DC, MC, Visa accepted • CAA; IGNS; NSRS; UCI Member

Shelburne
Harbour House Bed & Breakfast
Wolfgang Schricker, 187 Water Street, Box 362, Shelburne, B0T 1W0
Tel & Fax (902) 875-2074
E-mail musiced@atcon.com
Hwy 103, Exit 26 to Water St.; corner of Water & Harbourview • Three o/n units, one shared B&S • Cot available • Children under 12 yrs free • Non-smoking only
FEATURES: German spoken • Piano • Air-conditioning
RATES: $45 (1), $55 (2), $10 add'l person (STC) • Off-season rates • Full breakfast • Open June 15-July 10 and Oct. 1-15 • Visa accepted • NSRS Member

Shelburne
Toddle Inn Dining Room Bed & Breakfast
Tony Caruso, 163 Water Street, Box 837, Shelburne, B0T 1W0
(902) 875-3229
Hwy 103, Exit 25 or 26 • Four o/n units, one private B&S, one shared B&S • Children under 6 yrs free • Non-smoking only
FEATURES: Dining room open to the public from 7:30 am to closing
RATES: $50-$60 (1-2), $10 add'l person (STC) • Full breakfast • Open April 1-Dec. 24 • AE, Dis, MC, Visa accepted • NSRS Member

Sherbrooke
Days-a-go Bed & Breakfast
Randy & Linda Peck, 15 Cameron Road, Box 71, Sherbrooke, B0J 3C0
(902) 522-2983
Rte. 7, west side • Recently renovated older home (c. 1920), furnished with antiques • Three o/n units, one shared B&S • Not suitable for small children • No pets, please • Non-smoking only
FEATURES: Quiet rural setting on hobby farm means fresh eggs for breakfast • Enclosed sunporch with view of Sherbrooke Village and St. Mary's River • Professional guide available for hunting and fishing
RATES: $45 (1), $50-$55 (2), $10 add'l person (STC) • Full breakfast 7:30-9:30 • Open year-round • Visa accepted • NSRS Member

Sherbrooke
St. Mary's River Lodge ★★★
Fred & Ursula Schupbach, Box 39, Sherbrooke, B0J 3C0
(902) 522-2177
Fax (902) 522-2515
Adjacent to historic Sherbrooke Village and beautiful public picnic area at St. Mary's River • Six o/n units, private B&S • Cable TV/VCR in rooms
FEATURES: Licensed dining room serves breakfast, lunch and dinner with fine Swiss specialties • Take-out meals and patio dining
RATES: $42-$72 (1), $48-$78 (2), $6 add'l person (STC) • Open year-round • MC, Visa accepted • NSRS Member

Sherbrooke
Vi's Bed & Breakfast
Violet Fraser, 8041 Main Street, Box 164, Sherbrooke, B0J 3C0
(902) 522-2042
In town centre • Two o/n units, one shared B&S • Cable TV in living room • Smoking outside only
RATES: $40 (1), $45 (2) • Full breakfast 7:30-9:30 • Open June 1-Oct. 1

Shubenacadie
White House Guest Home
Robert & Rosalita MacMillan, Shubenacadie, B0N 2H0
(902) 758-3784
Rte. 224, fifteen minutes from airport • One o/n unit, private B • Cable TV • Not suitable for children
RATES: $40 (2) (STC) • Breakfast on request $3.50 • Open June 1-Sept. 30 • Off-season by reservation • NSRS Member

Smith's Cove
Harbourview Inn ★★★
Mona & Philip Webb, Box 39,
Smith's Cove, B0S 1S0
(902) 245-5686
Fax (902) 245-4828
5 km (3 mi) east of Digby, Exit 24
or 25 off Hwy 101 • Turn-of-the-
century country inn and annex •
Seven o/n units, private B&S; two
suites • Cable TV in suites and
lounge • No pets, please • Non-
smoking rooms available
FEATURES: Wheelchair accessibility • Laundromat • Dining room •
Playground • Tennis court • Outdoor
swimming pool • Tidal beach •
Vacation packages
*RATES: $60-$90 (1-2), $79-$149
(suite) • Breakfast 7:30-9:30 • Open
June-Oct. 15 • MC, Visa accepted •
UCI; NSRS Member*

South Haven
An Seanne Mhanse B&B
Laverne Drinnan, South Haven,
RR 2, Baddeck, B0E 1B0
(902) 295-2538
Hwy 105, 12 km (7.5 mi) east of
Baddeck, 2 km (1.5 mi) west of Exit
11 • Built in 1906 • Three o/n units,
one shared B • Non-smoking only
FEATURES: Bicycle storage
*RATES: $40-$55 (1-2), $15 add'l
person (STC) • Family rates • Full
breakfast • Open April-Nov. • MC,
Visa available • NSRS Member*

Spencer's Island
Spencer's Island Bed & Breakfast
Margaret Griebel, RR 3, Parrsboro,
B0M 1S0
(902) 392-2721
Rte. 209 to Spencer's Island, turn

off at Spencer's Beach sign • Three
o/n units, two shared B&S • TV and
radio in library • Non-smoking only
*RATES: $30 (1), $40 (2) (tax incl.)
• Full breakfast 7-10 • Open June-
Sept.*

Springfield
Frog Pond Bed & Breakfast
Larry Richardson, 717 Highway 10,
Springfield, B0R 1H0
(902) 547-2359
Hwy 101, Exit 18, 40 km (24 mi) on
Rte. 10 • Two o/n units, one shared
B&S • Cot available • No smoking
in rooms, please
FEATURES: Garden with lawn and
frog pond • Lake swimming •
Walking trails • Cross-country ski-
ing and skating in season
*RATES: $35 (1), $40 (2), $10 add'l
person • Full breakfast 7-9 • Open
year-round • NSRS member*

St. Andrew's
Peggy's Bed & Breakfast
Margaret Halloran, RR 3,
St. Andrew's, B0H 1X0
(902) 863-3805
Hwy 104, Exit 35 to Rte. 316S, 6.5
km (4 mi) • Three o/n units, two
shared B&S • TV in living room •
No smoking in rooms, please
*RATES: $30 (1), $40 (2) • Full
breakfast at guests' convenience •
Open May 1-Oct. 31*

St. Ann's
McGovern's of Hummingbird Hill Bed & Breakfast
Jean & Jim McGovern, St. Ann's, RR 4, Baddeck, B0E 1B0
(902) 929-2880
Hwy 105, Exit 11, 9 km (5.5 mi) north on Cabot Trail • Overlooking St. Ann's Harbour and North River • Two o/n units, one shared B&S • TV/VCR in living room
FEATURES: French spoken • Movies available
RATES: $40 (1), $50 (2) • Full breakfast 8 • Open year-round • NSRS Member

St. George's Channel
Marble View Bed & Breakfast
Anne Martin, The Points, RR 2, West Bay, B0E 3K0
(902) 345-2281/227-7147
24 km (15 mi) from St. Peter's on the Bras d'Or Trail in Richmond County • Secluded setting on the shores of the Bras d'Or Lake • Two o/n units, one shared S
RATES: $35 (1), $45 (2) (STC) • Open May 15-Oct.15 • MC, Visa accepted

St. Joseph du Moine
Conti's Bed & Breakfast
Arthur & Jacqueline Conti, 309 Bazile Road, Box 43, St. Joseph du Moine, B0E 3A0
(902) 224-2697
Three o/n units, one shared S • TV in living room • Non-smoking only
FEATURES: Panoramic views of ocean, islands, lakes and mountains • Spectaular sunsets • French spoken • Arrangements for whale-watching, deep-sea fishing

RATES: $32 (1), $40 (2), $10-$15 add'l person • Full breakfast 8 • Open May 15-Oct. 15 • MC, Visa accepted

St. Joseph du Moine
Pilot Whale Bed & Breakfast
Cheryl Power, Bazile Road, St. Joseph du Moine, B0E 3A0
(902) 224-2592
Fax (902) 224-1540
Rte. 19, on Cabot Trail • New log home • Four o/n units, one private B, one shared B&S • TV in living room • No pets, please • Non-smoking only
FEATURES: Double fireplace • Mountain views
RATES: $50-$65 (1), $55-$75 (2) • Off-season rates • Full breakfast • Open May 15-Oct. 31 • MC, Visa accepted • NSRS Member

Stellarton
MacDonalds Bed & Breakfast
James & Rena MacDonald, 292 South Ford Street, Box 831, Stellarton, B0K 1S0
(902) 752-7751
Hwy 104, Exit 24, ten minutes from New Glasgow • Three o/n units, one shared B
RATES: $35 (1), $40 (2), $10 add'l person (STC) • Full breakfast • Open June-Nov. • NSRS Member

Stewiacke
Interval Pines Bed & Breakfast

Joyce Barak, 487 St. Andrews Street, Box 415, Stewiacke, B0N 2J0
(902) 639-2835
Hwy 102, Exit 11 • Large home, secluded and private, in the St. Andrew's River valley • One o/n unit, shared B&S; one family suite • Cable TV in living room
FEATURES: Trout fishing
RATES: $35-$45 (1-2) (tax incl.) (STC) • Continental breakfast 7-9 • Open June 1-Sept. 30 • Off-season by reservation

Stewiacke
Sprucehaven Bed & Breakfast

Harold & Doreen Purdy, 5397 Highway 289, RR 2, Upper Stewiacke, B0N 2P0
(902) 671-2462
Hwy 102, Exit 12 to flashing light at Brookfield, then to Upper Stewiacke, 26.5 km (16 1/2 mi) • Two o/n units, private B&S • Clock radio in rooms • Cable TV/VCR in living room • No pets, please • Non-smoking only
FEATURES: Library with board games • Evening snack
RATES: $35 (1), $45 (2) • Continental breakfast 7:30-9 • Open June 1-Oct. 15 • Visa accepted • NSRS Member

Summerville Beach
Summerville Beach Retreat B&B

June Lohnes-Davis, RR 1, Port Mouton, B0T 1T0
(902) 683-2874
Toll free 1-800-213-5868

From Hwy 103, Exit 20, 2 km (1.2 mi) • Three o/n units, one shared B; four chalets • Clock radio in rooms • Cable TV/VCR • Non-smoking only
FEATURES: Wheelchair accessibility • Outside deck • Screened spa • Two minutes from beach with lots of privacy • Call for a vacation video
RATES: $45-$60 (1-2), $99-$129 (chalet) • Off-season rates • Full breakfast • Open May 1-Sept. 30 (chalets year-round) • Visa accepted • NSFCV; NSRS Member

Sydney
Century Manor Bed & Breakfast

Roberta MacIntyre, 212 Whitney Avenue, Sydney, B1P 5A4
(902) 567-1300
Hwy 125, Exit 8, George St. to second traffic light, right on Cottage Rd, left on Whitney Ave. • Victorian-style home • Two o/n units, one shared B&S • Clock radio in rooms • Cable TV in den • No pets, please • Non-smoking only
RATES: $40 (1), $45 (2) • Full breakfast 8-9 • Open May 1-Oct. 31 • Off-season by reservation • NSRS Member

Sydney
Cormorant Tourist Home B&B

Hazel Campbell, 2042 Kings Road, Sydney, B1L 1C4
(902) 539-5979
Hwy 125, Exit 6W to Rte. 4, 4 km (2.5 mi) on right • Panoramic view of Blackets Lake and mountains • Two o/n units, one shared B&S • Cable TV • No smoking in rooms, please
FEATURES: Small boat launch
RATES: $41 (1), $45 (2) • Full

breakfast • Open May 15-Oct. 15 •
MC, Visa accepted

Sydney
Gathering House
Bed & Breakfast ★★ ½
Jean & Ken Phillips, 148 Crescent
Street, Sydney, B1S 2Z8
(902) 539-7172
Fax (902) 539-6665
Easy access from Kings Rd. (Hwy
104 or 105), George St. (Rte. 125) •
Victorian home, furnished with
antiques, overlooking Wentworth
Park • Three o/n units, two shared
B&S • Cable TV/VCR in family
room
FEATURES: • Veranda • Pet thera-
py available • Sunday park concerts
• Off-street parking
RATES: $40 (1), $45-$55 (2), $15
add'l person • Full breakfast 7:30-9
• Open year-round • Off-season by
reservation • NSRS Member

Sydney
Old Country Post Office
B&B
Dr. Pushpa Rathor, 3 Strathcona
Street, Sydney, B1R 1X7
(902) 539-8033
Two o/n units, one shared B&S; one
suite • Non-smoking only
FEATURES: A unique experience
with palm reading and stress-reduc-
tion meditation available with hostess, who is also an artist, writer and
musician
RATES: $45 (1), $50 (2), $60
(suite) • Breakfast 7-9 • Open May
1-Oct. 31 • Off-season by reservation

Sydney
Park Place
Bed & Breakfast
Evanel McEwen, 169 Park Street,
Sydney, B1P 4W7
(902) 562-3518
Fax (902) 567-6618
E-mail
lemcewen@highlander.cbnet.ns.ca
Website
http://www.bbcanada.com/81.html
Exit 8 from Hwy 125, take George
St. to second traffic lights, turn right
on Cottage Rd., and then left on
Park St. • Victorian house • Three
o/n units, one shared B&S • Cable
TV and radio • Non-smoking only
RATES: $40 (1), $45 (2) (STC) •
Full breakfast 7-9 • Open May-Oct.
• Off-season by reservation • MC,
Visa accepted • NSRS Member

Sydney
Purcell Place
Bed & Breakfast
Robert & Annette Purcell, 596
Coxheath Road, Sydney, B1R 1R6
Tel & Fax (902) 562-4865
2.2 km (1.5 mi) off Keltic Dr. •
New brick home • One o/n unit, pri-
vate B&S • Non-smoking only
FEATURES: French spoken
RATES: $55 (1-2) • Full breakfast
7-10 • Open July 1-Aug. 31 • Off-
season by reservation

Sydney
Rigby House
Bed & Breakfast
Darlene Mallen & Bernard
Villeneuve, 66 Rigby Road, Sydney,
B1P 4T6
(902) 564-8346
Hwy 125, Exit 8, turn left on
George St., 2.5 km (1.5 mi), right
on Cottage Rd., three blocks to
Rigby Rd. • Three o/n units, one
shared B&S • Cable TV in rooms
and family room • Non-smoking
only
FEATURES: French spoken •
Heated outdoor swimming pool
RATES: $40-$50 (1), $50-$60 (2) •
Full breakfast 8-9:30 • Open year-
round • Visa accepted • NSRS
Member

Sydney
Rockinghorse Inn ★★★
Margaret Glabay, 259 Kings Road,
Sydney, B1S 1A7
Tel & Fax (902) 539-2696
Toll free 1-888-664-1010
Registered heritage property, fur-
nished with antiques • Eight o/n
units, six private B, two shared B;
one honeymoon suite • Cable TV in
common area • No smoking in
rooms, please
FEATURES: Dinner on request •
Library of steelworkers and miners
of Cape Breton • Sunroom
RATES: $69-$95 (2), $20 add'l
person • Full breakfast 8-9 • Open
year-round • AE, MC, Visa accepted
• NSRS Member

Sydney
White Maples
Bed & Breakfast
Pamela Roberts, 258 Curry Street,
Howie Centre, Sydney, B1L 1G3
(902) 564-4674
Hwy 125, Exit 6 to Rte. 4, 5 km (3
mi) to Howie Centre; or Rte 4, 6 km
(3.5 mi) past Sydney River Tourist
Bureau • One o/n unit, shared B&S
• Cable TV in room • No pets,
please • No smoking in room, please
RATES: $35 (1), $40 (2) (STC)•
Full breakfast 7-9 • Open May 15-
Oct. 15

Sydney Forks
Christie's
Bed & Breakfast
Olive Christie, 2486 Kings Road,
Sydney Forks, B1L 1A1
(902) 564-9364
Hwy 125, Exit 6, 7 km (4.5 mi)
towards St. Peter's • Three o/n
units, one shared B&S • Cable TV
/VCR in recreation room • Children
under 12 yrs free • No smoking in
rooms, please
FEATURES: Very private lot •
Pool table and games available •
Model ship display
RATES: $30 (1), $39 (2), $15 add'l
person • Full breakfast 8-10 • Open
June 1-Nov. 15

Sydney Mines
Annandale
Bed & Breakfast ★★★
Meg Sargent & Scott Phillips,
157 Shore Road, Sydney Mines,
B1V 1A9
(902) 544-1052
Toll free 1-800-565-2660
Hwy 105, Exit 21 to Rte. 305N, 3
km (2 mi) • Victorian house (c.
1880), furnished with antiques •

Four o/n units, one shared B&S • Cable TV/VCR and telephone in lounge • Pets with permission • No smoking in rooms, please
FEATURES: Veranda with ocean view • Croquet • Five minutes from Newfoundland ferry
RATES: $38-$48 (1), $45-$60 (2) (STC) • Full breakfast 7:30-9 • Open year-round • Dec.-March by reservation • MC, Visa accepted

Sydney Mines
Garland Stubbert's Bed & Breakfast ★★★
Garland Stubbert, 117 Shore Road, Sydney Mines, B1V 1A5
(902) 736-8466
Hwy 105, Exit 21 to Rte. 305N, 2.5 km (1.5 mi) from Newfoundland ferry • Three o/n units, one shared B&S • Cable TV in lounge • No smoking in rooms, please
FEATURES: Large deck overlooking harbour • Barbecue and camp stove available
RATES: $45 (2), $16 add'l person (STC) • Full breakfast 7-9 • Open May 1-Oct. 31 • NSRS Member

Sydney Mines
Gowrie House Country Inn ★★★★
C.J. Matthews & K.W. Tutty, 139 Shore Road, Sydney Mines, B1V 1A5
(902) 544-1050
Fax (902) 736-0077
Toll free 1-800-372-1115
Hwy 105, Exit 21 to Rte. 305N, 3 km (2 mi) • Historic Georgian-style house (c. 1820), furnished with antiques • Ten o/n units, private B&S; one cottage • Cable TV in some rooms • Pets with prior permission • No smoking in rooms, please

FEATURES: Dinner on request • English gardens • Veranda and decks
RATES: $99-$139 (2), $169 (cottage), $15 add'l person, $35 (MAP) • Breakfast 7:30-9:30 • Open May 1-Oct. 30 • MC, Visa accepted • IGNS; NSRS; UCI Member

Tangier
Paddler's Retreat B&B
Scott Cunningham & Gayle Wilson, Mason's Point Road, Tangier, B0J 3H0
Tel & Fax (902) 772-2774
Fisherman's home (c. 1860) with ocean view • Three o/n units, one shared B&S • Non-smoking only
FEATURES: Hot tub • Saltwater swimming • Sea kayaking tours, courses and rentals
RATES: $35 (1), $45 (2), $10 add'l person • Full breakfast 7:30-9 • Open May 1-Oct. 31 • MC, Visa accepted

Tantallon
Glen Haven Bed & Breakfast
Thelma Bowness, 241 Indian Point Road, Site 4, Box 3A9, RR 1, Tantallon, B0J 3J0
(902) 823-2358
Hwy 103, Exit 5 to Rte. 333, 7 km (4.5 mi) on right • Two o/n units, one shared B&S • Cable TV in one room and sitting room
FEATURES: Outdoor heated salt-water swimming pool
RATES: $40 (1), $60 (2), $10 add'l person • Full breakfast • Open June 1-Oct. 1 • MC, Visa accepted • NSRS Member

Tantallon
Stillwater Lake Bed & Breakfast

Elaine MacInnis, 40 Stillwater Lake Drive, Tantallon, B0J 3J0
(902) 826-1105
Fax (902) 826-2435
Hwy 103, Exit 5; or Hwy 102, Exit 3, Hammonds Plains Rd. to Stillwater Lake Dr. • Two o/n units, one shared B&S • Cable TV/VCR in living room • No pets, please • Non-smoking only
FEATURES: Sun deck overlooking lake • Bonfire pit • Lake swimming and fishing • Canoe available • Skating, cross-country skiing and snowshoeing in season
RATES: $45 (1), $55 (2) • Full breakfast 7-9 • Open year-round

Tantallon
Teddy Bear Bed & Breakfast

Thomas Betts, 22 Whynacht's Point Road, Box 2548, RR 2, Tantallon, B0J 3J0
(902) 826-7960/2138
Hwy 103, Exit 5, follow Peggy's Cove signs to Rte. 333, 4 km (2.5 mi) to Whynacht's Point Road • Overlooking a quiet cove • Four o/n units, one shared B&S; one suite • Cable TV/VCR and telephone in common room • Children under 12 yrs free • No scents, please • No pets, please • Non-smoking only
FEATURES: Rooms at ground level for easy access; ideal for asthmatics or sensitive individuals • Scent-free home
RATES: $50 (1), $60-$80 (2), $75-$85 (suite), $10 add'l person • Full breakfast 8 • Open year-round • NSRS Member

Tarbotvale
Greer's Cabot Trail Bed & Breakfast

Bob & Ann Greer, RR 4, Tarbotvale, B0E 1B0
(902) 929-2115
Turn in at Tarbotvale, cross the bridge and go up the hill • Close to Gaelic College, half-hour drive from Baddeck • Three o/n units, two shared B&S • No pets, please • Non-smoking only
FEATURES: Special dietary needs considered
RATES: $40 (1), $47-$50 (2) (STC) • Full breakfast • Open June 15-Sept. 30 • MC, Visa accepted • CBBBA; NSFC; NSRS Member

Tatamagouche
Forest Haven Guest House and Café

Heike Caspers, 8627 Highway 311, Balfron, B0K 1V0
(902) 657-2962
Fax (902) 647-2477
Five minutes from Tatamagouche • Four o/n units, two shared S • TV in leisure room • Pets permitted, usually on leash • Non-smoking only
FEATURES: German spoken • Bakery, craft and souvenir shop on site • German and Canadian cuisine
RATES: $45-$55 (1-2) (STC) • Weekly rates • Breakfast 7-10 • Open year-round • MC, Visa accepted

Tatamagouche
Mountain Breeze Farm Bed & Breakfast

Hannelore & Herbert Deffren, RR 4, Tatamagouche, B0K 1V0
Tel & Fax (902) 657-3193
Hwy 6 to Maple Ave. in Tatamagouche, first left onto Truro Rd., 3 km (2 mi) • Three o/n units,

one shared B&S • Non-smoking only
FEATURES: Sun deck • Barbecue • Sauna and whirlpool • Vacation packages
RATES: $40 (1), $45 (2) • Full breakfast 7-10 • Open year-round • MC, Visa accepted • NSRS Member

Tatamagouche
Train Station Inn ★★★
Shelley & James LeFresne, Station Road, Box 67, Tatamagouche, B0K 1V0
(902) 657-3222
Restored century-old train station with railway cars • Five o/n units in station, private B&S; three mini-suites in train cars • Cable TV/VCR in some rooms and living room • Cots available
FEATURES: Laundry facilities • Kitchen facilities • Air-conditioning (suites) • Outdoor skating in season • Nature walks on old rail bed • Bicycles available
RATES: $40-$55 (1), $47.60-$68.75 (2), $98 (suite), $5-$10 add'l person (STC) • Continental breakfast 8-10 • Open year-round • AE, Dis, MC, Visa accepted • NSRS Member

Timberlea
Sheldrake House
Bed & Breakfast
Clinton & Melanie Schick, 3331 St. Margaret's Bay Road, Timberlea, B3T 1J1
(902) 876-5026
Fax (902) 876-5041
Hwy 103, Exit 4 to Rte. 3W, first left (Grebe St.), left on Partridge Lane, second house on right • Former Sheldrake Rod and Gun Club (c. 1923), on two acres of landscaped grounds • One o/n unit,

private B&S • Cable TV, telephone and fireplace in room • Non-smoking only
RATES: $85 (1), $89 (2), $10 add'l person • Full breakfast 7-9 • Open year-round • Reservation and deposit required • NSRS Member

Toney River
Ella Rose
Bed & Breakfast ★★ ¹/₂
Jim & Catherine Bowering, 4133 Highway 6, Toney River, RR 4, River John, B0K 1N0
(902) 351-3479
20 km (12.5 mi) from Pictou Rotary, towards River John • Lovely old farmhouse (c. 1890) • Three o/n units, one shared B&S • Clock radio in rooms • TV/VCR in living room • No smoking in rooms, please
FEATURES: Beach access • Craft shop
RATES: $45 (1), $50 (2) • Full breakfast 8-11 • Open May 1-Sept. 30 • Visa accepted • NSRS Member

Truro
Blue House Inn B&B
Doug & Enid Jennings, 43 Dominion Street, Truro, B2N 3P2
(902) 895-4150
Two o/n units, two shared B&S • Cable TV, radio and fan in rooms • Cable TV/VCR in living room • No alcohol • Non-smoking only
FEATURES: Kitchen facilities • Piano in living room
RATES: $35 (1), $45 (2), $10 add'l person (STC) • Full breakfast 7:30-9 • Open July 1-Aug. 31

Truro
Elizabeth House
Bed & Breakfast ★★★
Betty Kelly, 401 Robie Street,
Truro, B2N 1L9
(902) 893-2346
Hwy 102, Exit 14 • Three o/n units,
one shared B&S • Cable TV in
lounge • Non-smoking only
FEATURES: Sun deck off guest
rooms • Evening tea with homemade sweets
*RATES: $35 (1) $40 (2) (STC) •
Full breakfast 7-9 • Open year-
round • NSRS member*

Truro
Iron Duck
Bed & Breakfast
George & Barb Rockwell, 242 Kent
Road, Box 75, Truro, B2N 5B6
(902) 895-3005
Hwy 102, Exit 14, left on Rte. 236,
2 km (1 mi) to Kent Rd. • Peaceful
setting on edge of town, with flower
and vegetable gardens • Two o/n
units, one shared B&S • Clock radio
in rooms • Cable TV/VCR in living
room • Pets on premises • No pets,
please • Non-smoking only
*RATES: $40 (1), $45 (2) • Full
breakfast 8 • Open June 1-Oct. 30*

Truro
Silver Firs
Bed & Breakfast ★★★ ½
Bev & Grant Richardson, 397
Prince Street, Truro, B2N 1E1
(902) 893-0570
Fax: (902) 897-1900
Three o/n units, private B; one suite
• Colour cable TV in suite and
lounge • Children over 12 yrs wel-
come • Non-smoking only
*RATES: $50-$60 (1), $75-$95 (2),
$105-$135 (suite), $15 add'l person*

*• Full breakfast 8-9:30 • Open May
15-Oct. 15 • Off-season by reservation • Visa accepted • IGNS Member*

Truro
Suncatcher
Bed & Breakfast
Ruth & Gerry Mailloux, 25 Wile
Crest Avenue, North River, RR 6,
Truro, B2N 5B4
(902) 893-7169
Near Hwys 102 and 104; please call
for directions • Two o/n units, one
shared B • Cable TV in family room
• Cot available • No pets, please •
Non-smoking only
FEATURES: French spoken •
Evening snacks
*RATES: $35-$45 (1-2), $8 add'l
person • Full breakfast at guests'
convenience • Open year-round •
NSRS Member*

Tusket
Plum Tree
Bed & Breakfast ★★★
Jill & Larry Trask, Box 115, RR 1,
Tusket, B0W 3M0
(902) 648-3159
E-mail ltrask@ns.sympatico.ca
Hwy 103, Exit 33, follow signs •
140-year-old home • Three o/n
units, one shared B&S • Cable TV
in living room • No pets, please
FEATURES: Sun deck with barbe-
cue • Picnic tables • Garden •
Walking trails
*RATES: $35 (1), $40-$60 (2), $5
add'l person • Continental breakfast
• Open May 1-Nov. 1 • NSRS
Member*

Tusket
Vaughn Lake Bed & Breakfast

George & Dale Duncanson, RR 1, Tusket, B0W 3M0
(902) 648-3122
Fax (902) 648-0012
Fifteen minutes from Maine ferries; from Hwy 103, Exit 33 at Tusket, follow signs, 3.5 km (2.5 mi) • Four o/n units, one shared B&S, one shared 1/2 B • Cable TV in living room • Children welcome
FEATURES: Kitchen facilities • Sun deck • Swimming • Paddle boat
RATES: $35 (1), $40 (2), $100 (whole house) • Full breakfast 7-10 • Open May 15-Nov. • Visa acccepted • NSRS Member

Upper Clements
Cheshire Cat B&B

Betty McKaigue, RR 2, Annapolis Royal, B0S 1A0
Tel & Fax (902) 532-7655
Four o/n units, private S; five housekeeping suites • Cable TV in suites and lounge • Children under 6 yrs free
FEATURES: View over Annapolis River • Twenty wooded acres with hiking trails • Bird-watching
RATES: $40 (1), $45-$60 (2), $45-$70 (suite), $10 add'l person • Full breakfast 7-9 • Open May 15-Oct. 15 • Visa accepted • NSRS Member

Victoria Beach
Golden Anchor Inn B&B

Bertha & Bill Titus, Victoria Beach, RR 2, Granville Ferry, B0S 1K0
(902) 532-2960
25 km (15 mi) west of Annapolis causeway • Three o/n units, one private 1/2 B, two shared B&S • Clock radio and ceiling fan in rooms • TV in lounge • Cots available
FEATURES: View of Bay of Fundy and sunsets • Kitchen facilities • Picnic tables
RATES: $33-$38 (1), $38-$43 (2), $45-$50 (family), $10 add'l person • Continental breakfast 8-9 • Open May 15-Oct. 15 • Visa accepted • NSFC; NSRS Member

Vogler's Cove
Shorebirds B&B

Judy & Len Brown, 8728 Route 331, Vogler's Cove, B0J 2H0
(902) 677-2056
Hwy 103, Exit 16 • Three o/n units, one shared B&S • Children over 12 yrs welcome • No pets, please • Non-smoking only
FEATURES: Sitting room for reading, games or music • Scenic view of harbour
RATES: $35 (1), $45-$50 (2), $12 add'l person • Full breakfast • Open June 15-Sept. 15 • MC, Visa accepted • NSRS Member

Wallace
Crumpetty Tree
Bed & Breakfast ★★★
Joyce Langille, 1154 Wallace River West Road, RR 3, Wallace, B0K 1Y0
(902) 257-2610
Three km (2 mi) west of Wallace • Farmhouse (c. 1836) on banks of Wallace River • One o/n unit, private B&S • Cable TV in lounge • Cots and crib available • Children under 3 yrs free
FEATURES: Piano in lounge • Canoe available • Bicycles available • Picnic table and barbecue
RATES: $35 (1) $50 (2), $5-$10 add'l person (tax incl.) • Full breakfast • Open June 1-Sept. 30 • Visa accepted • Reservations preferred • IGNS; NSRS Member

Wallace
Highland Cattle Farm
Windygates
Bed & Breakfast
Lieselotte Merzbach, 129 North Shore Road, Box 266, Wallace, B0K 1Y0
Tel & Fax (902) 257-2251
Rte. 6, 3 km (2 mi) from Wallace towards Tatamagouche, left on North Shore Rd. • One o/n unit (suite), private B • Cable TV and radio in room • No pets, please • Non-smoking only
RATES: $60 (1-4), $15 add'l person, $7.50 add'l child under 12 yrs • Full breakfast 7-10 • Open year-round • NSRS Member

Wallace
Jubilee Cottage
Country Inn ★★★ ¹/₂
Daphne Dominy, Box 148, Wallace, B0K 1Y0

Tel (902) 257-2432
Fax (902) 257-2510
Toll free 1-800-481-9915
Off-season (506) 529-1912
Rte. 6 • Lovingly restored 1912 home • Three o/n units, private B&S • Cable TV/VCR and piano in parlour • Non-smoking only
FEATURES: Ocean view • Licensed dining room • Evening snack • Horseshoe pit and lawn croquet • Migratory stopover for Great Blue Herons and Canada Geese
RATES: $60-$69 (2), $10 add'l person • Off-season rates • Full breakfast • Open May 9-Oct. 13 • MC, Visa accepted • Cancellation policy • IGNS; NSRS Member

Waterville
Orchard Hill House
Country Inn ★★★ ¹/₂
Kim & Norma Banks, RR 1, Waterville, NS, B0P 1V0
(902) 538-9750
Website
http://www.achilles.net/~bb/675.html
Hwy 101, Exit 14, 12 km (7.5 mi) west towards Berwick; or Hwy 101, Exit 15, south on Rte. 360 to Rte. 1, turn left, 2.5 km (1.5 mi) • Century-old one hundred-acre produce and dried-flower farm • Three o/n units, private B&S • Cable TV in lounge • No pets, please • Non-smoking only
FEATURES: Dining room • Guest living room with fireplace • Garden • Walking trails • Volleyball • Bird-watching • Farm market
RATES: $53 (1), $58 (2), $8 add'l person • Full breakfast • Open April 1-Oct. 31 • MC, Visa accepted Cancellation policy • NSRS Member

Wentworth
All Seasons
Bed & Breakfast
Mary Musseau, 14371 Highway 104, Wentworth Valley, B0M 1Z0
(902) 548-2064
Four o/n units, two private S, one shared B&S • Clock radio in rooms • Cable TV in living room • Cot available • Non-smoking only
RATES: $33-$45 (1), $45-$55 (2) $8 add'l person • Full breakfast at guests' convenience • Open year-round • MC, Visa accepted • NSRS Member

West Arichat
Maison Émile-Mouchet
B&B
Maurice D. LeBlanc, General Delivery, West Arichat, B0E 3J0
(902) 226-9740
E-mail nmw@web.net
Hwy 104, Exit 46 to Rte. 320E, follow to Rte. 206E, to West Arichat • Well-preserved home (c. 1865) • Three o/n units, one shared B&S • No pets, please
FEATURES: Salt water shoreline • Bicycles available
RATES: $50 (1-2), $7.50 add'l person • Full breakfast 7-9 • Open year-round

West Dover
Joanne's
Bed & Breakfast
Joanne Publicover, 6922 Route 333, West Dover, B0J 3L0
(902) 823-3006
View of West Dover Harbour from deck • Two o/n units, one shared B&S • Cable TV in rooms and sitting room • Non-smoking only
RATES: $55 (1-2) (tax incl.) • Full breakfast 7-9 • Open April 15-Oct. 15

West Dover (Middle Village)
Oceanside Inn
Bed & Breakfast
Tom & Dorothy Code, General Delivery, Peggy's Cove, B0J 2N0
Tel & Fax (902) 823-2765
On Rte. 333, 5 km (3 mi) east of Peggy's Cove at Middle Village Road, West Dover • Two o/n units, private B; one suite (whirlpool) • Cable TV/VCR in some rooms and sitting room • No pets, please • Non-smoking only
FEATURES: Private nature trails • Ocean swimming • Sandy beach • Row boats
RATES: $65-$110 (2), $10 add'l person (STC) • Full breakfast 8 • Open May 15-Oct. 15 • Off-season by chance or reservation • NSRS Member

West Jeddore
Jonah By The Sea B&B
Dora & Bill Jonah, 1854 West Jeddore Road, Jeddore, B0J 1P0
Tel & Fax (902) 889-3516
From Rte. 7, exit at Head of Jeddore to West Jeddore Road, eight minutes to mouth of harbour • Country home (c. 1900) in quaint fishing village • Three o/n units, one shared S • TV • No pets, please • Non-smoking only
FEATURES: View of ocean, Jeddore Rock and light • Private beach • Walking trails • Clam-digging, bird-watching and fishing
RATES: $35-$50 (1-2), $10 add'l person (STC) • Full breakfast 8-9 • Open May-Oct. • Off-season by reservation • Visa accepted • NSRS Member

Westport
Westport Inn B&B
Roland & Nancy Swift, Box 1226,
Westport, Brier Island, B0V 1H0
(902) 839-2675
Fax (902) 839-2245
Brier Island, Rte. 217 • Six o/n
units, one private B, one shared
B&S • TV/VCR in lounge
FEATURES: Licensed dining room
*RATES: $35-$55 (1-2), $10 add'l
person • Full breakfast • Open May
1-Oct. 31 • AE, MC, Visa accepted*

White Point
Two Tittle
Bed & Breakfast
Cyril & Marguerite Dunphy, 2119
White Point Village, RR 2,
Whitepoint, B0C 1G0
(902) 383-2817
Exit off Cabot Trail onto alternate
scenic route at Neil's Harbour or at
White Point Rd. • Waterfront prop-
erty • Three o/n units, two shared
B&S • TV in lounge • No pets,
please • Non-smoking only
FEATURES: Patio overlooking
Aspy Bay • Hiking trails • Sandy
beach
*RATES: $35 (1), $45-$48 (2) (STC)
• Full breakfast 7:30-8:30 • Open
year-round • CBBBA; NSRS
Member*

Whycocomagh
Mary Smith
Bed & Breakfast
Mary Smith, 21 Lakeview Drive,
Whycocomagh, B0E 3M0
(902) 756-2157
Hwy 105, turn on Main St. and fol-
low signs • Two o/n units, one
shared B&S • TV in living room •
Cats on premises
RATES: $35 (1), $45 (2) (tax incl.)

*• Full breakfast 8 • Open May 15-
Oct. 15 • NSRS Member*

Wilmot
Maggie K
Bed & Breakfast
Sandra & Thor Kittilsen, 747
Stronach Mountain Road, RR 2,
Kingston, B0P 1R0
(902) 765-3715
Hwy 101, Exit 17 to Rte. 1W, right
on Stronach Mtn. Rd., 3 km (2 mi)
on left • Panoramic view of
Annapolis Valley • Two o/n units,
one shared B&S • Cable TV/VCR
in living room • Designated smoking area
*RATES: $40 (1), $45 (2) • Full
breakfast 7-9 • Open May 1-Sept. 30
• Visa accepted • NSRS Member*

Windsor
Angels Wrest
Bed & Breakfast
Lynda & Bob Davies, 257 Victoria
Street, Windsor, Box 37, Curry's
Corner, B0N 1H0
(902) 798-2149
Late-Victorian home • Two o/n
units, one shared B&S; one suite •
Non-smoking only
*RATES: $35 (1), $35-$48 (2), $8
add'l person • Full breakfast 7:30-
9:30 • Open year-round • Visa
accepted • NSRS Member*

Windsor
Boegel's
Bed & Breakfast ★★★
Sharon & Terry Boegel, 145 Dill
Road, RR 1, Windsor, B0N 2T0
(902) 798-4183
Fax (902) 798-1063
Hwy 101, Exit 5, Rte. 14W towards
Martock to Dill Rd; or Exit 5A
(Wentworth St.) towards Martock to

King St. to Hwy 14 • Quiet scenic area on the edge of town • Three o/n units, one shared B&S • Clock radio and ceiling fan in rooms • Cable TV/VCR in living room • Cat on premises • Non-smoking only *FEATURES:* Fax service • 8 km (4.8 mi) to Ski Martock • Twenty minutes from Wolfville *RATES: $35 (1), $40-$50 (2), $10 add'l person • Off-season rates • Full breakfast 7:30-9:30 • Open year-round • MC, Visa accepted • NSRS Member*

Windsor
Clockmaker's Inn ★★★
Veronica & Dennis Connelly, 1399 King Street, Curry's Corner, Windsor, B0N 1H0
Tel & Fax (902) 798-5265

 Victorian home • Four o/n units, one shared B&S, one shared 1/2 B • Cable TV in lounge • Crib available • No pets, please • Non-smoking only *FEATURES:* Provincial heritage property furnished with antiques • Baby grand piano • Video library of classical music • Bicycles • Barbecue *RATES: $40 (1), $50 (2), $10 add'l person • Full breakfast 7:30-9:30 • Open year-round • MC, Visa accepted • IGNS; NSRS Member*

Windsor
Fiddlehead Inn B&B
Mala McGuire, 307 King Street, Windsor, B0N 2T0
Tel & Fax (902) 798-2659
Hwy 101, Exit 6, right at stop sign then first left (between museum and church) • Georgian-style home •

Three o/n units, private B&S • Cable TV/VCR in den • No pets, please • Non-smoking only *FEATURES:* Outdoor swimming pool • Ski packages *RATES: $46 (1-2), $52-$58 (suite) • Full breakfast 7:30-9 • Open year-round • Visa accepted • IGNS; NSRS Member*

Wolfville
Elisha Dewolf House (Kent Lodge) Bed & Breakfast
The Moores, 450 Main Street, RR 2, Wolfville, B0P 1X0
(902) 542-5609
Hwy 101, Exit 10 or 11 • Registered heritage property (c. 1760) with antique furnishings and collections • Two o/n units, one shared B&S • Pets on premises • No pets, please • Non-smoking only *FEATURES:* Contemplative gardens with unique seating *RATES: $45-$55 (1), $50-$60 (2) • Full breakfast 7:30-9:30 • Open May 1-Oct. 31*

Wolfville
Garden House Bed & Breakfast
Brian & Lisa McKenzie, 150 Main Street, Box 412, Wolfville, B0P 1X0
(902) 542-1703
Heritage home (c. 1830) at edge of town • Three o/n units, one private S, one shared B&S • Smoking outdoors only *RATES: $45-$55 (1), $50-$60 2), $10 add'l person • Continental or full breakfast 8:30 • Open May 1-Oct. 31 • MC, Visa accepted • NSRS Member*

Wolfville
Gingerbread House Inn ★★★ ½
Pat & Hedley Duffield, 8 Robie Tufts Drive, Box 819, Wolfville, B0P 1X0
(902) 542-1458
Fax (902) 542-4718
E-mail
gingerbread@valleyweb.com
Winner of the Nova Scotia Government Award for Excellence in House Design and Restoration • Four o/n units, private B&S or S; two suites (whirlpool) • TV, clock radio and ceiling fan in rooms • No pets, please • Non-smoking only
RATES: $59-$89 (1-2), $109-$139 (suite), $15 add'l person • Off-season rates from $44-$99 • Full breakfast 8-9:30 • Open year-round • Visa accepted • Cancellation policy • IGNS; NSRS Member

Wolfville
Seaview House Bed & Breakfast
Loretta Premi, 8 Seaview Avenue, Wolfville, B0P 1X0
(902) 542-1436
Fax (902) 542-2873
Hwy 101, Exit 10 or 11 to Main St., Wolfville, to Seaview Ave. • Restored Victorian home • Three o/n units, one private B, one shared B • Cable TV/VCR in guest lounge • Smoking on porch only
RATES: $45-$65 (1-2), $10 add'l person • Full breakfast 8-9:30 • Open May-Sept. • Off-season by reservation • Visa accepted • NSRS Member

Wolfville
Tattingstone Inn ★★★★ ½
Betsey Harwood, 434 Main Street, Wolfville, B0P 1X0
(902) 542-7696
Fax (902) 542-4427
Toll free 1-800-565-7696
Registered heritage poperty • Ten o/n units, private B&S; one cottage • TV, clock radio and telephone in rooms • No pets, please • Non-smoking only
FEATURES: Licensed dining room • Air-conditioning • Outdoor heated swimming pool • Tennis court • Gardens • Vacation packages
RATES: $85-$128 (1-2), $148 (cottage) • Breakfast 8-9:30 • Open year-round • AE, MC, Visa accepted • 48-hour cancellation policy • CAA; NSRS; TNS Member

Wolfville
Victoria's Historic Inn and Carriage House ★★★★
Urbain & Carol Cryan, 416 Main Street, Box 308, Wolfville, B0P 1X0
(902) 542-5744
Toll free 1-800-556-5744
Registered heritage property (c. 1893) • Fifteen o/n units, private B&S; four suites (Jacuzzi) • Cable TV and telephone in rooms • No pets, please • Non-smoking only
FEATURES: Licensed dining room by reservation
RATES: $79-$149 (2) • Breakfast 8-9:30 • Open year-round • DC, MC, Visa accepted • CAA; NSRS; UCI Member

Yarmouth
Clementine's
Bed & Breakfast
Evelyn & Ron Gray, 21 Clements
Street, Yarmouth, B5A 2B9
(902) 742-0079
Three o/n units, three shared B •
Cable TV in lounge • Not suitable
for children • No pets, please • Non-
smoking only
*RATES: $50-$60 (1-2) • Full
breakfast • Open May-Nov.*

Yarmouth
Harbour's Edge
Bed & Breakfast (c. 1864)
Esther & Gil Dares, 12 Vancouver
Street, Yarmouth, B5A 2N8
(902) 742-2387
Registered heritage property on two
acres with spectacular view of
Yarmouth Harbour • Three o/n
units, private B&S • Non-smoking
only
*RATES: $65-$75 (1-2), $10 add'l
person • Full breakfast 8-9:30 •
Open year-round • MC, Visa
accepted*

Yarmouth
Murray Manor
(c. 1820) ★★★
George & Joan Semple, 225 Main
Street, Yarmouth, B5A 1C6
Tel & Fax (902) 742-9625
Website
http://www.grtplaces.com/ac/murray/

Gothic-style
heritage proper-
ty • Three o/n
units, one
shared B&S,
one shared 1/2 B • Non-smoking
only
FEATURES: Acadian French spoken • Gardens and greenhouse •

Close to ferry, bus, airport, shops
and museums
*RATES: $50 (1), $60 (2) • Full
breakfast • Open year-round • Visa
accepted • NSRS Member*

Yarmouth
Victorian Vogue
Bed & Breakfast
Dawn-Marie Skjelmose,
109 Brunswick Street, Yarmouth,
B5A 2H2
(902) 742-6398
Sea captain's Queen Anne Revival-
style home • Five o/n units, one pri-
vate B, two shared B • Non-smok-
ing only
*RATES: $40 (1), $50-$65 (2) (STC)
• Full breakfast • Open year-round •
MC, Visa accepted • NSRS Member*

Chapter 4

Prince Edward Island

Alberton
Briarwood Inn ★★ ½
Gary & Debbie Inman, Box 215,
Alberton, C0B 1B0
(902) 853-2518
Off Rte. 12 on Matthews Lane •
Award-winning heritage home on
Dock River • Three o/n units, one
shared B, one shared S; six cottages
• Cot available
FEATURES: Boating, clam-digging and swimming on premises •
Golf course, fun park and beaches
nearby • Laundry facilities
*RATES: $45 (2), $15 add'l person •
$275 (weekly), $500-$650 (weekly,
cottage), $60 add'l person • Off-
season rates Oct.1-May 31 •
Continental breakfast • Open year-
round • Visa accepted*

Alberton
Cold Comfort Farm ★★★
Marilyn Wells, Box 105,
Alberton, C0B 1B0
(902) 853-2803
Rte. 12 near Alberton • Three o/n
units, one shared B
FEATURES: Hundreds of books in
library • Surrounded by gardens •
Beach on premises • Solitude or
conversation • Dinner on request
*RATES: $45 (2), $10 add'l person •
$270 (weekly), $50 add'l person •
Breakfast • Open June 15-Sept. 15 •*

Alberton
Island's End Inn
Lloyd Gavin, Box 88, Tignish,
C0B 2B0

(902) 882-3554
On Rte. 12 at Seacow Pond, 6 km
north of Tignish • Quiet location
overlooking Gulf of St. Lawrence •
Four o/n units, private B&S; five
housekeeping suites • Cable TV in
rooms • Cots available • Children
under 12 yrs free • Pets welcome
FEATURES: Deep-sea fishing,
Irish moss harvesting nearby • Walk
to beach • Short drive to Wind Test
Site and restaurant at North Cape
*RATES: $45-$60 (2), $5 add'l per-
son • $280-$385 (weekly), $25 add'l
person • Open May 1-Oct. 31 • MC,
Visa accepted*

Alberton
Poplar Lane
Bed & Breakfast ★★ ½
Dick & Gaya Dykerman, Box 257,
Alberton, C0B 1B0
(902) 853-3732
Turn left off Main St. onto Poplar
St. at end of road • Built in 1912,
set in quiet location • Three o/n
units, one shared B&S • Cable TV •
Pets permitted, usually on leash
FEATURES: Dining room within
walking distance
*RATES: $35 (2), $7 add'l
person (no GST) • Continental
breakfast • Open June 1-Sept. 15*

Albion Cross
Needles and Haystacks
Bed & Breakfast ★★ ½
Fred Foster, RR 2, St. Peters Bay,
C0A 2A0
(902) 583-2928

Toll free 1-800-563-2928
E-mail ffoster@cycor.ca
Rte. 327, 500 m off Rte. 4 • Large
1880s home surrounded by farm
country • Four o/n units, one shared
B, one shared S • Pets permitted •
Non-smoking only
FEATURES: Antique furnishings •
Sun deck with hot tub • Ideal for
cycling, walking and bird-watching
• White beaches, restaurants and
golf course nearby • Information on
eastern PEI attractions available
*RATES: $50 (2), $7 add'l person •
$300 (weekly), $42 add'l person •
Breakfast • Open June 1-Oct. 31 •
Off-season by reservation • MC,
Visa accepted • Reservations
preferred • TIAPEI Member*

Augustine Cove
Shore Farm
Bed & Breakfast ★★ ¹⁄₂
Mrs. Roy Cutcliffe, Port Borden-
Carleton, RR 1, Augustine Cove,
C0B 1X0
(902) 855-2871
Rte. 10, 8 km (5 mi) east of
Confederation Bridge • 200-acre
farm with private beach • Three o/n
units, two shared B&S, one private
B • Not suitable for children • No
pets, please • Non-smoking only
*RATES: $40 (2), $5 add'l person •
Breakfast extra • Open May-Oct. 31*

Baltic
Shady Lawn
Bed & Breakfast ★★ ¹⁄₂
Florence & Burrows MacPhail,
RR5, Kensington, C0B 1M0
(902) 836-5580
Toll free 1-800-275-7972
Website
http://www.bbCanada.com/75.html
Rte. 103, 10 km (6 mi) from
Kensington • Century home in farm-

ing commu-
nity with
quiet, shad-
ed, spacious
lawns • Five
o/n units,
one shared B&S, one shared S;
one housekeeping suite • TV in
family room • Cot and crib available
• Pets on leash permitted • Non-
smoking only
FEATURES: Gardens • Horseshoe
pit • Sand box • Restaurants and
attractions nearby • Five minutes to
beach
*RATES: $35-$50 (1-2), $60-$80
(suite) •$390- $530 (weekly, suite)
$8-$15 add'l person • Visa accepted
• Off-season rates Oct. 1- May 30 •
Full breakfast • Open year-round •
KATA; LATA Member*

Bay Fortune
The Inn at
Bay Fortune ★★★ ¹⁄₂
David Wilmer, Souris RR 4, C0A 2B0
(902) 687-3745
Fax (902) 687-3540
Off-season 49 Bond Street,
Hartford, CT, USA, 06114;
(860) 296-1348
Former summer home of Broadway
playwright Elmer Harris and late
actress Colleen Dewhurst (Marilla,
Anne of Green Gables) • Twelve
o/n units, private B&S, some with
sitting area and fireplace
FEATURES: Licensed dining
room; recommended by *Where to
Eat in Canada* as "without question
the best on the Island" •
Overlooking Fortune Harbour, with
the Northumberland Strait beyond •
Dinner only • Wheelchair accessible
*RATES: $120-$180 (2), $25 add'l
person • Full breakfast • Open May
23 to mid-Oct.*

Bay Fortune

Odds & Ends
Bed & Breakfast ★★ ½
June Underhay, Souris RR 4,
C0A 2B0
(902) 687-2980
Quiet family home on 100-acre farm
with view of Northumberland Strait
• Three o/n units, one shared B&S
FEATURES: Flower and vegetable
gardens • Laundry facilities •
Kitchen facilities • Deck • Barbecue
• Picnic table • Lawn • Golf, fine
dining and beaches nearby
*RATES: $40-$50 • Breakfast •
Open June 15-Nov. 30*

Belle River

J.R.'s Bed & Breakfast
Arthur & Jan Roome, Belle River
RR 1, C0A 1B0
(902) 962-2183
On Belle River Wharf Rd., off
TransCanada Hwy • Century farm-
house on three landscaped acres •
Two o/n units, one shared B&S, pri-
vate 1/2 B • Cable TV/VCR • Pets
permitted
FEATURES: Minutes from Wood
Islands ferry
*RATES: $42-$45 (1-2) •
Continental breakfast • Open May
1-Oct. 15*

Bideford

Hilltop Acres
Bed & Breakfast ★★★
Mrs. Janice (Wayne) Trowsdale,
Box 3011, Ellerslie, C0B 1J0
(902) 831-2817
Rte. 166, Lady Slipper Dr., 3 km (2
mi) west of Tyne Valley •
Renovated 1930s country home on
75 acres • Three o/n units, one
shared B&S • TV in sitting room •
Pets allowed • Non-smoking only

FEATURES: Living/dining room
for guests • Croquet • Whirlpool tub
• Complimentary evening beverage
• Excellent for cycling and walking
• Balcony overlooks Goodwood
River and Malpeque Bay
*RATES: $40-46 (1-2) • $260-$300
(weekly) • Discount on second and
subsequent nights • Breakfast •
Open June 1-Sept. 30 • Off-season
by reservation • PEIBBA Member*

Birch Hill

MacLean's
Bed & Breakfast ★★ ½
Mrs. Esther MacLean, RR 1,
Richmond, C0B 1Y0
(902) 831-2570
Toll free 1-800-288-8112
Near junction of Rte. 131 and
Rte. 12 (Lady Slipper Dr.) • Three
o/n units, one shared B&S, one
shared 1/2 B.• TV/VCR • Cot and
crib available
FEATURES: Near dinner theatre •
Greenwood Provincial Park and golf
course nearby • Beach on property
*RATES: $40 (2), $10 add'l person •
$240 (weekly), $60 add'l person •
Breakfast • Open May 1-Oct. 31 •
TIAPEI Member*

Bonshaw

Saw & Sickle
Bed & Breakfast ★★★
Paul & Wendy Naylor, RR 1,
Bonshaw, C0A 1C0
(902) 675-4004
Toll free 1-800-377-5792
On Green Rd. • New home on six
acres, balcony and wrap-around
deck with view • Two o/n units, one
shared B&S • Non-smoking only
FEATURES: Ideal for walking,
canoeing, fishing, skiing and snowshoeing • Outdoor hot tub

*RATES: $55 (2), $10 add'l person •
Off-season rates • Breakfast • Open
year-round*

Bonshaw
Strathgartney
Country Inn
Cathi & Blair McPhail, General
Delivery, Bonshaw, C0A 1C0
(902) 675-4711
Toll free 1-800-267-4407
On TransCanada Hwy, 15 minutes
west of Charlottetown • Green-
gabled 134-year-old farmhouse-
turned-inn • Nine o/n units, eight
B&S, two S; one housekeeping suite
• Non-smoking only
FEATURES: Licensed dining room
with musical comedy evenings •
Beaches, golfing and theatre nearby
*RATES: $49-$125 (2) • Breakfast •
Open year-round • AE, MC, Visa
accepted*

Borden-Carleton
Carleton Cove Farm
Tourist Home
Gordon & Carol Myers, RR2,
Albany, C0B 1A0
(902) 855-2795
On Rte. 10, 5 km (3 mi) from
Borden ferry in Carleton Siding •
Ninety-six acres of mixed-farm
property • Three o/n units, one
private B&S, one shared B&S •
TV in rooms • Cots available • Pets
permitted, usually on leash •
Non-smoking only
FEATURES: Complimentary
evening snack • Restaurant 4 km
(2.5 mi) • Shed for bicycles •
Whirlpool • Tour of farm on request
• Beach 6 km (3.7 mi)
*RATES: $35-$40 (2), $7 add'l
person • $210-$240 (weekly), $42
add'l person • Off-season rates •
Breakfast • Open year-round*

Borden-Carleton
MacCallum
Bed & Breakfast
Mrs.(A.A.) Grace MacCallum,
Borden-Carleton, C0B 1X0
(902) 855-2229
3 km (1.8 mi) from Borden ferry •
Quiet country home • Two o/n units,
one shared B • TV in living room •
Cot available
FEATURES: Piano in living room •
Restaurants and attractions nearby •
Bicycle storage • Beach 5 km (3 mi)
• Excellent for late arrivals and
early departures • Ample parking
*RATES: $40 (2), $5 add'l person •
Breakfast extra • Open June 1-
Sept. 30*

Brackley
Blossom Haven Cottage
& Tourist Home
Susanne Manovill, Brackley Beach,
C1E 1Z3
(902) 672-2714
Fax (902) 672-2518
E-mail manovill@upei.ca
On Rte. 6, west off Rte. 15 • Two
o/n units, one shared B&S; one cot-
tage
FEATURES: Picnic table and bar-
becue • Two bicycles and helmets
for guests' use • German spoken
*RATES: $32-$35 (1-2), $60 (cot-
tage), $5 add'l person • $210-$325
(weekly), $30 add'l person (no GST)
• Off-season rates before June 30
and after Aug. 31, excluding
Victoria and Labour Days • Open
May 1-Sept. 30*

Brackley
Brackley Bay Tourist Home and Cottages ★★★
Ronald & Jeanne Brewster, Brackley Beach, RR 9, Winsloe, C1E 1Z3
(902) 672-2660
Rte. 15 • Quiet home overlooking bay • Four o/n units, one private B, two shared B&S; three cottages • Cable TV in rooms • Children under 5 yrs, half-price • No pets, please • Non-smoking only
FEATURES: Picnic tables, barbecues, playground on premises • Deep-sea fishing, golf course, theatre and restaurants nearby • 1 km (.6 mi) to National Park beaches
RATES: $60-$75 (2), $100 (cottage), $10 add'l person • $350-$600 (weekly), $50 add'l person • Minimum stay (cottage) three days • Off-season rates (10% off) before July 1 and after Labour Day • Full breakfast • Open May-Sept. 30

Brackley
Brackley House Bed & Breakfast ★★ ½
Len & Carol Lang, Brackley Point Road, RR 9, Winsloe, C1E 1Z3
(902) 566-2268
Rte. 15 (Brackley Point Rd.) • Century-old country home with spacious grounds, garden and sun deck • Three o/n units, one shared B&S • Cable TV/VCR in sitting room • Cot available • No pets, please • Non-smoking only
FEATURES: Close to airport, Charlottetown's theatre district and National Park beach
RATES: $30 (1), $50-$60 (2), $10 add'l person (tax incl.) • Full breakfast • Open May 1-Sept. 1

Brackley
Lenrose Farm ★★★
Leonard & Rosemary MacCormack, Brackley, RR 9, Winsloe, C1E 1Z3
(902) 368-8242
Across from airport and close to beaches and Charlottetown • Working horse farm • One o/n unit, private B&S; one housekeeping suite
FEATURES: Furnished with antiques • Beaches nearby
RATES: $40 (1-2), $50 (suite), $5 add'l person • $240-$310 (weekly), $25 add'l person • Continental breakfast • Open June 1-Sept. 1

Brackley
Blue Waters Tourist Home ★★ ½
Lee & Judy Seaman, Brackley Beach, RR 9, Winsloe, C1E 1Z3
(902) 672-2720
Toll free 1-800-616-9436
Situated on ten acres, overlooking Brackley Bay and National Park • Five o/n units, two shared B&S; three cottages • Cable TV
FEATURES: Heated swimming pool and whirlpool • Barbecues • Spacious deck and lawn • Kitchen facilities
RATES: $39-$49 (1-2), $5 add'l person • $245-$330 (weekly), $675-$875 (weekly, cottage) • Open June-Sept. (cottages open May-Oct.) • TIAPEI Member

Brackley Beach
Linden Lane Guest House ★★ ½
Margaret MacCormack-Sosnkowski, Britain Shore Road, Brackley Beach, C1E 1Z3
(902) 672-3091
Built in 1820 of PEI sandstone in

secluded Linden garden • Four o/n units, one shared B&S • Children over 12 yrs welcome • Pets permitted, usually on leash • Non-smoking only
FEATURES: French and German spoken • Cyclists welcome • Romance packages
RATES: $42-$52 (1-2), $10 add'l person • Breakfast • Open June-Sept. 30

Brackley Beach
Windsong Farm Bed & Breakfast ★★ ½
Jean & John Huak, Brackley Beach, RR 9, Winsloe, C1E 1Z3
(902) 672-2874
Off-season 17 Langley Road, Falmouth, MA, USA, 02540; (508) 540-3244
Rte. 6 • Charming 1860s farmhouse near Rustico Bay • Four o/n units, two shared B&S • Cable TV • Children over 12 yrs welcome • Non-smoking only
FEATURES: Furnished with antiques • Sun porches • Ocean beaches nearby
RATES: $55-$65 (1-2), $15 add'l person • Minimum stay two nights in July and Aug. • $330-$390 (weekly), $90 add'l person • Off-season rates June and Sept. • Full breakfast

Brooklyn
Redcliffe Farm Bed & Breakfast
Vera Bates, RR 1, Montague, C0A 1R0
(902) 838-2476
Toll free 1-800-663-3799
On Rte. 317, ten minutes from Wood Islands ferry • Tastefully renovated 200-year-old farmhouse on sheep farm • Three o/n units, one shared B&S • TV • Pets permitted, usually on leash

FEATURES: Dinner with advance notice during 2-3 night stays • Porcelain reproduction dolls handmade on premises
RATES: $42-$50 (2), $10 add'l person • Breakfast • Open June 15-Oct.1

Cable Head
Cable Head Bed & Breakfast ★★ ½
Doug & Elizabeth Borman, St. Peters Bay, C0A 2A0
(902) 961-3275

Rte. 16, 2 km (1.2 mi) north of Rte. 2 • Modern home in unique setting • Three o/n units, one private B, two shared B&S • Cots and crib available • Children welcome • Pets permitted • Non-smoking only
FEATURES: Laundry facilities • Licensed dining room 10 km (6.2 mi) • Barbecues and picnic tables • Beautiful sandy beaches nearby • Driving range on property • Twenty minutes to championship golf courses • Airstrip on property for fly-in guests • Jacuzzi
RATES: $45-$55 (2), $8 add'l person • $270-$330 (weekly), $35 add'l person • Off-season rates Sept. 15-June 23 • Continental breakfast • Open year-round • PEIBBA Member

Cape Traverse
Glennhaven
Bed & Breakfast
Ed Cutcliffe, RR 1,
Borden-Carleton, C0B 1X0
(902) 855-2729
Hwy 1 to Mowatt's Tourist Mart,
turn right, 1 km (.6 mi) until paved
road bears left • Christian home •
Three o/n units, one shared B&S •
Non-smoking only
FEATURES: 4 km (2.5 mi) from
ferry and new bridge; 2 km (1.2 mi)
to safe tidal beach
*RATES: $17-$50 (1-2), $10 add'l
person • $75- $250 (weekly), $50
add'l person • Continental breakfast
• Open year-round*

Cape Traverse
Goodwin's
Tourist Home ★★ ½
Evert & Gayle Goodwin, Box 2603,
RR 1, Borden-Carleton, C0B 1X0
(902) 855-2849
Four o/n units, one shared B, one
shared S • Cable TV in rooms • Pets
welcome
*RATES: $35-$50 (1-2), $10 add'l
person • $210-$300 (weekly), $60
add'l person • Off-season rates after
Oct. 15 and before May 15 •
Breakfast • Open year-round*

Cape Traverse
MacWilliams'
Tourist Home
& Cottages ★★
Mrs. Donald MacWilliams, RR 1,
Borden-Carleton, C0B 1X0
(902) 855-2855
Off Rte. 10 • Country setting overlooking Northumberland Strait •
Two o/n units, one shared B&S; one
cottage; one mobile home • Adults
preferred • Non-smoking only

FEATURES: Verandas • Picnic
tables • Flower gardens • Beach on
premises • Strait crossing, tourism
restaurant and stores nearby
*RATES: $40 (1-2), $75 (cottage,
mobile home) • $270-$500 (weekly),
$30 add'l person • Open June 1-
Sept. 30*

Cavendish
Chinny-Chin-Chin
Elaine Miller, Forest Hills Park
Road, Cavendish, C0A 1N0
(902) 963-2377

1.6 km (1
mi) west on
Rte. 6 from
Rte. 6 and
Rte. 13 traf-
fic lights,
turn left opposite small white church
onto Forest Hill Park Rd., first
house on left • Located in centre of
Cavendish • One o/n unit, one
shared B&S; one cottage • TV •
Telephone • Non-smoking only
FEATURES: Large grounds •
Picnic table • Bicycle storage •
Close to beach • Two golf courses
next door • Horseback riding
*RATES: $50 (2), $140 (cottage) •
$325-$800 (weekly) • Continental
breakfast • Open June 1-late Sept.*

Cavendish
Country House Inn
Ruth Brewer & Dede Brewer-
Wilson, Gulf Shore Road,
Cavendish National Park, RR 2,
Hunter River, C0A 1N0
Tel & Fax (902) 963-2055
Toll free 1-800-363-2055
Overlooking Gulf of St. Lawrence •
Century country home furnished with
antiques and quilts • Five o/n units,
private and shared B&S; two house-
keeping suites • Non-smoking only

FEATURES: Piano • Breakfast on sun-porch • Two living rooms • Guest fridges • Bicycling • Walk on cliffs or beaches • Guests exempt from Park entry fees
RATES: $45-$55 (2), $80 (suite), $10 add'l person • $300-$530 (weekly), $50 add'l person • Continental breakfast • Two-night minimum stay

Cavendish
Cavendish Country Inn & Cottages ★★★
Donald & Lynn McKearney, Box 762, Cornwall, C0A 1H0
(902) 963-2181
Toll free 1-800-454-4853
E-mail donald.mckearney@sympatico.pe.ca
Website http://www.peisland.com/countryinn/cottages.html
On Rte. 6, east of Cavendish intersection • Eight o/n units, private B&S; thirteen cottages • Cable TV/VCR in rooms • Pets permitted, usually on leash • Non-smoking only
FEATURES: Minutes to beach and attractions • Laundry facilities • Heated swimming pool • Jacuzzi • Playground • Barbecues • Fax service • Golf and family packages
RATES: $85-$140 (2), $95-$199 (cottage), $10 add'l person • Off-season rates (up to 50% off) before June 23 and after Labour Day • Continental breakfast • Open May 1-Oct. 31 • Cancellation policy

Cavendish
Cavendish Wild Rose Country Inn
Gloria Dorgan, Cavendish Road, RR 2, Hunter River, C0A 1N0
(902) 963-3324
Toll free 1-800-794-3324
Rte. 6, 3 km east of Cavendish intersection • New country inn near tourist attractions • Six o/n units, private B&S • Cable TV in rooms • Non-smoking only
RATES: $65-$85 (1-2), $8 add'l person • Off-season rates available • Continental breakfast • Open year-round

Cavendish
Clark Homestead Bed & Breakfast ★★ ½
Chesley & Shirley Clark, RR 1, Hunter River, C0A 1N0
(902) 963-2723
Rte. 6 • Located in the heart of Cavendish • Three o/n units, one private 1/2 B, one shared B&S • Cable TV • Non-smoking only
FEATURES: Short walk to Green Gables, Cavendish Beach and major attractions • Cozy family room
RATES: $45-$55 (2) • Off-season rates before July 1 and after Aug. 31 • Continental breakfast • Open April 15-Oct. 15

Cavendish
Kindred Spirits Country Inn and Cottages ★★★★
Al & Sharon James, Cavendish, C0A 1N0
Tel & Fax (902) 963-2434
E-mail ajames@peinet.pe.ca
Rte. 6, Memory Lane • Country estate beside Green Gables House and Golf Course, decorated with antiques and crafts • Fourteen o/n units, private B&S (three with Jacuzzi); thirteen cottages • Cable TV in rooms • Non-smoking only
FEATURES: French spoken • Laundromat • Parlour lobby with fireplacee • Pool and whirlpool • Beach 800 m
RATES: $65-$140 (2), $125-$165 (suite), $115-$185 (cottage), $5-$15 add'l person, • Weekly and family rates • Off-season rates before June 15 and after Labour Day • Continental breakfast • Open May 15-mid-Oct. • MC, Visa accepted • CAA Member

Cavendish
MacLure Bed & Breakfast ★★ ½
John & Naomi MacLure, Cavendish Road, C0A 1N0
(902) 963-2239
Rte. 6, 3 km east of Cavendish intersection • Three o/n units, one shared B&S, one shared S • Cable TV in rooms and sitting room • Non-smoking only
FEATURES: Near Green Gables, beaches and golf course
RATES: $35-$45 (2), $5 add'l person • Off-season rates before June 29 and after Sept. 2 • Breakfast extra • Open year-round

Cavendish
Marco Polo Inn ★★ ½
Dr. K.G. Ellis, Box 9, Hunter River, C0A 1N0
(902) 963-2352
Toll free 1-800-665-2652
Off-season (902) 964-2960
Rte. 13, 2 km (1.2 mi) south of Cavendish Beach • Six o/n units, private B&S • TV in rooms
FEATURES: Licensed restaurant • Heated swimming pools • Marco Polo Land facilities available
RATES: $54-$60 (2), $4 add'l person • Off-season rates before June 23 • Breakfast • Open June 9-Sept. 7 • MC, Visa accepted • TIAPEI Member

Cavendish
Montgomery's House Bed & Breakfast
Montgomery Drummond, Cavendish, C0A 1N0
(902) 963-3287
Off-season 2 Altavista Crescent, Charlottetown, C1E 1M9; Tel & Fax (902) 894-4248
500m from beach in National Park with spectacular views of the Gulf • Two o/n units, one private B&S, one shared S • Cable TV in rooms • Non-smoking only
RATES: $65-$80 (2), $15 add'l person • Off-season rates before June 15 and after Aug. 31 • Open May 1-Sept. 30

Cavendish
Our Lady of the Way Tourist Lodge
Les Rogerson, 12 Maple Avenue, Charlottetown, C1A 6C9
(902) 963-2024
Toll free 1-888-963-5239
On Rte. 13, 1.5 km (1 mi) south of

Cavendish Beach • Ten o/n units, five shared B&S, three shared S • TV in rooms • Cot available • Pets permitted, usually on leash
FEATURES: Bilingual • Sun-deck • Picnic area • Licensed dining 1 km (.6 mi)
RATES: $35-$70 (1-4) • Off-season and weekly rates • Open June 15-Sept. 30 • BA, MC, Visa accepted

Cavendish
Parkview Farm Tourist Home and Cottages ★★ ½
Alvin & Eleanor MacNeill, Cavendish, RR 2, Hunter River, C0A 1N0
(902) 963-2027
Fax (902) 963-2935
Rte. 6, 2 km (1.2 mi) east of Cavendish intersection • Active 420-acre dairy farm overlooking ocean • Four o/n units, 2 shared B&S, one shared 1/2 B; seven cottages • Colour TV • Cots available • Pets permitted, on leash • Non-smoking only
FEATURES: Ocean view • Golf, restaurant and Green Gables nearby • Walk to beach 360m
RATES: $35-$45 (2), $110 (cottage), $5-$6 add'l person • Continental breakfast extra • Open year-round (cottages open May-Oct.) • MC, Visa accepted • TIAPEI Member

Cavendish
Shining Waters Country Inn ★★★
Peter & Kathleen Ryan; Marilyn & Philip Wood, Cavendish, C0A 1N0
(902) 963-2251/2758
Rte. 13 • Historic inn overlooking ocean and PEI National Park • Ten o/n units, private B&S • TV in rooms • Non-smoking only
FEATURES: Traditionally known as Rachel Lynde's house (*Anne of Green Gables*) • Parlour • Fireplaces • Antiques • Deck • Exercise equipment • Pool and whirlpools • Beach nearby
RATES: $75-$85 (2), $10 add'l person • Off-season rates and weekly rates available • Continental breakfast • Open May-Oct. • AE, DC, ER, MC, Visa accepted

Cavendish
Sunrise Farm Tourist Home ★★ ½
Garth & Donna MacNeill, Cavendish, RR 2, Hunter River, C0A 1N0
(902) 963-3088
On Rte. 6, 2 km (1.2 mi) east of Cavendish intersection • New Cape Cod home on active dairy farm overlooking the ocean • Two o/n units, one shared B&S • TV • Non-smoking only
FEATURES: Barbecue • Picnic table • Five-minute walk to beach • Close to attractions, restaurants, golf course and Green Gables
RATES: $35-$45, $5 add'l person • Off-season rates Labour Day-June 21 • Continental breakfast on weekends extra • Open year-round

Cavendish
Willow Cottage Inn ★★★
Edward & Ann Morris, Cavendish, C0A 1N0
(902) 963-3385
Rte. 6, on Memory Lane • Family-owned inn beside Green Gables House and Golf Course • Seven o/n units, private B&S; three cottages • TV/VCR in sitting room • Non-smoking only
FEATURES: Maid service • Sitting room with books and fireplace • Air-conditioning • 800m to beach
RATES: $65-$100 (2), $90-$115 (cottage), $5-$10 add'l person • Off-season rates • Full breakfast • Open May 15-Oct. 1 • MC, Visa accepted

Central Bedeque
Pine-Lawn Bed & Breakfast ★★ ½
George & Marina Campbell, Box 3944, Central Bedeque, C0B 1G0
(902) 887-2270
1 km (.6 mi) off Rte. 1A • Comfortable, quiet home overlooking acres of farmland • Three o/n units, one shared B, one private B&S • TV/VCR • Cot available • No pets, please • Non-smoking only
FEATURES: Wheelchair accessibility • Spacious deck • Barbecue and picnic table • Piano • Panoramic view of Bedeque Bay • Bird-watching
RATES: $35-$45 (2), $10 add'l person • $240-$270 (weekly) • Open May 1-Oct. 31 • Visa accepted

Charlottetown Area
Abegweit Tourist Home ★★ ½
Gail Jenkins, 19 Blythe Crescent, Charlottetown, C1A 8C7
(902) 892-2793
Three o/n units, one shared B&S • TV/VCR • Pets permitted, on leash
FEATURES: Wheelchair accessibility • Close to shopping and restaurants
RATES: $25-$30 (2), $7 add'l person • Open May 15-Oct. 15

Charlottetown Area
Abide Awhile Tourist Home ★★
Bruce & Evelyn Younker, 256 Mount Edward Road, Charlottetown, C1A 5T7
(902) 892-8811
Three o/n units, one shared B&S • TV/VCR • Pets permitted, usually on leash
FEATURES: Partial wheelchair accessibility • Close to shopping, restaurants and downtown
RATES: $25-$30 (2), $5 add'l person • Open May 15-Sept. 7

Charlottetown Area
Allix's Bed & Breakfast ★★★
Rita Allix, 11 Johnson Avenue, Charlottetown, C1A 3H7
(902) 892-2643
Quiet residential area • Two o/n units, one shared B&S • TV in living room • Non-smoking only
FEATURES: Use of living room • Close to restaurants, shopping, churches and Victoria Park
RATES: $45 (2), $12 add'l person • $270 (weekly), $72 add'l person • Off-season rates Sept. 1-April 30 • Full breakfast • Open year-round • TIAPEI Member

Charlottetown Area
Aloha Tourist Home
Maynard MacMillan, 234 Sydney Street, Charlottetown, C1A 1H1
(902) 892-9944
Century home facing Hillsborough day park • Three o/n units, one shared B&S • TV in rooms
FEATURES: Two fully equipped kitchens • Garage for bicycles and pets • Bus or airport pickup can be pre-arranged • Close to all amenities
RATES: $32-$38 (2), $4 add'l person • Off-season rates Oct 1-May 14 (25% off) • Open year-round

Charlottetown Area
Altavista
Bed & Breakfast ★★ ¹/₂
Ada & Stuart Drummond, 2 Altavista Crescent, Charlottetown, C1E 1M9
Tel or Fax (902) 894-4248

Beautiful waterfront home • One o/n unit, private B; one suite • TV in rooms • No pets, please • Non-smoking only
FEATURES: Canoeing on premises • Biking area • Waterfront deck • Five minutes to downtown • Fifteen minutes to beaches
RATES: $75-$85 (2), $15 add'l person • Breakfast • Open May 15- Oct. 15

Charlottetown Area
Amanda's Tourist Home
Laura MacLauchlan, 130 Spring Park Road, Charlottetown, C1A 3Y6
(902) 894-9909
Two o/n units, one shared B&S •
Cot available
FEATURES: Close to restaurants, shopping and Confederation Centre
RATES: $30 (2), $10 add'l person • Off-season rates • Open year-round

Charlottetown Area
Ambrose
Tourist Home ★★
Nora McLeod, 17 Passmore Street, Charlottetown, C1A 2B8
(902) 566-5853
Toll free 1-800-665-6072
Off University Ave. • Large duplex in city centre • Six o/n units, three shared B&S; one housekeeping suite • TV in rooms
FEATURES: Transportation provided to and from bus station and airport
RATES: $30-$40 (2), $55 (suite), $5-$10 add'l person • Off-season rates before July 1 and after Sept. 6 • Breakfast extra • Open May-Oct. • MC, Visa accepted

Charlottetown Area
Anchor's Aweigh ★★ ¹/₂
Mary Y. Hopgood, 45 Queen Elizabeth Drive, Charlottetown, C1A 3A8
(902) 892-4319
Near Victoria Park; directly across from Viceroy Ave. • Waterfront property overlooking North River • Two o/n units, one shared B&S • TV • Non-smoking only
FEATURES: Use of living room • Large deck • 2 km (1.2 mi) from amenities
RATES: $45 (2) • Full breakfast • Open year-round • TIAPEI Member

Charlottetown Area
Anne's Ocean View Haven Bed & Breakfast
R. Anne Olson, Kinlock, Box 2044, Charlottetown, C1A 7N7
(902) 569-4644
Toll free 1-800-665-4644
Six minutes east of Charlottetown off Rte. 1 • Peaceful country home in seascape setting • Four o/n units, private B&S; one suite • Cable TV and fridges in rooms • Trained pets permitted • Non-smoking only
FEATURES: Wheelchair accessibility • Views of fields, countryside and seascape • Packed lunches on request • Sun room • Garden patio • Maid service • Guest kitchen with stove and microwave • North shore beaches 20 minutes • Packages available
RATES: $75-$95 (2), $120 (suite), $10 add'l person • Full breakfast • Open year-round • ATOPEI Member

Charlottetown Area
Auberge Stratford Inn ★★ ½
Louise Lalonde, 27 Hopeton Road, Stratford, C1A 7G2
(902) 569-4849
Charming Edwardian-era inn en route to ferries and minutes from Charlottetown • Three o/n units, private B&S • Cable TV/VCR in sitting room
FEATURES: Charming garden and veranda • Billiards • Evening meals available • Beaches nearby • French spoken
RATES: $45-$75 (1-2) • $320-$400 (weekly) • Off-season rates Oct. 1-May 31 • Breakfast • Open year-round

Charlottetown Area
Beairsto Tourist Home ★★
Mrs. Ralph Beairsto, 42 Greenfield Avenue, Charlottetown, C1A 3N4
(902) 894-8055
Quiet residential area • One o/n unit, private B • No pets, please • Non-smoking only
FEATURES: Walking distance to downtown Charlottetown, theatres, shopping, Confederation Centre, park boardwalk and bus stop
RATES: $30 (2) • Off-season rates Sept. 1-May 1 • Open year-round

Charlottetown Area
Binstead Bed & Breakfast ★★★
Susan Partridge, Heartz Road, Charlottetown, C1A 7J7
(902) 894-9642
Toll free 1-800-333-5412
On Rte. 1A, six minutes to Charlottetown • Georgian-style mansion (c. 1833) overlooking Hillsborough River in peaceful landscaped setting • Four o/n units, private B&S, B or Jacuzzi; one suite • Cable TV • Cots available • No pets, please • Non-smoking only
FEATURES: Balcony and veranda with views • Central to most attractions • Sandy beaches
RATES: $75-$95 (2), $150 (suite), $10 add'l person • Continental breakfast • Open June 1-Oct. 1 • Reservations recommended • MC, Visa accepted • TIAPEI Member

Charlottetown Area
Birchill Bed & Breakfast ★★ ½
Bob & Yvonne Santer, 14 Birch Hill Drive, Charlottetown, C1A 6W5

(902) 892-4353
Three o/n units, one shared B&S,
one shared S • TV • Telephone •
Non-smoking only
FEATURES: Sun room •
Complimentary drinks on arrival •
Lock-up for bicycles • Close to
shopping, theatre, university, city
centr and beaches
*RATES: $45 (2), $7 add'l person •
$270 (weekly), $42 add'l person •
Breakfast • Open June 15-Sept. 15 •
PEIBBA Member*

Charlottetown Area
The Black Duck
Francesca Hart, RR 4, Cornwall,
C0A 1H0
(902) 892-0906
On Rte. 148 (York Point Rd.) •
1800s farmhouse in secluded paradise,
minutes from Charlottetown • Three
o/n units, one shared B&S one
shared S • Pets welcome • Non-
smoking only
FEATURES: Partial wheelchair
accessibility • Flower gardens •
Berry picking • Private river beach •
Homemade snacks
*RATES: $35-$50 (1-2), $8 add'l
person • Weekly rates • Full breakfast • Open May-Sept.*

Charlottetown Area
Blanchard
Heritage Home ★★ ¹/₂
Florence Blanchard, 163 Dorchester
Street, Charlottetown, C1A 1E4
(902) 894-9756
Three o/n units, one shared B&S
*RATES: $18-$30 (1-2) • Off-season
rates • Open May-Oct. 31*

Charlottetown Area
Cairns' Tourist Home
Helen Cairns, 18 Pond Street,
Charlottetown, C1A 2P2
(902) 368-3552
Three o/n units, one shared B&S •
Non-smoking only
*RATES: $24-$26 (1-2), $8 add'l
person • Open year-round
• TIAPEI Member*

Charlottetown Area
Callaghan Tourist Home
Mary J. Callaghan, 51 Dorchester
Street, Charlottetown, C1A 1C8
(902) 894-3502
Two o/n units, one shared B&S
*RATES: $25 (2) • Off-season rates
• Open year-round*

Charlottetown Area
Campbell's Maple
Bed & Breakfast ★★★
Mrs. Maida Campbell, 28 Maple
Avenue, Charlottetown, C1A 6E3
(902) 894-4488
Toll free 1-800-276-5288
Comfortable home with living room
& deck available to guests • Two
o/n units, two shared B&S; one
family suite • Non-smoking only
FEATURES: Five minutes from
airport, ten minutes from down-
town, fifteen minutes from north
shore beaches
*RATES: $55 (2), $10 add'l adult,
$5 add'l child • Full breakfast •
Open May 24-Oct. 31 • TIAPEI
Member*

Charlottetown Area
The Carriage House Bed & Breakfast ★★ ½
Don & Mary Large, 37 Grafton Street, Box 1265, Charlottetown, C1A 7M8
(902) 368-1426
Toll free 1-888-207-5444
Fully-restored historic home (c. 1820), one block from Confederation Plaza • Three o/n units, two private B, one shared B&S; one suite • Cable TV/VCR in lounge • Cot available • Non-smoking only
FEATURES: Antique furnishings • Office equipment available • Off-street parking
RATES: $55-$85 (1-2), $125 (suite), $10 add'l person • Weekly rates • Continental breakfast • Open year-round • Reservations required Oct. 1-May 1 • MC, Visa accepted

Charlottetown Area
Chez-Nous (A Tender Treasure) Bed & Breakfast ★★★ ½
Paul & Sandi Gallant, Ferry Road, RTR 4, Cornwall, C0A 1H0
(902) 566-2779
Fax (902) 628-3852
Toll free 1-800-566-2779
On Rte. 248, ten minutes west of Charlottetown • Five o/n units, private B • Cable TV and telephone in rooms • Pets permitted
FEATURES: Picnics • Solarium-enclosed dining room • Veranda • Bicycles • Jacuzzi
RATES: $70-$90 (2), $20 add'l person • Full breakfast • Open year-round

Charlottetown Area
Colonial Charm Inn
Gary MacDougall, 9 Euston Street, Charlottetown, C1A 1V5
(902) 892-8934
Toll free 1-800-239-5127
Award-winning colonial-style home • Four o/n units, one shared S, one shared B • TV in rooms • Non-smoking only
FEATURES: Close to downtown shopping, restaurants, tennis courts, bike rentals, Victoria Park, Confederation Centre and waterfront
RATES: $55-$105 (2), $12 add'l person • $330-$630 (weekly), $72 add'l person • Off-season rates Sept. 30-May 31 • Breakfast • Open year-round • MC, Visa accepted

Charlottetown Area
Cosy Country Bed & Breakfast ★★ ½
Paul & Carolyn Whelan, 8 Ferguson Drive, Stratford, C1B 1B7
(902) 569-3748
Quiet, spacious home with a view of Charlottetown • Three o/n units, one shared B&S, one shared 1/2 B • Pets permitted • Non-smoking only
FEATURES: Minutes to downtown restaurants, theatre or beaches
RATES: $30-$50 (1-2) •
Continental breakfast • Open June 22-Sept. 10

Charlottetown Area
A Country Home ★★★ ½
Norman & Phyllis Hall, RR 10, Winsloe, C1E 1Z4
(902) 368-2340
Toll free 1-800-265-4255
Off Rte. 1 (Upton Rd.), just west of Charlottetown • Restored heritage home nestled amidst mature trees

and flowers on spacious grounds • Four o/n units, private B&S; one cottage

FEATURES: Spacious deck with water view • Guest sitting room • Horses • Piano • Five minutes to airport and downtown • Short drive to all attractions
RATES: *$55-$75 (2), $15 add'l person • $330-$450 (weekly) • Full breakfast • Open year-round • Nov.-April by reservation • PEIBBA Member*

Charlottetown Area
Duchess of Kent Inn ★★★

Sharyn Dalrymple, 218 Kent Street, Charlottetown, C1A 1P2
(902) 566-5826
Toll free 1-800-665-5826
Downtown heritage home (c. 1875) with three-storey corner turret • Six o/n units, two private B, two shared B&S, one shared S; three suites • TV/VCR • Telephone • No pets, please • Non-smoking only
FEATURES: Furnished with antiques • Kitchen available • Laundromat nearby • Bicycle storage • Restaurants, Confederation Centre, shopping, museums and churches nearby
RATES: *$55-$85 (2), $85-$115 (suite) • Breakfast extra • Open year-round • Dec.-April by reservation • HIAC; PEIBBA; TIAPEI Member*

Charlottetown Area
The Dundee Arms ★★★

Terry Grandy, 200 Pownal Street, Charlottetown, C1A 3W8
(902) 892-2496
Fax (902) 368-8532
E-mail dundee@isn.net
Website
http://www.grtplaces.com/ac/dun-arms/index.html
Turn-of-the-century mansion in Olde Charlottetown • Eight o/n units, private B&S; two suites • Cable TV and telephone in rooms • Non-smoking only
FEATURES: Antique furnishings and period decor • Licensed dining room and pub • Off-street parking
RATES: *$100-$145 (1-2) • Off-season rates mid-Oct.-May 31 • Open year-round • Major credit cards accepted*

Charlottetown Area
Elmwood Heritage Inn ★★★★ ¹/₂
Carol, Jay, Megan & Ross
Macdonald, Box 3128,
Charlottetown, C1A 7N8
(902) 368-3310
Fax (902) 628-8457
Website
http://www.grtplaces.com/ac/elm-wood
North River Rd. • Victorian home
(c. 1880) with elm-lined drive, built
by architect W.C. Harris for Island
premier • Three o/n units, private
B&S; one housekeeping suite •
Cable TV/VCR and telephone in
rooms • Non-smoking only
FEATURES: Eight working fire-places • Private balcony overlooking
park-like setting • Antiques, quilts
and artwork on display • Bicycles •
Four blocks to Victoria Park and
harbour; twelve blocks to downtown
*RATES: $90-$150 (2), $15 add'l
person • Off-season rates Oct.1-May
1 • Breakfast • Open year-round •
DC, ER, MC, Visa accepted • TIA-PEI Member*

Charlottetown Area
Evergreen Bed & Breakfast ★★★
Don & Sheila Sinclair, 34 Admiral
Street, Charlottetown, C1A 2E6
(902) 892-7652
One o/n unit, private B&S with
Jacuzzi • TV • Smoking permitted
outdoors only
*RATES: $65 (2) • Full breakfast •
Open June 30-Oct. 15*

Charlottetown Area
Fitzroy Hall ★★★
Helen & Reg Doucette, 45 Fitzroy
Street, Charlottetown, C1A 1R4

(902) 368-2077
Fax (902) 894-5711
Recently restored Victorian mansion
(1872) • Five o/n units, private
B&S; one suite, Jacuzzi • Cable TV
in rooms • No pets, please • Non-smoking only
FEATURES: Bilingual • Antique
furnishings • Walking distance to
Province House, Confederation
Centre, Beaconsfield and waterfront
*RATES: $85-$120 (2), $18 add'l
person • Weekly rates available •
Off-season rates Oct. 1-June 1 •
Full breakfast • Open year-round •
AE, ER, MC, Visa accepted • CAA,
TIAPEI Member*

Charlottetown Area
Gallant's Overnight Guest Home
Mrs. St. Clair Gallant, 196
Kensington Road, Charlottetown,
C1A 7S3
(902) 892-3030
Fax (902) 368-1713
Four o/n units, two shared B&S,
one shared 1/2 B • Non-smoking
only
FEATURES: Free transportation
from airport, bus station and return
trip into city • Large backyard
*RATES: $20-$25 (1-2), $10 add'l
person, $140-$175 (weekly) •
Breakfast • Open year-round • TIA-PEI Member*

Charlottetown Area
Hamilton House
Prof. Iain & Annette Galloway,
44 Brighton Road, Charlottetown,
C1A 1T7
(902) 368-1849
Toll free 1-800-905-9042
Stately home next to Victoria Park •
Three o/n units, one shared B&S;
one suite • Cable TV in sitting room

• Non-smoking only
FEATURES: Walking distance to
city centre and Province House •
Reading and sun rooms • French,
German, Spanish and some
Japanese spoken • Language lessons
available • Packed lunches, tennis
racquets and bicycles on request
RATES: $68-$95 (2), $110 (suite) •
Breakfast • *Open year-round* •
Reservations required Sept.-June

Charlottetown Area
Heart's Content ★★ ¹/₂
Joan Cumming, 236 Sydney Street,
Charlottetown, C1A 1H1
(902) 566-1064
In Olde Charlotte Town • 1860s
heritage home overlooks tree-shad-
ed Hillsborough Square • Four o/n
units, two shared B&S • Cable TV
in parlour • Non-smoking only
FEATURES: Comfortable antique
furnishings • Parlour • Bilingual •
Garage for bicycles • Short stroll to
sights, shopping and waterfront
RATES: $39 (2), $8 add'l person •
$250 (weekly) • *Off-season rates
before June 25 and after Labour
Day* • *Continental breakfast* • *Open
year-round* • *MC, Visa accepted*

Charlottetown Area
Heritage Harbour
House Inn ★★★
Bonnie Hennessey Brammer,
9 Grafton Street, Charlottetown,
C1A 1K3
(902) 892-6633
Toll free 1-800-405-0066
Restored early 1900s house in quiet
area of Olde Charlotte Town • Four
o/n units, two shared B&S •
TV/VCR in living room • Non-
smoking only
FEATURES: Bicycle storage •
Victoria Park, restaurants, theatre

and downtown shopping two blocks
away • Off-street parking
RATES: $65 (2), $10 add l person •
Weekly rates available • *Continental
breakfast* • *Open June 1-Sept. 30* •
PEIBBA Member

Charlottetown Area
Heron's Moor ★★★
Carolyn & Jim Molyneaux, Box 41,
Cornwall, C0A 1H0
(902) 566-2606
Toll free 1-800-567-2458
Four o/n units, two private B, two
shared B&S • TV/VCR
FEATURES: Kitchen facilities •
Sitting room • Barbecue • Backyard
• Hot tub • Harbour view • Minutes
from Charlottetown • Scenic tours
available
*RATES: $50-$80 (1-2), $10 add'l
person* • *Weekly rates available* •
Continental breakfast • *Open May 1
-Oct.1*

Charlottetown Area
Hillhurst Inn ★★★ ¹/₂
Scott Stewart & Jane Toombs,
181 Fitzroy Street, Charlottetown,
C1A 1S3
(902) 894-8004
Heritage property (1897) located in
the heart of historic Charlottetown •
Nine o/n units, private B&S •
TV/VCR • Non-smoking only
FEATURES: Sitting/reading room •
Period furnishings and Island art
throughout • Bicycles and windsurf-
ing equipment available
*RATES: $90-$130 (2), $18 add l
person* • *Open year-round* • *Nov.-
May by reservation* • *Continental
breakfast* • *MC, Visa accepted* •
TIAPEI Member

Charlottetown Area
Hillside House ★★★★
Ken & Marilyn Roper, 25 Hillside
Drive, Charlottetown, C1A 6H9
(902) 892-3640
Toll free 1-888-892-3640
Private home two miles from city
centre • One o/n unit, private B&S •
Non-smoking only
FEATURES: Laundry facilities •
Suite has lounge with TV/VCR and
breakfast nook • Bicycle storage •
Off-street parking
*RATES: $90 (2), $10 add l person •
$540 (weekly) • Continental break-
fast • Open year-round • Off-season
rates Sept. 1-June 15*

Charlottetown Area
Hilltop View
Tourist Home ★★
Mrs. Violet Maund, 10 Duncan
Heights, Charlottetown, C1A 6L7
(902) 894-8393
Three o/n units, one shared B&S;
one housekeeping suite • Non-
smoking only
FEATURES: Free transportation to
and from airport and bus station •
Shopping centre, downtown, golf
course, churches and beaches nearby
*RATES: $20-$30 (1-2), $35 (suite)
$5-$10 add'l person • $180 (week-
ly), $25 add'l person • Continental
breakfast • Open year-round • TIA-
PEI Member*

Charlottetown Area
The Inns
on Great George ★★★ ½
Joy Houston, 58 Great George
Street, Charlottetown, C1A 4K3
(902) 892-0606
Fax (902) 628-2079
Toll free 1-800-361-1118
Olde Charlotte Town's cluster of
five Georgian-style buildings with
inn-keeping traditions dating back
to 1811 • Five o/n units, private
B&S; three housekeeping suites •
Cable TV and telephone in rooms •
Non-smoking only
FEATURES: Partial wheelchair
accessibility • Furnished with
antiques • Licensed dining room
*RATES: $85-$125 (2), $135-$205
(suite) • Off-season rates Oct. 1-
May 30 • Breakfast • Open year-round*

Charlottetown Area
Kenny's Tourist Home
John & Mary Kenny, 171 Bunbury
Road, Stratford, C1A 7G9
(902) 569-3437
Three o/n units, one shared B&S •
TV • Pets permitted, usually on
leash • Non-smoking only
*RATES: $30 (2), $10 add'l person •
Continental breakfast • Open May
24-Sept. 30*

Charlottetown Area
MacInnis
Bed & Breakfast ★★★
Jean MacInnis, 80 Euston Street,
Charlottetown, C1A 1W2
(902) 892-6725
Located in downtown Charlottetown
• Elegant 1892 heritage home with
decorative veranda and large elm
trees • Four o/n units, two shared
B&S, one shared S • Cable TV in
rooms • Cot available • No pets,
please • Non-smoking only
FEATURES: Shed for bicycles •
Beautiful flower beds • Two blocks
to Confederation Centre, Province
House, Olde Charlotte Town,
restaurants and Victoria Park
*RATES: $32-$50 (1-2), $10 add l
person • Weekly and off-season
rates available • Continental breakfast • Open year-round*

Charlottetown Area
MacKeen's
Tourist Home ★★ ½
Mrs. Rowena MacKeen, 176 King
Street, Charlottetown, C1A 1C1
(902) 892-6296
Toll free 1-800-668-6296
150-year-old home, centrally located in Olde Charlotte Town • Two
o/n units, one shared B&S, one two-
room suite • Cable TV
FEATURES: Large yard • Picnic
table • Sunroom • Air-conditioning •
Shed for bikes • Close to downtown
and waterfront
*RATES: $40-$50 (2-3), $5 add'l
person • $240-$300 weekly, $30
add'l person • Continental breakfast
• Open year-round • TIAPEI
Member*

Charlottetown Area
MacLeod's
Bed & Breakfast ★★ ½
Mrs. Gordon E. MacLeod, 29 Esher
Street, Charlottetown, C1A 5G3
(902) 892-1458
Within walking distance of downtown Charlottetown • Quiet, private,
friendly, residential property on spacious treed lot • Three o/n units, two
shared B&S, one family room • TV
room available • Non-smoking only
FEATURES: Sun deck • Flower
gardens • Walking distance to
downtown, theatre, golf course,
marina, waterfront park, harness
racing and restaurants
*RATES: $35-$50 (2), $10 add'l
person • Breakfast on request •
Open May 15-Oct. 31 • TIAPEI
Member*

Charlottetown Area
The Maples
Guest Home
Mrs. Earl W.B. Foster,
124 St. Peters Road, Charlottetown,
C1A 5P4
(902) 892-1383
Two o/n units, one shared B&S
FEATURES: Licensed dining room
200m • 18-hole golf course 800m,
harness racing 2 km
*RATES: $25 (2), $6 add'l person •
Weekly rates available • Continental
breakfast • Open June 25-Sept. 10*

Charlottetown Area
The Mill House ★★ ½
Mrs. Susan Mill, 89 Beach Grove
Road, Charlottetown, C1E 1J3
(902) 368-3450
Three o/n units, one shared B&S •
Non-smoking only
FEATURES: Patio deck with bar-
becue • Large backyard • Centrally
located for beaches, shopping, the-
atre • Bicycle storage
*RATES: $30 (2), $5 add'l person •
$180 weekly, $30 add'l person •
Continental breakfast • Open year-
round*

Charlottetown Area
Obanbrae Farm Bed & Breakfast
Brian & Dora MacKinley, 69 York Point Road, RR 4, Cornwall, C0A 1H0
(902) 566-4163
Rte. 248, 3 km (1.8 mi) west of Charlottetown • Two o/n units, one shared B&S • Cable TV/VCR in living room • Pets welcome, usually on leash
FEATURES: Kitchen privileges • Beef show cattle and donkeys
RATES: $35-$40 (1-2), $4 add'l person • $210-$240 (weekly) • Continental breakfast • Open June 1-Oct. 1

Charlottetown Area
Obanlea Farm Century Tourist Home ★★ ½
Mildred MacKinley, RR 4, Cornwall, C0A 1H0
(902) 566-3067
Off TransCanada Hwy on Rte. 248 (York Point Rd.) 3 km (1.8 mi.) west of Charlottetown • Family farm, 1100+ acres, potatoes, beef cattle and donkeys • Three o/n units, two shared B&S • Non-smoking only
FEATURES: Award-winning registered Herefords • Hosts will assist in planning your Island holiday
RATES: $35-$45 (2), $4 add'l person • Weekly rates available • Continental breakfast • Open May 1-Oct. 15 • Phone reservations welcome • PEIBBA; TIAPEI Member

Charlottetown Area
Pye's Village Guest Home ★★★
Everett & Mildred Boyle, Box 87, Cornwall, C0A 1H0
(902) 566-2026
On TransCanada Hwy, 10 km (6.2 mi.) west of Charlottetown • One o/n unit, private B&S; one private

S; one two-room suite • TV/VCR in living room • Non-smoking only
FEATURES: Close to golf course • Attractions nearby • Close to beaches, restaurants and theatre
RATES: $30-$35 (2), $5 add'l person (no GST) • Breakfast extra • Open year-round

Charlottetown Area
Reddin House ★★★
Paul & Joyce Newcombe, 90 Brighton Road, Charlottetown, C1A 1V1
Tel & Fax (902) 892-7269
E-mail pnewcombe@peinet.pe.ca
Historic 1915 home nestled in beautiful surroundings of Victoria Park • Two o/n units, one shared B&S, one shared S • Smoking on patio only
FEATURES: Bicycles and tennis racquets available • Walking trails, tennis courts and swimming pool nearby • Five blocks to downtown area, shops and churches • Twenty-minute drive to beaches
RATES: $55-$60 (2) • Weekly rates available • Breakfast • Open year-round • TIAPEI Member

Charlottetown Area
Reflections Art Studio
Bed & Breakfast ★★ ½
Elaine & Bill Monteith,
31 Woodland Boulevard, Box 6863,
RR 4, Cornwall, C0A 1H0
(902) 566-3609
Two o/n units, one shared B&S •
Cable TV • Non-smoking only
RATES: $55 (2) • *Off-season rates*
• *Full breakfast* • *Open year-round*

Charlottetown Area
River Winds ★★★
The Robertsons, 9 Colonel Gray
Drive, Charlottetown, C1A 2S4
(902) 892-2285
Fax (902) 566-1188
Elegant riverside home in Brighton,
five minutes from city centre • One
o/n unit, private B&S (Jacuzzi) •
Cable TV • Dog on premises • Non-
smoking only
FEATURES: Flowers abound •
Bicycles available
RATES: $70 (2) • *Off-season rates*
available • *Breakfast* • *Open year-
round*

Charlottetown Area
Rose Garden ★★★ ½
Mary Ellen MacLean, 254 Mount
Edward Road, Charlottetown, C1A
5S4
(902) 892-8277
Cellular (902) 628-3249
Toll free 1-800-656-5490
Off-season (902) 836-3200
Two o/n units, private B&S • Non-
smoking only
FEATURES: Minutes to beaches,
airport and horseback riding • Fresh
flowers daily • Honeymoon pack-
ages
RATES: $75-$85 (1-2), $10 add'l
person • *Continental breakfast* •

Open May 1-Oct. 31 • *Reservations*
recommended • *Deposit required* •
Cancellation policy

Charlottetown Area
St. Avards
Bed & Breakfast
Ginny Cheverie, 97 Kensington
Road, Charlottetown, C1A 5J3
(902) 894-4697
Three o/n units, one shared B&S
RATES: $25-$35 (2), $10 add'l
person • *Continental breakfast* •
Open May 1-Sept. 30

Charlottetown Area
The Shipwright
Inn ★★★★
Jordan & Judy Hill, 51 Fitzroy
Street, Charlottetown, C1A 1R4
(902) 892-5151
(902) 368-1905
Fax : (902) 628-1905
E-mail shiprite@isn.net
Restored 1860s heritage home origi-
nally owned by shipwright James
Douse, operated by award-winning
owners of the former Edwardian •
Four o/n units, private B&S • Cable
TV/VCR and telephone in rooms •
No pets, please • Non-smoking only
FEATURES: Partial wheelchair
accessibility • Fireplaces • Antiques,
art, quilts • Air-conditioning •
Luxury suite available • Off-street
parking • Secluded garden •
Computer, fax, modem available
RATES: $95-$140 (2), $20 add'l
person • *Off-season rates available*
• *Breakfast* • *Open year-round* •
MC, Visa accepted

Charlottetown Area
Southview
Tourist Home ★★★
Betty & Ray Peters, 8 Shelby Court,

Charlottetown, C1E 1R5
(902) 566-4719
New Cape Cod home situated in quiet rural setting close to golf courses and beaches • Two o/n units, one private B&S, one private B • Non-smoking only
FEATURES: Free airport pick-up • Cozy family room with fireplace • Seven minutes to downtown, waterfront • Bicycles available
RATES: $50-$55 (2) • Off-season rates Nov.-April • Breakfast • Open year-round

Charlottetown Area
Sunset View Bed & Breakfast
Gene & Jean MacDonald, RR 5, Charlottetown, C1A 7J8
(902) 569-1206
Two o/n units, private B&S • Non-smoking only
RATES: $40-$45 (1-2), $5 add'l person • Open June 15-Sept. 15

Charlottetown Area
A Taste of Home ★★ ½
Peggy Barnes, 33 Marianne Drive, Cornwall, C0A 1H0
(902) 566-9186
Rural setting • Four o/n units, one shared B&S, two shared S • Non-smoking only
FEATURES: Homemade muffins and bread • Patio with hot tub • Private backyard • Close to golf courses, beaches and Charlottetown • Free airport pickup
RATES: $35-$45 (2), $8 add'l adult, $5 add'l child • Weekly rates available • Full breakfast • Open May 1-Nov. 30

Charlottetown Area
Tea Hill Bed & Breakfast ★★★
Jean Drake, RR 1, Charlottetown, C1A 7J6
(902) 569-2366
Rte. 1A • Two o/n units, one shared B&S • TV in rooms • No pets, please • Non-smoking only
FEATURES: Panoramic view of Hillsborough Bay • Walk to park and beach • Minutes to Charlottetown
RATES: $45 (1), $16.50 add'l person • $275 (weekly), $100 add'l person • taxes incl. • Off-season rates Labour Day to June 20 • Full breakfast • TIAPEI Member

Charlottetown Area
Tighnabruaich
Joanne & Harry Rennie, Cornwall, C0A 1H0
(902) 566-5908
Two o/n units, one shared B&S
RATES: $30 (2) • Continental breakfast • Open year-round

Charlottetown Area
The Waterview Bed & Breakfast ★★★
Pilar Shephard, 3 Malahu Drive, Charlottetown, C1A 8A5
(902) 892-2053/1953
Magnificent modern home featuring works of art and beautiful antiques • Two o/n units, private B&S • Non-smoking only
FEATURES: Secluded sandy beach with access to safe swimming
RATES: $85-$95 (1-2) • Open June 1-Oct. 1

Chepstow
Bed and Breakfast by the Sea ★★ ½
Anna & Frankie McIntosh, Box 223, Souris, C0A 2B0
(902) 687-1527
Off-season (902) 687-2321)
On Rte. 16, east of Souris • Spacious house in quiet area overlooking water • Three o/n units, one shared B&S • TV/VCR • Cot available • Non-smoking only
FEATURES: Short walk to white, sandy beach • Minutes to Magdalen Islands ferry
RATES: $50 (2), $5 add'l person • $300 (weekly), $30 add'l person • Off-season rates before July and after Labour Day • Full breakfast • Open May 18-Thanksgiving

Cherry Valley
Cherry Tree House Bed & Breakfast ★★ ½
Elsie & Josef Scheier, RR 3, Vernon Bridge, C0A 2E0
(902) 651-2010
Just off TransCanada Hwy on Cherry Valley Cove Rd. • Older home (c. 1870), quiet farming area • Three o/n units, one shared B&S • Dog on premises • No pets, please • Adults preferred • Non-smoking only
FEATURES: German spoken • 20 minutes east of Charlottetown; 30 minutes from Wood Islands ferry
RATES: $38-$44 (2) • $176-$220 (weekly) • Breakfast • Open June 1-Sept. 30

Churchill
Churchill Farm Bed & Breakfast ★★ ½
Waldron & Jeanette MacKinnon, RR 3, Bonshaw, C0A 1C0
(902) 675-2481
On TransCanada Hwy 19 km (11.8 mi.) west of Charlottetown • Five o/n units, two shared B&S, one 1/2 B • No pets, please • Non-smoking only
FEATURES: Complimentary tea, coffee, snack in evening • Less than two hours from either end of Island • Beaches, lobster suppers, golf courses nearby
RATES: $25-$30 (2), $5 add'l person, (no GST) • $120-$180 (weekly) • Breakfast extra • Open year-round • TIAPEI Member

Clinton
Red Road Country Inn ★★★
Priscilla Petrofsky, RR 6, Kensington, C0B 1M0
(902) 886-3154
Toll free 1-800-249-1344
New accommodations on 45 acres in the heart of Lucy Maud Montgomery's inspirational setting • Eight o/n units, private B&S
FEATURES: Fresh-made breads and jams • Wooden row boat rentals • Minutes from Green Gables, beaches and golf courses
RATES: $85-$115 (2), $8 add'l person • Off-season rates available • Open year-round • TIAPEI Member

Covehead Road
Elaine's Farm
Bed & Breakfast

Elaine Wooldridge, Covehead Road,
RR 1, Little York, C0A 1P0
(902) 672-2430
Rte. 25, 14 km (8.7 mi) northeast of
Charlottetown • One-hundred-acre
horse and cattle farm in quiet surroundings • Two o/n units, one
shared B&S • TV • No pets, please
FEATURES: Churches, golf
course, ocean and bay beaches five-
minute drive away • Close to harness racing and other Charlottetown
attractions
RATES: $30-$35 (2) (no GST) •
Off-season rates after Sept. 1 •
Breakfast • Open June 20-Oct. 15

Crapaud
Torfness Christian
Bed & Breakfast

Anne Abernethy, Box 4907,
Sherwood Forest, Crapaud,
C0A 1J0
(902) 658-2759
Two o/n units, one shared B&S •
Non-smoking only
RATES: $32-$40 (1-2) •
*Continental breakfast • Open May 1
-Oct. 31*

Darnley
Cal-Mar
Bed & Breakfast ★★ ½

Carl Rogers, RR 1, Kensington,
C0B 1M0
(902) 836-3058
Toll Free 1-800-844-5183
Waterfront location • Two o/n units,
one shared B&S • TV • Non-smoking only
FEATURES: Partial wheelchair
accessibility • Malpeque's panoramic sunsets • Beach • Clam-digging •

Bird-watching • Swimming pool
RATES: $35-$45 (1-2) • $225-$275
(weekly) • Off-season rates Sept 15-
June 1 • Breakfast • Open year-
round

Darnley
Sea Breeze
Bed & Breakfast ★★ ½

Fran Harding, RR 1, Kensington,
C0B 1M0
(902) 836-5275
Toll Free 1-800-835-9251
Rte. 20 • Modern home, quiet scenic
location • Three o/n units, one
shared B&S • TV in living room •
Adults preferred • Non-smoking
only
FEATURES: Homemade muffins •
Restaurants nearby • Sandy beaches
& attractions nearby • Secure bicy-
cle storage
RATES: $35-$45 (1-2) • Breakfast •
Open May-Nov. • PEIBBA Member

Dunedin
Dunedin Lodge ★★★

John & Anne Read, Cornwall, RR
2, Dunedin, C0A 1H0
Tel & Fax (902) 675-3292
Three km (.8 mi.) from
TransCanada Hwy on Rte. 247 •
Island-stone home on West River •
Three o/n units, one shared B&S
(whirlpool), one shared S • Cable
TV • Partial wheelchair accessibility
• Not suitable for children under 10
yrs.
FEATURES: Laundry facilities •
Coffee • Barbecue • Deck • Golfing,
canoeing, fishing, swimming and
dining nearby • 20-25 minutes to
Cavendish and Borden, 10 minutes
to Charlottetown
RATES: $50-$75 (2), $5 add'l per-
son • Full breakfast • Open June 2-
Sept. 30

Dunstaffnage
The Little Blue Shed
Bed & Breakfast
& Cottage
Nancy MacFarlane, Dunstaffnage,
RR 3, Charlottetown, C1A 7J7
(902) 892-8024
At junction of Rtes. 2E and 6 • Two
o/n units, one shared B&S; one cottage • Non-smoking only
*RATES: $45 (2) • $275 (weekly),
$350 (cottage, weekly) • Off-season
rates Sept.-May • Open year-round*

Earnscliffe
Esther's Farm Home
and Cottages ★★
Esther Mutch, RR 3, Vernon,
C0A 2E0
(902) 651-2415
Off TransCanada Hwy on Rte. 267,
24 km (1.5 mi) east of
Charlottetown • Quiet country home
with beef cattle and pheasants on
300 acres • Three o/n units, one
shared B&S; two housekeeping
suites • Cot and crib available • Pets
permitted, usually on leash •Non-
smoking
FEATURES: Complimentary tea,
coffee • Housekeeping units available
• Clam digging on private beach
within walking distance
*RATES: $30 (2), $40 (suites), $5
add'l person • $175 (weekly), $245
(suite), $25-$30 add'l person •
Breakfast extra • Open year-round •
TIAPEI Member*

East Bideford
Burleigh's
Bed & Breakfast ★★ ½
Pauline & James Burleigh, RR 2,
Ellerslie, C0B 1J0
(902) 831-2288
Toll free 1-800-259-4054

Two km (1.2 mi.) off Rte. 12 on
Rte. 163 (Lennox Island Road) •
Quiet relaxing location by the scenic
Bideford River • Three o/n units,
one shared S, one private
B&S • Cot available • TV • Non-
smoking only
FEATURES: Complimentary
evening snack, home cooking •
Screened patio • Beach • Swimming
• Canoeing and paddle boat for
guests' use • Golf courses and
attractions nearby
*RATES: $40-$50 (2), $10 add'l
person • $250-$295 (weekly), $50
add'l person • Full breakfast • Open
June 1-Oct. 15 • Reservations
accepted after May 1 • TIAPEI
Member*

Fairview
McIsaac's
Bed & Breakfast ★★ ½
Barbara McIsaac, Cornwall, RR 2,
Fairview, C0A 1H0
(902) 675-2567
Century farm, 20 minutes from
Charlottetown, overlooking West
River • Two o/n units, one shared
B&S • TV in sitting room •
Telephone and radio in rooms
FEATURES: Near golf courses and
Fort Amherst-Port LaJoie historic
park • Private beach • Kitchen privi-
leges • Laundry facilities
*RATES: $30 (2) • Continental
breakfast • Open June 1-Sept. 30*

French River
Beach House Inn
Brenda & Barry Philp, RR 2, French River, C0B 1M0
(902) 886-2145
Toll Free 1-800-605-2458
Off Rte. 2 on Cape Rd. • Scenic location with views of ocean, sand dunes and coastal lighthouse • Six o/n units, one shared B&S, one shared S • Pets permitted • Non-smoking only
FEATURES: Beach on premises • Candlelight dinners by reservation
RATES: $45-$65 (2), $10 add'l person • Off-season rates Sept. 3-June 21 • Full breakfast • Open May 1-Oct. 31

Frenchfort
Miller's Farm
Bed & Breakfast ★★
Janet Miller, RR 3, Frenchfort, Charlottetown, C1A 7J7
(902) 629-1509
Toll Free 1-888-629-1509
On Rte. 260, 3 km (1.8 mi.) off Rte. 2 E • Quiet, yet centrally located • Three o/n units, one shared B&S • Non-smoking only
FEATURES: Water view from veranda • Picnic table • Shady lawn • Thirty minutes to Cavendish, National Park and golfing • Near Charlottetown
RATES: $30 (2) • Full breakfast • Open May 15-Oct. 15 • PEIBBA Member

Georgetown
Clippity Clop Acres
Audrey Firth, Georgetown, C0A 1L0
(902) 652-2447
Lovely cottage on horse farm overlooking Cardigan River • One o/n unit, private B&S; one cottage • Pets welcome
FEATURES: Riding lessons and horseback riding • Kennel on premises • Swimming pool
RATES: $50 (2), $10 add'l person • $400 (weekly, cottage) • Full breakfast • Open May 1-Oct. 15

Georgetown
Sea Song
Bed & Breakfast ★★ ½
Hilary & Wanda Cheverie, Box 123, Montague, C0A 1R0
(902) 652-2235
Rte. 3, north of Georgetown on Burnt Point Rd. • Ocean-front secluded country home with panoramic views • Two o/n units, one shared B&S • Cable TV/VCR in lounge • Not suitable for children • Non-smoking only
FEATURES: Private deck • Beachcombing • Excellent swimming • Golf course nearby
RATES: $55 (2) • $300 (weekly) • Continental breakfast • Open year-round

Greenwich
Greenwich Dunes
Bed & Breakfast
Betty Lou Tilley & Brenda Lee Doyle, RR 1, St. Peters, C0A 2A0; Off-season RR 1, Hunter River RR 1, C0A 1N0
(902) 621-0674
(902) 961-3370
Fax (902) 384-2961
Rte. 313 • Century home overlooking St. Peters Bay on the Island's north shore • Three o/n units, one shared B&S, one shared B • Non-smoking only
FEATURES: Tea room • Quilt shop • Deck with view of bay • Close to Greenwich Dunes and

miles of pristine beaches
*RATES: $35-$55 (1-2) • $1,000
(weekly; house) • Breakfast • Open
June 28-Sept. 2*

Hampton
Beachside
Bed & Breakfast
Jean & Cecil Dunbar, RR 2,
Cornwall, C0A 1H0
(902) 658-2693
Two o/n units, one shared S • TV •
Non-smoking only
FEATURES: Beach on premises
*RATES: $25 (2) • Breakfast extra •
Open May 15- Sept. 30*

Hampton
Bradway Inn ★★ ½
Helen Bradway, RR 1, Hampton,
C0A 1J0
(902) 658-2178
Off-season 66 Carmel Lane,
Feeding Hills, MA, USA, 01030
(413) 786-1282
Century home with beautiful view •
Three o/n units, one shared B&S,
one private S
FEATURES: View of
Northumberland Strait, overlooking
Victoria • Twenty-five minutes to
Charlottetown, Summerside, Borden
and Cavendish
*RATES: $40-$50 (2), $5 add'l per-
son • $240-$300 (weekly), $30 add'l
person • Family rates available •
Full breakfast • Open June 1 to
Labour Day*

Harrington
Harrington House
Bed & Breakfast ★★★
Ron & Evelyn MacIntyre, RR 9
Winsloe, C1E 1Z3
(902) 672-2788
Three o/n units, one private B&S,

one shared B&S • TV/VCR in guest
parlour
FEATURES: Furnished with
antiques and period reproductions •
Minutes to Charlottetown, National
Park beaches, restaurants, fine craft
shops and theatre
RATES: $45-$65 (2) • Weekly rates
• Full breakfast • Open July 1-Aug. 31

Harrington
Proude Traditions ★★★
Gail & Ken Campbell, Harrington,
RR 9, Winsloe, C1E 1Z3
(902) 984-5448
Rte. 15, 5 km (3 mi) past airport •
Centrally-located century home was
visited during 1959 Royal Tour of
Queen Elizabeth and Prince Philip •
Two o/n units, private B&S • Non-
smoking only
FEATURES: Near golf courses,
harness racing, beaches and fine
dining
*RATES: $65 (2), $10 add'l person •
$360 (weekly), $70 add'l person •
Open year-round*

Harrington
Wilbert's
Bed & Breakfast ★★★
Herbert & Vivia Wilbert, RR 9,
Winsloe, C1E 1Z3
(902) 368-8145
Toll free 1-800-847-8145
6 km (3.7 mi) north of airport •
Fifteen minutes from Charlottetown
• Quiet home in pleasant rural set-
ting with ducks and chickens •
Three o/n units, one private B, one
shared B&S; one housekeeping suite
• Cot available • Non-smoking only
FEATURES: German spoken •
Nature trails • Home-made jam and
muffins • Near major attractions:
Brackley Beach, Cavendish, golf
course and lobster suppers
*RATES: $30 (1), $45-$48 (2-4),
$45-$50 (suite), $8-$10 add'l per-
son • Weekly rates available • Full
breakfast • Open June 1-Sept. 15 •
MC accepted • TIAPEI Member*

Hunter River
Bent Willow
Bed & Breakfast ★★
Evelyn Chemko, RR 3, Hunter
River, C0A 1N0
(902) 964-2597
One o/n unit, private B&S • Cable
TV in room
*RATES: $40-$50 (2), $10 add'l
person • Off-season rates Sept.-June
• Continental breakfast • Open year-
round • Reservations required Oct.-May*

Hunter River
Cousins Village Inn
Bethany Cousins-Grant, Box 100,
Hunter River, C0A 1N0
(902) 964-3457
Toll Free 1-800-328-4606
Website
http://www.isn.net/~farnorth/inn

Beautiful spacious home on hill
overlooking scenic village of Hunter
River • Three o/n units, two shared
B&S • Pets permitted, usually on
leash • Non-smoking only
FEATURES: Walking trails •
Swimming pool • Centrally located
for touring Island
*RATES: $45-$55 (2) • $300-$370
(weekly) • Full breakfast • Open
June 30-Sept. 4*

Hunter River
The Daylily
Bed & Breakfast ★★ ½
Susan Le Maistre & Dave Johnston,
Box 83, Hunter River, C0A 1N0
(902) 964-3177
Well decorated, large older home •
Three o/n units, one private S, one
B&S • TV • Cot, crib and play area
available • Children welcome • No
pets, please • Non-smoking only
FEATURES: Bilingual • Beautiful
gardens • Located in serviced vil-
lage, surrounded by rolling hills •
Fifteen minutes to beaches and
Island attractions
*RATES: $45-$50 (2), $5-$10 add'l
person • $275-$325 (weekly), $25-
$50 add'l person • Off-season rates
June 16-27 and Sept. 1-12 • Third
night's stay half-price • Continental
breakfast • Open June 16-Sept.12 •
Visa accepted*

Hunter River
Jean's Overnight Guests
Jean MacDonald, Hunter River,
RR 2, C0A 1N0
(902) 964-3197/2470
On Rte. 13 (Rennies Road) • Dairy
farm • Three o/n units, one shared
B&S • Cable TV in sitting room
*RATES: $30 (2), $5 add'l person •
Open May-Sept.*

Hunter River
Just Another Farm Tourist Home ★★
Gezinus & Akkelien Vos, RR 1, Hunter River, C0A 1N0
(902) 964-3498
On Rte. 2 in central PEI • Dairy farm with beautiful view • Three o/n units, one shared B&S • Pets permitted, usually on leash
FEATURES: Dutch spoken • Kitchen facilities • Licensed dining room 1 km (.6 mi) • Barbeque • Ocean beach 16 km (10 mi) • Guests are welcome to watch cows being milked
RATES: $35-$40 (2), $5 add'l person • Continental breakfast • Open May 15-Sept. 15 • TIAPEI Member

Huntley
Trail's Inn ★★
Gary & Delores Beaton, Huntley, Alberton PO, C0B 1B0
(902) 853-4057
Off Rte. 152, on Mill Rd. • Two o/n units, one shared B&S • Cable TV in sitting room • Pets welcome • Non-smoking only
RATES: $40 (2) • $250 (weekly) • Open year-round

Kensington
Carson's Guest Home ★★ ½
Doreen M. Carson, Malpeque Road, RR 1, Kensington, C0B 1M0
(902) 836-5220
One o/n unit, private B&S • Cable TV in room • Non-smoking only
RATES: $30 (2) • $180 (weekly) • Continental breakfast • Open April-Nov.

Kensington
Pickering's Guest Home
Mrs. Heber Pickering, 4 Russell Street, Box 71, Kensington, C0B 1M0
(902) 836-3441
Two o/n units, one shared B&S
RATES: $20 (2), $5 add'l person • $120 (weekly) • Open May-Oct.

Kensington
Victoria Inn and Housekeeping Suites ★★★
Raymond O Brien, 32 Victoria Street East, Box 717, Kensington, C0B 1M0
(902) 836-3010
Toll Free 1-800-439-6769
Renovated turn-of-the-century home with period furniture • Two o/n units, private B&S; four housekeeping suites • Cable TV in rooms
FEATURES: Four-poster beds • Sun porch • Barbecue • Picnic area • Treed lawns and gardens • Centrally located for cycling • Close to beaches, golf course and attractions
RATES: $70 (2), $60 (suites), $5 add'l person • $360-$450 (weekly), $25 add'l person • Breakfast • Open June 15-Sept. 15 • MC, Visa accepted

Kingsboro
The Blue Panda
Bob Evans & Jack Bryant, RR 2,

Kingsboro, C0A 2B0
(902) 357-2155
Off-season 35 Tress Road, Prospect, CT, USA, 06712; (203) 758-6109
Relaxed atmosphere among kindred spirits • Five o/n units, one shared B&S • Cable TV in sitting room
FEATURES: Spectacular views • Privacy • Kitchen privileges • White sandy beach at Basin Head 3 km (1.8 mi)
RATES: $45-$50 (2) • Weekly and single rates available • Breakfast • Open July 1-Aug. 30 •

Kingsboro
Keus' Bed & Breakfast
Anna & Michael Keus, RR2 Kingsboro, Souris, C0A 2B0
(902) 357-2028
Off Rte. 16 E • Two o/n units, one shared B&S • Cable TV in sitting room• Non-smoking only
RATES: $40 (2), $5 add'l person (taxes incl.) • Breakfast • Open June 1-Sept. 30

Kingsboro
Robertson's Bed & Breakfast ★★
Lorna Robertson, RR 2, Souris, C0A 2B0
(902) 357-2026
10 km (6.2 mi) east of Souris • Five o/n units, two shared B&S • Non-smoking only
FEATURES: 2 km (1.2 mi) from Basin Head Fisheries Museum • White, sandy beach nearby
RATES: $25-$40 (2), $5 add'l person (taxes incl) • Breakfast • Open June 15-Sept. 30

Kingsboro
Singing Sands Inn
Don & Alexandra McCallum, RR 2, Souris, C0A 2B0
(902) 357-2371
Toll free 1-800-667-2371
Off-season Box 1097, Station Q, Toronto, Ontario, M4T 2P1; (416) 488-3538
Rte. 16, 11 km (6.6 mi) east of Souris and Magdalen Islands ferry • Eight o/n units, private B&S; five housekeeping suites • Cable TV in rooms • Children under 12 yrs free • Pets welcome with prior permission • Non-smoking only
FEATURES: Heated swimming pool and spa • Par-3 chipping golf • Playground, barbecues and games • Canoes and bicycles available • Deep-sea, lobster and tuna fishing arranged • Nature trails and bird-watching • Licensed restaurant and lounge • French spoken
RATES: $52-$67 (2), $6 add'l person • $312-$402 (weekly), $35 add'l person • Off-season and senior citizens' rates • Continental breakfast • Open May-Oct. • MC, Visa accepted

Little Pond
Ark Inn ★★★
RR 4, Souris, C0A 2B0
(902) 583-2400
Fax (902) 583-2176
Toll free 1-800-665-2400
Off Rte. 310 • Secluded retreat in natural surroundings • Seven o/n units, private B&S • No pets, please
FEATURES: Partial wheelchair accessibility • Dinner on request • Licensed • Views from 4 km (2.5 mi) walking trail • Private sandy beach • Two world-class golf courses nearby
RATES: $70-$95 (2), $110 (suite), $10 add'l person • Off-season rates

during June and Sept. • *Breakfast* •
Open June 15-Sept. 6 • *AE, MC,*
Visa accepted

Little Pond
Little Pond Country Store Bed & Breakfast ★★★

Eugene E. & Jessie M. Noyes, RR
4, Souris, Little Pond, C0A 2B0
(902) 583-2892
Two km (1.2 mi) off Rte. 310
(Kings Byway) • Lovely historic
home in tranquil countryside •
Three o/n units, one shared B, one
shared S • Cot and crib available •
Non-smoking only
FEATURES: Nature trails • Flower
gardens • Large Island-stone fire-
place • Breakfast served in cozy
country kitchen • Country store to
browse in • Beach 2 km (1.2 mi) •
Famous for Island cheese
RATES: *$45 (2), $8 add'l person* •
Weekly rates • *Full breakfast* • *Open
June 15-Sept. 30*

Little Sands
Bayberry Cliff Inn Bed & Breakfast ★★★

Nancy & Don Perkins, Little Sands,
C0A 1W0
(902) 962-3395
Rte. 4, 8 km (5 mi) east of Wood
Islands ferry • Waterfront property,

30 ft. from
cliff • Four
o/n units,
private B&S
• Cable TV
• Not suit-
able for children under 5 yrs. • No
pets, please • Non-smoking only
FEATURES: Rooms located in two
remodelled post & beam barns •
Decorated with antiques • Rustic

decor and quilts • Restaurants nearby • Large screened porch & deck •
Swimming • Seal-watching, winery
and vineyards and craft stores close by
RATES: *$75-$125 (2), $15 add'l
person* • *Weekly rates available* •
Full breakfast • *Open May 15-Sept.
30* • *MC, Visa accepted* • *One
night's deposit required* • *Early
reservations suggested*

Long Creek
Alice's Meadow View ★★ ½

Alice Taylor, Box 55, Cornwall,
C0A 1H0
(902) 675-2358
Long Creek, Rte. 19A • Quiet century home • Four o/n units, one
shared B&S • Cable TV • Pets permitted • Non-smoking only
FEATURES: Laundry facilities •
Evening snack • Kitchen facilities •
Barbeque • Flower garden • 1.6 km
(1 mi) off Blue Heron Drive, 20 km
(12.5 mi) from Charlottetown • Near
beaches, golf courses, churches and
restaurants
RATES: *$27-$31 (1-2), $7 add'l
person* • *Full breakfast* • *Open May
15-Oct. 31*

Long River
Memory Lane Guest Home ★★ ½

Fred & Barbara Doughart, RR 2,
Kensington, C0B 1M0
(902) 886-2767
Two o/n units, one shared B&S •
Pets permitted, usually on leash
RATES: *$35-$50 (2-4)* • *Open year-
round* • *TIAPEI Member*

Malpeque
Fox House
Bed & Breakfast

Greg Weeks, Box 488, Kensington,
C0B 1M0
(902) 836-5371
Rte. 20 at Malpeque • Heritage
home • Four o/n units, two shared S
FEATURES: French and Japanese
spoken • Picnic baskets available •
Mountain bikes • Close to beaches •
Custom tours
*RATES: $65 (2) • $390 (weekly) •
Off-season rates May 15-June 2 and
Sept. 10-Oct. 31 • Full breakfast •
Open May 1-Oct. 31 • Reservations
recommended*

Malpeque
Keir's Shore Inn ★★★★ ½

Steve Stratos & Colleen Bogdon,
Box 7615, Malpeque, C0B 1M0
(902) 836-3938
On Rte. 20, at Malpeque, 10 km
(6.2 mi) from Kensington • Restored
colonial heritage house (1790) with
waterfront location on Malpeque
Bay • Six o/n units, private B&S •
Children over 12 yrs welcome • No
pets, please • Non-smoking only
FEATURES: Library • Parlour •
Sun room • Porch • Beach on
premises
*RATES: $85-$130 (2), $20 add'l
person • Off-season rates • Full
breakfast • Open May 24-Sept. 30 •
AE, MC, Visa accepted*

Malpeque
Malpeque
Bed & Breakfast

Chris & Susan Hawkins, Box 7606,
RR 1, Kensington, C0B 1M0
(902) 836-5359
Rte. 20, Malpeque • Century home
with restful flower garden • Four

o/n units, one private B&S, two
shared B&S; one cottage • No pets,
please • Non-smoking only
FEATURES: Near Cabot Beach
and local attractions
*RATES: $45-$50 (2), $5-$10 add'l
person • $300 (weekly, cottage) •
Full breakfast • Open June 30-Aug. 31*

Margate
Thompson's
Tourist Home ★★ ½

Don & Valerie Thompson, RR 6,
Kensington, C0B 1M0
(902) 836-4160
Toll free 1-800-567-7907
Northeast 5 km (3 mi) on Rte. 6
from Kensington, exit left on
Thompsons Point Rd., 1.4 km (.8
mi) • Large, restored farmhouse on
three acres, overlooking picturesque
river • Five o/n units, one shared
B&S •TV/ VCR in family room •
Pets permitted, usually on leash
FEATURES: Period furnishings •
Near Green Gables and attractions •
Cavendish nearby
*RATES: $35 (2), $5 add'l person •
$220 (weekly), $35 add'l person •
Continental breakfast • Open June 1
-Sept. 30*

Marshfield
Rosevale Farm
Bed & Breakfast ★★ ½

Athol & Doris MacBeath, RR 3,
Marshfield, Charlottetown, C1A 7J7
(902) 629-1341
Rte. 2E, 3 km (1.8 mi) from
Charlottetown • Active dairy farm •
Two o/n units, one shared B&S •
Non-smoking only
FEATURES: Theatre and beaches
nearby • Centrally located for Island
touring
*RATES: $45 (2) • Off-season rates
before June 15 and after Sept. 15 •*

*Full breakfast • Open May 1-Oct.
15 • MC accepted • PEIBBA; TIA-
PEI Member*

Marshfield
Woodmere
Bed & Breakfast ★★★
Doris Wood, RR 3, Marshfield,
Charlottetown, C1A 7J7
Tel & Fax (902) 628-1783
Toll free 1-800-747-1783

 On Rte. 2E, 6
km (3.7 mi)
from
Charlottetown
• Colonial
home with standard-bred horses
grazing in fields • Four o/n units,
private B&S • Cable TV in rooms •
Non-smoking only
FEATURES: Fragrant rose gardens
• Minutes to airport, golf course,
harness racing, dining, theatre and
beaches • Central to all attractions
*RATES: $65 (2), $10 add'l person •
Weekly rate = one night free • Off-
season rates Sept. 15-June 15 • Full
breakfast • Open year-round • MC,
Visa accepted • TIAPEI Member*

Maximeville
Chez Évangéline
Bed & Breakfast ★★
Évangéline Gallant, Box 35, RR 3,
Wellington, C0B 2E0
(902) 854-3097
Rte. 11 (Lady Slipper Dr.) in
Région Acadienne • Three o/n units,
one shared B&S, one shared 1/2 B •
Cable TV in sitting room • Crib
available • Pets permitted, usually
on leash
FEATURES: Bilingual • Barbecue
on request • Beach nearby
*RATES: $30 (2), $5 add'l person •
$175 (weeekly), $25 add'l person •
Open June 1-Sept. 30*

Mayfield
Holly's Bed & Breakfast
Holly Gauthier, Mayfield, RR 2,
Hunter River, C0A 1N0
(902) 963-3033
Three o/n units, one shared B&S
*RATES: $35 (2), $6 add'l person •
Open June 12-Sept. 15*

Meadow Bank
MacFadyen's Farm
Bed & Breakfast ★★ ½
Dolphie & Dingwell MacFadyen,
RR 2, Cornwall, C0A 1H0
(902) 566-2771
On Rte. 19 • Two o/n units, private
B&S • Cable TV • Non-smoking
only
FEATURES: Hostess will assist
guests in planning the perfect Island
vacation • Kitchen privileges
*RATES: $35-$40 (1), $6 add'l per-
son (no GST) • Continental breakfast • Open May 1-Oct. 30*

Melville
Valleyview Farm
Bed & Breakfast ★★ ½
Valerie VanHee, RR 1, Belfast,
C0A 1A0
(902) 659-2887
Rte. 207 • Country living in a mod-
ern setting just minutes from Wood
Islands ferry, Belfast Highland
Greens and pool • Three o/n units,
one shared B&S, one shared S
*RATES: $45-$50 (2), $7 add'l per-
son • $300-$335 (weekly), $48 add'l
person • Open May 15-Oct. 30*

Mill River East
Gard's Belhaven ★★ ½
Harold & Norma Gard, RR 1,
Alberton, C0B 1B0
(902) 853-2922
(902) 859-1756
Off Rte. 2W, adjacent to Mill River
Golf Course • Three o/n units, one
shared B, one shared S • Pets wel-
come
*RATES: $40 (2) • Full breakfast •
Open June 1-Oct. 31*

Millview
Smith's Farm Bed & Breakfast ★★ ½
Mrs. Louise Smith, Vernon Bridge
PO, Millview, C0A 2E0
(902) 651-2728
Toll free 1-800-265-2728
On Rte. 3, 2 km (1.2 mi) off
TransCanada Hwy • Four o/n units,
two shared B&S • TV and piano in
living room • Cot available • Non-
smoking only
FEATURES: Complimentary tea •
Five-minute drive from
Charlottetown • Walking trail •
Bicycle storage • Thirty minutes
from Wood Islands Ferry
*RATES: $30-$35 (2), $5 add'l per-
son • $180-$210 (weekly), $50 add'l
person • Continental breakfast extra
• Open May 1-Nov. 15 • FVBB;
TIAPEI Member*

Milton
Miltonvale Bed & Breakfast ★★★½
Verna & Ken Coles, RR 10,
Winsloe, C1E 1Z4
(902) 368-1085
On Rte. 2, 13 km (8 mi) west of
Charlottetown • New home in quiet
scenic surroundings • Two o/n units,
private B&S • TV in family room •

Non-smoking
only
FEATURES:
Golf and fish-
ing nearby •
Twenty-
minute drive to beaches
*RATES: $55 (2), $10 add'l person •
$330 (weekly), $60 add'l person •
Off-season rates before June 30 and
after Aug. 31 • Breakfast • Open
May 15-Oct. 31 • Off-season by
reservation*

Miscouche
Lecky's Bed & Breakfast ★★ ½
Allen & Dorothy Lecky, Box 273,
Summerside, C1N 4Y8
(902) 436-3216
Victorian home (c. 1905) with period furnishings • Six o/n units, two
shared B&S • Not suitable for children under 10 yrs • No pets, please
FEATURES: Wrap-around lower
deck; upper deck overlooks meadow
• Acadian museum, fishing, golfing
and canoeing nearby
*RATES: $50-$60 (1-2), $10 add'l
person • $280-$350 (weekly), $40
add'l person • Off-season rates
before June 14 and after Sept. 30,
Full breakfast • Open year-round*

Montague
Boudreault's White House Tourist Home ★★ ½
Zita Boudreault, RR 2, Montague,
C0A 1R0
(902) 838-2560/3417
Toll free 1-800-436-3220
On Rte. 17 (Kings Byway), 1 km (.6
mi) south of Montague • Quiet,
friendly atmosphere • Four o/n
units, one shared B&S, one shared S
• TV room available • Telephone •
Cots available

FEATURES: Bicycle storage • Restaurants nearby • Two eighteen-hole championship golf courses, swimming, banks, theatres, deep-sea fishing and seal-watching cruises nearby
RATES: $40-$45 (2), $10 add'l person • Family rates • Full breakfast • Open June 15-Oct. 15

Montague
Edgecombe's En Suite Bed & Breakfast ★★★½
Arlene & Dennis Edgecombe, 533 Robert Clements Drive, Box 575, Montague, C0A 1R0
(902) 838-2610
Toll free 1-800-835-5054
Executive suite near waterfront • One o/n unit, private B&S (five-piece) • TV/VCR in room • Children under 12 yrs free • Pets on premises • Non-smoking only
FEATURES: Bicycles for guests' use • Near golf courses, beaches, Confederation Trail and seal-watching • Romance packages
RATES: $79 (2), $20 add'l person • $450 (weekly) • Off-season rates by reservation Oct. 1-May 1 • Full breakfast • Open year-round • Visa accepted

Montague
Parker's Bed & Breakfast ★★★
Bill & Olive Parker, Box 398, Montague, C0A 1R0
(902) 838-3663
Toll free 1-800-511-8786
South on Rte. 17 • Nestled in small-town setting of "Montague the Beautiful" • Four o/n units, two shared B&S • Cable TV in rooms • Cot available • No pets, please • Non-smoking only
FEATURES: Partial wheelchair

accessibility • Living room and decks available to guests • Bicycle storage • Golf, swimming, restaurants, aquatic centre, seal-watching, and churches nearby
RATES: $50 (1), $10 add'l person • Full breakfast • Open May 15-Oct. 15 • BBOL; PEIBBA; Pantel Member

Montague
The Pines Bed & Breakfast ★★★
Al & Anne Coneen, Box 486, Montague, C0A 1R0
(902) 838-3675

 31 Riverside Dr., two blocks off Main St. • Century home on two-acre lot • Four o/n units, two private B, one shared B • Cable TV • No pets inside, please • Non-smoking only
FEATURES: Partial wheelchair accessibility • Laundry facilities available • Common room • Patio • Barbecue • Picnic table • Croquet and horseshoes • Bicycle storage • Close to aquatic centre, restaurants, churches, museum, crafts, golf courses, river cruises and seal-watching
RATES: $40-$45 (2), $10 add'l person • $250-$300 (weekly), $70 add'l person • Full breakfast • Open May 15-Oct. 15 • MC accepted • TIAPEI Member

Montague
Windows on the Water Café and Inn ★★★
Dr. Lester Jinks & Dr. Dawn Shea, 106 Sackville Street, Montague, C0A 1R0
(902) 838-2080
Century-old restored building • Three o/n units, private S • Non-smoking only
FEATURES: Antique furnishings and quilts • Views of Montague Harbour • Licensed dining room
RATES: $70-$90 (2), $10 add'l person • Off-season rates • Breakfast • Open year-round

Morell
Kelly's Bed & Breakfast
Mary S. Kelly, RR 2, Morell, C0A 1S0
(902) 961-2389
On Rte. 2 • Former telephone office still houses old magneto switchboard and telephone memorabilia • Five o/n units, two shared B&S • Pets permitted • Non-smoking only
FEATURES: Laundry facilities • Bicycle storage • Barbecue • Picnic table • Flower gardens • Fishing • Restaurant and stores nearby • Only 4 km (2.5 mi) to The Links at Crowbush Cove or to Lakeside's sandy ocean beach
RATES: $40 (2), $8 add'l person • $230 (weekly), $45 add'l person • Breakfast • Open June 1-Oct. 31

Morell
Parish House Bed & Breakfast
Patrick & Joan Desmarais, RR 2, Morell, C0A 1S0
Tel & Fax (902) 961-2490
On Rte. 322, 6 km (3.6 mi) from Morell • Former convent, now peaceful country home • Four o/n units, one shared B&S, one shared S • Non-smoking only
FEATURES: Ten minutes from Crowbush Cove Links and Lakeside Beach • French spoken • Tea and biscuits served in evening
RATES: $35 (2), $8 add'l person • $210 (weekly), $45 add'l person • Continental breakfast • Open June 1-Oct. 30

Morell
A Village Bed & Breakfast ★★★
Daphne MacAdam, Box 71, Morell, C0A 1S0
(902) 961-2394
Located midway between Charlottetown & Souris, on Rte. 2; Main Street, across from Esso station • Three o/n units, two shared B&S, one private B • Non-smoking only
FEATURES: Laundry facilities • Patio • Barbecue • Bicycle storage • Churches, restaurants and stores within walking distance • Short drive to links at Crowbush Cove, trout and deep-sea fishing
RATES: $35-$45 (2), $8 add'l person • $210-$270 (weekly) • Off-season rates • Breakfast • Open year-round • Reservations preferred between Sept. 30 and May 1 • HBDTA; PEIBBA; TIAPEI Member

Mount Stewart
Cottage Laine Bed & Breakfast
Elaine Clark, Box 54, Mount Stewart, C0A 1T0
(902) 676-2827
On Rte. 2, 20 km (12.5 mi) east of Charlottetown across from Irving • Century home overlooking the village of Mount Stewart • Three o/n

units, one shared B• No pets, please • Non-smoking only
FEATURES: Tea room • Craft shop • Five minutes to beaches and Links at Crowbush Cove
RATES: *$35 (2), $5 add'l person • $210 (weekly), $35 add'l person • Continental breakfast • Open June 1- Sept. 30*

Murray Harbour North
Lady Catherine's Bed & Breakfast ★★★
Tom Rath & Colleen Dempsey, RR 4, Montague, C0A 1R0
(902) 962-3426
Toll free 1-800-661-3426
E-mail bronte@ladyc.ca
Website
http://www.peinet.pe.ca/ladyc

On Rte. 17 (Kings Byway), southeast of Montague • Large Victorian country home • Four o/n units, one shared B&S, one shared S • Non-smoking only
FEATURES: Evening meals available from Oct.-May by reservation • Dietary concerns accommodated • Handmade quilts • Relax on verandas overlooking Northumberland Strait • Bicycles and fishing rods available • Beaches, craft shops, golf course and seal-watching tours nearby • Recommended by *New York Times'* Frugal Traveller.
RATES: *$40-$60 (1-2) • Full breakfast • Open year-round • MC, Visa accepted • TIAPEI Member*

Murray River
Mary Catherine's Bed & Breakfast Guest Home ★★★
Catherine Mary Foley, General Delivery, Murray River, C0A 1W0
(902) 962-3437
Toll free 1-800-227-6406
On Main Street, 500m past post office • Two o/n units, one shared B&S, one private B; one suite; two cottages • TV/VCR in rooms • No pets, please • Non-smoking only
FEATURES: French spoken • Laundry facilities • Bicycle storage • Minutes from shopping, dining, marina, seal- and bird-watching tours, deep-sea fishing and swimming • Close to seal colony, mini-golf course and ferry • RV parking
RATES: *$55 (2), $60 (cottage), $125 (suite), $8 add'l person • $395 (weekly, cottage), $60 add'l person • Full breakfast • Open year-round*

New Glasgow
Clyde View Guest Home ★★ ½
Wanda Dickieson, RR 2, Hunter River, C0A 1N0
(902) 964-2651
Off Rte. 13, across from PEI Preserve Co. • Three o/n units, two shared B&S • Non-smoking only
FEATURES: Private dock on River Clyde • Sunroom overlooking flower garden • Piano
RATES: *$45 (2) • $275 (weekly) • Off-season rates Sept. 15-Oct. 15 • Continental breakfast • Open June 1-Oct. 15 •*

New Glasgow
Country View Farm Tourist Home
Ada & Richard B. Smith, New Glasgow, RR 2, Hunter River, C0A 1N0
(902) 964-2660
Three o/n units, one shared B • Pets permitted
RATES: $25 (2), $5 add'l person • Open June 15-Oct. 15 • TIAPEI Member

New Glasgow
My Mother's Country Inn ★★★
Nellie Andrew-Ingleman & Ragnar Ingleman, New Glasgow, Box 172, RR 2, Hunter River, C0A 1N0
(902) 964-2508
Toll free 1-800-278-2071
On Rte. 13 • Recently refurbished historic home (c.1850) on fifty acres of rolling hills and woodland • Seven o/n units, six B&S; four cottages • Cable TV • Non-smoking only
FEATURES: Partial wheelchair accessibility • Trout stream • Mill pond • Trails • Fishing and boating • Five minutes from Cavendish Beach and National Park
RATES: $65-$125 (2), $100-$135 (cottage); $10-$20 add'l person • Weekly rates • Breakfast • Open June 1-Sept. 15 • TIAPEI Member

New Haven
Safe Haven Guest House ★★ ½
Maryann Chaisson & Wayne Campbell, RR 3, Cornwall, C0A 1H0
(902) 675-2623
On TransCanada Hwy at New Haven • Old, refurbished farmhouse

(1908) • Three o/n units, two shared B&S • Cat on premises • Non-smoking only
FEATURES: Home baking and preserves • Dinner on request • Country walks • Close to beach, fishing, festivals and theatre • Fifteen minutes to Charlottetown, twenty-five minutes to Borden and thirty minutes to Cavendish
RATES: $35-$45 (2), $10 add'l person • Off-season rates • Full breakfast • Open year-round • Reservations accepted

New Perth
Schellen's Bed & Breakfast ★★ ½
Sharon & Martin Schellen, RR 6, Cardigan, New Perth, C0A 1G0
(902) 838-2396
Toll free 1-888-838-2396
On Rte. 3, 2 km (1.2 mi) west of Poole's Corner • Cape Cod home on five-acre lot • Three o/n units, one shared B&S • Cable TV/VCR • Non-smoking only
FEATURES: Eighteenth-century-style furniture hand-crafted on site • Close to golfing, beaches, scenic drives and restaurants • Craft demonstrations
RATES: $50 (2), $15 add'l person • Full breakfast • Open June 1-Sept. 30 • Visa accepted

New Perth
VanDyke's Lakeview Bed & Breakfast ★★ ½
Lorraine & John VanDyke, RR 3, Montague, C0A 1R0
(902) 838-4408
On Rte. 3 • 102-acre farm overlooking man-made lake • Four o/n units, two shared B&S (one Jacuzzi), one shared 1/2 B • Cable TV/VCR in sitting room

FEATURES: Octagonal dining/living room built in 1885 • Large patio • Walking trails along lake • Close to beaches, golf courses and trail riding
RATES: $25-$50 (2), $10 add'l person • $175-$300 (weekly), $60 add'l person • Continental breakfast • Open May 1-Oct. 31

Newtown Cross
Linden Lodge Country Inn ★★ ½
Don & Shammi Toll, Belfast PO, C0A 1A0
(902) 659-2716
Rte. 211, midway between Wood Islands ferry and Charlottetown • Lovely heritage home in spacious grounds surrounded by shimmering fields of grain • Five o/n units, two shared B&S • Cable TV/VCR • Non-smoking only
FEATURES: Near beaches, fishing, Provincial Park and Orwell Corner Historical Village • Hiking trails • Period furnishings in rooms
RATES: $45-$55 (2), $10 add'l person (no GST) • $270-$330 (weekly) • Full breakfast • Open June 15-Oct. 1 • Visa accepted

Nine Mile Creek
Laine Acres Tourist Home Bed & Breakfast ★★ ½
Florence & Milton MacLaine, RR 2, Cornwall, C0A 1H0
(902) 675-2402
Rte. 19 (Blue Heron Drive) • Three o/n units, one shared B&S • Cable TV
RATES: $24-$30 (1-2) • Breakfast extra • Open June 1-Sept. 30

Nine Mile Creek
Unicorn Inn ★★★
Joan Taylor, RR 2, Cornwall, C0A 1H0
(902) 675-3247
Fax (902) 675-2367
Rte. 19 (Blue Heron Drive) • Updated Victorian farmhouse overlooking St. Peters Island and Hillsborough Bay • Two o/n units, private B&S • Cable TV/VCR in sitting room
FEATURES: Saturday evening "Pub Nights" on request • Library
RATES: $65 (2) • Off-season rates • Open year-round

North Carleton
Captain's Lodge ★★★
Jim & Sue Rogers, Seven Mile Bay, RR 2, Albany, C0B 1A0
(902) 855-3106
Toll free 1-800-261-3518

Off Rte. 10 down a country lane • Sea captain's house (c. 1850) • Three o/n units, one shared B&S, one private B • Non-smoking only
FEATURES: Furnished with antiques • Sitting room • Evening desserts • Sun porch, veranda • Horseshoe pit • Gardens • Hammock • Cycling • Walk to beach • Confederation Bridge 7 km (4.3 mi)
RATES: $60 (2) • Off-season rates before June 15 and after Sept. 15 • Full breakfast • Open June 1-Oct. 15 • MC, Visa accepted • GTA, PEIBBA, TIAPEI Member

North Carleton
Muttart's Bed & Breakfast and Cottage ★★ ½
Everett and Freda Muttart, RR 2, Albany, C0B 1A0
(902) 437-6403
Toll free 1-800-253-1749
On Rte. 10 • Two o/n units, one shared B&S; one cottage
FEATURES: Laundry facilities • Wheelchair accessibility (cottage) • Camp-fire pit • Beach • Clam-digging • Wind-surfing • View of Northumberland Strait, Borden and The Link
RATES: $40 (2) • $500 (weekly, cottage), $50 add'l person • Continental breakfast • Open year-round

North Granville
Hilltop House
Ina & Michelle Dionne, RR 1, Breadalbane, North Granville, C0A 1E0
(902) 886-2059
Toll free 1-800-704-8756
Charming Victorian farmhouse in scenic hillside setting with river view • Three o/n units, one shared B&S; one housekeeping suite • Not suitable for children • Non-smoking only
FEATURES: Parlour available • Beautiful area for walking, bird-watching, cycling and golf • Near Cavendish lobster suppers
RATES: $45 (2), $55 (suite) • $290-$360 (weekly) (taxes incl.) • Continental breakfast • Open June 15-Sept. 7 • TIAPEI Member

North Lake
Lakeville Bed & Breakfast & Cottage ★★ ½
Mrs. Elora Rose, RR 1, Elmira, C0A 1K0
(902) 357-2206
Off Rte. 16 on North Lake Harbour Rd. • Two-hundred-acre potato and grain farm overlooking North Lake • Three o/n units, two shared B&S; one housekeeping suite; one cottage • Cable TV • Children welcome • Pets permitted, usually on leash
FEATURES: Deep-sea fishing arranged • Partial wheelchair accessibility • Walk to beach
RATES: $35-$45 (2), $50-$70 (suite), $130 (cottage), $8 add'l person • $240-$300 (weekly), $350-$490 (suite), $900 (cottage), $30-$50 add'l person (no GST) • Off-season rates • Breakfast extra • Open June 10-Nov 10, (cottage open year-round)

North Milton
Country Garden Inn Bed & Breakfast ★★★ ½
Velda Buell, RR 10, Winsloe, C1E 1Z4
(902) 566-4344
Toll free 1-800-308-9259
On Rte. 7, 5.4 km (3.3 mi) north of Rte. 2 • Country inn on ten acres • Four o/n units, private B&S (one Jacuzzi) • TV/VCR • No pets, please • Non-smoking only
FEATURES: Central to most attractions, ten minutes to Cavendish and North Shore beaches
RATES: $75-$105 (2) • Full breakfast • Open year-round

North Rustico
Andy's Surfside Inn ★★
Andy G. Doyle, Box 5,
Charlottetown, C1A 7K2
(902) 963-240
Off-season (902) 892-7994/0844
On Doyle's Cove in National Park •
Eight o/n units, four shared B&S •
Cable TV
FEATURES: Transportation to and
from Charlottetown available •
Laundry facilities • Kitchen facili-
ties • Ocean view • Antique furnish-
ings • Gas barbecue • Bicycles •
Sandy beach on premises
*RATES: $35-$50 (2), $10 add'l
person (no GST or park entry fee) •
$2000 (weekly, whole house) • Off-
season rates in June, Sept. and Oct.
• Continental breakfast • Open
June 1-Oct. 30*

North Rustico
North Rustico Cottages & Inn ★★
Walter, Marie, Dwight & Heather
Houston, RR 2, Hunter River, C0A
1N0
(902) 963-2253
Toll free 1-800-285-8966
On Rte. 6 • 1840s home overlooking
harbour • Four o/n units, one shared
B&S; one suite • Cable TV
FEATURES: Swimming pool •
Laundry facilities • New patio deck
*RATES: $50-$95 (1-3), $10 add'l
person • Off-season rates before
July 5 and after Aug. 24 •
Continental breakfast • Open June
15-Sept. 30*

North Rustico
Orchard View Farm Tourist Home ★★
Ronald & Heather Toombs, North
Rustico, RR 2, Hunter River, C0A
1N0
(902) 963-2302/2300
Toll free 1-800-419-4468
Rte. 6, 4 km (2.5 mi) east of
Cavendish • Nine-hundred-acre cen-
tury hog farm with grain and soy-
beans • Four o/n units, two shared
B&S, one shared 1/2 B, one
whirlpool B • Cable TV/VCR • Pets
permitted • Non-smoking only
*RATES: $35-$45 (2), $5 add'l per-
son • Special rates June 15-30 and
Aug. 21-31 • Open June 1- Oct. 1 •
MC, Visa accepted*

North Tryon
K.A.T.W.E.N. Tourist Lodge
Cathy & Wendall Muttart, RR 2,
Albany, C0B 1A0
(902) 855-2675
Off Rte. 1 on North Tryon Cross
Rd. • Three o/n units, one shared S •
TV • Non-smoking only
*RATES: $35 (2) • $210 (weekly) •
Open June 1-Sept. 30*

Orwell Cove
Ar Dachaidh
Bed & Breakfast
Audrey Currie, RR 2, Vernon
Bridge, C0A 2E0
(902) 659-2028
Off TransCanada Hwy at Orwell Cove
• Panoramic water view • Two o/n units,
private B&S; one housekeeping suite •
Pets welcome • Non-smoking only
FEATURES: Box stalls for horses •
Write for brochure
*RATES: $65-$110 (2), $10 add'l
person • Off-season rates Oct. 1-
May 31 • Open year-round*

O'Leary
The MacDonald
Home ★★★
Adrienne & Stanley MacDonald,
568 Main Street, Box 129, O'Leary,
C0B 1V0
(902) 859-3457/2606
Fax (902) 859-3834
Toll free 1-800-565-3457
Large early 1900s heritage home •
Two o/n units, one shared B&S •
Cable TV in parlour • Telephone •
Cot and high chair available • No
pets, please • Non-smoking only
FEATURES: Recognized by PEI
Museum and Heritage Foundation •
Antiques • Fireplace • Grand piano
in parlour • Whirlpool for guest use
*RATES: $45-$55 (2) • $200-$250
(weekly) • Off-season rates •
Breakfast • Open year-round • MC,
Visa • TIAPEI Member*

Orwell Cove
MacLean's
Century Farm
Tourist Home ★★
Edison & Lucille MacLean, Vernon
Bridge PO, C0A 2E0
(902) 659-2694

Two km (1.2 mi) off Rte. 1, midway
between Charlottetown and Wood
Islands • Overlooking Orwell Bay •
Three o/n units, one shared B&S,
one shared 1/2 B
FEATURES: This is a three-
hundred-acre working family farm
*RATES: $30-$34 (1-2), $7 add'l
person • $195 (weekly), $30 add'l
person • Breakfast extra • Open
year-round • TIAPEI Member*

Panmure Island
Partridge's
Bed & Breakfast ★ ¹/₂
Mrs. Gertrude Partridge, Panmure
Island, RR 2, Montague, C0A 1R0
Tel & Fax (902) 838-4687
Toll free 1-800-284-7551
Six o/n units, three private S, one
shared B&S • Cots and crib avail-
able • Cable TV • Children under 6
yrs free • Pets permitted
FEATURES: Kitchen and laundry
privileges • Barbecue • Picnic tables
• Bicycles, row boat and canoe free
to guests • Near white, sandy beach
*RATES: $40-$50 (2), $10 add'l
person • $240-$300 (weekly), $60
add'l person • Continental breakfast
• Open June 1-Oct. • TIAPEI
Member*

Park Corner
Beds of Lavender ★★ ¹/₂
Hank & Clara Williams,
Kensington, RR 2, Park Corner,
C0B 1M0
(902) 886-3114
Off-season 47 Mohican Road,
Cornfield Point, Old Saybrook, CT,
USA, 06475; (860) 388-2587
On Rte. 20 (Blue Heron Drive), 8
km (5 mi) north of New London •
New home with Shaker-style fur-
nishings overlooking Lake of
Shining Waters • Three o/n units,

one shared S, one shared 1/2 B •
Cot available • No pets, please •
Non-smoking only
FEATURES: Complimentary
evening snacks
*RATES: $40-$50 (2), $10 add'l
person (no GST) • Continental
breakfast • Open mid-June-mid-Oct.
• TIAPEI Member*

Pinette
Midge's
Bed & Breakfast
Eleanore & Gaston Laquerre,
Pinette, RR 3, Belle River, C0A 1B0
(902) 659-2333
Three o/n units, one shared B&S
FEATURES: Beach on premises
*RATES: $30 (2), $10 add'l person •
$180 (weekly), $60 add'l person •
Breakfast • Open May 1-Oct. 31*

Red Point
Green Shutters ★★ ¹/₂
Rachel Rupnow, Red Point, RR 2,
Souris, C0A 2B0
(902) 357-2538
On Rte. 16E • Fully-equipped
century-old farmhouse in beautiful
country setting • Three o/n units,
one shared B&S, one shared S •
Non-smoking only
FEATURES: Short walk to Basin
Head and other fine beaches •
Whole house available for rent
*RATES: $25-$35 (1-2), $5 add'l
person (tax incl.) • Breakfast • Open
year-round*

Rice Point
Straitview Farm
Bed & Breakfast ★★ ¹/₂
Louis & Marina Burdett, RR 2,
Cornwall, C0A 1H0
(902) 675-2071
Website http://bb.proton.com

On Rte. 19, 24 km (15 mi) from
Charlottetown • Three o/n units, one
shared B&S • Cot available • Non-
smoking only
FEATURES: Explore our nature
trail • Farm pets
*RATES: $30 (2), $5 add'l person •
$200 (weekly), $35 add'l person •
Breakfast extra • Open May 1-Oct.
30 • TIAPEI Member*

Richmond
Mom's
Bed 'n' Breakfast ★★ ¹/₂
Mrs. Erma Gaudet-MacArthur,
Richmond, C0B 1Y0
(902) 854-2419
Toll free 1-888-666-7999
At intersection of Rte. 2W and Rte.

127, 3 km
(2 mi) off
Lady
Slipper Dr.
• Heritage
home (c.
1875) •
Four o/n units, two shared B&S,
one shared 1/2 B, one private S • No
pets, please • Non-smoking only
FEATURES: PEI Ambassador
Certificate of special tourism recog-
nition • Two verandas • Parlour with
piano • Dining room with antiques •
Bicycle storage • Close to beaches
and golf course
*RATES: $45-$80 (2-5), $10 add'l
person • Off-season rates in June
and Oct. • Breakfast • Open June-
Oct. 15 • PEIBBA; TIAPEI Member*

Roseneath
Roseneath Bed & Breakfast
Brenda & Edgar Dewar, RR 6, Cardigan, C0A 1G0
(902) 838-4590
Toll free 1-800-823-8933
E-mail rosedew@peinet.pe.ca
Off Rte. 4, near Poole's Corner • Quiet 1870s home with antiques and collectibles • Veranda overlooks Brudenell River • Four o/n units, one shared B&S, two shared S • Cat on premises • No pets, please • Non-smoking only
FEATURES: Morning coffee in room • Evening tea • Bicycles and fishing rods available • Nature trails throughout property • Seal-watching cruises, Crowbush Cove and Brudenell golf courses nearby
RATES: $55-$65 (2) • Full breakfast • Open June 1-Sept. 30

Rusticoville
Cois Farraige ★★★¹/₂
B. Montgomery, RR 2, Hunter River, C0A 1N0
(902) 963-3148
Toll free 1-800-605-7480
Rte. 6, 10 km (6.2 mi) east of Cavendish • Restored century home, on shore frontage with view of Rustico Bay from deck • Three o/n units, two private B&S, one private S and Jacuzzi B• Cable TV • Children over 10 yrs welcome • Non-smoking only
FEATURES: Minutes from golfing, deep-sea fishing, craft stores and famous lobster and seafood suppers • Beach on premises • Cois Farraige means "beside the sea"
RATES: $55-$65 (2), $10 add'l person • $370-$440 (weekly) • Off-season rates • Full breakfast • Open May 1-Sept. 30

St. Catherines
Buena Vista Farm
Judith Gay, RR 2, Cornwall, C0A 1H0
(902) 675-3363
Horse farm overlooking scenic river • Three o/n units, one shared B&S • Cable TV in rooms • Pets permitted • Non-smoking only
FEATURES: Equestrian park, golf courses, sandy beaches, canoe rentals, provincial parks, attractions and historic sites nearby • Fifteen minutes to Charlottetown • Thirty minutes to Green Gables House
RATES: $35-$50 (2) • Open June 1-Sept. 30

Skinners Pond
Keefe's Farm Tourist Home
Mrs. Freda Keefe, RR 2, Tignish, C0B 2B0
(902) 882-2686
Two o/n units, one shared B&S • Pets permitted
FEATURES: Meals available
RATES: $25 (2), $3 add'l person • Open year-round

Souris
Church Street Tourist Home ★★
Jimmy Hughes, 8 Church Street, Box 381, Souris, C0A 2B0
(902) 687-3065
Toll free 1-800-242-8361
Corner of Church and Main St. at Ultramar station • Three o/n units, one shared B&S • Cable TV in sitting room • Telephone • Cot available
FEATURES: Dining room 90m • Ten-minute walk to Magdalen Islands Ferry • Sandy beaches, water-skiing and surfboarding nearby

• Migratory bird-hunting in season
RATES: $35 (1-2), $5 add'l person
• *Weekly rates* • *Open April 1-Jan. 31*

Souris
The Matthew House Inn ★★★★
Kimberly & Franco Olivieri, Box 151, Souris, C0A 2B0
(902) 687-3461
On Breakwater St., Harbourside, near Magdalen Islands ferry • Award-winning Victorian Heritage inn • Six o/n units, private B&S or S • TV/VCR and telephone in rooms • Non-smoking only
FEATURES: Fresh flowers from cutting gardens • Italian, French, Spanish and Portugese spoken • Licensed dining by reservation • Period art • Four fireplaces • Library and parlour • Porches • Mountain bikes, spa and exercise room • Harbour boatslip and coastline cruises available • Antique shop • Maps to secluded beaches, fishing spots and cycling trails provided
RATES: $95-$145 (2), $25 add'l person • *Weekly rates* • *Full breakfast* • *Open May 15-Oct. 15* • *Major credit cards accepted* • *TIAPEI Member*

Souris
The Nautical Nook Bed & Breakfast ★★★
Brian & Marie Mossey, Box 635, Souris, C0A 2B0
(902) 687-3329
Toll free 1-800-405-6487
Decorative, clean and spacious home with spectacular view of Souris Harbour • Three o/n units, one shared B&S, one shared 1/2 B • Cable TV • Non-smoking only
FEATURES: Enjoy your stay with this friendly fishing family •

Minutes to beaches • Ten minutes from Magdalen Islands ferry
RATES: $50 (2), $8 add'l person • *Continental breakfast* • *Open year-round* • *Off-season by reservation*

Souris
A Place to Stay Inn ★★
Jay & Betty Hannan, 9 Longworth Street, Box 607, Souris, C0A 2B0
(902) 687-4626
Toll free 1-800-655-STAY
Nine o/n units, three shared B&S • Cable TV in lounge • Pets permitted • Non-smoking only
FEATURES: Laundry facilities • Kitchen facilities • Licensed dining hall • Barbecue • Deck • Dormitory available • Mountain bike rentals • Minutes to beaches and Magdalen Islands ferry • Activity packages available
RATES: $45-$55 (1-2), $10 add'l person, $18 (dormitory) • *Off-season rates* • *Open year-round* • *Reservations required after Oct. 15* • *MC, Visa accepted* • *TIAPEI Member*

South Lake
The Sandpiper
Bed & Breakfast ★★★ ½
Murray & Linda Giguère-Fraser,
RR 1, South Lake, C0A 1K0
(902) 357-2189
On Rte. 16 • Quiet home with magnificent ocean view, 2 km (1.2 mi)
off Confederation Trail • Three o/n
units, one shared B&S • Cable TV •
Non-smoking only
FEATURES: Partial wheelchair
accessibility • Bilingual • Barbecue
and picnic table • Bird carvings and
tole painting on display • Minutes to
Singing Sand beaches • Fifteen minutes to Magdelen Islands ferry
*RATES: $50 (2), $10 add'l person •
$325 (weekly), $50 add'l person •
Breakfast • Open year-round*

South Melville
Share Our Home
Bed & Breakfast
Renate Ostick, Mill Road, South
Melville, RR 1, Crapaud, C0A 1J0
(902) 658-2221
Quiet location in the Bonshaw Hills
• Two o/n units, one shared B&S •
Non-smoking only
FEATURES: Beach nearby •
Thirty-minute drive to ferries, Green
Gables and Charlottetown
*RATES: $35-$40 (1-2), $10 add'l
person • $210-$240 (weekly), $60
add'l person • Senior citizens' dis-
count • Open June 15-Sept. 15*

South Rustico
Barachois Inn ★★★★
Judy K. & Gary MacDonald, Box
1022, Charlottetown, C1A 7M4
(902) 963-2194
Church Rd., Rte. 243 • Victorian
house (c. 1870), recently restored
with antique furnishings and works

of art • Four o/n units, private B&S
or S • Not suitable for very young
children • No pets, please • Non-
smoking only
FEATURES: View of Rustico Bay
• 6 km (3.7 mi) from Cavendish
National Park and Green Gables
House; 17 km (10.5 mi) from
Charlottetown
*RATES: $110-$125 (2), $25 add'l
person • Off-season rates before
June 15 and after Sept. 15 • Full
breakfast • Open May 1-Oct. 31 •
MC, Visa accepted • Reservations
recommended, deposit required •
Cancellation policy • TIAPEI
Member*

Spring Valley
Green Valley Cottages
and Bed & Breakfast ★★ ½
Gerry & Debbie Bryanton, Spring
Valley, Box 714, Kensington,
C0B 1M0
(902) 836-5667
Toll free 1-888-283-1927
On Rte. 102, 5 km (3 mi) north of
Kensington • Located in picturesque
farmland • One o/n unit, private
B&S; seven cottages • No pets, please
FEATURES: Petting zoo • Nature
trails • Bonfires • Minutes from
beaches, deep-sea fishing and
Cavendish • Playground • Barbecues
*RATES: $50 (2), $66-$125 (cot-
tage), $5 add'l person • Weekly
rates • Continental breakfast • Open
May 15-Oct. 31*

Springhill
Ford's
Bed & Breakfast ★★ ½
David Ford, RR 2, Tyne Valley,
C0B 2C0
(902) 831-2487
Toll free 1-888-297-3113
MacArthur Rd., 1 km (.6 mi) off

Hwy 2; 2 km (1.2 mi) off Lady Slipper Dr., Summerside • Newly remodeled 1936 family home • Two o/n units, one shared B • Cable TV/VCR in sitting room • Cot available • Non-smoking only
FEATURES: Patio • Back Road Gallery 1 km (.6 mi) • Dinner theatre, and Mill River Golf Course nearby
RATES: $40 (2), $10 add'l person • $240 (weekly), $70 add'l person • Full breakfast • Open May 1-Dec. 1 • Visa accepted

St. Peters Bay
The Crab'n'Apple Bed & Breakfast ★★ ½

Richard Renaud & Seana Evans-Renaud, Box 9, St. Peters Bay, C0A 2A0
(902) 961-3165
Rte. 2, 1 km (.6 mi) west from junction Rte. 2 and Rte. 313 • Quaint home with beautiful view of St. Peters Bay • Three o/n units, one shared B&S • Cots and crib available • Children welcome • Pets permitted, usually on leash • Non-smoking rooms available
FEATURES: Large cedar sun room • Bilingual • Laundry facilities nearby • Meals available with packages or off-season • Twenty-minute drive to Atlantic salmon fishing, links at Crowbush Cove and Brudenell golf courses
RATES: $40 (2), $5 add'l person • $260 (weekly) • Off-season rates before June 26 and after Sept. 5 • Continental breakfast • Open year-round • Off-season by reservation • MC, Visa accepted • PEIBBA Member

Stanhope
Campbell's Tourist Home & Housekeeping Unit ★★ ½

Mary & Malcolm Campbell, RR 1, Little York, Stanhope, C0A1P0
(902) 672-2421
Two o/n units, one shared B&S; one housekeeping suite
RATES: $50 (2), $80 (suite), $10 add'l person • $275 (weekly), $400 (suite), $50 add'l person (tax included) • Continental breakfast • Open year-round • TIAPEI Member

Stanley Bridge
Aunt Barry's Victorian Bed & Breakfast ★★

Peg Jones, RR 1, Breadalbane, C0A 1E0
(902) 886-3147
Rte. 6 • Quiet Victorian home overlooking bay, just minutes from all attractions • Three o/n units, one shared B&S • Non-smoking only
FEATURES: Short walk to beach, deep-sea fishing and lobster fishing • Water views from every window
RATES: $35-$50 (1-2), $5 add'l person • $235-$340 (weekly), $30 add'l person • Continental breakfast • Open year-round

Stanley Bridge
Gulf Breeze Cottages and Bed & Breakfast ★★ ½
David & Dorothy Simpson, Stanley Bridge, C0A 1E0
(902) 886-2678
Toll free 1-800-416-5463
Rte. 224, off Rte. 6 • Quiet location near ocean beach and golf course • Three o/n units, one shared B&S, one shared 1/2 B; four cottages • Cots available
RATES: $33-$35 (2), $78 (cottage), $5-$6 add'l person • $490 (weekly, cottage) • Breakfast extra • Open May 1-Oct. 30

Stanley Bridge
The Smallmans ★★ ½
Helen Smallman, 329 Poplar Avenue, Summerside, C1N 2B7
(902) 886-2846/436-5892
E-Mail smallman@atcon.com
On Rte. 254, 3 km (2 mi) south of Stanley Bridge • Scenic, tranquil riverside setting • Three o/n units, one shared B&S; one cottage • TV/VCR available • Cot and crib available • No pets, please • Non-smoking only
FEATURES: Complimentary evening coffee • Barbecue • Picnic table • Bird-watching • Beach on premises • Boating and swimming • Near Cavendish, lobster suppers and other attractions • Green Gables nearby
RATES: $35-$45 (2), $85 (cottage, $10 add'l person • $550 (weekly, cottage), $60 add'l person • Off-season rates in June and Sept. • Breakfast • Open June-Sept. • ATO; KATA; NLTA; PEIBBA Member

Summerside Area
Birchvale Farm Bed & Breakfast ★★ ½
Arnold & Barbara Waugh, RR 3, Summerside, C1N 4J9
(902) 436-3803/888-7331
Toll free 1-800-463-3803
Three km (2 mi) off Rte. 1A on Rte. 120, between Rte. 1A and Rte. 107. • Twenty minutes from ferry and Cavendish • Active farm in family for six decades • Three o/n units, two shared B&S, one private 1/2 B • Cable TV • No pets, please • Non-smoking only
FEATURES: 13th year hosting guests
RATES: $28-$38 (2), $8 add'l person • Continental breakfast • Open May 1-Oct. 31 • Visa accepted • TIAPEI Member

Summerside Area
Blue Heron Country Bed & Breakfast ★★★
Willard & June Waugh, RR 3, North Bedeque, C1N 4J9
(902) 436-4843
Toll free 1-800-575-8233
On Rte. 1A, twenty minutes from ferry • Charming family farm • Four o/n units, one private B, one shared B&S, one shared S • Non-smoking only
FEATURES: Award-winning B&B • Evening snack • Western-style riding stable
RATES: $45-$55 (2), $10 add'l person • Breakfast • Open year-round • TIAPEI Member

Summerside Area
Country at Heart
Bed & Breakfast ★★ ½
Carl & Vivian Wright, RR 3, North
Bedeque, C1N 4J9
(902) 436-9879
Toll free 1-800-463-9879
Off Rte. 1A on Rte. 181 (Taylor
Rd.), 2 km (1.2 mi) east of
Summerside • Twenty minutes to
Borden ferry, thirty minutes to
Cavendish • Two-storey home in
peaceful farming community • Four
o/n units, one private B, one shared
B&S, one shared 1/2 B • Non-smok-
ing only
FEATURES: Complimentary
evening snack • Picnic table and
barbecue • Fans available • 2 km
(1.2 mi) to riding stables
*RATES: $40-$55 (2), $10 add'l
person • Off-season rates Sept. 15-
June 15 • Continental breakfast •
Open year-round • Visa accepted •
TIAPEI Member*

Summerside Area
The Cozy
Bed & Breakfast ★★ ½
Claudette Clement, 54 Granville
Street, Summerside, C1N 2Z2
(902) 436-4023
Heritage home in exclusive residen-
tial area • Two o/n units, one shared
B&S • Non-smoking only
FEATURES: Antique furnishings •
Easy access to beaches, boutiques,
restaurants
*RATES: $45-$55 (1-2) • Off-season
rates Oct. 1-May 31 • Full breakfast
• Open year-round*

Summerside Area
The "Island Way" Farm
Bed & Breakfast ★★ ½
Gordon & Ruth Anne Waugh, RR3,
Summerside, C1N 4J9
(902) 436-7405
Fax (902) 888-2385
Toll free 1-800-361-3435
Rte. 1A • Family farm, situated in a
tranquil setting on Wilmot River •
Four o/n units, two private S, one
shared S • Pets permitted, usually on
leash • Non-smoking only
FEATURES: Stately turn-of-the-
century farm home full of character
and charm of days gone by • Riding
stable • Footpath along shore bank •
Back roads for cycling • Crafts for
sale
*RATES: $45-$60 (2), $10 add'l
person • Breakfast • Open May 1-
Sept. 30 • TIAPEI Member*

Summerside Area
MacDonald's
Bed & Breakfast
Ms. Hazel MacDonald, 142 Walker
Avenue, Summerside, C1N 4W8
(902) 436-6878
Off Granville Street, behind
Country Fair Mall and Sears • Two
o/n units, one private B&S, one pri-
vate S • Non-smoking only
*RATES: $45-$50 (2) • $270-$300
(weekly) • Continental breakfast •
Open June 1-Sept. 30*

Summerside Area
Paneau Bed &Breakfast
Muriel & Gerard Gallant, 11 North Drive, Summerside, C1N 4E7
(902) 436-0543
Toll free 1-800-281-0171
Minutes from downtown; twenty-five minutes from Borden ferry • Century home with large shaded yard • Five o/n units, one shared B&S, one shared S • TV in living room • Guest telephone • Cot and crib available • Pets on leash permitted
FEATURES: Evening snacks • Outdoor games, deck and barbecue available • Home cooking
RATES: $30-$35 (2), $10 add'l person • $185-$210 (weekly) • Off-season rates before July and after Sept. 30 • Full breakfast • Open May 1-Nov. 30

Summerside Area
Silver Fox Inn ★★★
Julie Simmons, 61 Granville Street, Summerside, C1N 2Z3
(902) 436-4033
Toll free 1-800-565-4033
Historic house (1892) designed by architect W.C. Harris • Six o/n units, private B or B&S • Not suitable for children under 10 yrs • Non-smoking only
FEATURES: Spacious rooms with fireplaces, fine woodwork and period furnishings • Close to business and shopping district
RATES: $69-$84 (2), $10 add'l person • Off-season rates before June 1 and after Sept. 30 • Continental breakfast • Open year-round • AE, MC, Visa accepted • TIAPEI Member

Summerside Area
Willowgreen Farm Bed & Breakfast ★★ ½
Steven & Laura Read, 117 Bishop Drive, Summerside, C1N 5Z8
(902) 436-4420
Toll free 1-888-436-4420
Located behind The College of Piping • Family homestead with tranquil and relaxed atmosphere – a working farm "in town" • Four o/n units, one shared B, one shared S • Non-smoking only
FEATURES: Country walks • Crafts • Horses welcome
RATES: $35-$45 (2), $7 add'l person • $210-270 (weekly), $60 add'l person • Breakfast • Open year-round • MC, Visa accepted

Summerside Area
Wilmot Tourist Home
Elmer Gallant, 114 Gaudet Crescent, Summerside, C1N 5E1
(902) 888-2733/436-2522
Off Rte. 1A • Three o/n units, two shared B&S • Pets permitted
FEATURES: Partial wheelchair accessibility
RATES: $30 (2) • Continental breakfast • Open year-round

Tignish
Chaisson Homestead
Anita Chaisson, 156 Chaisson Road, Tignish, C0B 2B0
(902) 882-2566
One o/n unit, B&S; three cottages • Cot available • Pets permitted
FEATURES: Partial wheelchair accessibility • French spoken • Restaurant 800 m • Ocean beach 800 m
RATES: $35 (2), $35-$60 (cottage), $6 add'l person • $150-$350 (weekly, cottage) • Off-season rates before June 21 and after Aug. 31 • Breakfast • Open year-round

Tignish
Maple Street Inn
Bed & Breakfast ★★ ½
Jackie & Elmer Arsenault, 216 1/2
Maple Street, Box 96, Tignish,
C0B 2B0
(902) 882-3428
Three o/n units, one shared B&S •
Cable TV • Non-smoking only
*RATES: $30-$40 (1-2), $10 add'l
person • $180-$250 (weekly) • Full
breakfast • Open June 1-Oct. 31*

Tignish
Murphy's Tourist Home
& Cottages ★★
Richard Murphy, 325 Church Street,
Tignish, C0B 2B0
(902) 882-2667
Two o/n units, one shared B; five
cottages • Pets welcome, on leash
*RATES: $30 (2), $40-$55 (cottage),
$5 add'l person • $180-$280
(weekly), $15 add'l person • Open
May 15-Oct. 15 • MC, Visa accepted*

Tignish
Tignish
Heritage Inn ★★★
Edith DesRoche, Box 398, Tignish,
C0B 2B0
(902) 882-2491
Fax (902) 882-3144
Behind St. Simon and St. Jude
Church • Restored convent (c.1868)
with spacious grounds in quiet sur-
roundings • Seventeen o/n units, pri-
vate B&S • Cable TV in rooms •
Cots available • Children under 6
yrs free • Smoking rooms available
FEATURES: Partial wheelchair
accessibility • Laundry facilities •
Kitchen facilities • Close to North
Cape, parks and beaches • Walk to
museums, restaurants and shopping
• Hostel rooms available

*RATES: $65-$100 (1-2), $10 add'l
person • $390-$600 (weekly) • Off-
season rates before mid-June and
after Labour Day • Continental
breakfast • Open April-Oct. • Off-
season by reservation*

Tyne Valley
The Doctor's Inn
Bed & Breakfast ★★ ½
Paul & Jean Offer, Tyne Valley,
C0B 2C0
(902) 831-3057
Rte. 167, 30 km (18.6 mi) west of
Summerside • Landscaped village
home (c. 1860) • Two o/n units, one
shared B • Pets permitted
FEATURES: Three-acre market
gardens provide fresh vegetables •
Special dining by arrangement •
Recommended in *Where to Eat in
Canada 92–96* • Living room with
fireplace • Cross-country skiing in
winter • 4 km (2.5 mi) from Green
Park and river swimming
*RATES: $55 (2), $10 add'l person •
$330 (weekly), $60 add'l person •
Breakfast • Open year-round • MC,
Visa accepted*

Tyne Valley
Valleyview
Bed & Breakfast ★★ ½
Betty MacIsaac, Box 85, Tyne
Valley, C0B 2C0
(902) 831-3490
Two o/n units, one shared B&S •
Cable TV in living room • Pets per-
mitted, usually on leash • Non-
smoking only
FEATURES: Kitchen privileges •
Close to Green Park Provincial Park
and golf courses
*RATES: $35 (2) • $130 (weekly) •
Open June-Aug.*

Uigg
Dunvegan Farm Motel and Bed & Breakfast ★★ ½
Harold & Dorothy MacLeod, RR 2, Vernon Bridge, C0A 2E0
(902) 651-2833
Rte. 24, 30 km (18 mi) east of Charlottetown • Quiet farm home on 170 acres • Three o/n units, one shared B&S, one shared 1/2 B • Pets welcome, on leash
FEATURES: Partial wheelchair accessibility
RATES: $30-$35 (2), $5 add'l person • $180-$210 (weekly), $30 add'l person • Breakfast extra • Open May 15-Nov. 15 • Visa accepted

Urbainville
Chez Yvette Bed & Breakfast ★★★
Yvette Deschenes, Box 63, Urbainville, C0B 2E0
(902) 854-2966
Rte. 124 off Rte. 2 in the Evangeline Region • Four o/n units, one shared B&S, one shared S • Cable TV • Cots available • Non-smoking only
FEATURES: French spoken
RATES: $50 (1-2), $10 add'l person • $300 (weekly), $70 add'l person • Off-season rates Oct.-May • Continental breakfast • Open year-round

Victoria
Dunrovin Lodge, Cottages and Farm
Mrs. Kay MacQuarrie-Wood, Box 40, Victoria, C0A 2G0
(902) 658-2375
Pioneers in farm vacations (c.1802) • Two o/n units, one private B&S, one private B; seven cottages • Pets permitted, usually on leash

FEATURES: Family-operated • Babysitting services • Horseback riding • Beach on premises • Museum, playhouse, Provincial Park, clam-digging and recreational facility nearby
RATES: $40-$45 (2), $40-$50 (cottage), $20 add'l adult, $7 add'l child • $275-$350 (weekly), $110-$145 add'l adult, $45 add'l child • Family and senior citizens' rates • Open June 21-Sept. 20 • TIAPEI Member

Victoria
Orient Hotel ★★★
Darrell Tschirhart & Lee Jolliffe, Main Street, Victoria-by-the-Sea, C0A 2G0
Reservations: Box 162, Charlottetown, C1A 7K4
(902) 658-2503
Fax (902) 658-2078
Toll free 1-800-565-ORIENT
E-mail orient@pei.sympatico.ca
Website http://www.sympatico.ca/orient
Heritage inn (c. 1900) • Three o/n units, private B&S; three suites • Non-smoking only
FEATURES: Partial wheelchair accessibilty • Tea shop • Licensed dining by reservation • Views of countryside and shore
RATES: $75-$95 (2), $105-$115 (suite), $15 add'l person • Off-season rates before June 15 and after Sept. 15 • Full breakfast • Open May 15-Oct. 15 • AE, MC, Visa accepted • Deposit required • HIAC Member

Victoria
Victoria Village Inn
Pam Stevenson, Box 1,
Victoria-by-the-Sea, C0A 2G0
(902) 658-2483
Charming heritage inn (c. 1884) •
Six o/n units, one shared B&S, three
shared S • Pets permitted, usually on
leash • Non-smoking only
FEATURES: Fine linens and
duvets • Licensed • Post Office and
"The Actor's Retreat" coffee shop
on premises • Next door to the
Victoria Playhouse
*RATES: $65-$85 (2) • Off-season
rates • Open year-round • MC, Visa
accepted*

West Point
Red Capes Inn ★★ ½
Barry & Ada Ellis, RR 1,
West Cape, O'Leary, C0B 1V0
(902) 859-3150/2199
Toll free 1-800-321-0439
On west shore, Rte. 14 (Lady
Slipper Dr.), 4 km (2.5 mi) north of
West Point Lighthouse • Modern
home finished with pine, cathedral
ceiling, stone fireplace, "star wars"
gallery • Two o/n units, one shared
B&S; one suite • Cable TV/VCR in
lounge • Non-smoking only
FEATURES: Swimming • Beaches
and restaurant nearby • Free videos
*RATES: $45 (2), $70-$80 (suite)
(no GST) • Continental or full
breakfast • Open mid-May to
mid-Oct. • Reservations from May 6*

West Point
Stewart Memorial House
Bed & Breakfast ★★ ½
Audrey MacDonald, West Point,
C0B 1V0
(902) 859-2970/1939
On Rte. 14 (Lady Slipper Drive) •

New house modelled after Big
Philip Stewart original • Four o/n
units, one private B, one shared B •
Cable TV/VCR
FEATURES: Partial wheelchair
accessibility • Displays of artifacts,
geneology and history • Antiques,
mats and quilts • Evening coffee
and snacks available • 1 km (.6 mi)
to Cedar Dunes Provincial Park
*RATES: $50-$70 (2) • Weekly rates
• Off-season rates Oct. 16-June 15 •
Full breakfast • Open year-round*

West Point
West Point
Lighthouse ★★★
Carol Livingstone, RR 2, O'Leary,
C0B 1V0
(902) 859-3605
Toll free 1-800-764-6854
Website
http://www.maine.com/lights/oth-
ers.htm
Rte. 14 (Lady Slipper Drive) •
Canada's only functioning
(restored) lighthouse inn • Nine o/n
units, private B&S • Cable TV/VCR
in guest lounge • Children under 10
yrs $5 • Non-smoking only
FEATURES: Partial wheelchair
accessibility • Featured in Fodor's
Great Canadian Inns and on "Cross
Country Cooking" TV show •
Licensed dining room • Evening
sweets and coffee • Museum • Patio
deck • Whirlpool • Sandy ocean
beach on premises • Nature trails •
Clam-digging, fishing and biking •
Packages available
*RATES: $70-$120 (2), $10 add'l
person • $420-$840 (weekly) • Off-
season rates before June 15 and
after Sept. 9 • Breakfast extra •
Open May 31-Sept. 28 • AE, MC,
Visa accepted • Deposit required •
TIAPEI Member*

Winsloe North
Cudmore's Chumleigh Tourist Home
Marjorie Cudmore, RR 9,
North Winsloe, C1E 1Z3
(902) 368-1300
On Rte. 233 • Century home with antique furniture • Two o/n units, one private B&S, one private S
FEATURES: Kitchen facilities • Five minutes to beach; fifteen minutes to Charlottetown
RATES: $25-$30 (2), $5 add'l person • $150-$160 (weekly), $10 add'l person • Open May 20-Sept. 30

Woodville Mills
Woodlands Country Inn ★★★
Max Newby & Mary Cameron, RR 1, Cardigan, C0A 1G0
(902) 583-2275
Toll free 1-800-380-1562
E-mail woodlands@pei.sympatico.ca
On Rte. 311 (Kings Byway) • Award-winning heritage home • Elegant Victorian estate (c. 1881) • Four o/n units, one shared B&S, one shared S • Pets permitted, usually on leash • Non-smoking only
FEATURES: Period furnishings • French spoken • Library • Billiards room and table tennis • Movies • Picnics available • Barbecue pit • Bicycles • Private beach, boating, tennis and golf nearby
RATES: $60 (1-2), $10 add'l person • $380 (weekly), $60 add'l person • Full breakfast • Open June-Oct. 31 • PEIBBA Member